SECURITY in ASIA PACIFIC

SECURITY in ASIA PACIFIC

The Dynamics of Alignment

Thomas S. Wilkins

LYNNE
RIENNER
PUBLISHERS

BOULDER
LONDON

Published in the United States of America in 2019 by
Lynne Rienner Publishers, Inc.
1800 30th Street, Boulder, Colorado 80301
www.rienner.com

and in the United Kingdom by
Lynne Rienner Publishers, Inc.
Gray's Inn House, 127 Clerkenwell Road, London EC1 5DB

Library of Congress Cataloging-in-Publication Data
A Cataloguing-in-Publication record for this book
is available from the Library of Congress.

ISBN 978-1-62637-745-5

British Cataloguing in Publication Data
A Cataloguing in Publication record for this book
is available from the British Library.

Printed and bound in the United States of America

The paper used in this publication meets the requirements
of the American National Standard for Permanence of
Paper for Printed Library Materials Z39.48-1992.

5 4 3 2 1

Contents

Preface

This book has been a long time in the making. Its original genesis goes back to my early research on "coalition warfare" in which I developed a series of theoretical frameworks to conceptualize the behavioral dynamics of coalitions.

As my interests began to shift from the North Atlantic to the Asia Pacific region as a result of a two-year Kiriyama postdoctoral fellowship at the University of San Francisco Center for the Pacific Rim, and the POSCO fellowship at the East-West Center in Honolulu, I came to realize that such frameworks could be modified and elaborated upon to understand the security dynamics of alignment in this latter region. After emigrating to Australia to take up my present post at the University of Sydney, I began to build my knowledge of the various constellations of alignment in the region, beginning with the US alliance system and the Shanghai Cooperation Organisation, and then returning to fill in the gaps on ASEAN.

To do this thoroughly took time, including several research postings to the region in Singapore, Taiwan, Japan, and Hong Kong, plus innumerable shorter visits. Arriving at a monograph that provided not only deep theoretical foundations on the phenomenon of alignment, but also the requisite empirical knowledge across a vast region, has been a long journey, but one well worth pursuing, and continuing into the future.

* * *

Along this journey, I have accumulated a great many debts to colleagues, family, and friends, near and far. The list of names is too long to recount in its entirety, but I would like to make special mention of a few individuals who have particularly assisted me in one way or another with this work and my professional progress in general.

I begin with colleagues at the Center for the Pacific Rim at the University of San Francisco, where I was based for two years as a Kiriyama postdoctoral fellow. These include the center's director at the time, Barbara Bundy, and deputy director, Ken Kopp, as well as office manager Christine Elbers and events manager Pat Hatcher. Thanks also go to Chiho Sawada and Ted Melillo, interaction with whom also greatly enriched my postdoctoral experience in the United States. I also thank Choong-nam Kim of the East-West Center Honolulu for the POSCO postdoctoral fellowship at the East-West Center in Hawaii.

Following my postdoctoral study, I emigrated to Australia to take a position at the Centre for International Security Studies (CISS), then under Alan Dupont, at the University of Sydney. Colleagues in the Centre, past and present, provided further intellectual stimulation and support as the project progressed; particularly worth mention are Jingdong Yuan, Christian Enemark, Peter Curson, and Sarah Philips, among many others. I was fortunate to have had the most efficient center manager, Vivian Puccini-Scuderi, to rely upon to manage my transition to the working environment in Australia. My current colleagues in the Department of Government and International Relations (GIR), especially the former head, Colin Wight, and the former head of school, Simon Tormey, have also been of great support in my career at Sydney. There are a great many other colleagues at the University of Sydney, and across Australia in general, to whom I owe a professional or intellectual debt, among them especially Bill Tow, who acted as an invaluable academic mentor, and Malcolm Cook, who initiated me into the think-tank/policymaking world. The university has also been generous in providing funding support through a number of avenues for extended field trips to the Asia Pacific region and the international conferences, for which I am most grateful.

Outside of Australia I have had the benefit of working with supportive colleagues in Japan at the University of Tokyo—where I held Japan Foundation and Japan Society for the Promotion of Science fellowships—including Kiichi Fujiwara, Yasuhiro Matsuda, and Akio Takahara. In Hong Kong, now my second adopted country (thanks to my wife!), I owe thanks to Richard Hu and all the academic and professional staff of the Department of Politics and Public Administration at the University of Hong Kong (HKU), where I have been based as a visiting associate professor. In Singapore I must thank Ralf Emmers for hosting me as a visiting fellow under his Multilateralism in Asia Program, and all of the academic staff at the Rajaratnam School of International Studies (RSIS), Nanyang Technical University. In Taiwan, I extend my gratitude to my gracious hosts at the Department of Political Science, Taiwan National University, then headed by Yeh-lih Wang, where I was based as Taiwan Ministry of Foreign Affairs (MOFA) Fellow.

For specific assistance on various chapters, I thank all those colleagues across Asia Pacific who gave their time to enter into discussions or informal interviews relating to my research project, or who engaged with my ideas through diverse academic workshops and other forums. For reading earlier draft chapters, my thanks go to Ralf Emmers, Hiro Katsumata, and Christopher Roberts for ASEAN; Stephen Aris and Jingdong Yuan for Shanghai Cooperation Organisation chapters; and Emilian Kavalski for his comments on various earlier drafts. I could not have prepared this manuscript without the tireless dedication of my research assistant, Minako Ichikawa-Smart, and my research intern, Jiye Kim. Student intern Hugh Evans also did sterling work for me in the early stages. I would also like to extend my gratitude to Lynne Rienner, who had faith in my work, and acknowledge her assistant, Nicole Moore, for her support and patience.

Finally, I wish to thank my wife, Zoie Wong, for her tolerance and understanding, and for listening to my relentless updates on chapter progress! I also deeply appreciate all the support offered by my parents during the course of my academic career.

Any errors found in the following text are my responsibility alone.

1

Security Alignment in Asia Pacific: A New Approach

The Asia Pacific region is increasingly becoming the primary locus of world geopolitics and geo-economics.[1] Indeed, a recent Chinese white paper declared that "it has become the most dynamic region with the strongest potential in the world."[2] As a consequence, Robert Ayson claims that "no region matters more than Asia to the world's security."[3] Given the region's tumultuous past, combined with the huge advances made in terms of economic, political, and military power in recent decades, an accurate appreciation of its fundamental security dynamics is therefore a crucial undertaking.[4] Yet, analysts are sharply divided over the prospects for peace and stability in this pivotal region. While liberal international relations (IR) scholars point to the extraordinary level of "complex economic interdependence" and the plenitude of multilateral security institutions as a brake on conflict, realists take a dimmer view of the rapid military buildup that is occurring against a backdrop of simmering maritime, territorial, and historical disputes.[5] The extraordinary pace at which developments unfold leads Rémy Davison to add that the "Asia-Pacific is such a fluid and dynamic region that it demands constant reappraisal and reconsideration."[6] Indeed, the dynamism of the region can catch policymakers and analysts off guard, making improved understanding of these perplexing regional security structures of paramount importance. Hence, according to Mark Beeson, the "Asia-Pacific is arguably the most important, but also the most complex and contested, region on the planet."[7]

As this book neared completion in 2017–2018, a series of ostensibly ground-shaking events initiated by the new Republican administration of Donald Trump testified to the volatility of the region's politics and threatened to upend many long-held assumptions about the United States' future role. The inconsequential summit meeting in Singapore with North Korea in June 2018, following a war of words in the Twitter-sphere and the announcement of an incipient trade war with China, has grabbed the attention of policymakers and analysts. Indeed, Trump has done serious damage to US credibility in the Asia Pacific by disparaging Asian allies and withdrawing from the Trans Pacific Partnership (TPP).[8] As a result, commentators have signaled that the Barack Obama–era policy of restoring US power and purpose in Asia under the "pivot"/"rebalance" is now "dead."[9] Yet for all the *Sturm und Drang* of recent events, actual policy documents such as the US National Security Strategy[10] have conservatively upheld the core precepts of US engagement with Asia Pacific security, and analysts have consoled themselves that despite the unguarded rhetoric, real departures from these precepts have yet to be actually realized.[11] Fundamentally, strategic decisionmakers in the US bureaucracy remain committed to upholding US primacy in the Asia Pacific in the teeth of ever-rising Chinese power and assertiveness, only drawing into sharper relief the intensification of Sino-American rivalry and the competition for power and influence in the Asia Pacific that continues to unfold.[12]

Beijing of course has profited from the reign of political chaos in the White House to further advance its own strategic interests in the region.[13] The 2017 XIX Party Congress enshrined "Xi Jinping thought" as its guiding light, while the 2018 National People's Congress appointed him as apparent president-for-life.[14] Under this strong leadership, Beijing has moved rapidly to fill the vacuum left by US disarray, pushing ahead with its "One Belt, One Road" (OBOR) initiative and consolidating the projection of its power both globally and regionally, particularly in Eurasia and the contested South China Sea. In the space between this spiraling great power competition, the Association of Southeast Asian Nations (ASEAN) has sought to uphold its claim to "centrality" via its extended pan-regional organs, particularly the East Asia Summit (EAS) and the Regional Comprehensive Economic Partnership (RCEP), while having to struggle harder to remain relevant as power politics intensify, and as new Beijing-based initiatives, such as Conference on Interaction and Confidence Building Measures in Asia (CICA), threaten to displace some of its traditional roles. Though the "Trump factor" may be a novel and disruptive element in regional politics, in terms of underlying strategic dynamics, *plus ça change* seems an appropriate motif. Given that current times are as ever cloaked in uncertainty, instability, and unpredictability, it is perhaps wiser to take a step back from the focus on "eventism" that marks the age we now live in and undertake a rigorous examination of the deeper structural trends and dynamics, eschewing punditry and future-casting since such efforts have often resulted in little more than a departure into quasi-fiction.[15]

Thus, in line with this injunction and in order to assist in the process of understanding regional security, it is essential to select and deploy the appropriate analytical tools, based upon the relevant theoretical foundations within the discipline of IR as well as extradisciplinary approaches, to make sense of this diverse, unpredictable, and complicated security environment. Indeed, many concepts and theories are competing in the intellectual marketplace to gain analytical purchase on both the pan-regional "macro-processes" and the more narrowly defined issues ("microprocesses") across the Asia Pacific region. In addition to the principal application of the core research traditions of IR, namely, realism, liberalism, and constructivism, much of the literature applies notions of security "order" or "architecture" as framing concepts to interpret security relations in the region, as discussed further below.[16] All of these theoretical/conceptual instruments serve a useful purpose by enhancing our comprehension of the region's security trends, but they also entail some limitations, which will be illustrated in due course. These valuable efforts notwithstanding, serious lacunae in our knowledge persist, with Beeson maintaining that "of all the world's regions, the Asia-Pacific is arguably the least well understood."[17]

In this book, I present a new approach to conceptualizing security in the Asia Pacific region through the perspective of alignment. Though the term will be further extrapolated in detail below, it is sufficient now to indicate that by *alignment* I basically refer to "agreements between two or more states to undertake defense-related security cooperation."[18] This approach is designed to facilitate an understanding of the complex patterns of regional interaction and broader security directions from a new and different angle. Indeed, the alignment choices made by both major and minor states have a profound impact on regional security trends and the prospects for peace and conflict. As George Liska attests, "Alignments are always instrumental in structuring the state system, sometimes transforming it."[19] Anchored in the main research traditions of IR, and in some ways subsuming related framing concepts such as security order and architecture, this volume provides an alternate and novel approach using alignment theories to capture the key security dynamics of this pivotal region.

However, as the pages that follow demonstrate, our understanding of alignment theory itself is also long overdue for revision and improvement in order to better accommodate the non-alliance or "new" alliance forms of security cooperation that have risen to prominence in recent years. This is a pressing task given the wide proliferation of these new forms of alignment in the post–Cold War era, which are especially conspicuous in Asia Pacific. The region encompasses a range of bilateral strategic partnerships, minilateral groupings, issue-specific alignments and hybrid organizations, as well as the representative case studies examined in this volume.[20] Thus, to remedy the situation requires the aggregation of diverse bodies of conceptual literature pertaining to alignment and their reformulation into a comprehensive, cohesive, and structured format. This book therefore serves two purposes: presenting a reconstituted approach to alignment theory and applying the resulting frameworks to the key security groupings in the Asia Pacific region in order to gain a fresh appreciation of their workings.

To achieve this dual purpose, I first outline the three prominent patterns of alignment as they obtain in contemporary international politics: the alliance (redux), the security community, and the strategic partnership. This is followed by their corresponding conceptual and theoretical bases: intra-alliance politics, security community theory, and organizational theories. Through this exercise, an overarching analytical framework can be derived to structure a holistic understanding of such macroprocesses in regional security (see Figure 1.1). It is my aim to render a service to scholars and analysts by providing a comprehensive analytical tool kit that may be applied to a variety of alignment case studies, past and present. It is also a sine qua non that such a combined framework acknowledges the major transformation in the empirical nature and conceptual understanding of alignments that has occurred since the end of the Cold War. As will become quickly evident through the following discussion, much of the IR scholarship has neglected to keep pace with the transformation of alignment paradigms since that time. A failure to appreciate the changed nature and purpose of alignments in the twenty-first century potentially leads to the misapplication of obsolete paradigms and frameworks and, consequently, threatens to skew our understandings.

Figure 1.1 Methodological Approach

IDENTIFY		PROPOSE		APPLY
Alignment Paradigm		Theoretical Perspective		Empirical Case Study (Archetype)
Alliance (redux)	⇒	Intra-alliance Politics	⇒	TSD (Virtual Alliance)
Security Community	⇒	Security Communities Theory	⇒	ASC
Strategic Partnership	⇒	Organizational Theories	⇒	SCO (Strategic Partnership Network)

Note: TSD is the Trilateral Strategic Dialogue; ASC is the ASEAN Security Community; and SCO is the Shanghai Cooperation Organisation.

In order to illuminate regional security trends from a new perspective, the core of my analysis focuses on the three most prominent examples of such differing alignments in Asia Pacific: the Trilateral Strategic Dialogue (TSD)—a virtual trilateral alliance; the ASEAN Security Community (ASC)—a security community; and the Shanghai Cooperation Organisation (SCO)—a strategic partnership network. These "archetypes" serve as case studies against which the foregoing conceptual apparatus may be tested, and taken together, they constitute the key poles of security alignment in Asia Pacific. In this way, the analysis covers competing empirical archetypes across the region and matches them with specific alignment paradigms rooted in IR theory. Each paradigm, with its accompanying analytical framework, acts as a conceptual lens for understanding the relevant case study, while being specifically calibrated for understanding different archetypes of alignment. Though the theoretical and empirical terrain may be exceedingly complex, this book aims to show that it can be usefully structured in such a way as to facilitate an improved and systemic understanding of the security dynamics in the Asia Pacific region using alignment perspectives.

In the process of formulating and applying alignment paradigms to case study archetypes in Asia Pacific, I seek to shed light on the following issues: What are the key instruments of security cooperation, how can they be characterized, and how can their behavior be understood? What kinds of security challenges/threats do these alignments anticipate and how are they responding to them? What kind of "vision" does each of the alignment archetypes champion in Asia, and what will be the likely outcome of the contest between such competing visions for the future of the region? Along the way, I consider how existing approaches to framing regional security, as well as conventional alliance/alignment theory, may be supplemented and updated.

Security in the Asia Pacific Region: Background

The Asia Pacific Region

The definition of *Asia Pacific* is more of a debate than a fixture. As Joanne Wallis and Andrew Carr point out: "This debate over terminology reflects the fact that, as power shifts, so do regional identities and geographic boundaries. It also reflects the direction and attention of state power and diplomacy."[21] Before embarking upon any study of the Asia Pacific region it is therefore necessary to unpack the complex definitional problems that accompany the term and seek to arrive at a satisfactory working definition to support this study (including setting some boundaries to its empirical coverage). Indeed, this "definitional minefield" continues to vex scholars and policymakers alike and therefore cannot be avoided.[22]

Though it may at first appear a simple matter for geographers or cartographers, establishing a precisely demarcated definition of a given "region" is seldom straightforward in practice, and Asia Pacific is no exception. The United Nations has produced a "geoscheme" by which it assigns countries a subregional category, but it does not delineate Asia Pacific itself as a region.[23] To fashion a serviceable Asia Pacific descriptor would require the aggregation of subregional building blocks defined by the geoscheme as Northeast and Southeast Asia, Central Asia, South Asia, and Oceania. But even this would be inadequate to properly capture what most IR scholars would perceive as "Asia Pacific" since it does not account for the major role played by the United States. In some cases, these descriptors match some of the institutional apparatus, such as Asia Pacific Economic Cooperation (APEC) and EAS that form the region's security "architecture." Moreover, in addition to sometimes arbitrary geographical markers, Beeson advises us that a region "can also be conceived geopolitically, culturally, ideologically, and economically."[24] Thus, as Björn Hettne notes, "it is how political actors perceive and interpret the idea of region and notions of 'regionness' that is critical: all regions are socially constructed and hence politically contested."[25] This is of no small consequence for the study of regional security politics, as we shall discover. For example, different actors at different times have used or misused regional appellations, frequently for political or ideological purposes, such as the "Pacific Basin," the "Pacific Rim," "Pacific Asia," and most recently, the "Indo Pacific," while seldom supplying concrete definitions to accompany or justify these constructs.[26]

The best acceptable solution to this conundrum is to assume an appropriate understanding of a region based upon the specific task to be undertaken. Hettne, after all, argues that "there are no 'natural' regions: definitions of a 'region' vary according to the problem or question under investigation."[27] For example, Barry Buzan and others have sought to highlight their notion of a "regional security complex" (RSC) based upon an intermediate "level of analysis" between the international system and the state (unit) levels.[28] This, according to Buzan and Ole Wæver, is "a set of units whose major ['macro'] processes of securitization, desecuritization, or both, are so interlinked that their security problems cannot reasonably be analyzed or resolved apart from one and another."[29] Buzan himself subsequently demarcates what he calls an "Asian super complex" comprising three subcomplexes.[30] These subcomplexes are closely allied to the descriptors enumerated above, with the "North East Asian" and "South East Asian" subcomplexes identical to the UN geoscheme, except for the inclusion of Australia in the South East Asian sub-complex instead of "Oceania." These together form the "East Asian Regional Security Complex." The addition of the South Asian RSC makes up the "Asian super complex." The United States is considered an "extraregional actor," while Central Asia was excluded from his study at the time. However, T. J. Pempel notes that "many of the countries of Central Asia have explicit claims to regional importance particularly on security grounds."[31] Perhaps a more succinct, though still unavoidably qualified, demarcation is that provided by Robert Ayson in his dedicated study *Asia's Security*, which consists of "core" components such as "East Asia" and "borderlands" stretching into Russia/Central Asia, Australia, and of course, the United States.[32]

Using the UN geographical definition as a starting cartographical template and then adjusting it with the functional notion of RSC from a security perspective gets us closer to the approach adopted in this book. Although in basic conformity with Ayson's interpretation of Asia and its borderlands, as Ajin Choi and William Tow propose, "the concept of 'region' in this context is understood no more as predetermined but instead as porous. Beyond geographic proximity, the region can be reconstituted by *reflecting patterns of states' interaction and power*."[33] In identifying subregional groupings based on the alignment of certain states, the definition of the region acts as a stage upon which the actors (states and alignments of states) act out their respective roles and through which we can ascertain the macroprocesses at work. As David Shambaugh notes:

> its traditional geographic subcomponents—North East Asia, South East Asia, South Asia, Central Asia, and Oceania—are no longer useful intellectual constructs for dividing and distinguishing the macro-processes occurring throughout the region. In the twenty-first century, these five subregions are all interconnected and interdependent at numerous levels.[34]

What matters most then is not a precise demarcation of the region or RSC as initially stated above, since these simply provide the stage upon which macroprocesses involving regional/cross-regional alignment groupings form and interact. In this study, the focus is therefore upon the member states (and affiliated states) of the three core alignments identified in the case studies, set against the definitional backdrop that Buzan and Ayson have provided.

As a brief aside, some limitations to this study require notation, given that the Asia Pacific security landscape presents an "intimidatingly broad canvas."[35] There are some selective omissions of states that are important stakeholders and contributors to the regional security environment but do not yet form a fully integrated part of the three case studies examined. The main one is India, which proves a highly problematic fit for this study.[36] New Delhi is increasingly a major player in the strategic struggles to be played out in the wider Asia Pacific region; however, it is not yet fully aligned with any of the three main groupings, while retaining connections with each of them.[37] As David Envall and Ian Hall argue, "India's ability to shape regional order is inhibited by inherited, but still influential, attitudes in New Delhi that are skeptical about alliances."[38] This is a consequence of India's continued adhesion to its Nehruvian policy of "nonalignment," a concept discussed later. India, which will appear on the margins of each case study, thus presents us with an interesting conceptual and empirical conundrum: what is nonalignment; how can it be explained; to what degree does Indian interaction with each of the three case alignments influence them? Even more problematic, at the time of writing (in 2017), India was in the process of acceding to the SCO as a full member, the ramifications of which could substantially change the nature of this alignment.[39] Perhaps adding to the mystery of Indian strategic policy was its interest in closer affiliation with the TSD to form a "Quad" in 2007, a prospect that was revived in 2018. These decisions potentially raise questions of bewildering complexity in our understanding of Indian (non-)alignment policy going forward, and its effect upon the established alignments treated here.

Also, other states that are peripheral actors in the three security alignments considered here are not given direct detailed coverage in this study. South Korea, as a result of its "North Korea–locked" condition, and Taiwan, as a result of its "abnormal" international status, are treated here as "issues" that influence the behavior of certain alignments (i.e., as "flashpoints" mentioned below) rather than fully autonomous security actors in their own right.[40] I acknowledge these countries can and do contribute to regional security discourses and they are important in any consideration of the US "hub-and-spoke" alliance system, but they are not *core* members, since they are not "networked" (as are the TSD partners). Likewise, due to its distancing from the Australia–New Zealand–United States Security Treaty (ANZUS), New Zealand is not fully engaged with the TSD alignment.[41] They will, however, make reappearance, along with India, under the discussion of the "TSD-plus" notion.

The Rise of Asia Pacific and Its Security Implications

The Asia Pacific region is the most dynamic area of the world, having undergone a profound transformation over the past half century.[42] This transformation occurred in two distinct phases. In the first phase, Japan, with the assistance of the United States, not only recovered from its postwar devastation, but became a leading economic power by the 1970s.[43] A decade later it had been joined by the newly industrialized countries (NICs) or "Asian Tigers" of Taiwan, South Korea, Hong Kong, and Singapore.[44]

Toward the end of this first phase, commentators had begun to speak of a "Pacific Century," indicating a shift in geo-economic power away from the Euro-Atlantic region to the countries of the Pacific Rim, spearheaded by Japan, with the Tigers and the United States also in the van.[45] This phase came to an end with the burst of the Japanese "bubble economy" in the early-1990s and the subsequent Asian Financial Crash of 1997–1998.[46] However, while Japan and the Tigers held the world's attention, a new phase had already surreptitiously begun whereby economic reforms in China, and a decade later in India, paved the way for their meteoric rise to economic primacy in Asia, accompanied now by the "Little Dragons" of Asia: Vietnam, Indonesia, Thailand, and Malaysia.[47]

The second phase, defined more narrowly as "Asia rising," or even just "China rising," was dubbed by Kevin Rudd, former Australian prime minister, as an "Asia-Pacific Century."[48] This subtle rebranding to shift the accent to the *Asian* component of this phenomenon also reflects how the main "Pacific" elements of Australia, Japan, and the United States are no longer playing the driving role in this process, notwithstanding recent US policy under the Obama administration to "rebalance" and to enjoy another "Pacific Century," as previously articulated by former secretary of state Hillary Clinton.[49] Indeed, the focus of the new Asia Pacific Century is squarely on China, India, and the fast-developing parts of Southeast Asia.

As Daniel Baldino and his coauthors posit, "it is likely that an emerging global power shift in favor of Asia, particularly China and India, will continue" in the twenty-first century.[50] These remarkable and rapid changes mean we now face an international environment of extraordinary complexity and potential volatility. This metamorphosis of the geo-economic landscape has significant ramifications in the geopolitical and geostrategic arenas. The rise of China and India is triggering new rivalries and shifts in the regional balance of power.[51] Historically, according to realist theorist John Mearsheimer, the incorporation of rising great powers into the prevailing international order, such as that of Germany and Japan in the first half of the twentieth century, has been highly problematic and has repeatedly been accompanied by a devastating conflict.[52] Such powers are often seen as "revisionist" for their intentions to acquire greater geopolitical space, play a larger role in established institutions, or even a desire to overturn the pre-existing security order.[53] It follows that "if Mearsheimer's logic is correct, the US and China will have no choice but to behave aggressively—the rise of China will not therefore be peaceful."[54]

Over the past half century, regional order was predicated on a US-led hegemonic system underpinned by a portfolio of regional alliances and known as the "hub-and-spoke" or "San Francisco" system.[55] The relative decline of the United States has potentially weakened this system, and recent policies under the Trump administration appear to be undermining it still further. This has made it increasingly vulnerable to challenges from external powers such as China, the Democratic People's Republic of Korea (DPRK), and others.[56] The economic advancement of the rising Asian powers has translated into increased military budgets, expanded and modernized military establishments, and a greater willingness to wield them as a guarantee of national interests.[57] Naturally, the status quo powers—Japan, the United States, Australia—are forced to respond to potential challenges to their security interests, possibly sparking "security dilemmas" and a resultant region-wide arms race. This has the potential to ignite conflict between the various competing constituencies of the region. Areas such as the South China Sea and East China Sea, as well as other contested maritime territories, are often singled out as the most dangerous flashpoints, alongside the perennial unresolved disputes over the status of Taiwan and North Korea.[58]

In addition, there is widespread recognition that these orthodox security threats are accompanied by a plethora of what have been dubbed "nontraditional security" (NTS) threats. NTS issues such as environmental dangers or natural disasters, financial crises, demographic shifts, pandemic diseases, and transnational criminal organizations, as well as terrorism and proliferation, multiply the security agendas of all the powers, both major and minor.[59] Mely Caballero-Anthony argues that these "NTS issues increasingly define states' security agendas" and that this is spurring "the emergence of new cooperative mechanisms and the recalibration of existing institutions to address these challenges."[60] Indeed, as will become apparent in the course of the case studies in this book, each of the key alignments makes claims to be founded on, or calibrated toward, combating such nontraditional threats: a fact that is little taken into account in so-called traditional alliance/alignment theory. For example, Beijing has identified that "nontraditional security threats such as terrorism, natural disasters and transnational crimes have become more prominent."[61] The emphasis on the NTS credentials of the alignments covered in this book not only reflects an empirical shift in policymaking and the security agendas in the case studies but also indicates how conceptualization of contemporary alignment needs adjusting to better account for such developments.

Framing Concepts for Understanding Asia Pacific Security

As alluded to above, analysts have regularly employed one of two alternative macroconcepts to frame their analyses of Asia Pacific security: *order* and *architecture*. Though these are sometimes conflated with alignment, and more often with one another, they are actually quite distinct. First, security order is defined, according to David Morgan, as "dominant patterns of security management within [regional] security complexes."[62] The idea of security order is closely affiliated with notions of an "international society" formulated by Hedley Bull.[63] According to Muthiah Alagappa, this entails "rule governed interaction among states in their pursuit of private and public security goals."[64] Though substantial literature has grown up around this concept, it has either remained rather abstract for practical application or otherwise devolved back to the basic explanatory apparatus of realism, liberalism, and constructivism, with each of these traditions emphasizing instrumental, normative-contractual, or solidarist paths to achieving security order, respectively.[65] But this concept entails serious limitations, as Emanuel Adler and Patricia Greve testify:

> arguments about the varieties of international order abound in International Relations. These disputes include arguments about the security mechanisms, institutions, and practices that sustain international orders, including balance of power and alliances, hegemony, security regimes based on regional or global institutions, public, private, and hybrid security networks, as well as different kinds of security communities.[66]

Others argue that we cannot meaningfully speak of a regional security order in Asia Pacific at all. Michael Yahuda asserts that

> the diversity within the region and the fluidity of the security arrangements are indicative of the absence of what might be called a regional order. There is as yet no basis for the establishment of a regional order, if that is taken to mean the existence of stable relationships based upon accepted rules of conduct between states, of shared views about legitimacy of governments within states and of common assumptions about the interrelationships among regional and external states.[67]

Instead, what is more apparent is the existence of "divergent visions of regional order"[68] insomuch as they are championed by the three respective alignment blocs investigated here. Even as their rival visions of desired security order collide, we are left with coexistent elements of the former Cold War order and its evolution as well as a newly emergent order based upon rising powers: a situation best described by Nick Bisley as a "hybrid order."[69]

Second is the related concept of security architecture. William Tow and Brendan Taylor define the term *regional security architecture* as "an overarching, coherent and comprehensive security structure for a geographically defined area, which facilitates the resolution of that region's policy concerns and achieves its security objectives."[70] In practice, this security structure is largely predicated upon institutions: these may be formal multilateral security dialogue forums, as in the case of APEC or the EAS, or on the basis of alliance treaties, such as the US-Japan security treaty.

However, there is a vital distinction between inclusive institutional forums, such as APEC and EAS, and tighter institutional components, such as a US-Japan alliance. For example, the TSD, ASC, SCO, and Five Power Defense Arrangement (FPDA) are *exclusive* alignments as well as constituents of the broader regional architecture. When such identifiable alignments operate within larger inclusive regional institutional forums designed to facilitate security dialogue like the APEC or EAS, consensus can fall victim to the rivalry between alignments within them, rendering them little more than "talk shops." In other words, "Not far beneath the veneer of diplomatic common cause represented by cooperative mechanisms national rivalries remain."[71] Not only this, but analysts discern "'competing geometries' between 'exclusivist' bilateral and overly 'inclusivist' multilateral pathways" toward achieving security for the region.[72] As a consequence, instead of the kind of ideal form of security structure that Tow and Taylor allude to above, the majority of analysts consider Asia Pacific architecture "nascent," "fractured," "partial," or otherwise ineffective.[73] Architecture in the empirical sense is therefore makeshift enterprise that, according to Victor Cha, consists of "networks and patchworks of differently configured and overlapping bilaterals, trilaterals, quadrilaterals, and other multilateral groupings that stitched together define the regional architecture."[74] This results both in major practical impediments as well as conceptual drawbacks, since no dedicated body of theoretical literature to date has comprehensively and effectively grappled with the conceptual operation or application of security architecture as a distinctive macroprocess, though relevant elements of IR theory have been applied on an ad hoc basis.

As a consequence of these limitations, this book argues that alignment may serve as an alternative frame for better understanding the security dynamics of the Asia Pacific. Indeed, alignment is a crucially important facet of international politics and demands greater investigation among the IR scholarly community than it presently receives. All our great strategic thinkers, contemporary and historical—Kautilya, Sun Zi, Machiavelli, to name but a sample—have extolled the practice of alignment for political or military advantage.[75] Alignments are an integral part of the current international system and reach back as far as recorded history. Indeed, one scholarly project has chronicled every alignment of substance in the modern era, from 1848 to 2008.[76] But one can go back further into the annals to confirm that alignments are a perennial fixture of international politics. One only has to think of the fluctuating alignments among Greek city-states forged and broken continuously throughout the course of the Peloponnesian Wars (431–401 B.C.E.), to cite one example.[77] Indeed, the IR research tradition of realism, with alignment/alliance theorizing at its core, dates from this conflict, and recent scholarship has revived its lessons for application to Asia Pacific.[78]

"Alignment" in international politics is the process or condition of cooperating on an agreed issue, or spectrum of issues, between two or more states in the system, either within or outside a formal institutional context. Though economic alignment is perforce possible (e.g., free trade agreements; the Maastricht Treaty, 1993; or the Cairns Group, 1986), it is seldom, if ever, classified as such. Thus the phenomenon of alignment is considered first and foremost one of political "security cooperation." But as Bisley warns us, "'security cooperation' covers everything from large-scale and high-cost alliances to low key and commitment-free discussions."[79] Therefore, the best stand-alone definition of the term is supplied by Steven David: "Alignment occurs when a state brings its policies into close cooperation with another state to achieve mutual security goals."[80] This is the definition accepted in this book, and a fuller picture of all its nuances will be gained through the course of the theoretical chapters that follow.

However, in order to make our study of alignment fit for purpose, we must recognize that both empirically and theoretically we need to overcome conventional applications and understandings of alignment that often subsume it under the "alliance" label, which is but one (common) paradigm representing a wider phenomenon. Ward posits

> "Alignment" is a more extensive concept than alliance since it does not focus solely upon the military dimension of international politics. Degrees of alignments in political, economic, military, and cultural spheres present a multifaceted sculpture of national and supranational postures.[81]

Moreover, it should be recognized that twenty-first-century Asia Pacific is not nineteenth- or twentieth-century Europe.[82] Alyson Bailes et al. comment that "old-style alliances with a defined opponent are now rare, and most groups address themselves to the reduction of conflict (internally of externally) and to transnational challenges such as terrorism."[83] As a consequence, Tow notes that "alliances, alignments and coalitions need to be reconsidered theoretically in terms of how much they fit into this new environment."[84] This being the case, it is necessary to break free of the "alliance-locked" discourse and the theory that encumbers our extant knowledge of alignment in IR to rethink and retool our understanding of the phenomenon to fit the contemporary context, which includes revising our understanding of contemporary alliances themselves.

A New Constellation of Alignments in the Asia Pacific

As a corollary of the multiplication of security challenges faced by regional states, Hugh White claims that we are currently seeing a "rebalancing of strategic alignments" in the Asia Pacific.[85] Bruno Tertrais adds that new challenges "have strengthened many old alliances and have fostered the creation of new alignments."[86] I argue that this is largely centered on the three emerging, but as yet not fully crystallized, "poles" of alignment. Tow indicates that, in addition to the long-established presence of the ASC, the security environment in the Asia Pacific is characterized by "competing geometries" consisting of the "intensification of the SCO as a 'de facto' anti-Western grouping and the further development of US-led trilateral or other multilateral security dialogues as tacit instruments of containment against growing Chinese power."[87] These three alignments are correctly recognized as the main feature of the "regional security framework" by a Chinese white paper, which states: "In this region there are ASEAN-led security cooperation mechanisms and platforms such as the SCO . . . as well as [US] military alliances formed in history."[88]

Although each of the alignments operates within a larger context of grand strategic competition, it is particularly notable, officially at least, that each has strongly emphasized its intention to focus on NTS challenges. This foregrounding of alignments designed to combat NTS threats is a marked departure from previous military-defense-focused alliances/alignments of the past. Indeed, China and the SCO have explicitly derided Cold War–style traditional alliances, instead proffering their own preference for the strategic partnerships, which emphasize NTS cooperation and comprehensive security.[89] This distinction colors both the alignments and the theoretical approach employed here, which is designed to bring such novel developments into sharper relief.

In this book, I introduce the conceptual underpinnings of three of the most prolific paradigms of security alignment and those that dominate the Asia Pacific security landscape in various guises: alliance (redux), security community, and strategic partnership. In advancing new or revised models of these three security alignments, I seek to address shortfalls in our conceptual understanding within the discipline of IR and security studies. The book thus contributes toward compiling a comprehensive metaframework through which alignments may be systematically interrogated. Informed by this conceptual taxonomy of alignment, I then subject three case studies of TSD, ASC, and SCO to empirical scrutiny and evaluation, demonstrating how the analytical frameworks can enlighten us as to the purpose, structure, and prospects of the three principal security groupings in the region. It should be noted that though the case studies presented here appertain to the Asia Pacific region, the theoretical paradigms/frameworks themselves are equally transferable to the analysis of other regions. Having adopted alignment as an alternative to typical order- or architecture-based studies, this introduction now ends by briefly outlining the alignment paradigms and case studies to be investigated in the chapters that follow.

Structure of the book

Alliances

Chapters 2 and 3 are focused upon the most prominent form of security alignment—the alliance paradigm—particularly the ways in which it has metamorphosed. Chapter 2 introduces this paradigm of alignment and the debates as to its use and misuse in IR and policy discourse, and why it is in urgent need of updating (hence: redux). This is followed by the relevant analytical framework based upon an "intra-alliance politics" perspective, designed to account for allied behavior within the compact. Armed with this framework, Chapter 3 then applies these tools to the case study of the TSD "virtual alliance" to assess the analytical utility of the framework and its effectiveness in revealing the behavioral dynamics of this archetype. Reflecting US policy of "strengthening alliances as we attract new partners," the TSD is an alignment of maritime democracies based around a nucleus of cooperation between the US, Japan, and Australia, within the broader US hub-and-spoke alliance system.[90] This trilateral grouping represents intensified cooperation under the earlier banner of "rebalancing" between the United States and its two "core" allies, the so-called northern and southern "anchors" of the Pacific: Japan and Australia. Established as a senior official dialogue in 2002 and upgraded to the ministerial level in 2006, the regularization of trilateral cooperation complements and reinforces individual bilateral ties between the allies, including the new bilateral security declaration between Tokyo and Canberra.[91]

Though it is embedded in the familiar traditional alliance paradigm of the twentieth century, the TSD is rather different from the former bilateral hub-and-spoke security alliances between the United States and its partners.[92] First, it can be considered a good example of Ralph Cossa's "virtual" alliance archetype, in that it lacks a formal treaty and partially exists under the cover of other multilateral initiatives, such as coordination in APEC and ASEAN Regional Forum (ARF), and historical bilateral treaties. Second, it officially assigns equal priority to NTS threats such as weapons of mass destructions (WMD), terrorism, and natural disasters, while "hedging" against incipient strategic threats from China and the DPRK.[93] As Cossa argues, alliances "remain indispensable for managing traditional security challenges and provide the basis for dealing effectively with new non-traditional security issues."[94] This alignment, led by the current regional hegemon, therefore represents one of the three "poles" around which the regional security order revolves. If additional spokes of the US-bilateral "San Francisco" system (e.g., Republic of Korea) are added as well as tacit members (e.g., India, Taiwan), this would represent a "TSD-plus" model. Again, this reflects US determination to "strengthen and evolve our alliances and partnerships into an extended network."[95] Nevertheless, as the TSD remains a relatively understudied alignment formation, with most of the extant literature concentrating on bilateral relations, adding the minilateral/trilateral element here is therefore a valuable contribution.[96] As Tow reminds us, "Theoretical work on minilateral security remains sparse, and this is certainly the case with its trilateral component."[97]

Security Communities

Chapters 4 and 5 are dedicated to conceptualizing the security community paradigm of alignment with the so-called ASEAN Political-Security Community (APSC), or just ASEAN Security Community (ASC), as the test case.[98] Formed in 1967, ASEAN is a well-established grouping of both continental and maritime states spanning the lower part of East Asia down toward Oceania. Essentially, ASEAN in its various guises, the ASC in particular, represents a combination of geographically contiguous small and middle-sized states aimed at protecting their security interests and avoiding domination by the leading powers of the region such as the United States and China. The institution is based upon a variety of foundational documents such as the 1967 ASEAN Declaration, 1976 Treaty of Amity and Cooperation (TAC), and ASEAN Charter (2007), for example, and its official commitments to achieve the condition of a political and security community as well as socio-cultural and economic communities.[99] Its core purposes are to ensure intra-mural collaboration among its membership, which has expanded incrementally to encompass the whole Southeast Asian region, and to serve as a generator of regional stability extending across the whole Asia Pacific.

ASEAN has been widely studied before, and analyses of this security community to date have mainly presupposed the ASC to be an institution or a component of security architecture. In contrast to the other more novel case studies (TSD and SCO) presented in this volume, the ASC case relies more heavily upon existing research material. What is new about the approach employed in this book is the specific conception of the ASC as an *alignment*. As will be demonstrated in the analysis that follows, the ASC qualifies as an alignment of member states pursuing mutual security objectives. What is particularly notable is that since its inception, according to Davison, ASEAN "eschewed the structure of a traditional military alliance" and instead adopted a functionalist approach inspired by the European

Union (EU) to provide for its intramural security.[100] Strongly influenced by academic perspectives and Track II initiatives such as Council for Security Cooperation in Asia Pacific (CSCAP) and International Institute for Strategic Studies (IISS, Asia), it is also exemplary of an alignment calibrated toward NTS issues.[101]

In addition, this alignment of Southeast Asian powers has sought to export its security model on a wider regional plane. The ARF and EAS aim to create a pan-regional security dialogue, while the ASEAN+3 mechanism seeks to bind the major Asian powers to its own security model, founded upon the "ASEAN way" (or "ASEAN Consensus"). Thus, we see "ASEAN-plus" as a way for this alignment to secure the interests of its members through manipulating the wider security order. Although the ASEAN countries individually maintain significant military capabilities, they seek to employ more of a soft power approach in maintaining regional security. The challenge for the ASC is how to maneuver to defend its collective interests between the maritime and continental power blocs—namely, the TSD and SCO—that vastly exceed the economic and military power of Southeast Asia, and in the teeth of division between internal member states on how to respond to security challenges such as territorial disputes in the South China Sea, which potentially threaten its cohesion. This collective action problem indicates the difficulty of such a diverse group of states maintaining their unity as an identifiable alignment and undermines their effectiveness as a regional security provider on the broader pan-regional plane.

Strategic Partnerships

Chapters 6 and 7 introduce the most novel form of alignment, the strategic partnership, and proceed to apply the interdisciplinary analytical framework to the exemplary SCO case study.[102] The SCO strategic partnership (network) began with the establishment of the Shanghai Five in 1996, which was originally designed to resolve border disputes between the powers. Since its official foundation in 2001, the SCO has steadily expanded its remit and attracted outside parties as observers just as it has deepened and broadened its institutional structure, with India and Pakistan acceding to membership in 2017.[103] Formed around the nucleus of the bilateral Beijing-Moscow "strategic partnership," the SCO is an institutional umbrella for a diverse network of interlocking strategic partnerships between the two leading powers and their Central Asian neighbors. Overseen by regular summit meetings and governed by a burgeoning bureaucratic apparatus, the SCO concerns itself with security cooperation across a broad spectrum of traditional and NTS threats, with particular concern for terrorism, separatism, and religious fundamentalism (the "three evils").

While it prioritizes NTS cooperation, its activities extend to joint military exercises, economic integration, and efforts at cultural exchange. Beyond this, with Chinese and Russian leadership, the SCO advocates a new model of security relations for the Asia Pacific based on the "Shanghai spirit," representing an emergent "pole" of power in the region, in contrast to the previous more-established blocs.

I intimate throughout that this is a Beijing-led project since "it is certainly plausible to argue that the Chinese leadership sets the tone for the SCO."[104] But this should not be taken to exclude Russia as a major partner in the enterprise. As Stephen Aris contends, "Russia and China are often depicted as alternative power centers within the international system. Therefore the formation of a regional organization comprising both Russia and China has important connotations for global politics, security and economics."[105] As its influence extends to peripheral "observers" and "dialogue partners," we may also conceive of an "SCO-plus" model. As in the first case study, the SCO as a minilateral (or "plurilateral") alignment is understudied, with much of the literature concentrating on the Sino-Russian bilateral "core."[106] Conceiving of the SCO explicitly as an alignment is a valuable undertaking in allowing us to gain a more holistic appreciation of its workings.

In the final chapter of the book, I conclude that alignment offers a new perspective that can be either an alternative or a complement to existing perspectives aimed at enhancing our understanding of the Asia Pacific security environment. I also stress that our understanding of alignment in the twenty-first century and in Asia Pacific needs rethinking. Because each different paradigm is designed to capture a distinct form of alignment and supply the necessary framework through which it may be appropriately analyzed, I seek to advance alignment theorizing beyond its traditional roots in structural balance of power/threat literature.[107] The book therefore concludes with a review of the strengths of the analytical frameworks in appraising the Asia Pacific case studies, followed by brief examination of the connections between alignments (interalignment dynamics) and final reflections on how synergies between the analytical frameworks suggest potential advances toward a more unified body of alignment theory.

In sum, the book is designed to offer a theoretically sophisticated yet practically relevant framing device for understanding Asia Pacific security dynamics from the new perspective of alignment. For the first time, to the best of my knowledge, it gathers a full set of the major theoretical paradigms/frameworks and three pan-regional case studies in one volume to offer a comprehensive picture of security dynamics in the Asia Pacific. In this respect, it takes a "loftier" academic vantage point that focuses more on deeper structural trends and reproducible dynamics rather than more immediate policy fluctuations. It is hoped that the theoretical approaches taken will withstand inevitable empirical developments in the case studies and be flexible enough to accommodate them over the *longue durée*.

The Asia Pacific is increasingly viewed as both the engine of global prosperity and the likely location for the eruption of major power conflict, making an understanding of the macroprocess of security alignment of fundamental importance. As Davison attests, "That the region is of critical global significance, both strategically and economically, is beyond contestation."[108] Explaining the microprocesses within individual alignment cases (the TSD, ASC, and SCO) further deepens our understanding of their purpose, modus operandi, and prospects. This task is all the more pressing given that the twenty-first-century security landscape, including the new prominence of NTS issues, bears little resemblance to the Cold War bipolar era and the theoretical approaches for explaining alignments and their behavioral dynamics are long overdue for updating to reflect current empirical realities. With this book, I aspire to rectify some of these shortcomings and contribute to the progression of serious debates upon regional security and alignment behavior.

Notes

1. McGregor, *Asia's Reckoning*; Rachman, *Easternization;* Mahbubani, *The New Asian Hemisphere.*

2. State Council Information Office of the People's Republic of China, *China's Policies on Asia-Pacific Security Cooperation.*

3. Ayson, *Asia's Security*, p. 1.

4. Pike, *Empires at War;* Auslin, *The End of the Asian Century.*

5. Berger, "Set for Stability?"; Friedberg, "Ripe for Rivalry"; Desker, "Why War Is Unlikely in Asia"; White, "Why War in Asia Remains Thinkable."

6. Davison, "Introduction: The Asia Pacific Century?" p. 2.

7. Beeson, *Institutions of the Asia-Pacific*, p. xi.

8. Brands, *American Grand Strategy in the Age of Trump.*

9. Mehta, "'Pivot to the Pacific' Is Over, Senior U.S. Diplomat Says."

10. White House, *National Security Strategy 2017.*

11. Cossa and Glosserman, "The Pivot Is Dead, Long Live the Pivot."

12. Kaplan, *The Return of Marco Polo's World*; Navarro, *Crouching Tiger.*

13. French, *Everything under the Heavens*; Liu. *The China Dream.*

14. Economy, *The Third Revolution.*

15. Friedman, *The Next 100 Years*: Friedman and LeBard, *The Coming War with Japan.*

16. Alagappa, *Asian Security Order*; Tow and Taylor, "What Is Asian Security Architecture?"

17. Beeson, *Institutions of the Asia-Pacific*, p. xii.

18. Ciorciari, *The Limits of Alignment*, p. 1.

19. Liska, *Nations in Alliance*, p. 12.

20. Kim, "Asia's Minilateral Moment."

21. Carr and Wallis, "An Introduction to Asia-Pacific Security," p. 2.

22. Davison, "Introduction: Asia's 'Great Game'?" p. 4.

23. United Nations Statistics Division, "Composition of Macro Geographical (Continental) Regions, Geographical Sub-Regions, and Selected Economic and Other Groupings."

24. Beeson, *Institutions of the Asia-Pacific*, p. xiii.

25. Hettne, "Beyond the 'New' Regionalism," p. 544.

26. Wilkins, "'The New Pacific Century' and the Rise of China."

27. Hettne, "Beyond the 'New' Regionalism," p. 544.

28. Buzan, "The Level of Analysis Problem in International Relations Reconsidered."

29. Buzan and Wæver, *Regions and Powers*, p. 44.

30. Buzan, "Security Architecture in Asia," p. 147.

31. Pempel, *Remapping East Asia*, p. 26.

32. Ayson, *Asia's Security*, p. 13.

33. Choi and Tow, "Bridging Alliances and Asia Pacific Multilateralism," p. 23. Italics added.

34. Shambaugh, "China Engages Asia," p. 97. Italics added.

35. Beeson, *Institutions of the Asia Pacific*, p. 5.

36. Brewster, *India as an Asia Pacific Power*.

37. Nayar and Paul, *India in the World Order*.

38. Envall and Hall, "Are India and Japan Potential Members of the Great Power Club?" p. 64.

39. Sajjanhar, "India and the Shanghai Cooperation Organization."

40. Chase, *Taiwan's Security Policy*; Cole, *Taiwan's Security;* Heo, Roehrig, and Seo, *Korean Security in a Changing East Asia*; Smith, *Reconstituting Korean Security;* Snyder, *South Korea at the Crossroads*.

41. New Zealand Ministry of Foreign Affairs & Trade, *Statement of Intent 2011–2014*.

42. Crump, *Asia-Pacific*.

43. Vogel, *Japan as Number One*; Johnson, *MITI and the Japanese Miracle*.

44. Kim, *Four Asian Tigers*; Garran, *Tigers Tamed*; Clark and Roy, *Comparing Development Patterns in Asia*; Castells, "Four Asian Tigers with a Dragon Head."

45. See, for example, Borthwick, *Pacific Century*; Gibney, *The Pacific Century*.

46. Wood, *The Bubble Economy*; Woo, Sachs, and Schwab, *Asian Financial Crisis;* Haggard. *The Politics of the Asian Financial Crisis;* Goldstein, *The Asian Financial Crisis*.

47. Nanda, *Rising India*; Chellaney, *Asian Juggernaut*; Lam and Lim, *The Rise of China and India*; Kang, *Rising China*; Schlossstein, *Asia's New Little Dragons*; Tellis and Wills, *Strategic Asia 2005–2006: Military Modernization in an Era of Uncertainty*.

48. Mahbubani, *The New Asian Hemisphere*; Davison, "Introduction: The Asia Pacific Century?"

49. Clinton, "America's Pacific Century."

50. Baldino et al., *Contemporary Challenges to Australian Security*, p. 70.

51. Walton and Kavalski, *Power Transition in Asia*.

52. Mearsheimer, *The Tragedy of Great Power Politics*; Goldstein, *Rising to the Challenge*.

53. Johnston, "Is China a Status Quo Power?"

54. Baldino et al., *Contemporary Challenges to Australian Security*, p. 72.

55. Calder, "Securing Security through Prosperity."

56. Cooper and Shearer, "Thinking Clearly about China's Layered Indo-Pacific Strategy."

57. Tellis and Wills, *Strategic Asia 2005–2006: Military Modernization in an Era of Uncertainty;* Bitzinger, "Military Modernization in the Asia-Pacific"; Goldman and Mahnken. *The Information Revolution in Military Affairs in Asia.*

58. Kaplan, *Asia's Cauldron*; Le Mière, "The Return of Gunboat Diplomacy"; Pollack, *No Exit;* Glaser and Glosserman, *Promoting Confidence Building Across the Taiwan Strait*; Kim and Cohen, *North Korea and Nuclear Weapons.*

59. See Ayson and Ball, *Strategy and Security in the Asia-Pacific*; Collins, *Contemporary Security Studies*; Tow, *Security Politics in the Asia-Pacific*; Dupont, *East Asia Imperiled;* Emmers, Caballero-Anthony, and Acharya, *Studying Non-Traditional Security in Asia.*

60. Caballero-Anthony, "Non-traditional Security and Multilateralism in Asia," p. 307.

61. State Council Information Office, China, *China's Policies on Asia-Pacific Security Cooperation.*

62. Morgan, "Regional Security Complexes," in Lake and Morgan, *Regional Orders* p. 32;.

63. Bull, *The Anarchical Society.*

64. Alagappa, *Asian Security Order*, p. 24.

65. Ibid.

66. Adler and Greve, "When Security Community Meets Balance of Power," p. 59.

67. Yahuda, *The International Politics of the Asia-Pacific*, p. 11.

68. Goh, "Conceptualizing the Relationship Between Bilateral and Multilateral Security Approaches in East Asia," p. 181.

69. Bisley, *Building Asia's Security,* p. 99.

70. Tow and Taylor, "What Is Asian Security Architecture?" p. 96.

71. Bisley, *Building Asia's Security*, p. 90.

72. Tow and Taylor, *Bilateralism*, p. 4.

73. Maull, "The European Security Architecture"; Bisley, *Building Asia's Security.*

74. Cha, "The Geometry of Asia's Architecture," p. 112.

75. Kautalya, *The Arthashastra*; Machiavelli, *The Prince*; Sun Tzi, *The Art of War.*

76. Gibler, *International Military Alliances.*

77. Homer, *The Iliad*; Thucydides, *History of the Peloponnesian War.*

78. Allison, *Destined for War.*

79. Bisley, *Building Asia's Security*, p. 17.

80. David, "Explaining Third World Alignment," p. 234.

81. Ward, *Research Gaps in Alliance Dynamics*, p. 7.

82. Friedberg, "Will Europe's Past Be Asia's Future?"

83. Bailes et al., *The Shanghai Cooperation Organization,* p. iv.

84. Tow, "Alliances and Alignments in the Twenty-First Century," p. 13.

85. White, "Should Australia Form an Alliance with Japan?"

86. Tertrais, 'The Changing Nature of Military Alliances', p. 135.

87. Taylor and Tow, "Challenges to Building an Effective Asia-Pacific Security Architecture," p. 344.

88. State Council Information Office, China. *China's Policies on Asia-Pacific Security Cooperation.*

89. Ibid.

90. US Department of Defense, *Summary of the 2018 National Defense Strategy*, p. 5.

91. Ministry of Foreign Affairs, Japan, "Japan-Australia Joint Declaration on Security Cooperation."

92. Cha, *Powerplay*.

93. Stephen Smith, "Trilateral Strategic Dialogue: Joint Statement."

94. Cossa et al., *The United States and the Asia-Pacific Region*, p. 5.

95. US Department of Defense, *Summary of the 2018 National Defense Strategy*, p. 8.

96. Ota, *The US-Japan Alliance in the 21st Century*; Akaha and Arase. *The US-Japan Alliance*; Green and Cronin, *The U.S.-Japan Alliance*; Ikenberry and Inoguchi, *Reinventing the Alliance*; Bell, *Dependent Ally*.

97. Tow, "The Trilateral Strategic Dialogue: Minilateralism and Asia-Pacific Order Building," p. 25.

98. ASEAN membership includes Brunei, Burma, Cambodia, Indonesia, Malaysia, Laos, the Philippines, Singapore, Thailand, and Vietnam. See Association of Southeast Asian Nations, "ASEAN Member States."

99. Association of Southeast Asian Nations, "Overview," https://asean.org/asean/about-asean/overview.

100. Davison, "Introduction: Asia's 'Great Game,'" p. 8.

101. Council for Security Cooperation in Asia Pacific, "About Us"; International Institute for Strategic Studies, "IISS-Asia Singapore."

102. Members include China, Russia, Kazakhstan, Kyrgyzstan, Tajikistan, and Uzbekistan. Observers include India, Pakistan (now acceded to membership), Mongolia, and Iran. See Shanghai Cooperation Organisation, "Main Page."

103. Shanghai Cooperation Organisation, "Brief Introduction to the Shanghai Cooperation Organisation."

104. Aris, *Eurasian Regionalism*, p. 44.

105. Ibid., p. 1.

106. Wishnick, *Mending Fences*; Westad, *Brothers in Arms*; Luthi, *The Sino-Soviet Split*; Lo, "A Wary Embrace"; Lukin, *China and Russia*; Rozman, *The Sino-Russian Challenge to the World Order*.

107. Waltz, *Theory of International Politics*; Walt, *Origins of Alliances*.

108. Davison, "Introduction: Asia's 'Great Game,'" p. 4.

2

Alliances (Redux)

Alliances are certainly the most prominent form of alignment in the theoretical sense, if no longer, I argue, in the contemporary empirical realm. It makes sense to elucidate this core paradigm at the outset, since scholarly attention with regard to alignment behavior has been overwhelmingly focused on it and because many of its theoretical assumptions, explicitly or tacitly, form the foundations of the study of the alignment phenomenon as a whole. Thus, it should also be noted that much of our conceptual understanding of *alliance* applies either directly or tangentially to exposing the dynamics of other alignments, including the security community and strategic partnership. This is beneficial because the conceptualization of the latter two paradigms is still in comparative infancy.

This chapter initially defines the key characteristics of the alliance paradigm and intimates how it needs to be reconstituted before proceeding to outline the theoretical base, from which the appropriate analytical framework is derived. Chapters 4 and 6 dealing with the alternate paradigms (security community, strategic partnership) also follow a corresponding format.

What Is an Alliance?

Alliances occupy a central position in international politics and in the scholarly investigation into alignment. John Duffield, Cynthia Michota, and Sara Ann Miller assert that "for hundreds of years, great powers, and many smaller ones as well, have regularly formed, acted through, and sometimes broken alliances."[1] Indeed, they observe, "for smaller states with limited resources, reliance on alliances may be the only option."[2] But as a result of

23

the priority given to alliance pacts by US policymakers and their regional allies, they have come to assume what Rajan Menon dubs a "totemic significance."[3] We therefore suffer from a serious case of "alliance bias" in our thinking about alignment in the discipline of IR. Indeed, the cognitive hegemony exercised over the minds of commentators, policymakers, and scholars has consequently subsumed all other forms of alignment into its paradigm. The reversal of this process is a running theme throughout this chapter and those that follow, as I aim to restore greater balance, nuance, and versatility to alignment theories.

What is perhaps doubly surprising, given its centrality and relative conceptual hegemony over the alignment phenomenon, is that scholars for the most part have appeared uninterested in the radical changes that have occurred within the "traditional military alliance" paradigm and thus neglected the need to reevaluate the utility of its accompanying theoretical base. Both these aspects warrant serious attention in order to account for the way that traditional Cold War–era alliances such as the North Atlantic Treaty Organization (NATO) have metamorphosed in the twenty-first century. This chapter does not suggest that alliances are about to disappear as tools of alignment statecraft—far from it—but as Menon has argued in the *End of Alliances*, no new alliances have appeared over the past half century (the last being the Sino–North Korean alliance pact of 1961), and those that do persevere have evolved and transformed to meet new challenges.[4] Notwithstanding, the reemergence of great power rivalry in the international security environment may yet give a new lease of life to their original functions. And yet, as former US assistant secretary of state for East Asian and Pacific affairs Kurt Campbell reminds us, from now on "alliances will look and act differently than they used to."[5]

Arriving at a succinct definition of an alliance is no simple task. As Duffield, Michota, and Miller submit: "Unfortunately, the process of developing theories of alliances has been complicated by the use of widely varying definitions."[6] I have probed alliance definitions in depth elsewhere and the interested reader may consult this work.[7] I therefore simply state my preferred definition by Glenn Snyder: "Alliances are formal associations of states for the use (or non-use) of military force, in specified circumstances, against states outside their own membership."[8] This definition has yet to be bettered, while Robert Osgood's version is equally serviceable.[9] There are many much weaker alternatives that should be summarily discarded. The definition above is exemplified by the Cold War NATO/Warsaw Pact archetypes and the "industrial-age" alliance blocs from late nineteenth century up to World War I. It also applies to the US system of bilateral military defense pacts in the Asia Pacific, at least as they were initially conceived of in the 1950s.[10]

However, I share the view of other scholars that alliances in the empirical world have undergone dramatic transformations, to the extent that in some major cases they deviate significantly from this definition and now bear scant resemblance to the traditional Cold War alliance paradigm. As William Tow observes, almost a generation removed from the end of the Cold War, "the relevance of alliances remains a highly contentious issue in the study and conduct of international relations."[11] The prime archetypes of this traditional paradigm—namely, NATO and the Warsaw Pact—no longer conform to all its key precepts. The Warsaw Pact has dissolved, rendering an enormous body of literature and expertise redundant at a stroke, though its weaker successor, the Collective Security Treaty Organization (CSTO), draws a limited amount of attention.[12] NATO, on the other hand, has been fundamentally transformed from its original purpose of deterring or counterattacking the "Soviet threat": a development that poses serious challenges to the explanatory value of "traditional" alliance theory approaches. Indeed, although there is copious literature on military adaptation related to NATO and the US-bilateral alliances, this does not directly engage with reconceptualizing what an "alliance" means in the twenty-first century.[13]

The remaining alliances of today have mutated significantly and their revised purposes reflect the radically different international security landscape that they now inhabit in the post–Cold War era. Ralph Cossa and others note, "As instruments of national policy, alliances are dynamic elements that are in a constant process of evolution, adjusting roles, missions, and capabilities to adapt to an ever-changing international environment."[14] Indeed, in accord with changing emphases on nontraditional security (NTS) threats, in addition to "traditional" military-strategic ones, alliances have concomitantly embraced nonmilitary forms of cooperation. Seongho Sheen dubs such broader nonmilitary missions "soft alliance" tasks, in contradistinction to "hard alliance"/"hard balancing" tasks against military threats.[15]

As well as the transformative process witnessed in the formerly traditional alliance archetypes, new variants of the paradigm have been identified. The first of these was coined by Victor Cha in describing relations between Japan and Korea within the US-alliance system. The term *quasi alliance* refers to a situation in which "one in which two states remain unallied but share a third party as a common ally."[16] Notably, one important distinguishing feature was the "antagonistic" nature of the Japan-Korean alignment. This might also be applied to the case of Australian-Japanese relations in the 1950s or, as Campbell points out, countries allied to Washington among the Gulf States.[17] It is not clear if the "antagonistic" element is integral to the "quasi-alliance" variant, or whether it could simply be applied to any such case of trilateral indirect alignment of two parties through the third.

Secondly, Cossa coined the term *virtual alliance* (or tacit alliance)[18] to describe the same trilateral relationship, although the theoretical composition of this was left largely undeveloped.[19] Fortunately, Hans Morgenthau provided the essence of such a concept many years before: "It occurs when their interests so obviously call for concerted policies and actions that an explicit formulation of these interests, policies and actions in the form of a treaty of alliance appears to be redundant."[20] Other good empirical examples are the US-UK "special relationship," one that demonstrates properties of collaboration stronger than most formal alliances, and above all, the US-Japan-Australia Trilateral Strategic Dialogue (TSD) case study archetype discussed in this volume.[21]

Theoretical Base

As noted above, alliance theory is essentially the mainstream of all our "traditional" alignment theory. I will first consider this body of thought and its limitations, along with its challengers, before setting forth the key tenets of the modified "intra-alliance politics" approach to analyzing contemporary alliances.

Ken Booth posits that "the traditional and still predominant explanation of alliances arises out of balance-of-power considerations."[22] In the seminal work *Theory of International Politics*, Kenneth Waltz postulates that in an anarchic international system, states are faced with insecurity, so structural imperatives will compel states to balance one another's power in order to survive.[23] The need for "capability aggregation" can be met through internal mobilization or by the formation of alliances or "coalitions" in time of war. In the *Origins of Alliances*, Stephen Walt seeks to extend Waltz's balance of power (BOP) theory by arguing that simple power calculations alone cannot account for alliance behavior. Rather, "states form alliances primarily against threats. Threats in turn are a function of power, geographic proximity, offensive capabilities and perceived intentions."[24] It follows that once the opposing state ceases to be perceived as a threat, the raison d'être of the alliance no longer exists and it therefore dissolves. Walt also notes that some states, especially small ones, "bandwagon" rather than "balance" threats.[25] These combined propositions have become a well-known canon of realism, in all its permutations, and the foundation of so-called alliance theory. Since these theories are relevant as a backdrop to both alliance and alignment theory but exhaustively examined elsewhere, it is preferable to concentrate on the less-developed "intra-alliance politics" perspective here. Nonetheless, elements of the traditional approach are still manifest in the analytical framework supplied below.

Traditional alliance theories prima facie exhibit persuasive explanatory power. They remain recognizable as fairly parsimonious "theories" in the positivist sense of IR methodology and appear compelling measured against the empirical record. But they do exhibit major limitations and flaws. First, it is apparent that these theories are almost exclusively fixed upon explaining formation and dissolution of alliances and give considerably less attention to their actual maintenance and management. Their focus is on the system rather than the state level of analysis, and they are only concerned with structural explanations for alliance behavior. And yet there are major flaws in their structural-realist methodological integrity. For example, Walt's "modification" of BOP theory ("balance of threat" (BOT)) violates the former's concentration on the system level by relocating causality to state-level variables. Furthermore, his concentration on the explanatory variable of "perceptions" clearly has constructivist connotations. He, perhaps unwittingly, revealed the limitations of pure realist approaches and nonetheless opened the path for eclectic approaches toward alliance theorizing drawing on the other research traditions of IR.[26]

Moreover, institutionalist scholars point out that the primary assumptions of BOP/BOT theory now appear flawed, since we are clearly faced with the puzzle of explaining the continued existence of anti-Soviet alliances in Europe and Asia. They argue that "understood in realist terms, alliances should not outlive the threats they were created to address. . . . When threats disappear, allies lose their reason for cooperating, and [they] will break apart."[27] Since NATO and the main US alliances in Asia Pacific did not dissolve after the collapse of the Warsaw Pact and Soviet Union threat they were formed to counter, we are faced with a need to explain their continued persistence, in contravention of balance of threat theory. Approaching the problem from an institutionalist perspective, we can consider how alliance bureaucracies become entrenched and inertia thus prevails. In Celeste Wallander's words: "Alliances can be more than simply pieces of paper or aggregations of military power: as explicit, persistent and connected sets of rules prescribe behavioral roles and constrain activity, sometimes alliances are institutions."[28] Thus, such institutionalized alignments may be said to constitute part of the international "security architecture," as many advocates of the US alliance system assert. Moreover, alliances are costly to recreate and therefore serve as a useful "insurance policy" against unforeseen threats and their extant capacities can be readily redirected elsewhere, as evidenced by NATO's involvement in Libya and Afghanistan. Thus, Wallander justifiably concludes that "alliances that have specific institutional assets for dealing with instability and mistrust will be adaptable to environments without threats."[29]

This leads Duffield and others to go as far as to propose, "Some might argue that there is no puzzle to be explained because *NATO is no longer an alliance.* Rather it has been transformed into something else; perhaps a regional collective security arrangement or what Wallander and Keohane have called a security management institution."[30] When an alliance is transformed into a more generic "security provider," the gap between security alignment and security dialogue forum as distinctive parts of regional/global architecture becomes blurred.

Analytical Framework: Intra-alliance Politics

In order to analyze alliances, both in their traditional and evolved configurations, we need a new framework that combines the parsimonious system-focused balance of power theories and state-level variables. Moreover, given the recognition that contemporary alliances explicitly involve ideational factors as well as traditional material factors, an "analytical eclectic" approach deploying more recent liberal and constructivist lenses is also desirable.

The approach applied here has previously been dubbed by Glenn Snyder as the "intra-alliance politics" (IAP) or sometimes just "alliance politics."[31] It is more practically oriented and primarily concerned with the interaction between the states that form an alliance, thus filling the explanatory gaps left by the structuralist theories noted above.[32] By examining the internal alliance dynamics and how they interact with "external" factors, we are able to bridge some gaps in our understanding of the wider questions of alignment. According to John Duffield, intra-alliance politics examines "the ways in which alliance members differ from one another and [it] asks how these differences affect individual state as well as overall alliance behavior."[33] Operating at a unit level of analysis, it can be divided into materialist explanations based upon "expediency" (largely realist) and ideational explanations (largely liberal and constructivist) based on normative "values." This echoes the mantra of "shared values and interests," as encountered in contemporary government statements regarding alliance relationships. Together both "streams" dovetail to provide a compound explanation for the behavior of alliances and expected levels of cohesion.

Material Factors: Interest, Power, Insecurity

Interests. One of the key assumptions of realism, in its classical form, is that states will behave expediently to safeguard their material interests. According to Duffield, "alliances are one of the most valuable instruments for advancing a state's interests."[34] When core national interests are shared with other states, they have the option to combine in an alliance to realize them. Morgenthau affirms that "common interests are the rock on which all alliances are built."[35] Yet while alliances are founded on these shared interests, a state's particular national interests will only partially overlap with those of its allies. They will retain individual preferences or commitments that may be quite distinct or even conflicting with those of their allies. Each member will exhibit differing strategic, political, regional, historical, or cultural variables or preferences, for example. Moreover, if competing interests arise between states in an alliance, their ability to compromise will be dependent on how strongly these interests are held, measured against their stake in alliance preservation. While minor interests may be subject to grudging compromise or even discarded, core or "vital" national interests are seldom subject to negotiation.

How such interests are defined and the intensity with which they are adhered to is a question for policymakers. This calculus is also subject to revision. States constantly reevaluate their national interests according to circumstances, and a change in government of a particular state or the admission of a new member state into the alliance may completely alter their negotiating positions within the covenant. It should be noted that while policymakers may find it expedient to rhetorically advocate certain interests, they may covertly be pursuing other "unofficial" interests that are not always compatible. In the process of alliance diplomacy, negotiations are subject to the same rules of any interstate bargaining process, but framed within an institutionalized alliance context.

Finally, long-term membership of an alliance may generate new emphasis on collective alliance interests and cause member states to adopt the interests of other member states in order to mutually validate alliance cohesion and to stave off discord. The complex task of harmonizing and sublimating state interest for the collective good is the key challenge of alliance management. George Liska states that "to facilitate coalescence, the . . . [alliance members] . . . will emphasize pressing common interests, while ignoring or minimizing divergent interests among allies."[36] Harvey Starr observes that "it is expedient to submerge temporarily intra [alliance] conflicts to cooperate against common enemies."[37] If a particular state's national interest in maintaining the alliance ebbs, the institution could fall into abeyance. If national interests become completely out of sync with alliance goals, that member may leave or defect to an opposing alliance. Either way, Snyder concludes that "an alliance will be viable only to the extent that it reflects the interests of its members."[38]

Power. As mentioned previously, power calculations are integral to realist explanations of alliance formation, as evidenced in the BOP and BOT theories. This shows that alliances are fundamentally about capabilities aggregation. But for most major alliances, this has begun to broaden beyond purely military capabilities to incorporate other aspects of "state capacity," especially as an alliance becomes institutionalized. These may include diplomatic, organizational, or economic-technological expertise; man-power; niche capabilities; or simply a favorable geostrategic location. Ultimately, states assess the value of what a putative ally can confer upon them through the alliance and what might thus be denied to an opposing alliance.

But in the management phase of alliances, "power" assumes an internal dimension in regard to alliance leadership, decisionmaking, and conflict resolution. In this sense, a form of internal power balancing applies.[39] Other things being equal, a state's aggregate power, relative to its allies, should determine its ability to press its national interests and its capacity to shape the alliance agenda. "As a general rule," Duffield notes, "the views of the most powerful members will carry the greatest weight."[40] However, Louise Richardson disputes this truism: "The classical theorists of alliances tell us that in a conflict of interests between two countries of unequal power, be they allies or enemies, the stronger state will prevail. History and the world around us illustrate that this is simply not what happens in all cases."[41]

There are several factors that might "level the playing field" in the intra-alliance bargaining process between unequally powerful states. First, even the most dominant ally may be in some respects dependent on its weaker partners. These allies may well contribute important, if not indispensable, assets to the alliance, be it a geographically crucial location, niche capabilities, or much-needed political legitimization. In particular, Duffield argues that "the ability to grant or deny access to one's territory, bases, or airspace may be a powerful source of leverage."[42]

Second, the fundamental principle of burden-sharing within the alliance prescribes that each partner contributes their fair share in accord with their relative state capacity and military capabilities. An ally that contributes liberally can be expected to gain more leverage in alliance policy, while an inequitable distribution of roles and responsibilities among allies can generate disputes.[43] Last, it would not always be expedient for a powerful ally to overawe its weaker partners. Since relations between sovereign states are at least nominally equal, to do so would sow disaffection. If its national interests are totally ignored, a smaller ally might withdraw from the alliance or even defect to an opposing one.

Insecurity. According to conventional BOT theory, states are impelled to form alliances due to the predicament they face through the existence of an existential threat.[44] But intra-alliance politics reveals further important dynamics located at the state level operating between allies themselves. Snyder posits that "the greater the threat posed by an adversary, the greater the cohesion of the alliance."[45] Yet, differing levels of threat perceptions among allies may complicate alliance management. Duffield alerts us to the fact that "alliance members may hold conflicting views about the precise nature of the threat to be addressed, and even when they do agree, they may favor different responses."[46] As long as allies are in agreement that a pressing enemy threat obtains, the alliance will endure. If there is a diminution in the existential threat, even to just one member, alliance ties may weaken. In the event that the threat is unequivocally removed, collapsed, or defeated, the alliance itself will be terminated, according to BOT theory. Alastair Buchan asserts that "almost by definition, alliances have a limited life cycle. . . . National objectives change, the *threat* which made it worthwhile to subordinate some national interests to the evolution of a collaborative policy changes also, and the strains of the alliance become too great to bear."[47]

As noted above, the contemporary empirical record appears to disprove this theory. Alliances have somehow persisted in the apparent absence of a strategic threat. Institutionalists would argue that the bureaucratic "sunk costs" of creating such a comprehensive alliance organization or long-term allied relationship between members militates against its dissolution. First, alliances are difficult to disassemble and even more difficult to create from scratch. Thus, it is better to maintain them as an "insurance policy" prepared to meet the next emerging threat and to address NTS threats. Indeed, after the collapse of the Warsaw Pact in 1991, NATO actively sought out a replacement foe to justify its existence, including a resurgent Russia and a (dubious) strategic threat from the Middle East, before finally settling on intervention in the Balkans and beyond. As Vidya Nadkarni notes, "NATO's crisp Cold War mission has been replaced by open-ended nation building and soft security goals in 'out-of-area' theaters, in the Balkans in the latter half of the 1990s and in Afghanistan after 2001."[48] Second, alliances develop into "security management institutions," where they serve as a vehicle to manipulate security relations with one's allies as much as with the adversary. Indeed, Paul Schroeder asserts that "all alliances in some measure function as pacts of restraint (*Pacta de Contrahendo*), restraining or controlling the actions of the partners in the alliance themselves."[49] They thus become a fixture of the international landscape ("security architecture") and determinant of foreign policy between the allied states.

Intra-alliance politics determines that the security dilemma condition is applicable to the internal maintenance and management of the alliance as well. Charles Kegley and Gregory Raymond note that "fear of being betrayed looms large in the minds of makers of foreign policy, casting a shadow over every alliance."[50] Indeed, questions of mistrust and betrayal threaten alliance cohesion at every step, in what Snyder dubs an "intra-alliance security dilemma."[51] Member states inside the alliance are still subject to feelings of insecurity toward one another. This can be explained according to Snyder's "abandonment-entrapment" dyad. On the one hand, fears of abandonment arise when a certain member state feels that its allies have become untrustworthy and that they may defect from the alliance, leaving it alone to face the external threat. On the other hand, member states must guard against being "entrapped" by their allies. According to Snyder, "entrapment means being dragged into a conflict over an ally's interests that one does not share, or shares only partially."[52] Alliances can be "entangling;" the more committed a state is to the preservation of the alliance, the more vulnerable it is to entrapment. Snyder identifies that "the severity of the alliance security dilemma, and the intensity of its fears of abandonment and entrapment, is largely determined by the same three factors that are central components of alliance bargaining power: interests, dependence and commitment."[53]

Ideational Factors: Ideology, Domestic Politics, and Norms

Ideology. According to the IAP perspective, congruent "value-systems" serve as impetus toward alliance formation and a bonding agent in forging alliance solidarity.[54] Indeed, it could be argued that this has always been the case with historical alliances, though it is largely sidelined in the traditional theoretical approaches. What is more, some of the key realist propositions can be interpreted through this prism. For example, Duffield, Michota, and Miller argue that "similar value systems may generate common interests and common interpretations of what constitutes a threat."[55] As noted, in the contemporary world, alliances are often justified as much on the basis of their "shared values," as they are on their supposed expediency. Ideological affinities, based upon similar weltanshauungen (world views), are an important aspect of explaining alliance behavior. This concerns an "ideological solidarity transcending the limitations of material interests" and encompassing "common culture, political institutions, and ideals."[56]

First, this assumption predicts that states of compatible regime type are both more likely to ally and will find it easier to maintain alliance cohesion. Thus, "the choice of allies is also influenced by the internal political configurations of states apart from the general ideological preferences."[57] In other words, closed authoritarian states should be attracted to their autocratic counterparts, whereas open democratic states should likewise be drawn into alliance with their ideological brethren. Indeed, the political composition of liberal democratic states appears to be better suited to achieving and maintaining alliance consensus. In particular, liberal democracies, Thomas Risse-Kappen argues, have in place "institutions based on norms and decision-making procedures emphasizing timely consultation, compromise, and the equality of the participants."[58] They will therefore naturally tend to replicate this within alliance institutions and "ways of doing business." This political-ideological affinity may be further reinforced by common ethnic, linguistic, religious, and cultural patterns among allies. Duffield, Michota, and Miller conclude that "in view of such considerations, scholars have suggested that alliances among liberal democratic states are likely to be especially strong and resilient."[59]

Second, whatever the broad congruence of shared values at the forefront of alliance cooperation, it must be remembered that each member state will retain its own distinct national identity and idiosyncrasies that may undermine overall ideological unity. National differentiation between allies along racial, ethnic, religious, or historical lines can result in "cultural differences" that can "cause friction, misunderstanding, and cracks in cohesion," according to Wayne Silkett.[60] This will be particularly evident in an alliance that includes multiple regime types. This problem may also be exacerbated by a high level of heterogeneity within the states themselves, undermining such a member's ability to act as a coordinated or "unified actor" within the alliance.

If the alliance is to endure, it requires a tolerance and understanding of national and internal diversity. Mitigating the tensions this can cause requires a political and ideological investment from all members. The task is to inculcate allegiance to the collective by building a new alliance identity, a "we feeling" that will serve as a basis of allied solidarity, though "instrumental" in nature, in contrast with "transformative" identity found in security communities.[61] This may be enshrined or institutionalized into an alliance charter or, most commonly, a formal treaty between allies. Moreover, once so established, the alliance represents as an ideological "totem" itself, gaining a value and institutional momentum of its own since "alliances and alignments may produce intrinsic values other than security, such as prestige, domestic stability, and economic benefits."[62] Having bought into a common identity, states begin to define themselves in relation to the alliance and are shaped by its standards. Thus "a typical alliance ideology will define the basis, and by implication, the limits of allied solidarity; it will be formulated so as to add incentive to joint action and to screen intra-alliance strains and splits."[63]

Domestic politics. Liberal theorists, in particular, point to the prominent role played by domestic factors in the process of alliance management. As suggested above, from a liberal perspective, the state is far from the monolithic "unified rational actor" assumed in neorealist BOP theories. Instead, Andrew Moravcsik posits that "the state is not an actor but a representative institution constantly subject to capture and recapture, construction and reconstruction by coalitions of social actors."[64] The interaction between government foreign policy and domestic agendas is known as "intermestic politics" or a "two-level game."[65] Charles Kegley and Eugene Wittkopf note that "public opinion, interest groups, and the mass media are more visibly a part of the political process in democratic systems, and the public participates openly in an effort to penetrate and influence government structures in ways actively prevented in closed political systems."[66] In contrast to the advantages presumed to be enjoyed by democratic states through ideological affinities, in respect to the promulgation of a consistent and cohesive alliance bargaining policy, they may be disadvantaged. Michael Ward notes that "the organizational structure of the alliance is a powerful determinant of the extent of cohesion: democratic and pluralist alliance structures are presumed to promote reduced cohesiveness when compared to hierarchically organized autocratic organizations."[67]

On the basis of these assumptions, domestic politics may make itself felt in alliance management through the following dynamics. These are likely to be more apparent in open democratic states than closed autocratic regimes, since, theoretically at least, such systems are not accountable to public opinion or institutions. First, domestic politics and democratic values act as a constraint for leaders in negotiating the roles and responsibilities of their state's participation within an alliance. The more closely the executive's preferences and actions comply with those of society, the less autonomy they will have in alliance negotiations. Risse-Kappen argues that "references to domestic pressures and constraints are likely to occur frequently. After all, liberal systems have in common that their leaders are constrained by the complexities of democratic political institutions."[68] Second, the invocation of domestic constraints serves as a powerful rhetorical tool in bargaining with alliance partners. For example, Snyder argues "the statesman may find domestic constraints useful in establishing a credible minimum position in an alliance negotiation."[69] However, the exigencies of alliance commitment may also create difficulties for a national executive among their domestic constituency as they struggle to justify "alliance policy" to domestic political interests or public opinion. Lastly, the existence of transnational connections, or political "coalitions," between certain domestic constituencies within democracies may also generate additional considerations in alliance politics. Risse-Kappen asserts that "domestic politics as a bargaining resource ('two-level games') and transnational as well as trans-governmental coalition-building provide tools by which the democratic allies are likely to influence each other."[70] This type of "transnational penetration"—in other words, "the manipulation of one state's domestic political system by another"—may include cooperation between antigovernmental interest groups or lobbies or propaganda directed at one or more allies, or indeed the alliance itself.[71] This is an ever-present possibility in societies with a free press, but less so in societies where the media and the power of domestic groups are curtailed.

Norms. While realists typically account for alliance cohesion through national interest and the intensity of enemy threats, a liberal-constructivist approach emphasizes explanations based upon shared value-systems and the institutionalization of "norms" to govern intra-alliance behavior. [72] Even alliances that exhibit a high degree of ideological and political affinity are subject to a certain degree of "mistrust" between member states. In order to attenuate the "climate of mistrust," the alliance must work to establish and adhere to agreed "norms" of behavior.[73] According to Peter Katzenstein, norms may be defined as "collective expectations for the proper behavior of actors with a given identity. . . . [N]orms have 'regulative' effects that specify standards of proper behavior."[74] Alliance norms may be informally held promises, expectations, or obligations, or they may be formally codified into an alliance treaty or charter. Often both types coexist, but once norms are formalized as institutional rules for alliance behavior, they assume a greater authority and the penalties for violating them increase. Snyder predicts that "the greater the potency of alliance norms, the less costly and more reliable alliance management will be."[75] From a liberal perspective, they serve as a binding force or a form of confidence-building measure, reassuring the individual states within the alliance.

The literature on alliances refers to three fundamental norms appertaining to the management of intra-allied relations. These are the norms of *pacta sunt servanda*, reciprocity, and consultation. In the first instance, the legalistic injunction that "treaties must be obeyed" covers the conviction that allies will fulfill their obligations and deliver on their promises, and it serves as a form of alliance "constitution." This is usually codified in treaty form in more institutionalized alliances, but Cha notes that "states do not need formal alliance contracts to have such expectations [of mutual support] . . . and feelings of mutual obligation; such contracts only reinforce and formalize patterns that exist on the basis of perceived common interests."[76] Either way, Kegley and Raymond argue that "alliances are given force by the authority and respect allies ascribe to their promissory obligations."[77]

The second norm is "reciprocity," which, according to Robert Keohane, "refers to exchanges of roughly equivalent values in which the actions of the party are contingent on the prior actions of others in such a way that good is returned for good and bad for bad."[78] This norm reinforces the former by ensuring that alliance is based upon mutual and corresponding exchange of benefits between allies and that "burden-sharing" among members is equitable. Exchanges do not have to be exact quid pro quo and may include "diffuse" exchanges on totally unrelated matters.

Lastly, sustained consultation between allies is presumed to reinforce alliance cohesion. Wallander notes that "the basic obstacle to cooperation or exchange in social relations is uncertainty, and the basic way institutions reduce transaction costs arising from uncertainty is by providing information."[79] Therefore, frequent consultation and exchange of information, including intelligence, increases "transparency" and helps allies manage changes in the alliance by reducing the uncertainty that can generate suspicion.

Conclusion

The alliance paradigm and its accompanying theoretical literature stand at the center of alignment study. However, major shifts in the post–Cold War empirical landscape with regard to the complexion of alliances or alignment have called into question not only the nature of alliances but the validity and adequacy of the theoretical base through which they have typically been understood. Alliances surviving the Cold War period, such as NATO and the US bilateral system in Asia Pacific, are evolving beyond their original mission and radically adapting toward new tasks. Given such alliance transformations, alongside the identification of new "quasi" or "virtual" alliances, scholarly attention must be dedicated to modifying existing theoretical frameworks or creating new ones better fitted to understanding contemporary examples.

Built on the foundations of "traditional" alliance theories such as balance of power and balance of threat, the intra-alliance politics perspective presented here can serve as an appropriate analytical framework for examining all forms of alliance and also make substantive contributions to the appreciation of non-alliance alignments. Such an analytical framework, illustrated in Table 2.1, focuses mainly on the state level of analysis, while pitting "material factors" (interest and power), mainly derived from the realist tradition, against "ideational factors" (ideology, domestic politics), principally derived from the liberal and constructivist camps. Through this eclectic approach, we can more fully apprehend the key drivers in the alliance formation, management, and termination stages, in contrast to the relative parsimony of BOP theory. We can also identify how the above factors interact to create an "intra-alliance security dilemma," threatening allied cohesion. Realist and liberal-constructivists provide contrasting explanations of how such a dilemma can be overcome, arguing respectively that enemy "threat" and allied "norms" account for the maintenance of the alliance's integrity. These propositions will now be tested against the case study of the TSD, an archetype of virtual alliance, in the next chapter.

Table 2.1 Intra-alliance Politics Perspective

Theoretical Tradition	Realism	Liberalism Constructivism
Drivers	Material	Ideational
	"Expediency" interests, power	"Values" ideology, domestic politics
Result	Intra-alliance Security Dilemma	
Cohesion	Threat	Norms

Notes

1. Duffield, Michota, and Miller, "Alliances," p. 292.
2. Ibid.
3. Menon, *End of Alliances*, p. xi.
4. Ibid.
5. Campbell, "The End of Alliances?" p. 162.
6. Duffield, Michota, and Miller, "Alliances," p. 292.
7. Wilkins, "Alignment, Not Alliance."
8. Snyder, *Alliance Politics*, p. 4.
9. According to Osgood, an alliance is "a formal agreement that pledges states to co-operate in using their military resources against a specific state or states and usually obligates one or more of the signatories to use force, or to consider (unilaterally or in consultation with allies) the use of force in specified circumstances." Osgood, *Alliances and American Foreign Policy*, p. 17.
10. Cha, *Powerplay*.
11. Tow, "Alliances and Alignments in the Twenty-First Century," p. 12.
12. For example, see Sakwa, "Senseless Dreams and Small Steps."
13. Kamp and Langheld, "Military Adaptation of the Alliance"; Lindley-French, "Adapting NATO to an Unpredictable and Fast-Changing World"; Smith, "A Strategy for the U.S.-Japan Alliance."
14. Cossa et al., *The United States and the Asia-Pacific Region*, p. 32.
15. Sheen, "A Smart Alliance in the Age of Complexity."
16. Cha, *Alignment Despite Antagonism*, p. 3.
17. Campbell, "The End of Alliances?" p. 155.
18. Booth, "Alliances," p. 259.
19. Cossa et al. "The United States and the Asia-Pacific Region."
20. Morgenthau, "Alliances in Theory and Practice," p. 193.
21. Wilkins, "Towards a 'Trilateral Alliance'?"
22. Booth, "Alliances," p. 263.
23. Waltz, *Theory of International Politics*.

24. Walt, *The Origins of Alliances*, p. vi.

25. Ibid., p. 29.

26. Katzenstein, "Introduction: Alternative Perspectives on National Security," p. 27.

27. Wallander, "Institutional Assets and Adaptability," p. 705.

28. Ibid., p. 706.

29. Ibid.

30. Duffield, Michota, and Miller. "Alliances," p. 302. [Italics added]

31. Snyder, *Alliance Politics;* Wilkins, "Analyzing Coalition Warfare from an Intra-Alliance Politics Perspective"; Starr, *War Coalitions*.

32. I have applied "traditional" theories to the TSD case study elsewhere: Wilkins, "Coalition Formation and Management in the Asia-Pacific Region."

33. Duffield, *Power Rules*, p. 18.

34. Duffield, Michota, and Miller, "Alliances," p. 291.

35. Morgenthau, "Alliances in Theory and Practice," p. 197.

36. Liska, *Nations in Alliance*, p. 62.

37. Starr, *War Coalitions*, p. 21.

38. Snyder, *Alliance Politics*, p. 9.

39. Sheehan, *The Balance of Power*, p. 11.

40. Duffield, *Power Rules*, p. 20.

41. Richardson, *When Allies Differ*, p. 2.

42. Duffield, *Power Rules*, p. 21.

43. Hartley and Sandler, "NATO Burden-Sharing."

44. Booth and Wheeler, *The Security Dilemma*.

45. Snyder, "Alliances, Balance, and Stability," p. 125.

46. Duffield, *Power Rules*, p. 18.

47. Buchan, "Problems of an Alliance Policy," p. 295. [Emphasis added]

48. Nadkarni, *Strategic Partnerships in Asia*, p. 26.

49. Schroeder, "Alliances, 1815–1945," p. 230.

50. Kegley and Raymond, *When Trust Breaks Down*, p. 1.

51. Snyder, "The Security Dilemma in Alliance Politics."

52. Ibid., p. 467.

53. Snyder, *Alliance Politics*, p. 186.

54. Ironically, realists themselves contribute much toward ideational perspectives, including the role of ideology and norms, for example. Walt, *The Origins of Alliances*; Snyder. *Alliance Politics.*

55. Duffield, Michota, and Miller, "Alliances," p. 297.

56. Morgenthau, "Alliances in Theory and Practice," p. 189.

57. Snyder, "The Security Dilemma in Alliance Politics," p. 465.

58. Risse-Kappen, *Cooperation among Democracies*, p. 12.

59. Duffield, Michota, and Miller, "Alliances," p. 297.

60. Silkett, "Alliance and Coalition Warfare," p. 80.

61. Adler and Barnett, *Security Communities*.

62. Snyder, "Alliances, Balance, Stability," p. 133.

63. Liska, *Nations in Alliance*, p. 61.

64. Moravcsik, "Taking Preferences Seriously," p. 518.

65. Kegley and Wittkopf, *World Politics*, p. 59.

66. Ibid., p. 67.

67. Ward, *Research Gaps in Alliance Dynamics*, p. 31.

68. Risse-Kappen, *Cooperation Among Democracies*, p. 38.

69. Snyder, *Alliance Politics*, p. 133.

70. Risse-Kappen, *Cooperation Among Democracies*, p. 12.
71. Walt, *The Origins of Alliances*, p. 46.
72. Krasner, *International Regimes*.
73. Kegley and Raymond, *When Trust Breaks Down*.
74. Katzenstein, *The Culture of National Security*, p. 5.
75. Snyder, *Alliance Politics*, p. 363.
76. Cha, *Alignment Despite Antagonism*, p. 40.
77. Kegley and Raymond, *When Trust Breaks Down*, p. 1.
78. Keohane, *International Institutions and State Power*, p. 136.
79. Wallander, "Institutional Assets and Adaptability," p. 711.

3

The Trilateral
Security Dialogue

The first case study is exemplary of how alliances have undergone profound changes in the post–Cold War era.[1] Not only does the Trilateral Security Dialogue (TSD), as a "minilateral" form of security cooperation, represent a new trilateral configuration of Washington's Asian alliances in the "virtual" (i.e., non-treaty) mold, but its roles and capabilities reflect a progression beyond the typical military-defense remit to ostensibly encompass nontraditional security (NTS) issues. Furthermore, it exemplifies the emergence of alignment based on "order" and "values," arguably displacing the conventional threat-based raison d'être for alliances. As Yuki Tatsumi points out, "The US-Japan-Australia trilateral security relationship is also unique in its strong inclination to engage in preserving and buttressing the existing international order in the region."[2] By drawing upon the analytical framework outlined in the preceding chapter, we may gain conceptually informed insights into the nature, functions, and durability of the TSD alignment.

The augmented trilateral cooperation between the United States and its existing bilateral treaty allies, Japan and Australia, was catalyzed by the end of the Cold War in the 1990s and formalized in 2006, as scholars such as Tomohiko Satake and James Schoff have documented.[3] Rather than dwell too deeply on the narrative aspects of the case study or elaborate upon its bureaucratic structure, this chapter focuses on how to conceptualize and analytically interrogate this important development. Essentially, the emergence of trilateral cooperation represents Washington's efforts to transform its Asian alliances to meet new challenges, according to a dedicated Track II study by Cossa et al.[4] Since 2011, after long and futile diversions into the Middle East, the United States sought to "rebalance" its strategic focus to the pivotal Asia Pacific region, including attempts to strengthen and reinvigorate its venerable "hub-and-spoke" system of bilateral alliances. Otherwise known as the "San Francisco system," this web of alliances served the United States well during the Cold War and yet is now in need of reformation to adapt to new security challenges in a transformed strategic environment.[5] In addition to upgrading defense and security ties with individually willing allies such as Japan and Australia, the United States has sought to bring other amenable states such as India, Vietnam, and Singapore into loose alignment with its extant treaty allies, notably employing the separate "strategic partnership" mechanism discussed in Chapter 6. Moreover, it has sought to create more direct linkages between these allies themselves, in a process Ryo Sahashi and others refer to as "intra-spoke" cooperation or "networking the spokes."[6] Perhaps this is a belated attempt to unofficially multilateralize its alliance network in Asia, which never developed in parallel to the NATO model in Europe.[7]

What stands out from these interrelated processes is the emergence of what Michael Green calls new "strategic Asian triangles"—trilateral configurations usually based upon existing alliance relationships.[8] Indeed, according to Michael Auslin, "U.S. strategic thinking has begun to look beyond the traditional hub-and-spoke model. . . . Washington has initiated a variety of *trilateral dialogues* aimed at leveraging close U.S. alliance relationships into broader arrangements focused on regional concerns."[9] Such minilaterals do not seek to supplant the main bilateral security framework, which Cossa et al. call "an indispensable foundation upon which to build any future security strategy."[10] Instead, Tatsumi argues "Washington has sought to utilize these minilaterals in order to complement its bilateral alliances and to encourage cooperation among its allies and partners in the Asia-Pacific region."[11] As a result, she continues, "the trilateral security relationship among the United States, Japan, and Australia has quickly emerged as one of the most robust 'minilateral' cooperative relationships that the United States has with its allies."[12]

Implicit in this is the partial obsolescence of the original Cold War–era bilateral network. Some commentators indicate how countries such as Thailand, the Philippines, and even perhaps South Korea may be slipping from the US orbit.[13] These other bilateral security partnerships have been so "downgraded" that only "Australia and Japan remain 'core' bilateral allies," according to William Tow and Amitav Acharya.[14] This is not to suggest that these other security relationships are defunct. For example, the US maintains a major military presence in South Korea, but the 2015 National Security Strategy advocated the need to "reinvigorate our ties to the Philippines and preserve our ties to Thailand," since these allies have apparently begun to drift away from the United States.[15] These additional members of the hub-and-spoke system are consigned to a more passive and peripheral presence in US regional strategy in comparison to the trilateral core. Consequently, Tow notes that "US policy-planners need therefore to work effectively with their Japanese and Australian allies to identify how traditional alliance politics can be reconstituted to accommodate the monumental structural change now taking place in the Asia-Pacific."[16]

The US-Led "Virtual Alliance" as an Alignment

Since the "virtual alliance" variant of alignment deviates from the standard historical alliance paradigm and existing set of US bilateral treaty alliances, it is first necessary to probe into its definition and characteristics before proceeding to apply the intra-alliance politics analytical framework.

Defining the TSD as a "Virtual Alliance"

Auslin attests that "from the beginning, all three governments made it clear that the TSD was not conceived of as a formal alliance or even as a mechanism to replace the hub-and-spoke system under whose umbrella both the U.S.-Japan and U.S.-Australian alliances fit."[17] However, if we acknowledge that the TSD partners represent a new or different kind of "alliance" (alignment), how should we classify it? For Tow, "the TSD could be regarded as a 'minilateral' body, as Australia, Japan and the US are already bound together by precedents of bilateral alliance cooperation."[18] The terms "informal trilateralism," "bilaterally networked multilateralism," "virtual JANZUS" (Japan-Australia-[New Zealand]-United States), "little NATO," and "shadow alliance" have all been applied to this case study.[19]

I classify the trilateral "core" of the hub-and-spoke system as an exemplar of the "virtual alliance" archetype introduced in the previous chapter. This denominator captures the essence of trilateral cooperation well, since "a virtual alliance is an informal process involving two or more smaller allies who normally do not conduct extensive or formal security relations with each other to upgrade such relations through the coordinative efforts of a common senior ally."[20] Cossa adds that such an alignment involves three distinctive elements: "(1) formation of consultative security mechanisms reflecting common interests and values, (2) lack of formal treaty or legislative obligations, [and] (3) [a] tendency for such collaborators to diversify their various security collaboration in different institutions to avoid arousal of third party suspicions."[21] Let us examine how the TSD conforms to each of these parameters.

First, the raison d'être of the alignment articulated in the 2006 TSD foundational communiqué is based on "shared strategic interests" and the "common cause" of "longstanding democracies."[22] And the 2009 TSD statement asserts that "the three countries remain committed to the trilateral process as an effective forum for the promotion of their governments' shared values, ideals, and interests."[23] The alignment is thus predicated on a compound of common interests and shared values, which may be investigated through the analytical framework provided in the previous chapter.

Second, there is no formal trilateral treaty or mutual defense pact, characteristic of the traditional military alliance paradigm, though the individual security treaties are in force between Washington and Tokyo, and Washington and Canberra (i.e. ANZUS). This is a deliberate characteristic of the "virtual alliance" in that the convergence of interests and values are so pronounced as to render a treaty superfluous (e.g., US-UK alignment). Thus Snyder contends that "the negotiation of a formal alliance is simply an interaction episode [between allies] . . . it is usually secondary or incidental."[24] Moreover, Purnendra Jain and John Bruni observe that "there is genuine concern by the Japanese, Australian and United States governments not to be seen to be developing any formalized and open alliance."[25] Such a formal treaty alliance would undoubtedly be viewed as a provocation to those who viewed themselves as potential targets.

Third, and following from this, excepting the TSD ministerial meetings themselves and some military exercises, much of the trilateral coordination is carried out within the context of other interaction frameworks, both bilateral and multilateral. Official TSD meetings occur between the foreign and defense ministers of the three allies on a regular basis (2006, 2007, 2008, 2009, 2013, 2016, and 2017). This is supplemented by periodic heads of government meetings, whether bilateral or trilateral. Closely related to this are a number of working groups tasked with different security issues that operate under the officially separate but "parallel" Security and Defense Cooperation Forum (SDCF). James Schoff advises that "the overall goals of the SDCF are to enhance interoperability, build cooperative capacity with allies, and create more multilateral cooperation and capacity, not only with allies, but also with regional forums."[26] In addition to the "separate" upgrading of military-security ties between the US and Japan, the US and Australia, as well as Japan and Australia, through the Joint Declaration on Security Cooperation,[27] multilateral forums such as Asia Pacific Economic Cooperation (APEC), the ASEAN Regional Forum (ARF), and the Proliferation Security Initiative (PSI) are all opportunities to harmonize trilateral policies.[28] The "diffuse" or "scattered" institutional nature of the trilateral alignment is therefore indicative of Cossa's "virtual" model.

We may therefore discern, in many but not all contexts, formally or informally, the appearance and agency of a "virtual" triangle between these countries: a de facto security alignment without de jure alliance fixtures.

This is further validated in practice through key behavioral indicators, including collaboration on ballistic missile defense (BMD), joint interception of North Korean weapons of mass destruction (WMD) cargoes, and co-deployments in Iraq and Afghanistan, to be discussed in the main text below. Whether this "virtual" alignment will develop into a fully fledged traditional military alliance, as the Franco-British-Russian Triple Entente did between 1906 and 1917, remains to be seen. Thus, because of its novel "virtual" alliance manifestation, this alignment presents us with "a unique theoretical challenge for explaining trilateral security cooperation."[29]

Analytical Framework: Intra-alliance Politics Perspective

Having established the significance, context, and novelty of this new form of alignment, this chapter now proceeds to examine realist ("material") and liberal-constructivist ("ideational") interpretations of its formation, management, and prospects, collectively dubbed an "intra-alliance politics" perspective, in order to gain analytical purchase on this case study. This perfectly mirrors the widely stated official objectives of the TSD. As Green has observed, "trilateral forums were established to leverage *common values and interests* in order to shape the larger regional agenda for security cooperation."[30] Though traditional balance of power/threat theories inform the framework, since the TSD is an "offshoot" of the original 1950s threat-based treaties that existed prior to the post–Cold War emergence of the TSD, they are necessarily relegated to the background.

Material Factors: Interests, Power, and Insecurity

Interests. TSD ministerial meetings are designed to "exchange views on a number of regional and global issues of mutual interest" between the three allies.[31] In the broadest sense, this involves their "determination to work together to protect our shared strategic interests in promoting peace and stability in the Asia-Pacific region."[32] What this means is a commitment by these traditional allies and status quo powers to manage power transitions, safeguard their joint strategic space, and avoid costly regional conflicts or military competition.

This reflects a compound of interlocking strategic, geopolitical, and economic interests. The parties have constantly reaffirmed the "importance of the trilateral strategic partnership among these three countries to ensure a free, open, peaceful, stable, democratic, and prosperous Asia-Pacific and Indian Ocean region and world, based on the rule of law."[33] The implicit challenge to this extant security order rooted in the San Francisco system is the rise of China and other Asian powers.[34] Each of the partners both individually, bilaterally, and trilaterally has been critical of China's attempts to disrupt the peace in the South and East China Seas with their foreign ministers together declaring their "strong opposition to coercive unilateral actions that could alter the status quo and increase tensions."[35] Efforts to "socialize" Beijing into the Asia Pacific order, initially based upon multilateral institutions, have now coalesced into a united trilateral front in opposition to such actions.

To address these interests, the TSD allies are committed to extended cooperation across a number of "issue-areas." One of the earliest TSD joint statements affirmed that "the Asia-Pacific region, while undergoing a dynamic change in political and economic terms, is faced with a wide range of security challenges including 'non-traditional' security challenges such as the proliferation of weapons of mass destruction, terrorism, and natural disasters."[36] Though it is often difficult in practice to categorically distinguish a "traditional" from a "nontraditional" security issue, as the two often intersect or overlap, I will illustrate each of these in the discussion that follows.

First, as far as conventional alliance motivations of "threat-balancing" are concerned, official proclamations on this score are deafening in their silence. Since previous bilateral security pacts between Japan and Australia with the United States were predicated on a communist, specifically Soviet threat, the justification for their continuation and reformulation into a tightened triangular alliance remains unspoken. As we have seen in the motivations for alliance formation/continuance, maintaining allied capabilities as "insurance" against future threats is seen as only prudent. There are two interconnected traditional security aspects of the TSD. The first, as mentioned above and further examined below, is "hedging" against a scenario in which Beijing attempts to translate its growing power into a bid for regional hegemony: an occurrence that each ally remains implacably opposed to. Thus Tow claims that the TSD aims to "sustain an acceptable international balance of power against aspiring hegemonic competitors."[37]

Second, broader issues of maritime security have recently emerged as one of the key drivers of trilateral security cooperation, as the 2016 TSD statement indicates. Each of the allies seeks to keep the vital Sea Lines of Communication (SLOCs), so crucial to the economic lifeblood of the region, free from major disruption, be it from state or non-state actors such as pirates. Connected to this are joint concerns that maritime and territorial disputes, in which Japan is directly embroiled, could threaten this functioning equilibrium. Clashes between China and Japan over Senkaku Islands and with other Southeast Asian states in the South China Sea have the potential to ignite military confrontation. The 2016 TSD statement also registered "the importance of upholding the rules-based maritime order including in the Asia Pacific region" and expressed "serious concerns over maritime disputes in the South China Sea" by calling for an end to reclamation/militarization of islets, the upholding of UNCLOS international law, and freedom of navigation/over-flight.[38] To this purpose, Ken Jimbo notes that "maritime security and capacity building in Southeast Asian littoral states has become one of the primary pillars for Japan-US-Australia regional security engagement."[39]

Third, tying together the traditional danger of "rogue states" and WMD proliferation to non-state groups, the allies are focused on containing a potentially nuclear-armed North Korean regime. That Pyongyang continues its bellicose behavior through military provocation and aggression—such as ballistic missile testing; nuclear-weapons development; and firebrand rhetoric against Japan, the United States, and the Republic of Korea—remains an area of joint concern.[40] The WMD program of North Korea and others is targeted through joint efforts such as the PSI and the emergence of trilateral BMD cooperation discussed below. Naturally, the continued military modernization programs among the majority of states in Asia Pacific and consequent arms proliferation remain additional cause for concern. As allied capabilities improve at an incremental rate, this could affect the regional balance of power that currently favors the US bloc.

As we segue into NTS challenges, firstly, terrorist/insurgent groups such as Islamic State in Iraq and the Levant (ISIL) and al-Qaeda still retain the capacity to harm any of the trilateral partners and to generate regional instability through conflicts in Southeast Asia and the Pacific Island countries. The TSD affirms its commitment to providing direct and indirect assistance in containing these challenges. This can take the form of law enforcement, counterinsurgency/counterterrorism, or capacity-building and official development assistance initiatives, all of which the TSD aims to coordinate among the allied parties.[41] Additionally, the TSD commits the allies to cooperation on humanitarian assistance and disaster relief (HADR) efforts.[42] Each of the allies has recognized their susceptibility to catastrophic environmental disasters, as Hurricane Katrina, the Great East Japan Earthquake, and repeated flash floods and fires in Australia testify. In the event of the "triple disaster" suffered by Japan in 2011, US and Australian forces made unprecedented efforts to assist Tokyo in Operations Tomodachi and Pacific Assist. Such dangers continue to affect states around the region, and the TSD allies are best equipped to respond to these crises, as the "core group" relief efforts in response to the 2004 Indian Ocean tsunami illustrate. Since tripartite cooperation is never going to be explicitly associated with the notion of a traditional counterbalancing alliance, or more specifically, "containment" against rising China, Tow maintains that "the TSD's credibility will hinge largely on its success in defining and implementing non-traditional areas of security collaboration."[43]

Nevertheless, the national interests of individual states will never be in perfect alignment and, whatever the coincidence of mutual interests, differences will always exist to undermine allied cohesion or engender intraallied disputes. In the case of the TSD, the divergence of particular interests is minimal and often applies to differences in how to approach the pursuit of joint interests, in other words, "tactical" rather than "strategic" differences. Trade friction between Japan and the US, so prevalent in the 1980s, has now become muted and Japan and Australia signed a free trade agreement (FTA) known as "Economic Partnership Agreement" in 2014. However, while the 2016 TSD statement committed the partners toward resolving the TPP negotiations, now that the US has withdrawn from the agreement in 2017, this leaves Tokyo and Canberra contemplating going ahead without their senior ally under the Comprehensive and Progressive Agreement for Trans-Pacific Partnership.

Real dissention is only evident in more minor issues: periodic inflammation of Japanese domestic opposition to US basing on national territory, particularly in Okinawa; the relative importance of Japanese "abductees" in the denuclearization talks with North Korea; clarification over the level of allied support for US policy regarding Taiwan; and Australian and Japanese discord over international whaling issues. This broad degree of shared interest speaks to the cohesion and resilience of this alliance. Indeed, the preservation of the alliance as the best guarantor of security has become an "interest" per se for all the member states. Thus, as Snyder concludes, "Alliances and alignments may produce intrinsic values other than security, such as prestige, domestic stability, and economic benefits."[44]

Power. In the realist view, the primary payoff gained by allying is capabilities aggregation. This is equally true of the "virtual alliance" variant. By pooling power resources and active capabilities, the alliance is better equipped to counter both the traditional and nontraditional challenges to its combined interests. As the 2018 National Defense Strategy of the United States asserts:

> Our allies and partners provide complementary capabilities and forces along with unique perspectives, regional relationships, and information that improve our understanding of the environment and expand our options. Allies and partners also provide access to critical regions, supporting a widespread basing and logistics system that underpins the Department's global reach.[45]

Japan and Australia are also aware that this expanded alliance allows them to augment their power as a cost-effective substitute for massive "internal mobilization." For example, Canberra admits that "allies are fundamentally important to Australia's security, because we do not have the power or reach to protect many of our interests on our own."[46] And as Daisuke Akimoto calculates, "it would cost about 22 or 23 trillion yen if Japan defended itself without the US military presence."[47]

However, simply tallying the aggregated power of the three allies is not sufficient. Their joint capabilities must be coordinated to be effective tools of allied security policy, be it a traditional strategic threat or more diffuse NTS challenges. There is strong evidence that this is the case for the allies, both in a trilateral context and associated bilateral initiatives that serve to reinforce combined capabilities.

Each ally is individually engaged in a process of military modernization and force restructuring toward more mobile, flexible, and lethal capabilities.[48] Most importantly, their respective armed forces are increasingly procured and organized for joint allied interoperability. According to Sahashi, "Australia, Japan, and the United States also have operational advantages in the security realm because their military systems, structures, experiences, and norms have remained similar throughout much of the postwar era."[49] Indeed, Japanese and Australian naval forces are calibrated to operate most effectively alongside their US counterparts, with their platforms (such as Aegis BMD) and operating systems (e.g., avionics, weaponry) often being of US provenance. In addition, both Japan and Australia are currently upgrading their amphibious capabilities with new naval acquisitions, again reinforcing their military compatibility. The three countries regularly conduct trilateral military exercises, such as RED FLAG-Alaska and Pacific Bond. There are also larger multilateral exercises where all or individual allies participate, such as RIMPAC, KAKADU, MALABAR, and COBRA GOLD.[50] This is in addition to bilateral exercises such as the US-Japan Keen Sword (2010),[51] which took place in the vicinity of Japan's strategically crucial Nansei Islands, and the regular Nichi-Gō Trident exercises between Japan and Australia.[52] Prior to this, the three allies operated closely in operation Enduring Freedom in Afghanistan and Operation Iraqi Freedom, where the Australian Defence Force (ADF) and Japan Ground Self-Defense Force (JGSDF) were co-deployed in Samawah (2004–2006).

Thus Auslin concludes that "maintaining Japanese and Australian support for such joint exercises, and even expanding them into larger interdiction or ISR (intelligence, surveillance, and reconnaissance) exercises, is a goal for the U.S. government, and one that gives substance to the TSD."[53] On a larger strategic scale, Emma Chanlett-Avery and Bruce Vaughn record that "an integrated missile defense system, currently under consideration, may be among the most advanced of potential trilateral arrangements."[54] All of these mutually reinforcing trends, in trilateral, bilateral, or multilateral contexts, testify to the force-multiplying capacity generated by the trilateral alliance. These efforts were amply validated when the United States and Australia found themselves assisting with disaster relief operations in the aftermath of the Great East Japan Earthquake in 2011, as mentioned above.[55] As an aside, greater steps at trilateral integration were set back by Australia's decision not to procure Japanese boats for its future submarine program, opting instead for a French contractor.[56]

The intra-alliance politics perspective also alerts us to the expected power dynamics within the trilateral alliance. Measured in aggregate power and military capabilities, the United States is the strongest ally by far. Japan comes second, with Australia a distant third.[57] One would expect that Washington would both lead the alliance and dominate its decision-making process and strategic policies. This is true to a large degree, but several caveats apply to this initial judgment. Certainly, both Japan and Australia are highly dependent on their respective guarantees from the United States for their ultimate national security. The United States' extended nuclear deterrent notwithstanding, Japan and Australia are especially reliant upon US early warning, intelligence information, and technological cooperation.[58] This means that in both cases their "strategic role and influence is increasingly interdependent with American power and capabilities."[59] Washington has recently become more vocal in its calls for key allies to share a greater portion of the "defense burden" and to maintain a healthy level of defense expenditure: an exhortation that both countries have sought to comply with.[60]

However, this is not to say that they are entirely supine allies. The 2017 US National Security Strategy explicitly recognized "the invaluable advantages that our strong relationships with allies and partners deliver."[61] In particular, it regards access to Japanese and Australian "host nation support"—including territory, facilities, and incremental gains in military capabilities—as vital. Therefore, Stuart Harris and Richard Cooper argue that the relationships "are less unbalanced than is commonly thought."[62]

Now that a trilateral relationship has emerged, it will be interesting to watch for any instances where Japan and Australia combine their power and dependence to strengthen their joint hand against Washington in future negotiations, since it is held that "multilateral negotiations tend to be more effective than bilateral negotiations, which tend to be disadvantageous to the smaller power."[63] This was not possible under the former separate bilateral arrangements (quasi-alliance), but now Tokyo and Canberra have a direct bilateral security relationship through the 2007 Joint Declaration on Security Cooperation, it becomes potentially feasible, especially if they feel that US security guarantees are becoming less reliable. Thus far Green has recorded "numerous cases where Japan and Australia jointly urged the United States to engage in regional architecture" perhaps indicating a serious mutual effort on the part of Tokyo and Canberra to exercise this latent influence.[64]

Following from this de facto condition of allied interdependence is the question of "burden sharing," fundamental to all credible alliances. The axiom in intra-alliance politics is that an ally's relative contribution to the alliance translates into influence in the bargaining process and the shaping of allied strategy and policy. Back in 1990, Tokyo was aghast to learn that "checkbook diplomacy" paid no dividends in the Gulf War coalition. Australia understood this dynamic and has been perceived as a significant and reliable contributor to US "coalitions of the willing" in Afghanistan and Iraq, by which time Japan had learned the lesson. As a consequence of its economic difficulties and the cost of the war on terror, Washington has been less willing to assume the responsibility for allied defense unilaterally. Current US policy declares that "we expect [allies] to shoulder a fair share of the burden of responsibility to protect against common threats."[65] By unhesitatingly giving their support to the United States in the wake of the 9/11 terrorist attacks, making serious contributions to combat/support operations in the Middle East, and devoting substantial resources to counterterror and counterproliferation activities such as PSI, both Tokyo and Canberra have demonstrated their credibility and loyalty as US allies. In the changed Asia Pacific security environment, the absence of Cold War exigencies means that both partners have to "earn" rather than "free ride" on US security guarantees. All these factors make the three states more mutually interdependent and have served to reinforce the allied bond.

Insecurity. From the realist perspective, a condition of mutual insecurity and sense of shared threat are the catalysts that bring allies together and the adhesive that maintains allied cohesion. Given that the extant hub-and-spoke system of bilateral alliances was predicated upon opposition to the now-expired Soviet threat and the spread of communism, it is reasonable to question why a newly revitalized trilateral alliance is needed. After all, traditional alliance theory predicts that such threat-less alliances will be disbanded. Institutional explanations for alliance continuation are useful here, as is the realist notion of an "insurance policy" against the emergence of new threats. Thus, "when original threats predicating alliance formation disappear, other security problems may nevertheless remain or emerge. A major issue then arises to what extent existing alliance infrastructures are able to adapt."[66] Whether combating the NTS threats enumerated above or within the broader strategic context of strategic competition, all of the powers acknowledge that "these threats require cooperation and joint response."[67]

However, while alignment to counter NTS dangers is useful, it seldom justifies the deep level of defense cooperation, especially the war-fighting interoperability that is evident in the TSD. Realists are therefore alert to the rise of China as a potential rival and strategic challenger to the interests of the TSD allies, along with a resurgent Russia and ever-pugnacious Democratic People's Republic of Korea (DPRK).[68] Officially, "according to their communiqués, TSD partners see China as a source of constructive engagement in those policy contexts rather than as a threat to their mutual security."[69] Unofficially, however, each of the powers views trilateral security coordination as an expedient way to "hedge" against a revisionist and aggressive People's Republic of China (PRC) in the future. Zhu Feng notes that all the protestations of innocence notwithstanding, "the TSD is in effect an important effort to counterbalance China's rise and military buildup in the region: without the specter of a rising China, Washington, Tokyo, and Canberra would not have begun intensifying defense cooperation in the Asia-Pacific."[70] Firm evidence of this appears in the 2017 TSD Statement that draws attention to China's behavior regarding its maritime disputes in the South China and East China Seas.[71]

Alternatively, the TSD could actually be seen as a response to the Chinese-led alignment formation discussed in Chapter 6. As Tow points out, "it can also be interpreted as a response flowing from what Washington believes to be an imperative for strengthening offshore allied counterweights to recent Chinese and Russian coalition-building initiatives on the Asian land mass such as the Shanghai Cooperation Organization."[72] By consolidating its Japanese and Australian alliances alongside existing bilateral allies and strategic partners, the United States is able to dominate Halford Mackinder's maritime "inner crescent," later known as "rimland," to contain the power of a continental "heartland," a Eurasia-dominating alliance: a prospect that has been highlighted by China's institutional activism in this region, such as Belt and Road Initiative (BRI), (formerly OBOR), and Asian Infrastructure Investment Bank (AIIB).[73]

Beijing has assiduously rebutted such notions, arguing that it "poses no obstacle or threat to anyone" and that "China will never go for expansion, nor will it ever seek hegemony."[74] It has since refined its vision to include concepts such as "new state-to-state relations," "win-win" results, and "comprehensive security."[75] Nevertheless, analysts point to the rapidly increasing and nontransparent defense budget of the PLA and its acquisition of enhanced force projection capabilities.[76] Disaggregated from a clear insight into China's strategic intentions, an explicit "threat"[77] cannot yet be discerned, though there are occasional indicators of bellicose behavior, such as maritime clashes between Chinese vessels and those of Japan, whose claims of sovereignty are explicitly supported by the TSD.

Related to external threats, alliance analysts are preoccupied with determining the level of cohesion within any alignment. How durable will the alignment prove in the event of a serious confrontation? Tow argues that "the TSD can be used by Australia and Japan to institutionalize geopolitical reassurance from the United States and maintain alliance affinity with the Americans," thus mitigating the potential "intra-alliance security dilemma" of "abandonment versus entrapment."[78] Given its greater aggregate resources, if the United States were to face "abandonment" by Australia, or even Japan, the blow would be highly damaging but not necessarily fatal to US security posture in the Asia Pacific region. This is an extremely unlikely scenario, especially with regard to the latter. On the other hand, Kishore Mahbubani argues that Tokyo now worries deeply about abandonment by Washington, because "if that tie breaks, Japan could find itself strategically vulnerable in the face of three potentially unfriendly, if not adversarial, neighbors: China, Korea and Russia."[79]

To a lesser extent, Canberra worries about maintaining its relevance as a partner of the United States and about losing its great power protector. These fears have motivated both Tokyo and Canberra to deepen their alliance ties to the United States; to make a proportionately greater contribution both to this alliance and to US global strategies, such as the "war on terror"; and to pay obeisance to the Trump administration while under criticism for "unfair" exploitation of US security guarantees. Gary Smith and David Howe note that they can only rely on US "insurance" of their security if they are prepared to pay the "premium" of supporting their superpower ally when called upon.[80]

The counter-dynamic to this is the consequentially increased fear of "entrapment," whereby each of the allies worries they will be dragged into a conflict by their opposite numbers. There is already growing evidence that "China as a rising power has been a serious sticking point in the trilateral process."[81] Washington has served notice to both Tokyo and Canberra that it expects support in the event of Sino-American conflict, notably over the Taiwan Strait. When Australia on one occasion apparently distanced itself from this commitment, Richard Armitage warned that "if Washington found itself in conflict with China over Taiwan it would expect Australia's support. If it didn't get that support it would mean the end of the US-Australian alliance."[82] Further, one US official stated that "if Americans and Chinese are killing each other" over Taiwan, and "Japan doesn't support us, the alliance is dead."[83]

Trilateral perceptions of a putative "China threat," however, are complex and sometimes divergent. The fear of entrapment is also present in Washington, where decisionmakers worry that deteriorating Sino-Japanese relations fueled by growing nationalism and territorial disputes over the Senkaku/Diaoyu Islands, which are explicitly covered by the 1960 US-Japan security treaty, could drag them into a conflict. Tokyo continues to court Chinese displeasure over issues such as the Yasukuni Shrine and its wartime legacy in national textbooks.[84] Given their proximity to the PRC, perhaps the United States and Japan are in closer accord, having weathered Beijing's ire after they declared Taiwan a "common strategic objective."[85] However, Rory Medcalf thinks such fears of entrapment may be exaggerated: "The TSD is far short of an alliance: in no way does the dialogue oblige Australia or Japan to aid the other in the event of a military threat. The TSD does not entangle Australia in potential security contingencies facing Japan, such as confrontation with China or South Korea over contested waters and islands."[86]

This is a legitimate claim from a narrow legal-diplomatic point of view, but a compound of security imperatives as well as allied "norms" (see below) make Australian and Japanese support for the United States in most contingencies an almost foregone conclusion.

Ideational Factors: Ideology, Domestic Politics, and Norms

Ideology. In contrast to the realist interpretation of the TSD, Dibb recognizes that "alliances are not merely the product of rational calculations of national interests. They involve shared values, belief systems and a history of cooperation."[87] From a liberal-constructivist perspective, this type of ideological solidarity plays a key role in accounting for the formation and persistence of the tripartite alignment. In this respect, the affinity of the TSD partners in terms of worldview, ideals, and domestic systems is striking.

The ideology of these "like-minded states" is largely defined by what they stand for. Joint communiqués typically emphasize "the profound common values that guide our national policies: the maintenance of freedom, the pursuit of democracy, and respect for human rights."[88] Washington has been emphatic on this point, with former secretary of state Condoleezza Rice declaring that "the United States does have permanent allies: the nations with whom we share common values."[89] The basis of a shared ideological worldview is found in the similarities between the American, Japanese, and Australian domestic systems and cognate "regime-types." Indeed, the Australian government under John Howard actively promoted trilateral meetings as the coming together of "three great Pacific democracies."[90] The fact that each of these states is an "open" liberal democracy undoubtedly facilitates close relations. This conformity lends predictability and assurance to an alliance relationship, as Thomas Risse-Kappen argues.[91]

The contemporary policy discourse is paying increasing attention to the notion of such "values-based" alignment/alliance formations.[92] It is the ideological similarities and analogous domestic systems that instigate the TSD alliance. The alliance represents a concrete manifestation of the efforts to build a collective alliance identity. Indeed, the alliance acts as a touch point for shared values. Based upon mutual ideological values, the allies are opposed to any actor, state or non-state, that does not conform to liberal democratic principles and that seeks to disrupt the stability of the status quo through violent means, especially terrorists or "rogue" states with WMD. The TSD affirms that "as longstanding democracies and developed economies, our three countries have a common cause in working to maintain stability and security."[93]

To achieve this common goal, it highlights the importance of "supporting the emergence and consolidation of democracies" in its 2006 foundational statement.[94] Each of the partners has sought periodically to "export" these values as part of their foreign policy, primarily the United States, but David Fouse also notes Tokyo's attempt "to follow the path of 'value-oriented diplomacy' [to] help establish 'the arc of freedom and prosperity' along the outer rim of Eurasia."[95] Thus, Akihiko Tanaka observes, "TSD is a natural component of such value-oriented diplomacy."[96] However, ironically, this could generate conflict with China from a different vector to the conventional military threat enumerated above, as democracy promotion is viewed by the Beijing government as the "threat of peaceful evolution."[97] Zhu Feng concurs that "from China's perspective, one key danger of the TSD is that it may lead to the formulation of a 'democracy coalition' in the Asia-Pacific, one that is bound to be targeted at China by default."[98]

However, allied "regime-type" compatibilities should not be over-stated; national identities can still influence allied negotiations. The United States and Australia are certainly closer to each other on this score than they are to Japan, but when examined more closely, some distinctions emerge. Though Australia has imbibed much of American culture and economic practice and many have accentuated the affinities in order to smooth alliance management, it remains at heart strongly oriented toward a "European," particularly "British," identity and this is reflected in the Westminster parliamentary model and its social-democratic society.[99] The same popular "anti-American" zeitgeist that periodically affects America's European allies also obtains here, and has been accentuated through differences with the Trump administration. Participating in US military expeditions, though supported by the establishment and facilitated by close military ties, often has to weather the climate of domestic opinion.

In comparison, interaction with Tokyo presents some difficulties for both these allies and vice versa. Ralph Cossa and Brad Glosserman remind us that "it is tempting to see Japanese decision making and the resulting policies as a lot like our own . . . but that conclusion must be resisted. . . . Sensitivity to the nuances of Japanese politics and history is essential."[100] Though Japan was reengineered as a "Western" democracy during the US occupation period (1945–1952), it still operates in a uniquely "Japanese way" that deviates markedly from the Anglo-American political systems. Japan has in effect had "one-party" governance for most of the postwar period. The linkages of government with big business, synergized through the "state developmental" model, have in the past distinguished it from the more open/liberal trading societies of the other allies.[101] Moreover, Japan represents a different "civilization," and Japan's national identity is based upon a widespread belief in its own "uniqueness."[102] Thus, Akio Watanabe argues that Japan on the one hand and Australia and the US on the other are "almost diametrically different in historical and cultural backgrounds."[103] As what differentiates them historically, if not culturally, recedes into the past, however, one observes scant evidence that individual identities and national values seriously impede allied cooperation.

Domestic factors. As liberals predict, following from ideological issues, domestic politics play an important role in individual allied relations, especially in the US-Japan instance, and will continue to do so in the future. International alliances can generate policy problems for national governments, but they can also bring benefits such as domestic stability, and in the case of democracies, they are always subjected to critical public perceptions and domestic interest groups.

It was domestic political leadership that provided the impetus for upgrading the TSD to the ministerial level in 2006, upgrading and codifying the tripartite security alignment. Under the conservative governments of President George W. Bush and Prime Ministers Junichiro Koizumi and John Howard, large amounts of political capital were expended to consolidate the trilateral relationship. As Purnendra Jain notes, "For some years Australia, Japan and the US have been headed by national governments with a strong neoliberal orientation that to some extent serves to unite their interests on issue of international order and security."[104] Despite changes of government, the momentum of TSD cooperation has continued, indicating that the alignment enjoys bipartisan support in each partner country, though the advent of the Trump administration put it under initial strain.

There is strong evidence of intermestic politics operating in alliance negotiations, with numerous examples of allied politicians being "constrained" or "empowered" in allied bargaining as a result of domestic pressures. Japan is the most egregious case. Ironically, the "peace constitution" (which the US itself imposed upon a defeated Japan in 1947), particularly Article 9 that limits what its military forces can do, has become a brake on the augmented alliance cooperation that both allies seek. As Yoshihide Soeya identifies, "Japan's conception of security is fundamentally affected by *domestic constraints* and identity factors."[105] Though in the past Japanese leaders tapped into this and domestic antimilitarist impulses to find excuses not to offer more robust military support for the United States beyond national territorial defense, this dynamic is now changing, partly as Tokyo finds itself under increasing US pressure.[106]

With regard to more recent Liberal Democratic Party (LDP) governments, this pressure has actually assisted them in achieving their desired renaissance of Japan's international profile, where "Japan is demonstrating a willingness to play a more active role in global security issues."[107] A remarkable list of new security legislation has eroded the tightest constraints on the Japan Self-Defense Forces (JSDF) deployment overseas in support of allies, a fact further underlined by the most recent constitutional "reinterpretation" to allow for "collective defense" alongside allies, though in very circumscribed cases only.[108] Indeed, the nationalist government of Shinzo Abe has consistently sought to erode the fetters on Japan's "proactive contribution to international peace" and seeks to improve Japan's military capabilities indigenously and in cooperation with the United States.[109] Indeed, the support of allies in Washington and Canberra for all these initiatives as a way of strengthening alliance ties has provided political capital to domestic reform within Japan.

There have been countless examples of domestic politics interfering with US-Japan relations relating to the provisions of the alliance treaty and trade frictions, but the most persistent has been the difficulty in resolving disputes over the heavy military footprint that Okinawa currently endures. The Okinawa question is a double-edged sword. On one hand, Washington asserts that "the forward posture of US forces and our demonstrated ability to bring forces to bear in crisis are among the most tangible signals of our commitment to the security of our international partners."[110] On the other, some domestic constituencies view them as an infringement upon sovereignty, a nuisance or even a tempting invitation for an enemy to target their territory.[111] Recognizing the need to reduce the military burden that falls disproportionately upon Okinawa, the US-Japan Joint Declaration on Security in 1996 specifies significant troop reductions and relocation designed to resolve such friction henceforth.[112] Ironically, this agreement, yet to be properly implemented, has itself become a major source of disagreement and friction between the allies. The clearest example of this was when Democratic Party Japan Prime Minister Yukio Hatoyama was forced to resign due to his failure to reconcile his support for Okinawan anti-base constituencies with alliance supporters in Japan and the United States.[113]

Interestingly, just as Japan is seeking to reduce the physical American presence on its soil, Canberra accepted a "rotational" deployment of US Marines at its military facilities in northern Australia. The correlation between these developments illustrates the synergy of the TSD dynamics.

Trade frictions, procurement disputes over the jointly produced F-X warplane, and interference in the controversial "comfort women issue" by the US Congress have all served to strain US-Japan relations in the past.[114] Between Japan and Australia, the "whaling issue," concerning Japan's rights to hunt whales in Australia's exclusive economic zone (EEZ), serves as a bone of contention between their respective governments and publics. In 2016, Australia won its case against Tokyo in the International Court of Justice, but Japan has sought to circumvent the ruling.[115] And yet, this issue has always been subordinated to the overall need for good security relations.[116]

It should also be noted that the domestic realm within each of the respective countries is by no means monolithic. To give one example of Japan, a schism "between right idealists, centrists, and left idealists continues to run through Japanese politics today."[117] A similar dynamic exists between Democrat and Republican parties in the United States, and Liberal and Labor in Australia, though traditionally all of these have evidenced strong bipartisan support for their respective alliance relationships. Another "factor is public perceptions and how these influence alliance relationships especially in democracies."[118] Public opinion in these democracies can be more variable, however. To cite the case of Australia: "Maintaining support for the alliance is contingent upon Washington's success in convincing the Australian public of both the necessity and legitimacy of its policies."[119] The Australian government singularly failed to achieve this during the ill-fated "war on terror," when popular perceptions of the United States plummeted around the world, including among its closest allies, and advocating in support of a Trump administration will also face serious resistance among the public.

Norms. When explaining alliance cohesion, liberals/constructivists would prioritize the establishment and effectiveness of allied norms: for them, "threats matter, but *promises* also matter."[120] When we consider the existence of norms between the TSD allies, they seem all the more embedded and effective due to the long tradition of bilateral relations that preceded this recent triangular alliance. As Rosemary Foot notes, "norms can emerge in a variety of ways: spontaneously evolving, as social practice; consciously promoted, as political strategies to further specific interests; deliberately negotiated, as mechanisms for conflict management; or as a combination, mixing these three types."[121] Whatever their path of development, the intra-alliance politics framework identifies three main categories of norm-influenced behavior in alliances.

First, there is strong evidence to indicate that the norm of *pacta sunt servanda* obtains both to formal and informal obligations among the partners. There is no official *trilateral* treaty instrument between the TSD partners. The only formal defense treaties are the Mutual Security Treaty between the

United States and Japan and the ANZUS Treaty between the United States and Australia. These treaties theoretically commit the United States to come to the assistance of its allies in the event of an attack and vice versa, though in Japan's case "collective defense" scenarios are tightly circumscribed.[122] These treaties proved invaluable during the Cold War in reducing insecurity between allies and setting the parameters for mutual cooperation and assistance and continue to serve as mechanisms of an intra-allied cooperation that has been seamlessly extended to the new trilateral.

Because allied expectations and obligations are largely spelled out within the confines of existing treaties and the TSD, a new treaty is both unnecessary and likely to be seen as exclusionary or provocative by other states in the region. As Cossa's "virtual alliance" model implies, "a formal, official trilateral security alliance does not appear to be a serious option."[123] An informal sense of obligation is evident in the way that Tokyo and Canberra have consistently provided financial, diplomatic, or military assistance for the United States in the past and present. That the United States and Australia were immediately forthcoming with major assistance after the March 2011 disasters in Japan is also demonstrative of this dynamic. There was no formal requirement to offer this, but each ally perceived that the wider principle of *pacta sunt servanda* was crucial to maintaining good alliance relations.

There is ample evidence that the TSD members are committed to the norm of reciprocity, both direct and diffuse. While the United States has extended its protection to Japan, including its "nuclear umbrella," Tokyo has been obliging with financial and diplomatic support for US military activities and the "war on terror" in a "need to appease the Americans."[124] Japan has increased its share of the allied "defense burden" by dispatching JSDF assets and personnel to support coalition operations in the Middle East and has supported Australia in peacekeeping operations in Cambodia (1991), East Timor (1999), and South Sudan (2016). Moreover, the *US-Japan Defense Guidelines* indicate a multitude of ways in which the US Forces in Japan (USFJ) and the JSDF may share facilities and materiel through enhanced Acquisition and Cross-Servicing Agreements (ACSAs).[125] Japan and Australia have since signed their own ACSA, thus triangulating this process.

Australia has likewise obliged with diplomatic and military support for the United States. Canberra invoked Article IV of the ANZUS Treaty after 9/11 to send troops to Afghanistan and Iraq to participate in coalition efforts in those countries. In return, the United States has continued to extend technological cooperation to Australia, providing Canberra with powerful assets such as the Abrams battle tank and Apache attack helicopter, while both countries are receiving deliveries of the much-delayed F-35 Joint Strike

Fighter. The ANZUS Treaty provides a framework for Australia and the United States to share defense technologies, logistics, and intelligence. Aurelia Mulgan identifies the restructuring, particularly of the US-Japanese relationship, "to facilitate greater reciprocity in terms of the defense burdens assumed by each side."[126] There are two other good examples of diffuse reciprocity or quid pro quo on seemingly unconnected matters. First, Canberra has given diplomatic support for Tokyo's efforts to gain a permanent seat on the UN Security Council in return for Japan's support for Australia's presence in regional institutional processes. Also, the US-Australia FTA of 2005 was "widely viewed as a reward for Australian loyalty in the war on terrorism," according to Joseph Siracusa.[127] The TSD commits the parties to mutual condemnation of unilateral or coercive measures in the East China Sea, thus supporting Japan's administration of the Senkaku Islands. Both Canberra and Washington also condemned Beijing's unilateral attempt to establish an Air Defense Identification Zone (ADIZ) over this contested territory in 2013.[128] One notable setback for diffuse reciprocity, noted above, was the frustration of Japanese expectations to be the supplier of Australia's new submarine flotilla.

Consultation between the allies has proved crucial to maintaining allied cohesion and avoiding intra-allied suspicions through a "climate of trust." The alliance operates by the principle that "effective communication must build and maintain credibility and trust with friends . . . through an emphasis on consistency, veracity and transparency both in words and deeds."[129] The TSD forum provides the arena in which the three powers consult on security cooperation, exclusive of other states. The 2006 communiqué states that to strengthen trilateral cooperation, the states decided to enhance their exchange of information and strategic assessments on major international and regional security issues and developments.[130]

In addition, opportunities for consultation occur through bilateral channels or "policy networks." The Japan-US Security Consultative Committee and Australia-US Ministerial Talks provide additional bilateral consultation opportunities. Lastly, each of the allies interacts under the umbrella of multilateral fora such as the EAS, APEC, the ARF and the PSI, of which all three are members. As Cossa's "virtual alliance" model indicates, it is difficult to distinguish trilateral cooperation from participation in the multilateral initiative, a point reinforced by Desmond Ball.[131] Military exercises, both bilateral and multilateral, are exemplary of this dynamic. Trilateral exercises such as RED FLAG-Alaska and Pacific Bond, as well as the co-deployment of allied troops in Iraq and other PKOs, have bolstered understanding between the allies at the military-to-military level. According to Washington, they "foster an understanding of cultures, values and habits of other societies."[132] The capitals all recognize that "close and continuous policy and operational coordination at every level of government, from the unit tactical level through strategic consultations . . . is essential."[133]

Finally, intelligence sharing between the three allies has reached a high level, with the United States and Australia sharing information based on the United Kingdom–United States of America (UKUSA) Agreement and the Japanese and Australians having also signed an intelligence sharing agreement (ISA).[134] Wikileaks also intimates that US-Japan compacts on sharing intelligence and trilateral efforts have surreptitiously been upgraded. As Auslin affirms, "the U.S. is pushing for the enhancement of information exchange on these issues as well as for sharing strategic assessments with Japan and Australia in order to have similar regional pictures."[135] Tokyo has responded by tightening its intelligence handling procedures through the introduction of the State Secrecy Law ("Specially Designated Secrets Protection Law").[136] In addition, it has emerged that the Australian Secret Intelligence Service is training Japanese counterparts in espionage techniques.[137]

Conclusion

The TSD as a minilateral institution is indicative of the new shape of alliances in the twenty-first century, representing a de facto or "virtual trilateral alliance." It serves to knit together Japan and Australia as individual treaty-alliance "spokes" with the US "hub" into a "strategic triangle," at the same time as the bilateral Japan-Australia strategic partnership reinforces the triangle by overcoming the previous indirect "quasi-alliance" nature of their security relationship by bringing them into direct security alignment. These developments have created a new and revitalized trilateral "core" at the center of the extended US alliance system, which itself has mutated through the arguable de-emphasis of some peripheral allies, such as Thailand and Philippines, even as it has acquired new informal partners, such as India and Singapore.

In the absence of detailed inside knowledge of the discussions held at TSD meetings, we can analyze the resultant trilateral statements and infer from these its core concerns and objectives, referencing these against policies and strategies pursued by the allies individually, bilaterally, and trilaterally through other venues and means. This demonstrates that a "virtual alliance" conforms to a diffuse or informal institutional structure, in contrast to typically heavily institutionalized Cold War alliance mechanisms. In addition, the TSD as a case study exemplifies how alliance missions have broadened beyond the traditional enemy "threat" raison d'être to focus upon a wider range of NTS security issues. This focus has at least partially or officially supplanted an explicit enemy threat-based mission, though the

TSD is committed to upholding its vision of regional security order and retains the capacity to operationalize its latent capabilities to meet a newly emergent strategic threat ("hedging").

Analysts have pondered whether the moves toward consolidation of trilateral security cooperation through the TSD portend the emergence of a more formal military alliance pact along the traditional paradigm. As Beeson notes, there is no doubt that "America has sought to respond to the challenge of a rising China by reinforcing its alliance relationships with Australia and Japan."[138] Recent TSD statements in particular have taken a robust stance against Chinese activities in the South and East China Seas and a tougher deterrent stance against the DPRK nuclear program. As a result, Zhu Feng identifies that "Beijing has viewed any updates of the U.S. alliance system in the region as a pressing menace. From China's perspective, the TSD could very well become an Asian version of NATO—a turning of a 'hub-and-spoke' web of bilateral alliances with the United States into a multiple-ally institution."[139]

Yet this is a moot point as the virtual alliance paradigm serves many of the functions of a de jure military pact but forgoes the disadvantages of provocation and formal "entrapment." Moreover, Jain advises, "Possible impediments come from both external and internal sources and will make it difficult for the three nations currently in a formal dialogue process to transform their trilateral security relations into an institution, alliance or treaty that formally links the three partners strategically."[140] Nevertheless, even as it faces down the DPRK and engages in extensive NTS cooperation, careful reassurance is needed in order to assuage Beijing's concerns that its latent capability is not to be directly targeted at the PRC. As Tow notes, "Much will depend on the exercise of sensitivity by the TSD countries in their joint communiqués concerning Beijing's interests and legitimacy as a regional security actor."[141] The same applies to the notion of expanding the TSD into a quadrilateral format to include their mutual strategic partner, India. At present, this possibility remains uncertain and there is no direct alignment between the four powers.

As a new form of alliance-type alignment founded explicitly on shared interests and values, with the objective of deterring challenges to regional order, the application of the intra-alliance politics perspective provides a valuable tool to reveal the relative importance of realist and liberal-constructivist drivers behind security cooperation. Through this approach, we are able to gain superior analytical purchase on the TSD "virtual" alliance that cannot be provided by traditional balance of power/balance of threat theories alone. This chapter has demonstrated that the intra-alliance politics framework for analysis acts as an effective tool for unlocking the internal properties of an alliance and accounting for its variegated behavioral dynamics. Moreover, it has revealed that this alignment is genuinely shaped by a compound of common interests and shared values and that "insurance" against a potential threat and adherence to agreed allied norms keep it unified. By taking this dyadic analytical approach, we may conclude that "both realist and idealist explanations are useful in the proper applications."[142]

Notes

1. I would like to extend my thanks to Professors William Tow and Kiichi Fuji-wara for their support on this topic, through my invitation to relevant workshops and projects, and for their guidance and mentorship.

2. Tatsumi, "Introduction," p. 18.

3. Satake, "The Origin of Trilateralism?"; Schoff, "The Evolution of US-Japan-Australia Security Cooperation."

4. Cossa et al., "The United States and the Asia-Pacific Region," p. 32.

5. Calder, "Securing Security Through Prosperity."

6. Sahashi, "The Rise of China and the Transformation of Asia-Pacific Security Architecture," p. 145.

7. Cha, *Powerplay*. Acharya, *Why Is There No NATO in Asia?*

8. Green, "Strategic Asian Triangles."

9. Auslin, "Shaping a Pacific Future: Washington's Goal for the Trilateral Strategic Dialogue," p. 13. Italics added.

10. Cossa et al., "The United States and the Asia-Pacific Region," p. 32.

11. Tatsumi, "Introduction," p. 16.

12. Ibid., p. 15.

13. Wu, "Chinese Perspectives on Building an East Asian Community in the Twenty-First Century," p. 66.

14. Tow and Acharya, "Obstinate or Obsolete?" p. 18.

15. White House, *National Security Strategy of the United States of America* (2015), p. 7.

16. Tow, "Asia's Competitive 'Strategic Geometries,'" p. 46.

17. Auslin, "Shaping a Pacific Future," p. 18.

18. Tow, "Tangled Webs," p. 31.

19. Tow, "Contingent Trilateralism,"; Tow and Trood, "The 'Anchors'; Jain and Bruni, "Japan, Australia and the United States."

20. Tow, "Alliances and Alignments in the Twenty-First Century," p. 19.

21. Cossa, *U.S.-Korea-Japan Relations*.

22. US Department of State, "Trilateral Strategic Dialogue Joint Statement" (2006).

23. US Department of State, "Trilateral Strategic Dialogue Joint Statement" (2009).

24. Snyder, "Alliances, Balance, Stability," p. 124.

25. Jain and Bruni, "American Acolytes," p. 96.

26. Schoff, "The Evolution of US-Japan-Australia Security Cooperation," p. 43.

27. Wilkins, "From Strategic Partnership to Strategic Alliance?"

28. Ashizawa, "Australia-Japan-US Trilateral Strategic Dialogue and the ARF."

29. Tow, "Contingent Trilateralism."

30. Green, "Strategic Asian Triangles," p. 761. Italics added.

31. US Department of State, "Trilateral Strategic Dialogue," 2009.

32. US Department of State, "Trilateral Strategic Dialogue," 2006.

33. US Department of State, "Australia-Japan-United States Trilateral Strategic Dialogue Ministerial Joint Statement" (2017).

34. Goh, "Hierarchy and the Role of the United States in the East Asian Security Order"; Goh, "Great Powers and Hierarchical Order in Southeast Asia."

35. Ministry of Foreign Affairs, Japan, "Australia–Japan–United States Trilateral Strategic Dialogue Joint Statement" (2017).

36. "Japan–United States–Australia Trilateral Strategic Dialogue Joint Statement." Tokyo, June 27, 2008. https://www.mofa.go.jp/region/asia-paci/australia/joint0806 -2.html.

37. Tow, "The Trilateral Strategic Dialogue," p. 3.

38. Ministry of Foreign Affairs, Japan, "Japan-United States-Australia Trilateral Strategic Dialogue Joint Statement" (2016).

39. Jimbo, "Japan-US-Australia Cooperation on Capacity Building in Southeast Asia," p. 61.

40. Ministry of Foreign Affairs, Japan, "Japan–United States–Australia Trilateral Strategic Dialogue Joint Statement" (2016).

41. Ibid.

42. Envall, "Community Building in Asia?"

43. Tow, "The Trilateral Strategic Dialogue," p. 2.

44. Snyder, "Alliances, Balance, Stability," p. 133.

45. US Department of Defense, *Summary of the 2018 National Defense Strategy.*

46. Australian Department of Defence, *Defence 2000*, p. 33.

47. Akimoto, "Exercising the Right to Collective Self-Defense?" p. 157.

48. Australian Department of Defence, *2016 Defence White Paper*; Liff, "Japan's Defense Policy"; US Department of Defense, *Summary of the 2018 National Defense Strategy.*

49. Sahashi, "Australia, Japan, and US Trilateral Cooperation in the Regional Security Architecture," p. 93.

50. Chanlett-Avery and Vaughn, "Emerging Trends in the Security Architecture," p. 12.

51. Global Security, "Keen Sword"; Herndon, "Sun Sets on Keen Sword Exercise."

52. Australian Department of Defence, "Australia-Japan Bilateral Exercise Concludes."

53. Auslin, "Shaping a Pacific Future," p. 19.

54. Chanlett-Avery and Vaughn, "Emerging Trends in the Security Architecture," p. 13.

55. Samuels, *3.11: Disaster and Change in Japan.*

56. Gady, "Why Japan Lost the Bid to Build Australia's New Subs."

57. Lowy Institute, "Asia Power Index."

58. Desmond Ball argues that the UK-US intelligence-sharing agreement (1947/48) is the most valuable asset of Australia's alliance with the United States. See Ball, "The US-Australian Alliance."

59. Lyon and Tow, "The Future of the US-Australian Security Relationship," p. 26.

60. Rich, "Japanese Government Urges Another Increase in Military Spending"; Baldino and Carr, "The End of 2%."

61. White House, *National Security Strategy of the United States of America* (2017), p. 2.

62. Harris and Cooper, "The US-Japan Alliance," p. 55.

63. Chung, "Confidence-Building Measures in the South China Sea," p. 284.

64. Green, "Strategic Asian Triangles," p. 762.

65. White House, *National Security Strategy of the United States of America* (2017), p. 4.

66. Tow and Acharya, "Obstinate or Obsolete?" p. 25.

67. Australian Department of Defence, *Australia's National Security: A Defence Update* (2005), p. 13.

68. Luttwak, *The Rise of China vs. the Logic of Strategy*; Friedberg, *A Contest for Supremacy*.

69. Tow, "Tangled Webs," p. 31.

70. Feng, "TSD—Euphemism for Multiple Alliance?" p. 43.

71. Ministry of Foreign Affairs, Japan, "Australia–Japan–United States Trilateral Strategic Dialogue Joint Statement" (2017).

72. Tow, "Asia's Competitive 'Strategic Geometries,'" p. 37.

73. Mackinder, "The Geographical Pivot of History"; Spykman, *The Geography of the Peace*.

74. State Council Information Office, *China's National Defence in 2004*.

75. State Council Information Office, *China's Policies on Asia-Pacific Security Cooperation*.

76. US Office of the Secretary of Defense, *Military and Security Developments Involving the People's Republic of China 2016*.

77. Walt, *The Origins of Alliances*.

78. Tow, "Asia's Competitive 'Strategic Geometries,'" pp. 40–41.

79. Mahbubani, *Can Asians Think?* p. 120.

80. Smith and Lowe, "Howard, Downer and the Liberal's Realist Tradition," p. 468.

81. Jain, "Japan-Australia Security Ties and the United States," p. 529.

82. Quoted in Edwards, "Permanent Friends?" p. 45.

83. Lawrence, "Miles to Go," p. 23.

84. Qiu, "The Politics of History and Historical Memory in China-Japan Relations."

85. For Japan's counterstance, see Faiola, "Japan to Join U.S. Policy on Taiwan," p. A1.

86. Medcalf, "Squaring the Triangle," p. 28.

87. Dibb, "Australia–United States," p. 41.

88. Ministry of Foreign Affairs, Japan, "Japan-US Joint Declaration on Security: Alliance for the 21st Century."

89. Rice, "Rethinking the National Interest," p. 5.

90. Jain, "Japan-Australia Security Ties and the United States," p. 528.

91. Risse-Kappen, *Cooperation Among Democracies*.

92. Armitage and Nye, "The US-Japan Alliance," p. 15.

93. Ministry of Foreign Affairs, Japan, "Trilateral Strategic Dialogue Joint Statement Australia–Japan–United States" (2006).

94. Ibid.

95. Fouse, "Japan's 'Values-Oriented Diplomacy.'"

96. Tanaka, "Trilateral Strategic Dialogue," p. 37.

97. Ong, "'Peaceful Evolution,' 'Regime Change' and China's Political Security," p. 718.

98. Feng, "TSD—Euphemism for Multiple Alliance?" p. 45.

99. Smith and Lowe, "Howard, Downer and the Liberal's Realist Tradition," p. 460.

100. Ralph A. Cossa and Brad Glosserman, "US-Japan Defense Cooperation: Has Japan become the Great Britain of Asia?"

101. Johnson, *Japan, Who Governs?*; Johnson, *MITI and the Japanese Miracle*.

102. Berger, "From Sword to Chrysanthemum," p. 124.

103. Watanabe, "Japan and Australia," p. 11.

104. Jain, "Japan-Australia Security Ties and the United States," p. 525.

105. Soeya, "Japan: Normative Constraints Versus Structural Imperatives," p. 228. Italics added.

106. Singh, "The Development of Japanese Security Policy."

107. Hughes and Krauss, "Japan's New Security Agenda," p. 160.

108. *Japan Times,* "Abe Cites Need for Japan to Fully Exercise Right to Collective Self-Defense."

109. Hughes, *Japan's Foreign and Security Policy Under the "Abe Doctrine."*

110. US Department of Defense, *The National Defense Strategy of the United States of America* (2005).

111. See LaFeber, *The Clash.*

112. Ministry of Foreign Affairs, Japan, "Japan-U.S. Joint Declaration on Security: Alliance for the 21st Century."

113. Dudden, "Okinawa Today."

114. Lorell, *Troubled Partnership*; Morris-Suzuki, "Japan's 'Comfort Women.'"

115. *The Guardian,* "Malcolm Turnbull Tells Shinzo Abe He's Disappointed About Whaling Resumption."

116. Mossop, "Australia v. Japan"; *Economist,* "Not Whaling but Drowning."

117. Berger, "From Sword to Chrysanthemum," p. 139.

118. Cossa, *U.S.-Korea-Japan Relations: Building Toward a "Virtual Alliance,"* p. xx.

119. Dibb, "Australia–United States," p. 46.

120. Cha, "Complex Patchworks." Italics original. p. 49.

121. Katzenstein, *The Culture of National Security,* p. 21.

122. Akimoto, *The Abe Doctrine.*

123. Cossa, "U.S.-Japan-Korea: Creating a Virtual Alliance."

124. Berger, "From Sword to Chrysanthemum," p. 129.

125. The Acquisition and Cross-Servicing Agreement (ACSA) is indicative of the exchange of support, materiel, and training between the two nations.

126. Mulgan, "The US-Japan Security Relationship in a New Era," p. 140.

127. Siracusa, "John Howard, Australia, and the Coalition of the Willing," p. 45.

128. Australian Minister for Foreign Affairs, "China's Announcement of an Air-Defence Identification Zone over the East China Sea."

129. US Department of Defense, *Quadrennial Defense Review Report* (2006), p. 92.

130. US Department of State, "Trilateral Strategic Dialogue Joint Statement," (2006).

131. Ball, "Whither the Japan-Australia Security Relationship?"

132. US Department of Defense, *East Asia Strategy Report,* p. 15.

133. Ministry of Foreign Affairs, Japan, "Japan-U.S. Joint Declaration on Security."

134. Richelson and Ball, *The Ties That Bind.*

135. Auslin, "Shaping a Pacific Future," p. 12.

136. Repeta, "Japan's 2013 State Secrecy Act."

137. Malley, "Spies Like Us."

138. Beeson, *Institutions of the Asia-Pacific,* p. 71.

139. Feng, "TSD—Euphemism for Multiple Alliance?" pp. 43–44.

140. Jain, "Japan-Australia Security Ties and the United States."

141. Tow, "The Trilateral Strategic Dialogue," p. 7.

142. Starr, *War Coalitions,* p. 130.

4

Security Communities

The past two chapters have been concerned with the conceptual and empirical investigation of the alliance paradigm and its variants. This one is dedicated to expressly recognizing the "security community" as a form of security alignment quite distinct from the traditional alliance paradigm and setting forth a suitable analytical framework to probe into its workings. This framework will then be applied to the ASEAN case study in the next chapter. In comparison to the preceding alliance paradigm, the security community is a more novel form of security cooperation. However, a firm theoretical base, largely based upon sociological theorizing and situated primarily within the constructivist tradition of international relations (IR), exists around the concept. Security communities theory still rests first and foremost upon the foundational work of Karl Deutsch and his associates[1] and especially upon the dedicated constructivist approach advanced in the seminal work of Emmanuel Adler and Michael Barnett.[2] More recent scholarship has assisted in supporting attempts to reconsider security communities as alignments, and this has been duly incorporated in the following analysis. In this chapter, I do not seek to reinvent security community theory but rather to appropriately recalibrate it toward a more explicit alignment perspective. While retaining the essentials of conventional security community theory, I therefore reformulate and present these accordingly to specifically emphasize alignment properties and to accentuate their external dimensions alongside their intramural dynamics.

However, since security communities are not usually explicitly perceived as security alignments, the following section in which the term is defined and the concept unpacked necessarily incorporates further justification for doing so, since some scholars may bristle at this classification. This is needed to overcome the "territorial" nature of IR research traditions and the tendency to view alternative assumptions as challenges to their "home ground."[3] Indeed, part of the constructivist turn has been an effort to distance itself from the preoccupations of realism, in which alliances feature prominently, and to distinguish itself through the use of alternative descriptors and conceptual discourses. This has obscured the fact that both alliance theory and security community theory are united in their focus on the phenomenon of alignment.

What Is a Security Community?

In the orthodox security community paradigm, states align together to eliminate the recourse to violence within their designated political space. They achieve this by working together to change intramural perceptions in order to forge an exclusive common identity, or "we-feeling." This in turn will be built on mutual self-restraint and predicated on shared norms and practices. In brief, Raimo Väyrynen defines a security community as "a collective arrangement in which its members have reasons to trust that the use of military and economic coercion in their mutual relations is unlikely."[4]

The concept was first envisioned by Karl Deutsch and his associates in their 1950s study of the North Atlantic area, in which they identify the creation of a peaceful comity of states through gradual confidence-building and integration.[5] Deutsch established the main parameters of the security paradigm, which his intellectual successors have built upon. To quote him at length:

> A SECURITY COMMUNITY is a group of people that become "integrated."
>
> BY INTEGRATION we mean the attainment, with a territory, of a "sense of community" and of institutions and practices strong enough and widespread enough to assure, for a "long" time, dependable expectations of "peaceful change" among its population.
>
> BY SENSE OF COMMUNITY we mean a belief on the part of individuals within a group that they have come to agreement on at least this one point: that common social problems can and must be resolved by processes of "peaceful change."
>
> BY PEACEFUL CHANGE we mean the resolution of social problems, normally by institutionalized procedures, without resort to large-scale physical force.[6]

Space does not permit a thorough examination of all of the attributes, permutations, and debates relating to the concept.[7] One of the key aspects of Deutsch's original approach includes the important distinction between "pluralistic" and "amalgamated" security communities. If the states remain separate entities, such as in the North American Free Trade Agreement (NAFTA), this is denoted as a "pluralistic" security community.[8] If they surrender a measure of their national sovereignty to a supranational institutional apparatus, it becomes an "amalgamated" security community, such as the United States after the Civil War (1861–1865).[9]

It is important to stress that members of a security community are aligned with one another to jointly pursue a common (security) purpose, just like in alliances and strategic partnerships. As Deutsch contends, "the keeping of the peace among the participating units was the main political goal overshadowing all others."[10] It will be recalled that alignment is "a relationship between two or more states that involves mutual expectations of some degree of policy coordination on security issues under certain conditions in the future."[11] Hence, Emmanuel Adler and Patricia Greve posit that "actors that constitute security communities *align* consciousness in the direction of common enterprises, projects, and partnerships, thus turning security community into the day-to-day practice of peace."[12] That these members become engaged in "cooperative security" on the *inside* distinguishes them from nonmembers on the *outside* of the compact, who are not so aligned, even if these "outsiders" are not necessarily viewed as a "threat" or target. They thus fulfill the *exclusivity* criterion of alignment, in contradistinction to *inclusive* "security dialogue forums" such as the EAS or APEC. Until recently, the majority of the scholarship has emphasized only the internal or intramural dimension of security communities. However, by foregrounding their external orientation, with the aid of new additions to security community theory, we can bring the alignment dimension of such communities into sharper relief.

Moreover, security communities are closer to other forms of alignment than is generally acknowledged. Indeed, prolific writers on alliances and coalitions, such as Stephen Walt and Harvey Starr, have considered the notion of security community as integral to alignment study.[13] Others, such as Michael Williams, argue that alliances may incubate security communities, or, as in the case of Celeste Wallander's work mentioned in Chapter 2, that alliances may further "evolve" into such a community, in addition to their prior collective defense functions.[14] As Ondrej Ditrych points out, "in Deutsch's conception, [a security community] should emerge around a core and either a military alliance based on a common threat, or an economic alliance formed for a mutual benefit."[15] This convergence with other alignment paradigms points to valuable conceptual synergies and certainly warrants their inclusion in the wider corpus of alignment theorizing.

Further justification for the inclusion of security communities and the ASEAN case study in this book on alignment in the Asia Pacific relates to their close interconnection with associated framing concepts such as security "order" and "architecture," as noted in Chapter 1, therefore making them integral to any survey of regional security dynamics. First, Vincent Pouliot reminds us that "security communities are vehicles of international order."[16] Indeed, Deutsch's formulation of the concept was an effort to identify the means for "engineering a more peaceful and stable international order."[17] This connection particularly stands out in the recent work of Simon Koschut.[18] And second, since security communities will generally assume institutional form, emerging within a preestablished international organization (e.g., NATO), or generating new ones (e.g., ASEAN), they will represent tangible manifestations of security "architecture."[19] However, Wæver reminds us that the obvious but simplistic tendency to identify a security community as literally synonymous with the appropriate organization should be treated with caution.[20]

On a final note, it is important to draw attention to the apparently successful crossover of the concept from its origins in the academic world to the policymaking world.[21] It has been applied by policy practitioners to describe preexisting alignments, such as the Euro-Atlantic Community or NAFTA (US-Canada/US-Mexico relations).[22] Ditrych also observes that in "the official discourse of NATO . . . the alliance was then more and more conceived of as a *community* in a new opposition to the previous state of being only an *alliance*."[23] Australian prime minister Kevin Rudd also invoked the term as part of his (unsuccessful) attempt to build an "Asia Pacific [security] community" in 2008.[24] However, most important for the study at hand is the explicit adoption of the term by the ASEAN Secretariat. The officially declared ASEAN Security Community (ASC) is designed to promote "an ASEAN-wide political and security cooperation in consonance with the ASEAN Vision 2020 *rather than a defence pact, military alliance or a joint foreign policy*."[25] This crucial case study will be explored fully in Chapter 5, but the evidence above indicates how the security community concept may be supplanting the traditional alliance paradigm in the minds of some policymakers.

Theoretical Base

In comparison to alliances with their long-established pedigree, the "security community" is a relative newcomer to our repertoire of alignment paradigms.[26] What Deutsch embarked upon in the 1950s was left to languish during the remainder of the Cold War, until it was "rediscovered" in the 1990s and the term underwent a renaissance led by constructivist scholars. Though all security community scholars pay homage to Deutsch, this has not prevented fierce debate on interpreting and reinterpreting his writings.

As Koschut identifies: "The concept has been adopted and adapted by various 'schools' of IR theory, however, mostly to serve their own purposes."[27] Indeed, Chang has suggested three "interpretations" of the concept with the following distinctions: "Whereas the Deutschian security community is objective, the constructivist security community is more interpretative, with the instrumental security community somewhere in between."[28] He then proffers a fourth "model" for a "critical security community," based upon the theories of Robert Cox.

It is constructivism that has emerged as the dominant approach toward elucidating the security community paradigm. The 1998 work of Adler and Barnett was, in their own words, "the first sustained effort to lay firm foundations for the study of security communities."[29] Others have taken up the intellectual gauntlet to elaborate or refashion the concept, for the most part, along the constructivist line. New permutations of the security communities approach, as well as challenges to it, are emerging, as the more recent work of Adler, Collins, and Bellamy demonstrates.[30] Some scholars have explored its applicability to security architecture/international organizations, such as the Organization for Security and Co-operation in Europe (OSCE), and its conceptual linkage with interdependence/democratic peace, while M. J. Reese has concentrated on the role of great powers in relation to security communities.[31] However, according to the latter, "while theories of security community evolution have been plentiful, there has not yet been a substantial effort to study the inverse: security community dissolution."[32] This is changing, however, with the work of Simon Koschut looking at how "disintegration" could challenge this "progressivist bias."[33]

Security community theorists have been largely concerned with the internal dynamics of the phenomenon. However, considering more explicitly a community's relation to its external environment is not only important but augments my claim that it operates as an alignment. Just as all alliances have an *internal* orientation—as the intra-alliance politics perspective (above) shows—security communities will have an *external* one. As Adler and Barnett attest, "Security is becoming the condition and the quality of these communities; who is inside, and who is outside, matters most."[34] Deutsch did not explicitly address this question in his original writings, being content to investigate the internal dynamics of the North Atlantic area—an omission he acknowledges as a "side-step."[35] Thus, Väyrynen contends, "This approach tends to focus on the 'inside' of the security community and pay less attention to its relations with the external environment. However, in real life, the outside environment has an impact on the security community and it can, in turn, influence that environment."[36]

What propositions for the external behavior of security communities have been advanced? Adler and Greve identify that the "key question is whether security communities can be expected theoretically and seen empirically to act externally in the same way that they do internally, or whether they simply replicate the security dilemma on a higher level."[37] In the first instance, Deutsch and coauthors speculated that if security communities spread to envelop the entire system that a universal expectation of peaceful change would prevail. Hypothetically, "if the entire world was integrated as a security community wars would automatically be eliminated."[38] More conceivably, we are witnessing a proliferation of regional security communities that have reached the limits of their expansion and will eventually, if not already, share common borders. Reese suggests that if a constellation of large regional-based security communities develops, it "implies a possible future where relations between security communities, rather than individual states, will become the primary focus of international politics."[39] But in the second instance, the corollary of "we-feeling" inside the community is the creation of a "them-feeling" toward states outside its membership.[40] This development portends antagonistic regional security alignments, or "blocs," whether both are internally security communities or not. According to Reese, this is the "security community paradox": "that states must disavow the use of force with community partners while retaining the capability to employ force against extra-community states."[41] Only recently has the literature begun to seriously explore such concerns, as the work of Pernille Rieker illustrates.[42]

Any theoretical limitations and deficiencies in the paradigm have not prevented its widespread application to a number of empirical case studies. First, the North Atlantic Community, Deutsch's original case study, has generated fierce debate, as the work of Thomas Risse-Kappen and exchanges between Michael Cox and Vincent Pouliot illustrate.[43] Second, those involved in advancing and analyzing the European project have been greatly influenced by the security community paradigm.[44] Wæver considers Western Europe a "comprehensive" security community, though he prefers the descriptor "non-war community,"[45] something in-between the pluralistic and amalgamated categories. Within Europe, the Baltic subregion ("Norden") has also drawn major attention from scholars, as the works of Frank Möller and Peter Wallensteen and others testify.[46] Andrew Hurrell and Daniel Flemes have investigated South America;[47] Richard Higgott and Kim Richard Nossal have considered Australia. Michael Barnett and F. Gregory Gause III's analysis of Gulf States, and Farah Dakhlallah's work on the League of Arab States should also be noted.[48] Africa has also been examined by Benedikt Franke, Arie Kacowicz, and Naison Ngoma.[49] Lastly, Amitav Acharya, Alan Collins, and many others have analyzed ASEAN as a security community and sparked discussion over the applicability of the "European model" to Southeast Asia, all of which is considered in Chapter 5.[50]

Analytical Framework: "Security Communities"

Acharya reminds us that "security community" is not only a descriptive category but also an analytical tool.[51] While Deutsch did provide a first cut "transactionalist" framework for measuring the existence of a security community, this has not been widely adopted among security community theorists, although renewed interest in the original "Deutschian" approach is evident, particularly in the work of Michael Haas.[52] Instead, it is the framework advanced by Adler and Barnett that forms the point of departure for the following sections. They are concerned specifically with the "pluralistic" form of security community: "a transnational region comprised of sovereign states whose people maintain dependable expectations of peaceful change."[53] As noted above, their framework is anchored in a constructivist research tradition, which places it at odds with "traditional" structuralist alignment theories discussed in Chapter 1.[54] At its core, this approach recognizes that "international reality is a social construction driven by collective understandings, including norms, that emerge from social interaction."[55] Adler affirms that "security communities are socially constructed because shared meanings, constituted by interaction, engender collective identities. They are dependent on communication, discourse, and interpretation, as well as on material environments."[56]

There are two parts to the Adler and Barnett framework (see Figure 4.1). In the first, they explore the causal foundations of the concept through a three-tiered approach. This extrapolates on the role of "precipitating conditions"; "structure" (power, knowledge) and "process" (transactions, organizations, social learning); and "mutual trust/identity formation" in explaining why such communities come about and what drives their behavior. Together these provide explanations for "the production of dependable expectation of peaceful change."[57]

The second part of the framework is a more straightforward model of how security communities chart their evolution through three phases: nascent, ascendant, and mature. This part of the framework is a "conceptualization of the mechanisms and conditions by which security communities develop."[58] While the first part is conceptually dense, dealing with the epistemology and ontology, the second part distills many of its propositions into a more "applied" framework for analysis. Because the intent of this book is to provide practical frameworks for analyzing different alignments, I have opted, like most scholars, to concentrate upon the second part, drawing upon the first part in cases where explanatory issues require additional reinforcement. This methodology chimes with Niklas Bremberg's assertion that "the social construction of security communities is not primarily discursive but very much practical."[59] As previously noted, the

Figure 4.1 Security Communities: Analytical Framework

FIRST PART: Explanatory drivers

Economic and/or strategic

Recognition of an external, existential threat

Recognition of an internal threat

Tier 1

Precipitating Conditions

· Change in technology, demography, economics, the environment

· Development of new interpretations of social reality

· External threats

↓

Tier 2

Factors Conducive to the Development of Mutual Trust and Collective Identity

Structure:	Process:
Power	Transactions
Knowledge	Organizations
	Social Learning

↓

Tier 3

Necessary Conditions of Dependable Expectations of Peaceful Change

Mutual Trust	Collective Identity

↓

Dependable Expectations of Peaceful Change

continues

Figure 4.1 Continued

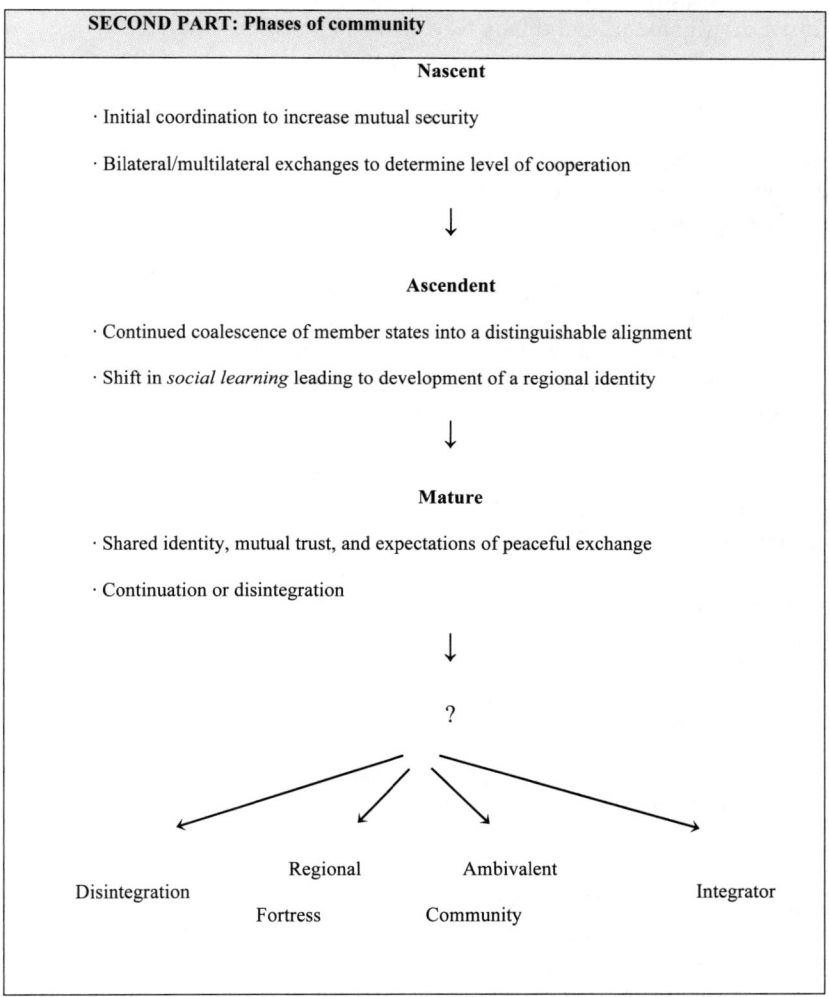

Source: Based on Adler and Barnett, "A Framework for the Study of Security Communities," p. 38.

framework above has been adapted from its antecedents accordingly toward the purpose of emphasizing security communities explicitly as forms of alignment, and this is reflected in its presentation.

Nascent Phase

The formative, or nascent, phase in the evolution of a security community can be explained by a combination of factors discussed in Adler and Barnett's original three-tier framework. They posit that "the trigger mechanisms for a security community are likely to have material and normative bases."[60] It is often tricky to clearly disaggregate these bases, though a general trend throughout the evolution of a security community is that initial "material" drivers are gradually transformed or replaced by "normative" ones in the course of its growth, as we shall see below.

First, it must be noted that security communities often come about due to unexpected fluctuations in the international system. Such unpredictable stimuli might include major shifts in the balance of military or economic power (e.g., hegemonic decline), cataclysmic events affecting material structures and normative or political mind-sets (e.g., a financial crash), or other transnational processes (globalization or regionalization). Any or all of these "structural" drivers result in a condition of "insecurity" among states. Thus,

> "in this initial phase, governments do not explicitly seek to create a security community. Instead they begin to consider how they might coordinate their relations in order to increase their mutual security; lower the transaction costs associated with their exchanges; and/or encourage further exchanges and interactions."[61]

Second, the crucible of common interests in the nascent community may be economic, strategic, or both. Indeed, "there will be a relationship between the establishment of international economic associations that are designed to encourage economic interchange and the presence of international arrangements that are intended to produce order and security."[62] Certainly, economic impulses toward division of labor/comparative advantage and free-trading incentives can all drive the process.[63] This leads Acharya to conclude that "economic interdependence may significantly facilitate the development of security communities."[64]

On the other hand, and in accord with "traditional" alignment theory, security communities may be forged by shared threat perceptions.[65] These may be focused on an existential foe, such as "communism," in which case the inside/outside (us/them) bifurcation is embedded in the very formation of the security community. Alternatively, a shared sense of internal domestic threats such as separatism and terrorism may act as a motivator. Importantly, Bremberg notes that "non-military security threats effect processes of security community-building."[66] But in contradistinction to alliance formation, states relating to each other in the community "reconfigure their perceptions of security by adopting logic different to that of the security dilemma."[67] Between such states, political-military threat drivers are often subsumed by the gradual appearance of "cooperative security" among the members and a broader understanding of security challenges in the later stages.[68]

In each of these cases, the interests of individual governments and state leaders, or "political entrepreneurs," may play a key role in bringing about the community. In this phase, Jennifer Mitzen asserts "security communities tend to be constituted around powerful core states that act as attractors."[69] Indeed, Reese surmises that "the complete absence of a great power patron is expected to pose an obstacle to the development and consolidation of a security community."[70] This may have implications for the ASEAN Security Community (ASC), examined in Chapter 5.

Third, the locus of such cooperation must be ascribed to a specified (sub)"region" that is a "regional security complex."[71] Alternatively, the security community building process can play a part in generating a cognitive sense of "region," where none heretofore existed.[72] We have looked at the problematization of "regions" in Chapter 1, but the important point here is that security communities must be inextricably linked with a relatively contiguous region for them to exist. At the nascent phase, this will involve a definitional or re-definitional negotiation among the states moving toward a community as to who "belongs" in their region and who does not.

Fourth, closely bound with the conception of "region" is institutionalization. Adler and Barnett claim that "in order to deepen and extend their interactions, to foster cooperation, and to verify in the absence of trust, states will frequently establish 'third parties,' that is, organizations and institutions that can observe whether the participating states are honoring their contracts and obligations."[73] As Neumann reminds us, the organization can sometimes become the embodiment both of its region and of the security community itself, as in the case of the European Union (EU), for example.[74]

Lastly, some scholars have pointed to the presence or absence of cognate political ideologies, particularly liberal democracy, in forging security communities. Adler and Barnett posit that "greater political, social, and ideological homogeneity can lead to greater interaction and association, and the development of new organizations and institutions."[75] Russett suggests that "common values" should be particularly salient in the case of liberal democracies.[76] This is because "liberal ideas are more prone to create a shared transnational civic culture, whose concepts of the role of government, tolerance, the duty of citizens, and the rule of law may shape the transnational identity of individuals of the community."[77] Furthermore, "as open societal and economic systems they will also have the advantage of familiarity with transnational networks, and exchange of peoples, goods, and ideas."[78] Though these claims have been disputed by Andrej Tusicisny,[79] this seems to explain the comparatively lower level of "community" among the authoritarian or closed states of the Gulf Cooperation Council (GCC) that Barnett and Gause found in their study.[80] The "mixed" nature of the ASEAN polities should therefore present an interesting puzzle on this score.

Ascendant Phase

Haas neatly postulates that "an 'ascendant' organization is one that has avoided war for perhaps a decade or more."[81] But theorists have been less specific in actually quantifying a security community in the ascendant phase. Ultimately, it is measured by increased levels of intramural "trust" directly linked to the foundation of common "norms" of behavior, which Jeffrey Legro defines as "collective understandings of the proper behavior of actors."[82] For Väyrynen, "a trusting relationship shapes identities, reinforces norms, and helps to overcome diverging interests of the members. Conversely, common identities and norm compliance obviously contribute to increasing trust and help to resolve interest conflicts."[83] But this can only be achieved by further advancement in several interlocking spheres. Coalescence into a meaningful alignment will be evidenced through stable and regularized institutional interactions, redefinitions of security, processes of socialization that result in higher levels of mutual trust, as well as development of a shared identity, which should ultimately lead to dependable expectations of peaceful change.[84]

First, we should expect to observe an amplification of institutional transactions at all levels. Basically, "the multiple channels that existed in the nascent phase are extended and intensified, and states and their societies are increasingly embedded in dense networks of relations collectively portrayed as "friendly."[85] The now cooperative linkages in one area will spill over into others, from economic collaboration to security cooperation, for example (or vice versa). According to Adler and Barnett, these "increased interactions, moreover, encourage the development of new social institutions and organizational forms that reflect diffuse reciprocity, shared interests, and perhaps even collective identity."[86] This process can occur through formal intergovernmental institutional interaction, but also more informally through what Alex Bellamy dubs a "transversal community" within. This is a "transnational civil society within the security community that blurs the boundaries between member states through much higher levels of border crossing and economic relations."[87] Thus, through intensified institutional interaction and by means of institutions themselves as sites on socialization, a common modus operandi (or "way of life") emerges with powerful actors occasionally "nudging" recalcitrant partners into conformity.[88] Therefore, Adler and Barnett conclude that "widening networks and intensified relations between and among societies, states, and organizations institutionalize cognitive structures and deepen mutual trust and responsiveness."[89]

Second, we should observe a reorientation of security thinking. States within the ascendant community begin to redefine security more in "regional" terms than "national" terms. Now "we expect that states have altered how they see their security and define the threat."[90] "Cooperative" rather than "competitive" security postures toward one another should begin to emerge. This ought to be materially evident through a discernible shift in military and defense posture between the members. Among the community members, we should observe changes in procurement patterns, military doctrines, tighter military-to-military relations, joint military exercises, and an openness in strategic planning and intelligence sharing, all of which signify that they have effectively ceased to actively prepare for war with one another. Bureaucratic structures originally intended for confidence-building measures (CBMs) and verification are gradually recalibrated and reoriented toward joint security cooperation.

Third, we will see shifts in identity, recognizable in public as well as elite opinion. Such social learning results in shifts in national affiliation or identity.[91] We see the beginnings of a newly shared "regional identity," based on mutual "trust." Adler and Barnett write, "Learning increases the knowledge that individuals in states have not just about each others' purposes and intentions but also of each others' interpretations of society, politics, economics, and culture; to the extent that these interpretations are shared and disseminated across national borders."[92] Tusicisny indicates that the disposition of "public opinion" is a relevant factor in building trust among communities.[93] Indeed, an important facet of developing such shared meanings and understandings will necessarily involve some element of generating a common regional "narrative," usually one that focuses on certain historical and cultural affinities, no matter how tenuous these may be in reality. Therefore, "to the extent that the actors locate themselves within a shared or congruent storyline they can be said to have a collective identity."[94] Bellamy dubs this phenomenon "frames." He argues, "These frames are the 'big stories' of the community, which identify its birth, its purpose and its membership in broad terms. We know a community when we see one because of its 'frames.'"[95] It is through the transactional/institutional, threat redefinition, and social learning processes that the security community is knitted together.

Mature Phase

Once these processes come to fruition, shared identity, mutual trust, and expectations of peaceful change within the community become entrenched, and war between its members becomes unthinkable. Ergo, "mutual trust and collective identity are necessary conditions of dependable expectations of peaceful change and, thus, of the security community."[96] A security community may now be said to have reached maturity. "A mature security community comes about when the norms at its heart become embedded or internalized by its member states."[97] Indeed, the EU is often held up as the model for attainment of this phase. Adler and Barnett supply a checklist for determining whether the security community has been achieved and whether it can be considered loosely or tightly "coupled." These "types" are distinguished by level of "depth of trust between states, the nature and degree of institutionalization of the governance system in the region, as well as whether states reside in formal anarchy or are on the verge of transforming it."[98] There are five aspects of "maturity" that require appraisal.

First, in a loose community, decisionmaking and conflict resolution procedures are resolved through multilateral consensus. "When a security community matures, 'mutual aid' and consultation becomes a matter of habit," in Bellamy's estimation.[99] Members trust that their interests will be protected and represented by the whole, and the interests of the community itself become a factor in individual national calculations. Now "purely egoistic interests are transcended," according to Väyrynen.[100] In a tight community, "rule is shared at the national, transnational, and supranational levels."[101] Through a degree of internationalization of authority, "shared and coordinated practices, and public policies, can further an informal system of rule."[102] This may include cooperation on law enforcement and other synchronization of best practice to harmonize domestic policies/regulations. Integration may even reach a level of a "multiperspectival polity," in John Ruggie's words, with rule shared at the national, transnational, and supranational levels.[103]

Second, borders will be unfortified, though "border checks and patrols are undertaken to secure the state against threats other than organized military invasion" from one's neighbors.[104] In a tightly coupled variant, citizens within the community are free to move among the member states without visa or other restrictions.

Third, changes in military planning reflect the sense that other members no longer conceivably present a potential military threat. There is no longer preparation for contingencies employing organized violence against one's comembers. Consider the abandonment on the eve of World War II of . American "Color Plan Red" in which the US military planned for war against Britain and Canada, as a prime example of this dynamic.[105] In the tight community, national militaries become integrated, with military capabilities (at least partially) pooled against mutual threats, as in the EU.

Fourth, the former developments are a corollary of changes in overall threat perceptions. As states identify with the community "self," intramural threats need no longer be considered but are now represented by threats to the community from an external "other." It is also clearly evident in "the differentiation between those within from those outside" as the "we" feeling inside is juxtaposed against the "them" feeling toward outsiders.[106] This shows that the security community has now morphed into a discernible alignment. Rivalries and conflicts may still appear, but these will be settled only through diplomatic means in accordance with the norms of the community. In a tight variant, reciprocal arms control and CBMs have now evolved into genuine "cooperative security" against internal threats to the community and those arising outside it. Thus, states can be expected to coordinate closely on policies on domestic and regional threats such as terrorism, separatism (since intrastate violence is still possible),[107] and other nonmilitary challenges, such as transnational crime or environmental security.[108]

Lastly, both loose and tight communities will be ideationally reinforced by the discourse employed to self-identify with the norms and standards of its combined membership, while state policy will be made in reference to what Adler calls "a community of practice."[109] Member states now behave in conformity with a community-constructed "logic of appropriateness," reaffirming "correct" behavior in accord with mutually agreed norms and discouraging the opposite.[110] Moreover, the security community will be validated by employment of "speech acts" to embed shared meanings and understandings in the political "discourse."[111] These will distinguish it from external parties who do not share such norms. In conclusion, "mature security communities may develop political agency in their own right and the transnational institutions housed within them may make rules and create generally accepted social knowledge."[112]

Whither the Security Community?

Once a security community has reached a mature phase, where does it go from there? It is impossible to truly tell if a case is "closed" according to Deutsch.[113] Particularly, as Ditrych points out, because communities may move through "zones of transition," coalescing and regressing at different times.[114] Nevertheless, there are two basic outcomes: disintegration or continuation, both of which can take several forms.

It must be remembered that security communities are susceptible to regression or disintegration at any phase in their development.[115] Given that they depend upon shared interest, values, and identity, founded on mutual trust, changes in these variables may act as centrifugal forces: "the same forces that 'build them up' can 'tear them down.'"[116] Since a security community is predicated upon peaceful relations between its members, obviously "war thus signals the breakdown of the community."[117] However, pioneering research by Koschut shows that "since security communities, in contrast to alliances or regimes, can be said to involve particularly strong bonds among its members this suggests that cases of disintegration naturally tend to be rare."[118] He argues that disintegration could result from external shocks, diminution in community resources (or overextension by expansion), institutional failure, disruption of normative interaction, or social "unlearning." He concludes that "security communities cease to exist when its norms are no longer followed and when collective meanings are no longer meaningful."[119]

At present the case for some form of continuation of the security community, once founded, is stronger and better documented. Reese contends that "the argument against regression [or disintegration] is that there are prohibitive social and material costs involved in destroying such a relationship, once it exists. Therefore, communities are thought to be durable due to their social foundation."[120] No one has considered the question of whether loose communities then evolve into tight ones, or if tight ones then become "comprehensive" (like the EU) or potentially "amalgamated." However, Bellamy provides three scenarios for the progression of (mature) security community behavior.

First, a successful community may become a "regional fortress." In this respect, a "security community may simply reproduce the logic of realism at the regional level constructing and reifying rigid boundaries between insiders and outsiders."[121] Thus, this becomes a fully fledged externally oriented alignment. In this instance, Reese argues, "This paradox is that states in a security community have on the one hand accepted that non-violent conflict resolution is an admirable norm for security behavior between themselves, but on the other hand continue to exist in a world where violent conflict with non-community members remains possible."[122] Though left unsaid, the possibility that this dynamic may proceed toward alliance formation needs investigating.

Second, a security community may expand its compass in accord with Deutsch's ideal that the conditions of security community "might be extended over larger and larger areas of the globe."[123] This is what Bellamy calls an "integrationalist" scenario.[124] As a precursor to acquiring new states, the security community will seek to "stabilize and pacify the extra-regional 'near abroad,' through socialization into community norms and practices."[125] Thus, "the mechanism of security community includes a disposition towards spreading the community outward through explicit or implicit practices of socialization or teaching."[126] This will entail, as in the EU/NATO case,

> the creation of partnerships, transnational security dialogues, or the constitution of regions around a focal point, for example, the Mediterranean or Baltic Seas. Widening the community that practices peace may follow a "logic of securitization" where sustaining the security mechanism is predicated on its spread (through formal or informal inclusion of the periphery).[127]

According to Wæver, "These practices may give security communities an 'empire-like quality.'"[128]

Finally, "ambivalent communities" basically occupy the middle ground, being neither exclusionary/hostile alignments nor making major efforts to expand their domain or influence their neighbors, in Bellamy's estimation. Loose communities "may be predicated on the idea of preserving the internal boundaries between states. In such cases, the security community may have little effect on either the quality of internal or external boundaries."[129]

Conclusion

Security communities have not typically been explicitly categorized as paradigm of alignment. As Väyrynen notes: "Conventional research on military alliances and other security organizations has paid hardly any attention to security communities despite the fact that the concept has existed at least for half a century. It has, therefore, remained largely non-integrated with the 'mainstream' theories of international relations."[130] Yet empirically such communities appear to be rising to the forefront of international behavior, as the North Atlantic, European, and other examples testify. Though it is seldom thought of as an "alignment" in the sense of alliances or coalitions, for reasons iterated above, it does qualify as such since it is defined by pooling of member's resources toward a shared security goal. For security communities, Adler asserts, "alignment . . . allows them to combine their material and ideational resources for the sake of what they jointly practice."[131] The initial objective is to bring about intramural expectations of security cooperation and the abolition of war as an instrument of settling disputes between members: "peaceful change." It morphs into an alignment as "we-feeling" increases and is juxtaposed with a "them-feeling" toward external parties. Thus, in contrast to traditional alliances, security communities develop from the inside out rather than the outside in.

The framework for understanding security communities, based upon Adler and Barnett but suitably modified to accentuate an alignment perspective, follows three phases of development: nascent, ascendant, and mature. However, as Acharya points out, none of these phases is entirely fixed or discrete. For Ditrych, "the degree of integration that makes it meaningful to speak of a security community is reached when, as a result of a sufficient density and intensity of transactions, a sense of community is achieved and institutions and practices developed."[132] As to its preservation, according to Adler and Greve, "The maintenance as well as decay or break-down of a security community is rooted in the mechanisms and practices that lie at the heart of dependable expectations of peaceful change."[133] At the center of security community are shared values, norms, and practices that serve to generate a common identity that bonds the alignment.

Significantly, the empirical record appears to demonstrate that such security communities become heavily institutionalized and often therefore take upon the embodiment of "security architecture" as well as becoming synonymous with the "region" they represent. Finally, of great interest to its incorporation into alignment theory is what Reese dubs the "security communities paradox"—they are built on an identity that includes a norm of nonviolence but they must, at the same time, retain the capability to use violence against states outside their membership.[134] Once a community is substantively in existence, its members must necessarily be aligned together in the face of a potentially hostile external environment.

Notes

1. Deutsch, Burrell, and Kann, *Political Community and the North Atlantic Area.*
2. Adler and Barnett, *Security Communities.*
3. Adler, "Imagined (Security) Communities," p. 251.
4. Väyrynen, "Stable Peace Through Security Communities?" p. 166.
5. Deutsch, Burrell, and Kann, *Political Community and the North Atlantic Area.* Some credit Richard van Wagenen with first coining the phrase: Van Wagenen, *Research in the International Organization Field,* pp. 10–11.
6. Deutsch, Burrell, and Kann, *Political Community and the North Atlantic Area,* p. 5.
7. Adler and Barnett discuss the "conceptual vocabulary" of the term at length in Adler and Barnett, "A Framework for the Study of Security Communities"; also Bellamy, *Security Communities and Their Neighbours.* For a comprehensive overview of literature see Koschut, *Normative Change and Security Community Disintegration.*
8. "It is uncertain whether NAFTA should be considered two independent security communities (separating the Mexican-American and Canadian-American relationships) or an integrated one," according to Reese, "Destructive Double Standards," p. 27.
9. Deutsch, Burrell, and Kann, *Political Community and the North Atlantic Area,* p. 6.
10. Ibid., p. 31.
11. Miller and Toritsyn, "Bringing the Leader Back In," p. 333.

12. Adler and Greve, "When Security Community Meets Balance of Power," p. 72. Italics added.

13. Walt, "Why Alliances Endure or Collapse," p. 168; Starr, "Democracy and War."

14. Williams, "From Alliance to Security Community."

15. Ditrych, "Security Community," p. 357.

16. Pouliot, "The Alive and Well Transatlantic Security Community," p. 121.

17. Adler and Barnett, *Security Communities*, p. 4.

18. Koschut, "Regional Order and Peaceful Change."

19. Franke, "Africa's Evolving Security Architecture and the Concept of Multilayered Security Communities."

20. Wæver, "Insecurity, Security, and Asecurity in the West European Non-War Community," p. 71.

21. Koschut, "Regional Order and Peaceful Change," p. 521.

22. Gonzalez and Haggard, "The United States and Mexico"; Shore, "No Fences Make Good Neighbors."

23. Ditrych, "Security Community," p. 353. Italics in original.

24. Wilkins, "Australia and Middle Power Approaches to Asia Pacific Regionalism."

25. Association of Southeast Asian Nations, "The Official Homepage of the Association of Southeast Asian States," June 14, 2012, http://www.aseansec.org. Italics added.

26. Or is it? Just because the term was not explicitly applied by scholars in the past does not mean that such communities did not objectively exist. Limited work has been done on the historical lineage of this form of alignment and this would be a worthy program for further research.

27. Koschut, "Regional Order and Peaceful Change," p. 524.

28. Chang, "Essence of Security Communities," p. 351.

29. Adler and Barnett, *Security Communities*, p. 6.

30. Adler, "The Spread of Security Communities"; Collins, *The Security Dilemmas of South East Asia*; Bellamy, *Security Communities and Their Neighbours*.

31. Adler, "Seeds of Peaceful Change"; Franke, "Africa's Evolving Security Architecture and the Concept of Multilayered Security Communities"; Tilly, "International Communities"; Russet, "A Neo-Kantian Perspective"; Reese, "Destructive Double Standards."

32. Reese, "Destructive Double Standards," p. 1.

33. Koschut, *Normative Change and Security Community Disintegration*, p. viii.

34. Adler and Barnett, *Security Communities*, p. 4.

35. Deutsch, Burrell, and Kann, *Political Community and the North Atlantic Area*, p. 20.

36. Väyrynen, "Stable Peace Through Security Communities?" p. 182.

37. Adler and Greve, "When Security Community Meets Balance of Power," p. 79.

38. Deutsch, Burrell, and Kann, *Political Community and the North Atlantic Area*, p. 5.

39. Reese, "Destructive Double Standards," p. 1.

40. Deutsch, Burrell, and Kann, *Political Community and the North Atlantic Area,* pp. 20–21.

41. Reese, "Destructive Double Standards," p. 1.

42. Rieker, *External Governance as Security Community Building.*

43. Risse-Kappen, *Cooperation Among Democracies*; Cox, "Beyond the West"; Pouliot, "The Alive and Well Transatlantic Security Community"; Massie, "Canada's (In)dependence in the North American Security Community."

44. Adler, "Europe's New Security"; Bellamy, *Security Communities and Their Neighbours*; Möller, "Capitalizing on Difference"; Mouritzen, "Peace for the Wrong Reason?"; Bremberg, "The European Union as Security Community-Building Institution."

45. Wæver, "Insecurity, Security, and Asecurity in the West European Non-War Community."

46. Möller, *Thinking Peaceful Change*; Wallensteen, *Towards a Security Community in the Baltic Region*; Wiberg, "The Nordic Security Community."

47. See also: Flemes, "Creating a Regional Security Community in Southern Latin America"; Hurrell, "An Emerging Security Community in South America?"

48. Higgot and Nossal, "Australia and the Search for a Security Community in the 1990's"; Barnett and Gause, "Caravans in Opposite Directions"; Dakhlallah, "The League of Arab States and Regional Security."

49. Franke, "Africa's Evolving Security Architecture and the Concept of Multilayered Security Communities"; Kacowicz, *Pluralistic Security Communities and "Negative" Peace in the Third World*; Ngoma, "SADC: Towards a Security Community?"

50. Acharya, *Constructing a Security Community in Southeast Asia*; Acharya, "Collective Identity and Conflict Management in Southeast Asia"; Collins, "Forming a Security Community."

51. Acharya, *Constructing a Security Community in Southeast Asia.*

52. Deutsch, Burrell, and Kann, *Political Community and the North Atlantic Area*; Ditrych, "Security Community," p. 352; Haas, *Asian and Pacific Regional Cooperation.*

53. Adler and Barnett, "A Framework for the Study of Security Communities," p. 30.

54. Wendt, "Constructing International Politics"; Wendt, "Anarchy Is What States Make of It"; Wendt, *Social Theory of International Politics*; Adler, "Seizing the Middle Ground"; Price and Reus-Smit, "Dangerous Liaisons?"; Hopf, "The Promise of Constructivism in International Relations Theory."

55. Adler and Barnett, *Security Communities*, p. 10.

56. Adler, "Imagined (Security) Communities," p. 258.

57. Adler and Barnett, *Security Communities*, pp. 29–30.

58. Ibid., p. 49.

59. Bremberg, *Diplomacy and Security Community-Building*, p. 137.

60. Adler and Barnett, "A Framework for the Study of Security Communities," p. 51.

61. Ibid., p. 50.

62. Ibid., p. 51.

63. Solingen, *Regional Orders at Century's Dawn.*

64. Acharya, *Constructing a Security Community in Southeast Asia*, p. 27.

65. Adler and Barnett, "A Framework for the Study of Security Communities," p. 50.

66. Bremberg, *Diplomacy and Security Community-Building*, p. 141.

67. Bellamy, *Security Communities and Their Neighbours,* p. 3.

68. Adler and Barnett, "A Framework for the Study of Security Communities," p. 50; Carter, Perry, and Steinbruner, *A New Concept of Cooperative Security*; Evans, "Cooperative Security and Intrastate Conflict"; Dewitt, "Common, Comprehensive, and Cooperative Security"; Agius, "Social Constructivism."

69. Mitzen, "Security Communities and the Unthinkabilities of War," p. 240.

70. Reese, "Destructive Double Standards," p. 1.

71. For discussion of this claim, see: Wæver, "Insecurity, Security, and Asecurity in the West European Non-War Community," p. 74.

72. Adler and Barnett, "A Framework for the Study of Security Communities," p. 33.

73. Ibid., p. 50.

74. Neumann, "A Region-Building Approach to Northern Europe."

75. Adler and Barnett, "A Framework for the Study of Security Communities," p. 51.

76. Russett, *Grasping the Democratic Peace*; Doyle, "Liberalism and World Politics."

77. Adler and Barnett, "A Framework for the Study of Security Communities," pp. 40–41; Kacowicz, "Explaining Zones of Peace."

78. Russet, "A Neo-Kantian Perspective."

79. Tusicisny, "Security Communities and Their Values," p. 437.

80. Barnett and Gause, "Caravans in Opposite Directions"; Barnett, *Dialogues in Arab Politics*.

81. Haas, *Asian and Pacific Regional Cooperation*, p. 142.

82. Legro, "Which Norms Matter?"

83. Väyrynen, "Stable Peace Through Security Communities?" p. 165. See also Kegley and Raymond, *When Trust Breaks Down.*

84. Acharya, *Constructing a Security Community in Southeast Asia*, p. 30.

85. Adler and Barnett, "A Framework for the Study of Security Communities," p. 53.

86. Ibid., p. 53.

87. Bellamy, *Security Communities and Their Neighbours,* p. 59.

88. Adler and Barnett, "A Framework for the Study of Security Communities," p. 53.

89. Ibid.

90. Ibid., p. 55.

91. Bellamy, *Security Communities and Their Neighbours,* p. 24.

92. Adler and Barnett, "A Framework for the Study of Security Communities," p. 54.

93. Tusicisny, "Security Communities and Their Values."

94. Adler and Barnett, "A Framework for the Study of Security Communities," p. 54.

95. Bellamy, *Security Communities and Their Neighbours,* p. 53.

96. Väyrynen, "Stable Peace Through Security Communities?" p. 167.

97. Bellamy, *Security Communities and Their Neighbours,* p. 9.

98. Adler, "Imagined (Security) Communities," p. 255.

99. Bellamy, *Security Communities and Their Neighbours,* p. 9.

100. Väyrynen, "Stable Peace Through Security Communities?" p. 159.

101. Adler and Barnett, "A Framework for the Study of Security Communities," p. 57.

102. Ibid.

103. Ruggie, "Territoriality and Beyond," pp. 172–174.

104. Adler and Barnett, "A Framework for the Study of Security Communities," p. 55.

105. Bell, "Thinking the Unthinkable," p. 789.

106. Adler and Barnett, "A Framework for the Study of Security Communities," p. 55.

107. Ayoob, "Defining Security."

108. Dupont, *East Asia Imperiled*; Buzan, Wæver, and de Wilde, *Security.*

109. Adler, "The Spread of Security Communities."

110. DiMaggio and Powell, "The Iron Cage Revisited"; see also: Bellamy, *Security Communities and Their Neighbours.*

111. Wæver, "Securitization and Desecuritization."

112. Bellamy, *Security Communities and Their Neighbours,* p. 9.

113. Deutsch, Burrell, and Kann, *Political Community and the North Atlantic Area,* p. 16.

114. Ditrych, "Security Community," p. 352.

115. Koschut, *Normative Change and Security Community Disintegration.*

116. Adler and Barnett, "A Framework for the Study of Security Communities," p. 58.

117. Adler and Greve, "When Security Community Meets Balance of Power," p. 71.

118. Koschut, *Normative Change and Security Community Disintegration*, p. 24.

119. Ibid., p. 6.

120. Reese, "Destructive Double Standards," p. 6.

121. Bellamy, *Security Communities and Their Neighbours,* p. 57.

122. Reese, "Destructive Double Standards," p. 2.

123. Deutsch, Burrell, and Kann, *Political Community and the North Atlantic Area*, p. 4.

124. Bellamy, *Security Communities and Their Neighbours,* p. 11.

125. Adler and Greve, "When Security Community Meets Balance of Power," p. 63.

126. Ibid., p. 72.

127. Ibid.; Wæver, "Insecurity, Security, and Asecurity in the West European Non-War Community."

128. Ibid.

129. Bellamy, *Security Communities and Their Neighbours,* pp. 57–58.

130. Väyrynen, "Stable Peace Through Security Communities?" p. 159.

131. Adler, "The Spread of Security Communities," p. 201.

132. Ditrych, "Security Community," p. 351.

133. Adler and Greve, "When Security Community Meets Balance of Power," p. 70.

134. Reese, "Destructive Double Standards," p. 7.

5

The ASEAN
Security Community

The ASEAN security community (ASC) is emblematic of the second paradigm of alignment, outlined in the preceding chapter (Chapter 4).[1] In 2017, ASC celebrated the fiftieth anniversary of its creation.[2] Having outlasted many other regional institutions, including military alliances such as the Southeast Asia Treaty Organization (SEATO), this achievement should not be underestimated.[3] Amitav Acharya, one of the foremost authorities on ASEAN, considers it as having served as a "force for stability and cooperation in Southeast Asia and Asia for the past four and a half decades."[4] Though it has its detractors, who have typically compared it unfavorably with the supposedly exemplary performance of the European security community, the ASC has nonetheless achieved considerable momentum as a key security provider in Asia Pacific. Indeed, such comparisons to the European Union (EU) can be misleading since Michael Leifer contends that "ASEAN was certainly not conceived as a political community along the lines of the European model."[5] In addition, the current troubles being experienced in Europe have tempered its status as the outstanding form of security community. Whatever its shortcomings, which will be duly noted, the ASC is a vital element of Southeast Asian security regionalism that has substantively extended its reach across the wider Asia Pacific arena. Thus, no study of pan-regional security dynamics can be complete without its inclusion.

The ASC case study is especially notable for its numerous intersections with the aforementioned framing concepts of "order" and "architecture," a recurring theme in the following analysis. In the first instance, in contrast to the typical realist (instrumental) order championed by the Trilateral Security Dialogue (TSD) alliance and broader US hub-and-spoke system, the ASC represents an alternative pathway to regional order. Even its critics acknowledge that it is "an association of states created to achieve the limited purpose of maintaining regional order."[6] Analysis of the ASC reveals a prioritization of a normative-contractual-type order among its constituent states, in conformity with the liberalist tradition. But in addition, its member states are externally aligned toward the purpose of building a wider pan-regional, "community-based" order through the so-called ASEAN-plus process. Thus, Ryo Sahashi identifies that ASEAN's aim is to "try to enmesh the great powers in regional institutions and norms where they are better able to control order building."[7] Nevertheless, some ASC members retain bilateral or multilateral defense ties with the United States or other powers, indicating that realist-instrumental thinking toward regional order firmly complements the normative vision of "community-building."

This brings us to the close interrelationship between the ASEAN-plus model and regional security architecture. ASEAN declares that it will "uphold ASEAN Centrality in engaging our Dialogue Partners and other external parties, especially in the evolving regional architecture."[8] Part of the ASC's raison d'être is its ability to define and superintend regional security processes in the teeth of the other two major alignment blocs described elsewhere in the book. The role of the ASC here is crucial as "Southeast Asian countries, despite living in the shadow of their more powerful neighbors such as India, China and Japan, have exerted a major influence on the development of Asian regional approaches to regional architectures."[9] The ASEAN-plus model includes a suite of regional organizations, such as the ARF, ASEAN+3, EAS, and ASEAN Defence Ministers Meeting Plus (ADMM+), all designed to engage parties external to the ASC. Indeed, according to Acharya, "ASEAN provides the institutional 'platform' within which the wider Asia Pacific and East Asian regional institutions are anchored. . . . without ASEAN, it would not have been possible to construct these wider regional bodies."[10] This ASEAN-plus model is considered at the end of this chapter in order to further corroborate the ASC's external orientation as an alignment. However, the chapter does not aim at a thorough review of the wider ASEAN-plus security architecture, since its primary focus is on ASEAN (the ASC) as an alignment itself. Notwithstanding these significant contributions, from a conceptual perspective, ASEAN remains "an essentially contested institution."[11] Therefore, before applying the analytical framework presented in the previous chapter, it is necessary to justify its qualifications both as a "security community" and as a form of "alignment," since neither proposition is universally agreed upon by the scholarly community. Also, since the relevant empirical material to be covered in this case study is quite extensive, space limitations preclude the provision of a dedicated historical narrative of ASEAN's development.[12]

Instead, details appertaining to the evolution of the organization are incorporated into the main analytical sections that follow.

The ASEAN Security Community as an Alignment

Defining ASEAN as a "Security Community"

There are compelling reasons for placing the ASC within the paradigm of a security community, both from the political and academic standpoints. First, it must be acknowledged that Southeast Asian policymakers have declared their intention to establish a security community and have explicitly labeled it as such. As part of ASEAN's Vision 2020, embodied in the Bali Concord II, the Secretariat declares, "The ASEAN Security Community (ASC) embodies ASEAN's aspirations to achieve peace, stability, democracy and prosperity in the region where ASEAN Member Countries live at peace with one another and with the world at large in a just, democratic and harmonious environment."[13] The official ASEAN policy of creating an ASC has been consistently enumerated in documents such as Plan of Action for a Security Community (2004) and ASEAN Charter (2007), and commitment toward creating an "ASEAN Community" (by 2020, at last count) has been regularly renewed at ASEAN summit meetings. The term is therefore firmly entrenched in government policy discourse, with Nicholas Khoo arguing that "the aspiration to become a security community has strengthened with time."[14] More specifically, the Plan of Action identifies three pillars needed to realize the ASC security community: an ASEAN Political Security Community (APSC), ASEAN Economic Community, and an ASEAN Socio-Cultural Community.[15] Because this book is concerned with security alignment, when the text refers to an "ASEAN Security Community" (ASC) as the referent for analysis, it is primarily concerned with the APSC, but also, to a lesser degree, with the economic and sociocultural pillars, which together can be considered more holistically representative of the security community paradigm. As Rizal Sukma attests, the "APSC is to serve as the umbrella for bringing ASEAN's political and security cooperation to a higher plane."[16]

Second, as indicated in Chapter 4, the overlap between the academic concept of security community and the state-driven regional project of a security community has been particularly striking in this case. Certainly, the ASC appears to conform toward the criteria set out by Karl Deutsch in the introduction of Chapter 4. It has overcome the internal "security dilemma" and created an array of common institutions mediated by shared practices, all aimed at achieving peaceful change among its common population. Most important, there has been no serious military confrontation between its member states since its foundation, though minor border skirmishes have occurred, as addressed below. As Christopher Roberts notes, "The policy documents surrounding ASEAN's aspiration to forge a security community, together with ASEAN's blueprints for regionalism more broadly, reflect Deutsch's definition of a security community."[17] Having met these generalized qualifications above, the application of the analytical framework below will further probe its characteristics, strengths, and weaknesses as an exemplar of the security community paradigm of alignment in detail.

Hiro Katsumata attests that "the Southeast Asians have set out the plan for an ASEAN security community, inspired by Karl Deutsch's security community literature."[18] In this respect, ASEAN is extraordinary in that the policymakers of Southeast Asian states have formulated their common political goals with strong reference to Track II academic channels and adopted much of the conceptual vocabulary of security community literature to shape their national policy. Christopher Roberts attests that "key components of ASEAN's associated blueprints have emulated certain constructivist ideas, [and] the end goals of the Association reflect half a century of scholarly work on the concept of a security community."[19] Yet despite the strong coincidence, See Seng Tan cautions us that when regional policy think tanks use the term "ASC," what they mean "is not quite the same as what scholars generally mean by a SC [security community], even though the two overlap quite a fair bit."[20] Lastly, to anticipate critique, there are a minority of scholars, led most prolifically by David Jones and Michael Smith, who claim that ASEAN is no more than an "illusion."[21] Others, such as Alan Collins, consider that ASEAN remains a "security regime" and not (yet) a security community.[22] A range of other writers raise questions about the ASC's credentials as a bona fide security community, or various aspects of this claim.[23]

Defining the ASC as an Alignment

Even if in accord with the proposition that the ASC represents a security community, some ASEAN specialists may balk at the specific characterization of the ASC as a *security alignment*. This is emphatically not, as the previous chapter has indicated, the same as suggesting it is a form of "alliance." As Sheldon Simon notes, both ASEAN and the ASEAN-plus model are "explicitly neither defense arrangements nor alliances."[24] However, I believe that it is feasible and meaningful to consider the ASEAN security community as a form of alignment for a number of reasons. The literature relating to the security communities paradigm elaborated in Chapter 4 recognizes either implicitly, or at times explicitly,[25] that security communities are states in alignment for a common security purpose, in accord with our general definition of alignment provided in Chapter 1.[26] On these bases, specific theoretical and empirical justifications related to the ASC can also be provided.

First, Acharya points to its "exclusionary attitude."[27] By definition, ASEAN membership is only open to states of the Southeast Asian region. Accordingly, attempts by non-regional states, such as Sri Lanka, to accede have been rebuffed. While he notes that "security communities are basically inward-looking constructs,"[28] as groups of states in alignment, they inhabit an exogenous environment in which they must interact collectively (or individually) with an external "other." As Etel Solingen identifies, "ASEAN's consensus was found to be pointedly driven by the need to portray a common external front that would strengthen ASEAN's position *vis-a-vis* major powers."[29]

Second, we can clearly observe various external alignment policies in practice. In the first place, at its inception, the ASC aimed at securing regional autonomy and noninterference from external powers, manifested through initiatives such as the Zone of Peace, Freedom, and Neutrality (ZOPFAN) in 1971 and the later declaration of a Southeast Asian Nuclear Weapons Free Zone (SEANWFZ) in 1995. This period was one of creating cohesion as an *internal* alignment in its subregion. But at least since the end of the Cold War, the ASC has acquired an identifiable *external* orientation as an alignment. This is most identifiable through its efforts to "shape" the external Asia Pacific security environment through institutions embodied in the ASEAN-plus model of regional security architecture noted above, which will be discussed in a dedicated section prior to the chapter's conclusions. The ASEAN Secretariat declares that "the ASC is open and *outward looking*, engaging ASEAN's friends and Dialogue Partners to promote peace and stability in the region.[30]

Thus, the ASC has coalesced as a distinguishable alignment, first through exclusion of external powers in its formative phase, then by collective engagement with such external powers as a relatively unified alignment actor in the post–Cold War period. These two dimensions have typically been compartmentalized, with "pure" security community theory focusing largely on ASEAN's intramural relations, while more empirical analyses have tended to look separately at the ASEAN-plus process. Instead, the purpose of the following analysis is to attempt to more explicitly recombine these two elements through the modified "security communities" framework presented in Chapter 4. By applying the framework below, which restores some realist/traditional alignment theory elements, to the analysis of how ASEAN relates to its external environment, we can gain a better appreciation of ASEAN's disposition as an alignment "actor."

Analytical Framework: Phases of Security Community

Though both neorealists[31] and neoliberals[32] have sought to employ their respective theoretical apparatus to understand the ASEAN experience, and Michael Haas has returned to a more orthodox twelve-point Deutschian/functionalist framework,[33] the following framework largely follows the mainstream constructivist approach. Yet, as the modified framework promulgated in the previous chapter demonstrates, the functionalist approach remains the foundation of the paradigm, and both realist and liberal elements, such as "threat perceptions" and "norms-building," have been incorporated explicitly into a more eclectic approach here.

In this chapter, I now proceed to analyze the ASC through three putative phases—"nascent," "ascendant," and "mature"—utilizing the analytical framework outlined in the previous chapter. In his seminal work *Constructing a Security Community in South East Asia*, Acharya, who followed a similar approach, cautions us that "it is important to note that the distinction between 'loose' and 'tight' security communities cannot be a sharp one and there may be considerable overlap between 'nascent,' 'ascendant' and 'mature.'"[34] Thus advised, I therefore proceed though these three phases in turn, followed by a dedicated section on the ASEAN-plus process, to further elaborate upon its external alignment orientation.

Nascent Phase

This section tracks the beginning of the ASEAN project, or "nascent stage" of the ASC, charting the key drivers behind its establishment. Though this history has been amply documented elsewhere, my presentation here differs from other works, as it puts the accent on alignment formation under the overarching structure of the security community paradigm. This section outlines the range of "precipitating factors" that propelled the grouping of five Southeast Asian states from a "security regime" toward the nascent stage of security community in the 1960s (but also considering if such factors also explain its expansion/completion in the 1990s). These include systemic factors, common interests, leadership, regionalism/institutionalism, and identity. However, it should be borne in mind throughout the following discussion that these factors cannot be neatly segregated, but instead are both concurrent and overlapping.

Systemic factors. The emergence of the ASC in the mid–Cold War period and its expansion in the post–Cold War period are largely tied to structural pressures exerted by a changing international system. In the post–World War II period, most of the Southeast Asian states gained independence from their European colonial rulers, often through a process of protracted conflict (e.g., Dutch police actions, Malayan Emergency). The newly independent countries emerged into the harshly competitive environment of the Cold War as "fragile states" that had to address urgent priorities of completing their individual nation-building projects and securing their borders against internal and external challengers. Alan Collins notes that beyond "immediate threats to the stability of the region, ASEAN was designed to be first and foremost an association of states engaged in nation building."[35] After independence, many of these states pursued policies of "nonalignment," as championed by Jakarta. But T. J. Pempel argues that "Southeast Asia's early wave of anti-colonialist nationalisms was overtaken by a collective realization of their common vulnerability to the larger regional powers."[36] With the security "overlay" of the European colonial powers lifted and the East-West competition threatening to destabilize various countries in the region, a modus vivendi was required to secure the autonomy for the region and present a stronger front to would-be external interlopers.

This predicament led to the development of a "security regime" for mediating and defusing intra–Southeast Asian conflicts in the early-mid 1960s. A subregional security dialogue was established, partly through the Association of Southeast Asia (ASA), successor to the stillborn "Maphilindo" grouping.[37] With the end of the Indonesian Konfrontasi policy toward Malaysia/Singapore in 1965, these organizations were supplanted by the creation of a totally new organization in 1967: ASEAN. Thus, as Acharya observes, "The attributes of an earlier stage of a security community, particularly at its "nascent" stage, may indeed resemble those of a security regime."[38]

After the founding Bangkok Declaration of 1967 gave birth to ASEAN, the original membership, despite occasional fractious relations, was able to concentrate on national development and region-building for much of the Cold War under the protective auspices of ASEAN. It has been argued by Ralf Emmers that the formation of the ASC was driven by "the coexistence of associative and balance of power dimensions within the same arrangement."[39] In the first instance, the initial ASEAN states specifically eschewed a traditional military alliance pact, despite the "threats" they faced, as discussed below. Instead, responses to the insecurity generated by the international system took the form of an "associative" security community effort. That Indonesia, and later Vietnam, would foreswear potential regional hegemony in favor of community-building shows their commitment to associative measures. Acharya and Tan state that "although Southeast Asians have recognized that the distribution of power does matter in regional stability, they have not advocated military balancing postures as the best way to ensure regional stability."[40]

In contrast, we must note a crucial "external" balancing dimension to the ASEAN alignment from the Cold War to the present. Like the development of the North Atlantic "Security Community" under the umbrella of the North Atlantic Treaty Organization (NATO) military alliance, the ASC itself was only able to forego military-alliance cooperation in Southeast Asia due to external sub-alignments with extraregional great powers. Throughout the ASC formation process, various ASEAN countries enjoyed a variety of alliance guarantees or other informal alignments with external powers. Mark Beeson notes that "it is hardly surprising that this fraught external strategic atmosphere would encourage the new and vulnerable states of Southeast Asia to seek strength in numbers or through alliances with more powerful actors."[41] The US alliance system protected Thailand and the Philippines (also through SEATO, until 1977), while the very presence of US forces in strength de facto shielded other countries from their potential foes. Britain also maintained forces in Southeast Asia until 1970 and is still committed to a collective defense agreement with Malaysia and Singapore under the Five Power Defense Arrangement (FPDA).[42] Thus, Southeast Asia was at no time without de jure or de facto military allies. As Emmers reminds us: "The security institutional equilibrium in Southeast Asia and beyond has consisted of formal and tacit bilateral alliances linking regional states to external players."[43] However, Acharya counters that these subsequently diminished in priority as an instrument of security management and came to be "seen as a means of last resort and hence a supplement to regional security understanding."[44] It should be noted, as an aside, that the ASC's deepening and internal/external expansion in the 1990s post–Cold War era can also be explained as "a consequence of strategic and economic uncertainty at the regional and global levels,"[45] as elaborated upon below.

Common interests. Systemic pressures therefore brought the founding members together to protect their shared national and regional strategic interests. It is thus fair to surmise that "the Association constitutes a form of cooperation among sovereign states that share common interests."[46] In terms of mutual strategic interests, according to Acharya, "ASEAN was also a product of *shared threat perceptions.*"[47] However, such threat perceptions do not neatly conform to traditional alignment theory predictions in the ASC case. After the resolution of Konfrontasi (accompanied by some minor spats between Malaysia and the Philippines over Sabah in the mid-late 1960s), the ASC project was motivated by the (then) *external* Vietnamese-communist threat in the 1960s–1970s. Emmers recounts that "ASEAN was established, according to a realist perspective, during the Second Indochina Conflict as a response to a Vietnamese and Chinese threat. Yet, in contrast to a realist interpretation of security cooperation,

ASEAN has never evolved into a formal or tacit alliance despite the presence of external threats since its formation in 1967."[48] Thus, despite occasional attempts to coordinate joint ASEAN military cooperation during
this period, no intraregional alliance emerged due to divergent perceptions of the Vietnamese/communist threat and the Southeast Asian states
preferred to rely upon extraregional bilateral/multilateral alliances as their
primary means of protection.

Instead, most of the ASEAN members were united in facing dangerous *internal* threats of separatism, insurgency, and terrorism, often with a
transborder element. Adler and Michael Barnett note that, in contrast to
the EU/NATO experience, "The ASEAN case points to the importance of
domestic rather than systemic security concerns, and shows how this led
to a particular set of ASEAN practices."[49] ASEAN states needed an
extended period in which to secure their newly independent states, which
in practice often amounted to securing the various ruling regimes.
Acharya outlines "a common sense of vulnerability to the enemy within,
particularly the threat of Communist insurgency . . . magnified by the
possibility of external backing" from China, Vietnam, or the Soviet
Union.[50] Thus internal and external threats were transnationally interlinked during the phase of alignment formation.

Particularly when one takes the latter explanation into account, it
becomes evident that though its members may have shared perceptions of
internal/external threat, ASEAN was not formed "against" something, as
per alliances, but rather "for" something: the creation of a secure and
prosperous regional home. Thus, Singapore's former foreign minister S.
Rajaratnam affirmed that "those who are outside the grouping should not
regard this as a grouping against anything, [or] against anybody."[51] As the
Indochina conflicts were wound down in the early 1990s and these countries became ASEAN members (along with Burma later), these previously
"external" threats were subsumed into the regional compact. As predicted,
threat perceptions served to strengthen a common sense of regional identity, since "although ASEAN countries were initially pushed to accept
regionalism in the face of a common fear of externally backed communism, this threat-driven utility . . . was sustained and reinforced by
decades of interaction and socialization."[52]

In addition to strategic interests, economic drivers are often held up
as precipitating factors in the formation of a nascent security community,
the European Coal and Steel Community being a case in point.[53] For
ASEAN, economic factors did not play exactly this predicted role, and
there are some divisions of opinion regarding the role of economic drivers
in the *initial* stages of ASEAN. According to Leifer, the formation of
ASEAN did not promote Southeast Asian economic intercourse but rather

allowed its members to "enhance political stability, both nationally and regionally, through the fullest allocation of national resources to economic development."[54] Despite periodic initiatives to move economic integration forward, the economic pillar did not emerge as a major driver of community-building since "fundamentally, ASEAN economies are competitive, not complementary, depending overwhelmingly on extra-ASEAN FDI [foreign direct investment] and exports to non-ASEAN states," according to Lee Jones.[55] Therefore Acharya concludes that "the relatively low priority attached by ASEAN to intra-regional trade also suggests an approach to community-building that is quite different from the path outlined by Deutsch."[56]

However, although economics were not a significant driver in the *original* formation of the ASC, once the *expansion* of ASEAN was complete in the 1990s, stronger efforts were made to strengthen this leg of the nascent community. Under the pillar of "economic community," an ASEAN Free Trade Area (AFTA) was promulgated in a bid to reduce intra-ASEAN tariffs, increase its competitiveness, and attract more external investment in 1992, supplemented in 1997 by the Chiang-Mai Initiative (CMI) and the nurturing of transnational "growth triangles."[57] Now, according to Jun Yan Chang, "Intra-ASEAN trade has more than doubled from 2004 to 2011, while the increase in the intra-ASEAN share of inward Foreign Direct Investment (FDI) is an even more staggering six-fold."[58] Moreover, the ASC has also looked at aligning its trade policies toward external parties. As Acharya notes, "ASEAN's economic objective was to improve its external economic climate through collective bargaining with its major trading partners."[59] This reinforced economic stance now forms part of the economic pillar of ASEAN policy alongside a number of ASEAN free trade agreements (FTAs) with external parties (notably the ASEAN-China FTA, 2010), serving to make the association a more unified economic entity (or ASEAN Economic Community).[60] This may find further expression in the Regional Comprehensive Economic Partnership (RCEP), when it is inaugurated, thus moving the heretofore "security" element of ASEAN-plus into the economic realm as well.[61] Simon therefore concludes that "its major achievement may well be its external orientation found in the free trade agreements with external powers."[62]

Leadership. The literature suggests that visionary leadership is required to instigate a nascent security community, either from a strong member state or a particularly proactive national government. After the ASA acquiesced in its own dissolution to be replaced by ASEAN, Jakarta played a "lead role," serving as the "core state" around which a new regional organization would be founded. At Bangkok's request, delegations from these four countries, plus Singapore, engaged in intensive but informal "sports-shirt diplomacy" to produce a declaration leading to the foundation of ASEAN.[63] The "founding fathers" of ASEAN therefore played a leading role in the establishment of the security community, as the framework predicts. Acharya declares, "There is no doubt that promoting a regional security community in the Deutschian sense was a primary objective of ASEAN's founders when they launched the grouping in 1967."[64]

Regionalism. The notion of region-building was central to the ASEAN enterprise, as Solingen reflects: "The claim, for instance, that ASEAN leaders had hoped to develop a regional identity where none existed seems quite plausible."[65] Acharya concurs that "ASEAN was a turning point in the *imagination* of Southeast Asia by its elites through a contrived sense of regionness" aimed at covering the whole of Southeast Asia.[66] As mentioned earlier, such a cognitive shift will often be concretely embodied by institutionalization.[67] As Adler and Barnett note, "To this end, region-building was a highly self-conscious exercise determined not only to increase economic and political transactions but also to encourage elite socialization in order to manage conflict."[68] This was reflected in the expansion to sequentially include those other regional states that were considered a "natural" part of the region: Brunei in 1984; then in the 1990s, Vietnam (1995), Laos and Myanmar (Burma) (1997), and Cambodia (1999), the so-called "CLMV" or "new ASEAN" countries. By this time, the ASC encompassed the entire Southeast Asian "region." It is especially noteworthy, as Roberts points out, that "ASEAN has aspired to forge an institutionalized form of regionalism akin to a security community"[69] and for ASEAN, "a security community represents the ideal outcome of a successful regionalist project."[70]

Identity. The final element illustrative of the precipitation of a nascent security community is the forging of a common identity based on shared values, from among a heterogeneous mix of Southeast Asian states. In contradistinction to much of the literature, which emphasizes the natural tendency for security communities to develop and flourish among liberal democratic states (see Chapter 4), ASEAN raised the question of whether an "illiberal" security community can exist and prosper, perhaps substituting a "shared developmentalist ideology" for genuine adhesion to mutually held values.[71] During its formation/expansion phase, ASEAN incorporated multifarious styles of governance ranging from (imperfect) democracies in Indonesia, Thailand, Cambodia, and Philippines; through "soft-authoritarian" regimes in Singapore, Malaysia, and Brunei; to relatively stringent authoritarian systems in Laos, Burma, and Vietnam. As a result of the admission of the CMLV countries in the 1990s, David Jones and Nicole Jenne argue that "widening membership actually weakened the grouping's coherence in terms of regime types."[72] This leads Narine to conclude that "ASEAN is a community based around the mutual benefits of shared rules, not a strong sense of collective identity."[73]

Ascendant Phase

Though security community scholars have not provided precise qualifiers for the ascendant phase of development, Haas determines that "an 'ascendant' organization is one that has avoided war for perhaps a decade or more."[74] More specifically, Acharya posits that this phase "is marked by tighter military coordination, lessened fears on the part of one actor that others within the grouping represent a threat, and a deepening of mutual trust along with beginnings of a cognitive transition towards intersubjective processes and collective identities."[75] But to determine this is by design rather than accident, more specific criteria need to be examined to look for evidence of purposeful efforts toward increased institutionalization, changing security postures, and socialization.

Institutionalization. Since its inception in 1967, ASEAN has become progressively more institutionalized. As security communities theory would predict, institutional cooperation in one sphere has naturally spilled over into other areas.[76] Pempel notes that since it was "begun as a non-communist arrangement to promote security among its members, ASEAN gradually expanded its collective mission to include economic, social, and cultural cooperation and development."[77] According to its Secretariat, the current ASC Plan of Action covers "political development, shaping and sharing of norms, conflict prevention, conflict resolution, and post-conflict peace building."[78] Specifically, Roberts enumerates the long list of policy goals promulgated by ASEAN to enhance political and security cooperation through "peace stability, democracy and prosperity in the region"; a "common regional identity"; a "rules-based community"; increased cooperation on maritime, transnational criminal, health, law enforcement, governance, and other "human security" issues; and a commitment to a single market.[79] In this respect, he concludes that "the accomplishment of ASEAN's goals would in fact exceed the requirements for a security community as defined in the literature."[80]

However, while ASEAN has expanded both its remit and institutional apparatus, Beeson contends that the "widening process has not been accompanied by a concomitant process of deepening."[81] The core governing institutions of ASEAN remain relatively weak. It is tied together by Heads of Government summits and annual meetings of ASEAN foreign and finance ministers, therefore remaining an emphatically intergovernmental body (*une Asie des états*). It is at this level that questions of "high policy" are discussed and agreed. As Pempel notes, "ASEAN operates not from any set of strict legal procedures that might be viewed as checks on national sovereignty but instead, most typically, by creating sequential issue-by-issue coalitions."[82] Getting consensus on controversial security issues is problematic given the size and diversity of the ASEAN membership. This has undermined apparatus such as the ASEAN Intergovernmental Commission on Human Rights, established in 2008, which though rhetorically endorsed by all, in practice has been frequently ignored. The widening of ASEAN membership through the addition of the CLMV countries has, according to Evelyn Goh, "further deepened the divides between the organization's original and more recent members, making a coherent regional stance even more elusive."[83] Since these countries are lacking in capacity to fully engage with ASEAN apparatus due to shortcomings in their internal national development, Acharya warns that "expansion has both enhanced and eroded ASEAN's progress toward a security community."[84]

ASEAN exhibits no strong transnational bureaucratic apparatus at its core, unlike the EU. The ASEAN Secretariat is small and poorly funded and the Secretary General exercises little supranational power.[85] There are a range of instruments organized around the ASEAN Charter (which made ASEAN a legal entity), including Coordinating Council, Community Council, and Committee of Permanent Representatives, all of which engage in a multitude of meetings, estimated at over 750 annually by some accounts.[86] As Roberts notes, the High Council was established as a mechanism for resolving intra-ASEAN disputes, but so far "the good offices of the High Council have never been invoked."[87] ASEAN authority itself is limited to areas of "low policy"—"issues of functional cooperation in areas like energy, tourism, the environment and agriculture"[88]—although theorists do point to the utility of such "communications" in building a "sense of community" (see below). Nevertheless, efforts are under way to bolster the multinational character of ASEAN and deepen its integration. On the important aspects of harmonizing regional laws and legislation, the ASEAN Law Ministers Meeting/ASEAN Senior Law Officials Meeting is charged with "gradual harmonization of national laws to catch up with the level of cooperation and integration amongst ASEAN member countries."[89]

Moreover, the ASC is decidedly an elite-driven project (see section on "leadership" above). Though ASEAN is strong on symbolism—summits, projects, logos, ASEAN People's Assembly—it appears that popular support for its multinational character is weak among its combined populations. The need to deepen popular support for and identity with the ASEAN project is to be addressed through the ASEAN Socio-Cultural Community pillar, and

ASEAN is now striving to be "people-orientated" and "people-centered" according to its 2017 Leader's Declaration.[90] According to Collins:

> If ASEAN is to become a security community it will need to generate a regional identity among the peoples of Southeast Asia and give them a stake in the association's development. So long as ASEAN remains a club for the governing elite then it will remain detached from the general populace and thus unable to create a sense of commonality or "we-feeling."[91]

This, he argues, can be based around civil society organizations (CSOs), since "CSOs can therefore act as conduits for the type of interaction Adler and Barnett note occurs in the ascendant stage."[92]

Changing security postures. An ascendant security community should be recognizable through its level of joint security cooperation, particularly shifts in its conception of security threats and the resultant changed military postures of its members. On this score, the ASC displays mixed progress. First, there is evidence, according to Avery Poole, that "they increasingly conceptualize their security as interdependent."[93] Indeed, Adler and Barnett claim that "cooperative security has become, or is becoming, part of [ASEAN's] collective identity."[94] This is exemplified by Blueprint for APSC, which extends the ASEAN understanding of security "beyond the requirements of traditional security but also takes into account non-traditional aspects vital to regional and national resilience, such as economic, socio-cultural, and environmental dimensions of development."[95]

Indeed, ASEAN and its Track II advisers have found that this broad conception of security is a relatively uncontroversial (a "lowest common denominator") approach to joint security cooperation and have embraced it with gusto. As Mely Caballero-Anthony notes, "a plethora of new cooperative efforts have emerged, geared mostly to addressing different NTS threats."[96] These nontraditional security (NTS) threats include issues such as transnational crime, unregulated population movements, environmental disasters, and infectious diseases.[97] With regard to mutual transnational threats, Indonesia, Malaysia, and Singapore have deployed trilateral patrols to counter piracy and terrorism in the Straits of Malacca (code-named Operation MALSINDO). Additionally, Hiro Katsumata points to a growing emphasis on "human security," as a result of the ASEAN task force responding to the 2008 cyclone in Myanmar. He states that "this can be regarded as another important step toward an ASEAN security community, since humanitarian assistance is an integral element of such a community."[98] Such joint security cooperation ranks as a significant achievement, yet it is notable that persistent internal security threats (such as insurgency in Mindanao) are excluded from ASEAN's "cooperative security" ambit on account of sovereignty and nonintervention norms. Indeed, ASEAN has struggled to confront the crisis posed by Myanmar's apparent expulsion of its Rohingya minority and other refugees fleeing government repression, seemingly attempting to "sweep it under the carpet" by limiting itself to vague references to the irregular movement of persons.[99] As well as undermining its rhetorical commitment to human security and human rights, it reflects the fact that "suppressing these challenges to regional security requires some erosion of the principle of non-interference in internal affairs."[100]

However, gains in "cooperative security" notwithstanding, traditional military threats remain a concern among the ASC and its individual members, and these have both internal and external dimensions. First, Nick Bisley points to a continuation of the "perception that the main threats to their security interests [come] from *beyond* Southeast Asia."[101] As William Cole and Erik Jensen argue, "China's rise, with its classic dangers and opportunities, has created pressure on ASEAN to develop a deeper, more integrated, and more consolidated identity."[102] But since the various diverse ASC members lack consensus on the prospective dangers posed by the People's Republic of China, meaningful multilateral defense integration has been slow to emerge. As an aside, as Roberts has shown, there has been a distinct lack of solidarity among ASEAN regarding the judicial dispute (which Manila won) over the Scarborough Shoal, and the unwillingness to uphold at the Permanent Court of Arbitration ruling in favor of one of its members did damage to its diplomatic credibility on this score.[103] Yet, in terms of harder defense cooperation within the ASC, a web of bilateral/minilateral contacts and "virtual" collective defense, often involving extra-regional allies, exists but has been circumscribed.[104] As Erik Beukel observes, "Indonesia, Malaysia, the Philippines, Singapore and Thailand have developed bilateral defense arrangements on intelligence sharing, border security, joint military exercises and the provision of training facilities."[105] Indonesia has also proposed a regional peacekeeping force, but this has yet to eventuate.[106] Jörg Friedrichs argues that the present situation is unsatisfactory: "When it comes to acute militarized conflict, however, ASEAN is simply not in a position to galvanize adequate action. ASEAN cannot do anything to defuse military incidents, such as when Chinese patrol boats harass Philippine or Vietnamese survey ships exploring for oil and gas."[107]

Second, critics have pointed to a residual degree of intra-ASEAN threat perceptions, due in part to a number of "shelved" territorial disputes between its member states. As Acharya points out, "there are lingering concerns about competitive arms acquisitions and an interactive contingency planning involving ASEAN members."[108] However, Raimo Väyrynen argues, "these weapons are seldom targeted specifically at other members of ASEAN; they are more an insurance against the uncertainties of the post–Cold War era and the potential instrument for the territorial disputes in the South China Sea and the rise of China."[109] Hence it is difficult to establish as proven fact "hostile intent" just from examining procurement trends. Indeed, as some analysts have indicated, many of these weapons procurements are a case of emulating one's neighbors and symbols of national prestige, rather than being deliberately calibrated toward their neighbors.[110] We need to examine the level of cooperation and the degree of confidence and "trust" between these forces. ASEAN member states' military forces have engaged in an unprecedented level of staff exchanges, joint training exercises, and other confidence-building measures (CBMs) designed to create a predictability and mutual reassurance of benevolent intentions toward one another.

Socialization. The de-emphasizing of neighboring member states as existential military threats identified above is part of a wider process of "socialization" (or "social learning") occurring through the ASC. Michael Green and Bates Gill assert that "there is clear evidence of socialization occurring across the new regional architecture in Asia."[111] As the analytical framework predicts, the organizational apparatus of ASEAN serves as a "site" for socialization to occur, by spreading and reinforcing shared values and norms and generating "we-feeling." As Acharya suggests, "most security communities are anchored in formal or informal institutions, including regimes, which promote norms and principles of conduct, constraints on unilateral preferences, facilitate information-sharing, and build predictability and trust."[112] The panoply of core ASEAN institutions and its extended range of pan-regional and Track II forums (such as Council for Security Cooperation in Asia Pacific) all contribute to the process of "socialization." This is manifested in the promulgation and diffusion of the so-called "ASEAN way," which embodies the principal operating "norms" of the ASC. Richard Stubbs outlines its main features: "the importance of neutrality; sovereignty and territorial integrity; the peaceful settlement of disputes; informal, non-confrontational negotiations; and the promotion of domestic stability and social harmony—which together underscore the importance of state autonomy and non-interference in the affairs of other states."[113]

These unifying norms proved useful in socializing new members, including potentially problematic states such as Vietnam and Myanmar, into the ASC through the joint subscription to shared identity or "we-feeling" rooted in said norms. The Secretariat claims that "since its inception in 1967, ASEAN has developed confidence and maturity to address issues of common concern as one ASEAN family."[114] On this attempt to build a common "narrative," Barnett and Adler note "how the painstakingly developed ASEAN way, with its particularistic symbols and processes of socialization, led to the notion that ASEAN constitutes a distinctive region."[115]

Once again, these achievements are circumscribed in various ways. First, for all the rhetoric and shared identity among ASEAN elites, this we-feeling seems to have so far failed to reach the level of popular opinion among member states, meaning the shared identity of the ASC lacks deep roots. As Collins notes, a real community requires "a positive identification among people that entails a sense of obligation and responsibility toward one another."[116] Second, based upon norms of sovereignty, noninterference, and nonbinding consultation and consensus, it is a weak reed upon which to found a security community. The ability to ensure compliance is lacking, thus allowing members to quietly ignore implementing ASEAN recommendations. Takeshi Yuzawa records the "effective manipulation of consensus decision-making by reluctant states . . . with each member exercising veto power."[117] Indeed, the results of the ASEAN way often pander to the more reluctant or recalcitrant members, resulting in little concrete action (the "lowest common denominator").

Third, some states in ASC do not always govern domestically in consistency with the supposed liberal principles of security community. As Cole and Jensen argue, "Asian nations do not seem to share the belief that liberal democracy is the prerequisite to security and development."[118] Not only has this led to some tensions between contrasting systems of governance among the more progressive and/or democratic members of the ASC and its more authoritarian counterparts, but also raised the question of the further advancement and durability of ASEAN as a security community. Indeed, Caballero-Anthony notes that "the ASPC represents a desire of ASEAN to move beyond functional security cooperation to develop a framework of regional governance based not only on practical necessities but also on normative considerations, such as notions of democracy, human rights, transparency and justice."[119]

Yet the desire of countries such as Indonesia, Thailand, and the Philippines for progress toward a "liberal democratic security community," a model outlined in the literature in the previous chapter, has created internal fissures among the ASC. These aspirations include substituting the core norm of "noninterference" for "flexible engagement." Jakarta in particular has advocated for a very liberal security community with a "regional peacekeeping force" and "human rights commission."[120] Much of this is likely to prove unacceptable to more authoritarian regimes in the ASC that have tended to honor these principles in the breach, shielded behind the norm of noninterference. Hence, Narine observes that "the Charter indicates a real and growing ideological divide within ASEAN. Democratic values have taken root in some ASEAN states and these countries do not wish to be alienated from the international democratic community."[121] However, progress toward such goals may be further impeded as Thailand has regressed back toward authoritarian military government and the Philippines' president Rodrigo Duterte persists with his "war on drugs."[122] Yet, Patricia Becker argues, using ASEAN as a test case, the absence of "democratic peace" does not mean the absence of "dependable expectations of peaceful change" or "we-feeling" even among illiberal states.[123]

Toward a "Mature" Security Community?

ASEAN's Vision 2020 document clearly enunciates its intention to move toward what we could fairly describe as a "mature" security community. It states: "ASEAN shall have, by the year 2020, established a peaceful and stable Southeast Asia where each nation is at peace with itself and where the causes for conflict have been eliminated, through abiding respect for justice and the rule of law and through the strengthening of national and regional resilience."[124] This section examines the prospects for the attainment of a mature security community in the future, assessing progress made so far, as well as deficiencies, before concluding with comments on the "continuation" or "disintegration" of the ASC. Acharya argues as follows:

> Several characteristics of a mature security community are present in Southeast Asia . . . these include multilateralism, discourse and language of community, cooperative (but not collective) security, and policy coordination against internal threats. But to describe ASEAN as a mature security community will be inaccurate in the absence of a high level of military integration, common definition of external threat, and unfortified borders.[125]

In other words, ASEAN evinces several, though not all, of the criteria that Adler and Barnett outlined as constitutive of a pluralist security community at a "mature" phase. Let us examine in more detail Acharya's claims and measure them against the indicators provided in the previous chapter. These include the following: "trust" and "we-feeling," collective interests and multilateralism, threat perceptions, military preparations, and language and discourse. Brief comment will also be made on the factors deemed to be absent.

Trust and "we-feeling." In accord with Adler and Barnett's description of the loosely coupled minimalist version of security community, we can observe that states within the ASC identify positively with one another, maintain a reasonable level of intramural "trust," and share a common identity (or "we-feeling"). Katsumata points to "the Southeast Asian countries' commitment to the habit of dialogue and consultation, aimed at enhancing a sense of mutual trust."[126] Acharya argues that "taken together, the practice of multilateralism, the ASEAN norms, the 'ASEAN way,' and the principle of regional autonomy constitute the basis of ASEAN's collective identity."[127] There are multiple and diverse mechanisms and patterns of interaction— such as ASEAN Charter, Treaty of Amity and Cooperation (TAC), and ADMM (ASEAN Defense Ministers Meeting)—that reproduce the security community and evidence of shared meanings and collective identity. There is also the expectation that states will practice "self-restraint," as is clear over unresolved intramural territorial conflicts, for example (except one instance, discussed later in this chapter).

But there are limits to this level of intramural trust in the security community. Critics argue that "the level of distrust within ASEAN remains surprisingly high."[128] Emmers notes that "despite long-term cooperation, intra-ASEAN relations have continued to be affected by persistent feelings of mistrust, bilateral disputes and contradictory strategic perspectives."[129] Also, Khoo is highly critical with regard to the strength of ASEAN norms.[130] Evidence of a lack of "we-feeling" and "mutual aid" mentality is also given by Narine, who posits that the Asian financial crisis, "[m]ore than any other event . . . underlined the very limitations of the ASEAN Way and the 'ASEAN identity' that was, supposedly, the product of decades of interaction."[131] On the other hand, ASEAN solidarity was well reflected in the generous responses of its members toward those states affected by the 2004 tsunami disaster, according to Heide Gentner.[132]

Collective interests and multilateralism. Looking at the extent that national interests are protected and represented by the whole and are effected through the practice of multilateralism, we discern mixed results. In general terms, Leifer notes that the ASEAN "fulfills the role of a diplomatic community holding a more or less uniform view on regional security issues."[133] While Roberts attests that the ASC does speak with a "collective diplomatic voice on the international stage,"[134] the member states are also studying a platform "for forming a more coordinated, and coherent ASEAN position on global issues of common interests and concern, based upon a shared ASEAN global view."[135] When engaging external parties, though individual members pursue bilateral issues, "all take into account the multilateral framework provided by ASEAN."[136]

There is certainly a strong sense of shared interest in terms of individual state sovereignty and regional autonomy among the compact. To that extent, each member's interest is interchangeable with that of the group. As a result, Avery Poole notes how these "ASEAN norms have a constitutive effect that, through interaction and socialization, serves to redefine the interests of member states."[137] Yet, the individual states retain a strong sense of narrowly defined national interest, which sometimes impedes intramural solidarity. This is hardly surprising given that the members of ASEAN are "remarkably divergent in terms of their colonial heritage, post-colonial political setting, level of economic development, ethnic composition, and linguistic/cultural make-up."[138] Thus Roberts concludes that "until the ASEAN members' political systems and values converge to become more compatible then significant *interest harmonization* and *policy coordination* will also be difficult to achieve."[139]

It is true that ASEAN exhibits an impressive array of multilateral activities, but it remains first and foremost based upon interaction between individual states within this framework. However, Acharya asserts, "It is widely understood and agreed within ASEAN that contentious bilateral disputes are best handled through bilateral channels; while the ASEAN multilateral framework serves as a social and psychological barrier to extreme behavior, it does not have to deal with such conflicts directly and openly."[140]

Notwithstanding, as Acharya notes, "the mere existence of disputes and conflicts within a group does not necessarily undermine its claim to be a security community."[141] Moreover, intramural disputes are "quite mild in nature" in comparison with disputes elsewhere in Asia such as the Senkaku/Diaoyu Islands or Arunachal Pradesh, for example.[142] However, in less-sensitive issue areas, particularly the prosecution of intramural security against NTS threats, an emerging but perhaps more committed multilateral response is evident, in supplement to various bilateral/mini-lateral linkages. Caballero-Anthony notes how ASEAN states are pooling their resources to increase their joint capacity to respond to these challenges.[143] More recently, however, the intensification of some members' external disputes has called into question their cohesion, with Roberts noting that "a lack of collective identification and integration [is] visible in the case of the South China Sea dispute, where a common position has not been maintained."[144]

The internationalization of authority representative of John Ruggie's "multiperspectival polity" is not likely to be achieved in the near future.[145] The ASC does not yet demonstrate a strong degree of shared governance among the national, transnational, and supranational levels and certainly cannot therefore be considered as a "tightly coupled" security community. Shared and coordinated practices and public policies are being slowly developed, but these do not affect core areas of state governance. As David Jones and Michael Smith identify, the "ASEAN Secretariat lacks any supranational capacity," in other words, "the organizational structure of ASEAN remains essentially *intergovernmental*."[146]

A move beyond a loose form of "cooperative security" toward genuine supranational "collective security" also remains a distant prospect. Leifer asserts that "within ASEAN, security has always been addressed through consultation and dialogue rather than through conventional collective security."[147] This point is reflected in the glacial progress toward preventive diplomacy both in ASEAN and the ARF.[148] As a result, Roberts concludes that "beyond limited functional cooperation, the diversity of strategic interests and alignments continues to constrain the feasibility of significant cooperation and integration between the ASEAN members."[149]

Threat perceptions. There has been a marked degree of change in intramural threat perceptions since the foundation of ASEAN. Acharya asserts that "it can be safely asserted that no ASEAN country seriously envisages war against another at present."[150] Though minor territorial disputes remain and occasional border frictions have emerged between ASEAN members, these are not likely to lead to the outbreak of a full-scale war and may have as much to do with the limits of state capacity to control such disputes effectively as it does deliberate intent.

The shared threat perceptions that unite ASEAN are threefold. First, several ASEAN states continue to face internal domestic security threats, such as terrorism, insurgency, and separatism, which endanger state authority and capacity. Tan observes that "ethno-nationalist and ethno-religious conflicts and domestic political crisis continue to color parts of the Southeast Asian landscape."[151] There has been some degree of intra-ASEAN cooperation against these, within the limits of the norms of noninterference and the sanctity of individual state sovereignty.

Second, as noted above, the ASC states have engaged in notable cooperation on nontraditional security threats, indicating policy coordination on internal threats, a characteristic of a "tight" security community.[152] Energy security and climate change are addressed multilaterally through the Cebu Declaration on East Asian Energy Security, the ASEAN Wildlife Enforcement Network in 2005, and the Asia-Pacific Partnership on Clean Development and Climate, in addition to antipollution agreements to deal with the forest-fire "haze" problem in Indonesia.[153] There has also been intra-ASEAN cooperation on counterterrorism, such as the ASEAN Convention on Counter-Terrorism in 2007. However, with regard to counterterrorism collaboration, Pempel notes, "Although different Asian governments have collaborated with one another against regional terrorist networks, the primary lines of cooperation have been between individual Asian countries and the United States."[154]

Third, as extra-regional power rivalries intensify between the other two alignment blocs of Asia Pacific, ASEAN has become cognizant of "external" threats to its security that compel it toward closer cohesion as a unified alignment bloc. As Stéphanie Martel notes: "The growing rivalry between the United States and China, and the rising level of tensions in the South China Sea since 2010, make traditional issues the main source of insecurity not only in the wider Asia Pacific region but for ASEAN itself."[155] Clearly, the ASC states see themselves challenged by China's assertive stance in the South China Sea, where the Philippines, Vietnam, and Malaysia have tried to uphold their territorial claims.

Yet, as noted earlier, member states have struggled to reach a common front on this issue. This was starkly illustrated in the ASEAN Minsters Meeting of 2012 where the chair, Cambodia, declined to issue a joint statement on the South China Sea dispute due to its financial dependence upon the People's Republic of China (PRC). This was a troubling incident for ASEAN, whereby "Manila and Hanoi accused Cambodia of putting its allegiance to Beijing ahead of its obligations to its regional partners and of pushing the 10-nation group to its most severe crisis in years."[156] Additionally, other ASEAN members refrained from giving full-throated support to Manila's effort to seek a ruling from the Permanent Court of Arbitration in the Hague. When it received a verdict in its favor, Rodrigo Duterte, the Philippines's incoming president, set aside this "win" to "avoid imposing upon China."[157] This apparent defection to China further undermined any effort toward a common front with ASEAN's other claimants, with serious implications for the organization's credibility.

Despite the existence of an ASEAN-China strategic Partnership for Peace and Prosperity, so far efforts to convince China to respect joint and individual national interests have not been successful. The attempts to convert the 2002 Declaration on Conduct (DOC) in the South China Sea into a Code of Conduct (COC) have not materialized due to lack of political will among members in the face of Chinese recalcitrance. As Roberts concludes, "ASEAN's institutions do not provide an adequate enabling environment to address the South China Sea dispute."[158] Now that the ASC has reached a sufficient degree of common internal security, it finds itself challenged again by threats emanating from outside the alignment itself.

Military preparations. Partly in relation to the previous indicators, the analytical framework seeks to identify a mature security community in a more concrete sense in terms of how far national territorial sovereignty is "protected" from or "surrendered" to one's neighbors. This can be detected in community attitudes toward military planning and border control. In the first instance, while ASEAN states do not actively plan for military conflict with one another, they have not made steps to integrate their militaries in a way that would make such conflict utterly impossible. It is hard to gather firm evidence for military plans appertaining to comembers. Though some may take Singapore's defense strategy vis-à-vis Malaysia as evidence of lack of security community, it is uncertain how "fresh" such plans really are.[159] This caveat notwithstanding, as noted above, intra-ASEAN military CBMs and joint exercises and operations have proceeded apace, though they remain far short of the goal of a common defense force. All member states clearly retain the right and capability to use force independently, with limited, if any, multilateral constraints. There is no system of "collective defense" and levels of military integration are low. Acharya reminds us that "ASEAN's practice of multilateralism does not extend to defense matters" and "ASEAN members are reluctant to make a serious attempt at military integration."[160] The organization has reiterated that it does not desire to form a military alliance.

This reluctance to pool sovereignty is also evident in border control. Citizens of ASEAN states do not have freedom of movement within the region as enjoyed by the EU citizens. Border posts and visa regulations remain in force, though some preferential agreements exist. Indeed, subregional economic zones have resulted in "freer movement of transnational capital, labor and technology."[161] There is also cooperation among some members to increase border security/interoperability in order to tackle terrorism, illegal movements, and transnational crime. Acharya records,

> Mutual cooperation against the transborder movement of communist guerrillas, including intelligence-sharing, mutual extradition treaties, and joint border patrols, and counter-insurgency operations served as an important basis for intra-ASEAN solidarity, while bilateral border committees set up to deal with insurgents proved useful as a direct channel for handling territorial disputes.[162]

Borders are not completely "unfortified" and there have been low-level skirmishes on the border of Thailand and Cambodia over a dispute involving claims to a historic temple at Preah Vihear. Therefore, "ASEAN countries are still dealing with intramural tensions and border disputes, as the Cambodian-Thai conflict recently showed."[163] ASEAN's Treaty of Amity and Cooperation (TAC) and 2000 Memorandum of Understanding (MOU) on a Joint Border Commission failed to resolve the dispute, though it should be noted that the ASEAN Secretary General was active in providing its "good offices" in defusing the crisis.

Language and discourse. Lastly, how much is the ASC experience indicative of the "discourse and language" of security community and to what degree does it embody a "community of practice"? Certainly, member states rhetorically invoke the language mutually agreed as appropriate to the community-building project at every opportunity. Collins attests "that ASEAN, at least in rhetoric, is on the path to forming a Deutschian security community is clearly evident in the use, within its declarations, of such language as, 'shared values and norms,' 'common identity,' 'sense of belonging' and even 'we-feeling.'"[164] Katja Freistein in particular draws attention to the ASEAN Charter as a "discursive monument" arguing that "most likely, the Charter will become the most important discursive point of reference for ASEAN's current and future activities."[165]

Yet, the intensity, if not the proliferation, of transnational linkages has proved short of those expected in a bona fide security community to date (presumably measured against the EU). Because of its failure to move beyond "norms"-based to "rules"-based community, Väyrynen concludes the following: "While a measure of common identity has emerged in ASEAN, the lack of democratic traditions and practices has failed to make it a 'liberal cognitive region' leading to a pluralistic security community."[166] Moreover, Alice Ba argues that "the admission of new [CLMV] members, however, destabilizes that process by introducing states that do not share the cognitive experiences or normative commitments of the original members," raising questions as to what kind of security community it is, and will become.[167]

External Dimension: ASEAN-plus

The framework presented thus far has drawn necessary attention to the interaction of external factors with the concomitant intramural process of community-building. Yet the foremost expression of the ASC's external alignment posture is evinced through the ASEAN-plus process. As alluded to above, once the internal "integration" process was completed through the accession of the CLMV countries to complete ASEAN's Southeast Asian regionalist project, the organization rapidly turned its attention outward to secure its common interests on the wider pan-regional plane. In this respect Narine argues, "the 1990s were a pivotal decade for ASEAN."[168] The motivation for strengthening the alignment and a new concentration on its external bearing were based upon the recognition that "individual ASEAN members lack structural power, but collectively they acquire . . . enough bargaining clout to command the attention of great powers and even to socialize them through regional institutions."[169] Thus, responding to the transformation brought about by the end of Cold War bipolarity, the ASC embarked upon an institutional drive that has since positioned it as the driving engine of the Asia Pacific region's security architecture.

Kishore Mahbubani attests that "ASEAN has played a key role, being single-handedly responsible for spawning a new alphabet soup of cooperation ventures: ARF, APEC, ASEAN+3, ASEM, and EAS."[170] It is this ASEAN-plus that marks the evolution of the ASC into a coherent alignment. As Herman Kraft notes: "This started ASEAN on its way to a significant shift in the evolution of its identity—from an association dedicated to keeping the Southeast Asian region free from being enmeshed in great power rivalries to one which accepted its 'centrality' in a wider East Asian and Asia-Pacific regionalism."[171] Lacking the strategic weight to balance or influence greater powers in the Asia Pacific, the ASC sought to channel its efforts instead toward socializing external powers into its own form of normative-contractual order, which it had heretofore implemented internally in the intramural community-building process. As Beukel contends, the ASEAN-plus model is "an attempt to extend the 'ASEAN way' to the rest of East Asia."[172] By incubating (or "brewing," in Katsumata's metaphor) internal norms, adjusting them and then exporting them region-wide, ASEAN seeks to create a larger and "indivisible" cooperative security process,[173] making it, in effect, an "Asia-Pacific way."[174] The instruments of this approach include the suite of institutions noted above, the ARF being the most studied example. As Taylor and Tow note, ASEAN created the ARF "to enmesh both American and Chinese regional security behavior within an Asian-centric version of regional order. By doing so, Southeast Asian elites modified the politics of balancing in their subregion and facilitated the coordination of great-power support for their own enterprise of building a security community."[175] In the "integrationist" security studies literature, the ARF has even been talked of as a putative pan-regional security community.[176]

The degree to which this attempt at "binding" or "enmeshing" greater powers and resolving security disputes through an external projection of ASEAN's institutional power is debatable. This has resulted in a strange paradox that "ASEAN regionalism is stronger in its external relations than in intra-ASEAN cooperation."[177] Noted skeptics such as Jones and Smith have delivered a blistering critique of the real, tangible effects of ASEAN's socialization program. They argue that although the PRC and others have learned to "talk the ASEAN talk"—adopting the language of "cooperative" security, for example, by signing the TAC and DOC—there is little evidence of great powers being restrained when their vital interests are at stake.[178] Matthew Davies also pointedly notes that "the ARF has never progressed beyond the first stage of evolution, confidence building, to deal substantively with the major regional issues via preventive diplomacy."[179]

Furthermore, as in ASEAN itself, "The ASEAN way of non-binding commitments has cultivated 'habits of non-implementation' in the ARF, making the cost of non-compliance extremely low."[180] Goh records that these efforts fall "well short of the kind of sustained cooperation and normative agreement needed for a new regional order."[181] As other major powers in the region strengthen alternative alignments such as the TSD and SCO, enthusiasm for the ARF may be dwindling, particularly with the

continued failure for the ARF, or ASEAN itself, to move toward meaningful action on the issue of "preventive diplomacy," let alone its ultimate aim
of "conflict resolution." Nonetheless, it is true that, as David Capie notes,
"despite deep skepticism of inclusive, soft institutionalism on the part of
some, ASEAN remains at the heart of regional cooperation."[182]

It should be noted, however, that these instruments of regional architecture must not be conflated with the ASC alignment itself. They are an extension of an internal process of "intramural security" toward an effort to
achieve "extramural security" on behalf of the ASEAN member states. As
Simon argues, Southeast Asia "contains no major powers with regional or
global reach."[183] According to Beeson, these efforts serve as an "example of
the way regional institutions can mediate external forces."[184] Nevertheless,
as alluded to above, the two are intertwined. Helen Nesadurai argues that
"centrality—the capacity to manage the wider regional order in ways beneficial to member states—rests on its internal cohesion."[185] Thus, the intramural and extramural dynamics of security community are strongly interlinked
and therefore need recombining to gain a more complete appreciation of this
alignment case study.

Conclusion

As the preceding analysis demonstrates, the ASC is best captured by the
security community paradigm of alignment and through a largely constructivist perspective. Acharya asserts that "without a constructivist understanding, it would be difficult to explain the emergence of ASEAN."[186] Because
it is not designed as a typical military alliance, this perspective better
accounts for the formation and internal dynamics of the ASC in contrast to
traditional structural-realist explanations for alignment. But the application
of the framework to the ASC case study does raise questions as to the need
for further modifying how the constructivist theoretical approach is opera-
tionalized. Particularly notable, as Acharya admits, is that "the ASEAN
experience somewhat blurs the distinction between nascent, ascendant and
mature security communities."[187] Indeed, this case study has indicated how
the analytical framework suffers from duplication/overlap of explanatory
variables across the different phases and the impossibility of making clear
and categorical distinctions as to which factors apply to which phase.

Also, as the approach taken in this book has shown, greater consideration needs to be given to accentuating security communities as having an
external dimension, as a unified alignment "actor." By looking at how the
community-building approach has been further extended outward by the
ASC alignment through the ASEAN-plus process, we can gain a better

appreciation of alternative forms of alignment behavior, in contrast to the other two paradigms/case studies considered in this book. As Khoo notes, rather than engage in alliance-style "balancing," "ASEAN and its security community advocates have sought to project the organization's norms of conflict resolution and identity convergence practices onto a wider regional canvas."[188] This claim notwithstanding, only by a (re)incorporation of the traditional/realist alignment theories into the framework, as the work of Emmers and others testifies, can we complete the composite picture of how the ASC is oriented as an identifiable alignment, since such factors have become more relevant as the ASC is forced to deal with more traditional security challenges such as maritime disputes in the South China Sea.

As Roberts attests, "the importance Deutsch placed on considerations such as *power* implied a more eclectic framework with the opportunity to accept some of the contentions of the neo-realist and neo-liberal paradigms."[189] He further notes that "various patterns of inter-state behaviour predicted by realism may be prominent at low levels of integration but suggests that a shift towards the patterns of behaviour predicted by neo-liberal institutionalism can become more prominent at higher integration."[190] Together, these adjustments allow us to more fully embrace the "shifting dynamics in ASEAN's intramural and extramural sets of foreign relations" instead of compartmentalizing them theoretically or empirically.[191] As Nesadurai notes, "Maintaining the analytical separation between the domestic and international realms," as has heretofore sometimes been the case in the literature, is not tenable.[192]

Finally, the security communities paradigm outlined in the Chapter 4 also proposes three future trajectories from the ASC as it seeks to remain relevant as a regional security provider. In order of probability, they are continuation, integration, and regional fortress. In the first instance, while debates rage regarding the achievements and durability of the ASC itself, Narine posits that "ASEAN's continuing role as a purveyor of regional norms seems assured."[193] War between ASEAN states appears extremely unlikely and any intramural conflicts that do emerge are most likely to be resolved through ASEAN-led diplomacy, even if the "preferred strategy of consensus diplomacy . . . manages problems rather than solves them."[194] Nevertheless, we can say with reasonable certitude that ASEAN members look forward to dependable expectations of peaceful change within their region and this is likely to continue.

Väyrynen suggests that "cooperation in the ASEAN framework may have progressed far enough that the risk of interstate warfare in the region has disappeared for good."[195] It is therefore difficult to envisage the disintegration of the ASC or the attendant ASEAN-plus model at this time. ASEAN is the most effective mechanism that the states of Southeast Asia have to protect their combined interests against external powers and to multiply their strength through a common front. To validate this, David Arase suggests, "Contrast this to what ASEAN members would confront if they were unaffiliated, individual countries living cheek by jowl, surrounded by major powers with competing interests in their region."[196] In this respect Keiichi Tsunekawa adds that "at present, ASEAN remains the most successful model of regional security cooperation in Asia."[197]

As noted, ASEAN has sought to consolidate its internal successes through an external "integrationist" strategy aimed at using ASEAN norms and institutions to secure the type of normative-contractual order across the wider Asia Pacific region. Indeed, the organization will likely expand to incorporate East Timor and possibly Papua New Guinea in due course. Moreover, Goh asserts that "by extending the ASEAN model to East Asia and the Asia Pacific, ASEAN has institutionalized and legitimized the interests of smaller states in restraining and normatively taming the excesses of great power."[198] Others, however, are more skeptical of its continued influence. Wu Xinbo argues that "although ASEAN helped kick off the process of regional cooperation, it simply lacks both the political and economic might to bring it to a [Asia Pacific] regional level."[199] Though the ASEAN-plus process has met with modest success to date, its continued relevance or "centrality" is increasingly challenged by both US and Chinese visions for regional security examined in Chapters 3 and 7. As Satu Limaye notes, "This orientation is trickier as the contest for power, order and relations across the region heats up."[200] Lastly, as M. J. Reese's proposition of security communities developing into "regional fortresses" seems predicated as an outgrowth of a security community that has reached a *mature* level, it is too early to apply this label to the ongoing ASC project. [201]

Notes

1. Much of the research on this case study was undertaken as a visiting fellow under the Multilateralism and Regionalism Programme at the Rajaratnam School of International Studies (RSIS) under the direction of Associate Professor Ralf Emmers at Nanyang Technical University. I am very grateful to Ralf and all the faculty of the RSIS (especially Tan See Seng, Mely Caballero-Anthony, Alan Chong, and Rajesh Basrur) and their administrative staff for making my stay there intellectually stimulating and logistically carefree. My thanks also go to Hiro Katsumata and Christopher Roberts for their comments on previous drafts.

2. Association of Southeast Asian Nations, "ASEAN Leaders' Declaration on the 50th Anniversary of ASEAN."

3. Buszynski, *SEATO: The Failure of an Alliance Strategy.*

4. Acharya, "ASEAN 2030," p. 3.

5. Leifer, "The ASEAN Peace Process," p. 28.

6. Jones and Smith, "Making Process, Not Progress," p. 149.

7. Sahashi, "The Rise of China and the Transformation of Asia-Pacific Security Architecture," p. 139.

8. Association of Southeast Asian Nations, "ASEAN Leaders' Declaration on the 50th Anniversary of ASEAN," p. 2.

9. Acharya, "The Strong in the World of the Weak," p. 173.

10. Acharya, "The Myth of ASEAN Centrality?" p. 274.

11. Acharya, "Arguing About ASEAN," p. 494.

12. This information can be found in an extensive literature, such as Acharya, *Constructing a Security Community in Southeast Asia*; Narine, "Forty Years of ASEAN"; Emmers, *Cooperative Security and the Balance of Power in ASEAN and the ARF*.

13. Association of Southeast Asian Nations, "ASEAN Vision 2020."

14. Khoo, "The ASEAN Security Community," p. 180.

15. Association of Southeast Asian Nations, "ASEAN Security Community Plan of Action."

16. Sukma, "The ASEAN Political and Security Community (APSC)," p. 136.

17. Roberts, *ASEAN Regionalism*, p. 2.

18. Katsumata, "Mimetic Adoption and Norm Diffusion," p. 571.

19. RSIS-Macarthur Conference on Regional Security Cooperation, "Building Institutional Coherence in Asia's Security Architecture," p. 5.

20. See Tan, "Southeast Asia in Search of Security Community," p. 3.

21. Jones and Smith, "Making Process, Not Progress."

22. Collins, "Forming a Security Community: Lessons from ASEAN."

23. Ba, "ASEAN Centrality Imperiled?"; Khoo, "Deconstructing the ASEAN Security Community."

24. Simon, "ASEAN and Southeast Asia," p. 242.

25. Adler and Greve declare, "actors that constitute security communities align consciousness in the direction of common enterprises, projects, and partnerships, thus turning security community into the day-to-day practice of peace." Adler and Greve, "When Security Community Meets Balance of Power," p. 72.

26. *Alignment* is defined "as a relationship between two or more states that involves mutual expectations of some degree of policy coordination on security issues under certain conditions in the future." Miller and Toritsyn, "Bringing the Leader Back In," p. 333.

27. Acharya, "Collective Identity and Conflict Management in Southeast Asia," p. 216.

28. Acharya, *Constructing a Security Community in Southeast Asia*, p. 192.

29. Solingen, "East Asian Regional Institutions," p. 35.

30. Association of Southeast Asian Nations, "ASEAN Security Community Plan of Action." Italics added.

31. Leifer, "The ASEAN Peace Process"; Emmers, *Cooperative Security and the Balance of Power in ASEAN and the ARF*.

32. Narine, "ASEAN in the Twenty-First Century."

33. Haas, "Successful Security Communities."

34. Acharya, "Collective Identity and Conflict Management in Southeast Asia," p. 202.

35. Collins, "Forming a Security Community," p. 212.

36. Pempel, *Remapping East Asia*, p. 10.

37. Taylor, "Malaysia, Indonesia—and Maphilindo."

38. Acharya, "Collective Identity and Conflict Management in Southeast Asia," p. 202.

39. Emmers, *Cooperative Security and the Balance of Power in ASEAN and the ARF*, p. 2.

40. Acharya and Tan, "Betwixt Balance and Community," p. 44.

41. Beeson, *Institutions of the Asia Pacific*, p. 19.

42. Storey, Emmers, and Singh, *The Five Power Defence Arrangements at Forty*.

43. Emmers, "Southeast Asia's New Security Institutions," p. 181.

44. Acharya, *Constructing a Security Community in Southeast Asia*, p. 224.

45. Roberts, *ASEAN Regionalism*, p. 8.

46. Emmers, *Cooperative Security and the Balance of Power in ASEAN and the ARF*, p. 3.

47. Acharya, "Collective Identity and Conflict Management in Southeast Asia," p. 203. Italics added.

48. Emmers, *Cooperative Security and the Balance of Power in ASEAN and the ARF*, p. 3.

49. Adler and Barnett, *Security Communities*, p. 20.

50. Acharya, "Collective Identity and Conflict Management in Southeast Asia," p. 203.

51. Cited in Emmers, *Cooperative Security and the Balance of Power in ASEAN and the ARF*, p. 14.

52. Acharya, "The Strong in the World of the Weak," p. 174.

53. Adler and Barnett, *Security Communities*, p. 43.

54. Leifer, "The ASEAN Regional Forum," p. 11.

55. Jones, "Explaining the Failure of the ASEAN Economic Community," p. 656.

56. Acharya, "Collective Identity and Conflict Management in Southeast Asia," p. 204.

57. Association of Southeast Asian Nations, *Agreement on the Common Effective Preferential Tariff Scheme for the ASEAN Free Trade Area*.

58. Chang, "Essence of Security Communities," p. 349.

59. Acharya, "Collective Identity and Conflict Management in Southeast Asia," p. 204.

60. Association of Southeast Asian Nations, "AFTA & FTAs."

61. Association of Southeast Asian Nations, "Regional Comprehensive Economic Partnership (RCEP)."

62. Simon, "ASEAN and Southeast Asia," p. 241.

63. Association of Southeast Asian Nations, "The Founding of ASEAN."

64. Acharya, "Collective Identity and Conflict Management in Southeast Asia," pp. 202–203.

65. Solingen, "East Asian Regional Institutions," p. 48.

66. Acharya, "Remaking Southeast Asian Studies," p. 481.

67. Adler and Barnett, *Security Communities*, p. 52.

68. Ibid., p. 20.

69. Roberts, *ASEAN Regionalism*, p. 7.

70. Ibid., p. 2.

71. Adler and Barnett, *Security Communities*, p. 41.

72. Jones and Jenne, "Weak States' Regionalism," p. 211.

73. Narine, "ASEAN in the Twenty-First Century," p. 412.

74. Haas, "Successful Security Communities," p. 142.

75. Acharya, *Constructing a Security Community in Southeast Asia*, p. 36.

76. Haas, *Beyond the Nation-State*.

77. Pempel, *Remapping East Asia,* p. 10.

78. Association of Southeast Asian Nations, "ASEAN Vision 2020," p. 2.

79. Roberts, "State Weakness and Political Values," p. 12.

80. Roberts, "State Weakness and Political Values."

81. Beeson, *Institutions of the Asia-Pacific*, p. 23.

82. Pempel, *Remapping East Asia,* p. 11.

83. Goh, "Great Powers and Hierarchical Order in Southeast Asia," p. 120.

84. Acharya, *Constructing a Security Community in Southeast Asia*, p. 123.

85. Haacke, "ASEAN's Diplomatic and Security Culture," p. 79.

86. Rüland, "Southeast Asian Regionalism and Global Governance," p. 97.

87. Roberts, *ASEAN Regionalism*, p. 176.

88. Beeson, *Institutions of the Asia-Pacific,* p. 25.

89. Cole and Jensen, "Norms and Regional Architecture," p. 249.

90. Association of Southeast Asian Nations, "ASEAN Leaders' Declaration on the 50th Anniversary of ASEAN," p. 1.

91. Collins, "Forming a Security Community," p. 222.

92. Ibid., p. 211.

93. Poole, "Cooperation in Contention," p. 5.

94. Adler and Barnett, *Security Communities*, p. 428.

95. Association of Southeast Asian Nations, "ASEAN Political-Security Community Blueprint."

96. Caballero-Anthony, "Non-traditional Security and Multilateralism in Asia," p. 320.

97. See Dupont, *East Asia Imperiled*; Caballero-Anthony and Emmers, "Understanding the Dynamics of Securitizing Non-Traditional Security"; Emmers, Caballero-Anthony, and Acharya, *Studying Non-Traditional Security in Asia*.

98. Katsumata, "Mimetic Adoption and Norm Diffusion," p. 564.

99. Lego, "Why ASEAN Can't Ignore the Rohingya Crisis."

100. Simon, "ASEAN and Southeast Asia," p. 228.

101. Bisley, *Building Asia's Security*, p. 35. Italics added.

102. Cole and Jensen, "Norms and Regional Architecture," p. 255.

103. Roberts, "ASEAN, the 'South China Sea' Arbitral Award, and the Code of Conduct."

104. Beukel, "ASEAN and ARF in East Asia's Security Architecture," p. 26.

105. Ibid.

106. Capie, "Evolving Attitudes to Peacekeeping in ASEAN."

107. Friedrichs, "East Asian Regional Security," p. 773.

108. Acharya, "Collective Identity and Conflict Management in Southeast Asia," p. 219.

109. Väyrynen, "Stable Peace Through Security Communities?" p. 122; see also: Beukel. "ASEAN and ARF in East Asia's Security Architecture," p. 7; Jones and Smith, "Making Process, Not Progress"; Khoo, "Deconstructing the ASEAN Security Community."

110. Loo, "Is There an Arms Race in Asia?"

111. Green and Gill, "Unbundling Asia's New Multilateralism," p. 20.

112. Acharya, "Collective Identity and Conflict Management in Southeast Asia," p. 201.

113. Stubbs, "The ASEAN Alternative?" p. 451.

114. Association of Southeast Asian Nations, "ASEAN Security Community Plan of Action." Italics added.

115. Adler and Barnett, *Security Communities*, p. 423.

116. Collins, "Bringing Communities Back," p. 280.

117. Yuzawa, "The Fallacy of Socialization?" p. 83.

118. Cole and Jensen, "Norms and Regional Architecture," p. 259.

119. Caballero-Anthony, "Non-traditional Security Challenges, Regional Governance, and the ASEAN Political Security Community (ASPC)," p. 41.

120. Roberts, "State Weakness and Political Values," p. 23.

121. Narine, "ASEAN in the Twenty-First Century," p. 376.

122. Mérieau, "Thailand's Deepening Authoritarian Rule"; Human Rights Watch, "Philippines: Duterte's 'Drug War' Claims 12,000+ Lives."

123. Becker, *Illiberal Security Communities*, p. 6.

124. Association of Southeast Asian Nations, "ASEAN Vision 2020."

125. Acharya, "Collective Identity and Conflict Management in Southeast Asia," p. 219.

126. Katsumata, "Establishment of the ASEAN Regional Forum," p. 189.

127. Acharya, "Collective Identity and Conflict Management in Southeast Asia," p. 213.

128. Narine, "ASEAN in the Twenty-First Century," p. 377.

129. Emmers, *Cooperative Security and the Balance of Power in ASEAN and the ARF*, p. 6.

130. Khoo, "Deconstructing the ASEAN Security Community."

131. Narine, "Forty Years of ASEAN," p. 420.

132. Gentner, "ASEAN: Cooperative Disaster Relief After the Tsunami."

133. Leifer, "The ASEAN Regional Forum," p. 3.

134. Roberts, *ASEAN Regionalism*, p. 7.

135. National Institute for Defense Studies, "Southeast Asia: Challenges in Creating an 'ASEAN Political-Security Community,'" p. 127.

136. Thayer, "The Rise of China and India," p. 326.

137. Poole, "Cooperation in Contention," p. 12.

138. Acharya, "Collective Identity and Conflict Management in Southeast Asia," p. 206.

139. Roberts, *ASEAN Regionalism*, p. 187. Italics original.

140. Acharya, "Collective Identity and Conflict Management in Southeast Asia," p. 208.

141. Ibid., p. 214.

142. Acharya, "Collective Identity and Conflict Management in Southeast Asia."

143. Caballero-Anthony, "Non-traditional Security Challenges, Regional Governance, and the ASEAN Political Security Community," p. 28.

144. Roberts, *ASEAN Regionalism*, p. 182.

145. Ruggie, "Territoriality and Beyond," p. 172.

146. Jones and Smith, "Making Process, Not Progress," p. 159. Italics added.

147. Leifer, "The ASEAN Regional Forum," p. 14.

148. Emmers and Tan, "The ASEAN Regional Forum and Preventive Diplomacy."

149. Roberts, *ASEAN Regionalism*, p. 177.

150. Acharya, "Collective Identity and Conflict Management in Southeast Asia," p. 214.

151. Tan, "Southeast Asia in Search of Security Community," p. 7.

152. Adler and Barnett, *Security Communities*, p. 57.

153. Association of Southeast Asian Nations, "Cebu Declaration on East Asian Energy Security"; Association of Southeast Asian Nations Wildlife Enforcement Network, "About Us"; Asia-Pacific Partnership on Clean Development and Climate, "Overview"; Association of Southeast Asian Nations, *ASEAN Agreement on Transboundary Haze Pollution.*

154. Pempel, *Remapping East Asia*, p. 270.

155. Martel, "From Ambiguity to Contestation," p. 556.

156. Higgins, "ASEAN Struggles to Cope with Rival Claims in the South China Sea."

157. Associated Press, "Philippines to "Set Aside" South China Sea Tribunal Ruling."

158. Roberts, "ASEAN, the 'South China Sea' Arbitral Award, and the Code of Conduct," p. 206.

159. See Huxley, *Defending the Lion City.*

160. Acharya, "Collective Identity and Conflict Management in Southeast Asia," p. 217.

161. Ibid., p. 215.

162. Ibid., pp. 203–204.

163. Tan, "Southeast Asia in Search of Security Community," p. 6.

164. Collins, "Bringing Communities Back," p. 288.

165. Freistein, "'A Living Document,'" p. 408.

166. Väyrynen, "Stable Peace Through Security Communities?" p. 123.

167. Ba, "On Norms, Rule Breaking, and Security Communities," p. 259.

168. Narine, "ASEAN in the Twenty-First Century," p. 373.

169. Acharya, "The Strong in the World of the Weak," p. 174.

170. Mahbubani, *The New Asian Hemisphere*, p. 84.

171. Kraft, "Driving East Asian Regionalism," p. 63.

172. Beukel, "ASEAN and ARF in East Asia's Security Architecture," p. 6.

173. Katsumata, "Establishment of the ASEAN Regional Forum."

174. Acharya, "Ideas, Identity, and Institution Building from the 'ASEAN Way' to the 'Asia-Pacific Way'?"

175. Taylor and Tow, "Challenges to Building an Effective Asia-Pacific Security," p. 332.

176. Garafano, "A Security Community for Asia?"

177. Akrasanee, "Issues in ASEAN Economic Regionalism," p. 72.

178. Yuzawa, "The Fallacy of Socialization?" p. 78; see also: Ba, "Who Is Socializing Whom?"

179. Davies, "Multilateralism and Security Communities," pp. 229–230.

180. Yuzawa, "The Fallacy of Socialization?" p. 82.

181. Goh, "Institutions and the Great Power Bargain in East Asia," p. 106.

182. Capie, "Explaining ASEAN's Resilience: Institutions, Path Dependency, and Asia's Emerging Architecture," p. 168.

183. Simon, "ASEAN and Southeast Asia," p. 225.

184. Beeson, *Institutions of the Asia-Pacific*, p. 2.

185. Nesadurai, "ASEAN During the Life of the *Pacific Review*," p. 948.

186. Acharya, "Collective Identity and Conflict Management in Southeast Asia," p. 206; Katsumata, "Establishment of the ASEAN Regional Forum"; Haacke, "ASEAN's Diplomatic and Security Culture," pp. 57–87.

187. Adler and Barnett, *Security Communities*, p. 219.

188. Khoo, "The ASEAN Security Community," p. 189.

189. Roberts, *ASEAN Regionalism*, p. 2.

190. Ibid., p. 7.

191. Roberts, "ASEAN, the 'South China Sea' Arbitral Award, and the Code of Conduct," p. 192.

192. Nesadurai, "ASEAN During the Life of the *Pacific Review*," p. 944.

193. Narine, "Forty Years of ASEAN," p. 426.

194. Simon, "ASEAN and Southeast Asia," p. 235.

195. Väyrynen, "Stable Peace Through Security Communities?" p. 123.

196. Arase, "Non-traditional Security in China-ASEAN Cooperation," p. 815.

197. Tsunekawa, "Building Asian Security Institutions Under the Triple Shocks," p. 85.

198. Goh, "Institutions and the Great Power Bargain in East Asia," p. 112.

199. Wu, "Chinese Perspectives on Building and East Asian Community in the Twenty-first Century," p. 64.

200. Limaye, "Why ASEAN Is Here to Stay and What That Means for the US," p. 2.

201. Reese, "Destructive Double Standards."

6

Strategic Partnerships

The strategic partnership as a discernible form of security align- ment emerged in the post–Cold War period. The term was first nominally employed by China and Brazil in 1993[1] to signify and enhance their bilateral relations and has subsequently been adopted by a diverse range of states/actors, including dyads such as Russia-China, US-India, and NATO-EU, among a host of others.[2] Such partnerships often appear in different guises, with some adding seemingly superfluous prefixes such as *comprehensive* or *global,* for example. But despite variations in the nomenclature used in individual cases, they basically amount to the same thing, which is simply referred to as *strategic partnership* throughout this book.

Until recently, our limited understanding of the term has coalesced around the Indian, Russian, and Chinese usage, though this is gradually changing.[3] Both the Beijing-Moscow strategic partnership, officially promulgated in 1996, and India's broad portfolio of such alignments serve as our exemplars of the phenomenon. Feng Zhongping and Huang Jing argue that "Beijing has been largely successful in employing strategic partnerships, a prominent instrument in its limited diplomatic toolkit, in order to guarantee a benign environment for its rise."[4] Interestingly, India, a state without traditional "allies," which spearheads the ideology of "nonalignment," is a notable adherent to this mode of security cooperation, with more than twenty partnerships. Yet, the strategic partnership model is now widely emulated by traditional Western powers, particularly Japan and Australia, who also enjoy their own bilateral partnership.[5] The belated embrace of the strategic partnership mechanism by the United States now indicates how alignment choices have substantially departed from the traditional Cold War military alliance pact. Ashley Tellis considers the US relationship with

India represents "a great example of how the evolving post–Cold War environment has demanded new kinds of strategic partnerships."[6]

Indeed, as Thomas Renard and Giovanni Grevi note, "The proliferation of partnerships over the last two decades exposes both the relevance of this trend and the great heterogeneity, and uneven value, of these relationships."[7] Subsequently, a European Strategic Partnerships Observatory has been created by a consortium of think tanks in order to "monitor the evolution of the EU's strategic partnerships" and to act as a sorting house on both the EU's multiplying partnerships and those of other major powers, such as China and Brazil, for example.[8] Now that the term is in widespread use as a descriptor of bilateral security cooperation, it is imperative that it receive more conceptual attention from international relations (IR) scholars. As Feng and Huang argue, despite their increasing centrality to alignment policy, "these partnerships remain largely unexplored in academic literature and policy debates, and the concept is still ill-defined."[9]

What Is a "Strategic Partnership"?

Like so many buzzwords in common currency, oftentimes its meaning is assumed to be self-evident and thus not requiring further specification or definition. For their part, IR academics on the whole seem to have circumspectly avoided grappling with this new concept, perhaps in the belief that if it is ignored it might fade from the international discourse, or possibly through discomfiture that it does not neatly fit extant models of security cooperation, such as the much-revered alliance paradigm. Some commentators have simply reached for the "alliance" label to apply to what are officially and explicitly described in state policy as "strategic partnerships."[10] As a consequence, our conceptual/theoretical knowledge of a form of security cooperation at the forefront of several leading states' security policies remains wholly inadequate. While there is a large body of literature spanning political analyses of various strategic partnerships, few of them make the effort to expressly define what it is they are investigating.[11] As Renard and Grevi note in the foreword to Feng and Huang's paper, what we need to know is, "How do partnerships fit the foreign policy of major countries? What are the goals of these partnerships and what is their output? What are the main features of strategic partnerships?"[12]

This section draws on the relevant literature from business and organization studies, as the disciplinary progenitors of the term, to indicate how definitions drawn from this field may be constructively adapted to an IR context.[13] Mirroring the familiar problem of essentially contested concepts in IR, consensus on definitional issues is hard to obtain. Lynn Mytelka laments, "But what exactly are strategic partnerships? . . . there is no single definition."[14] The resultant problems of misuse and miscomprehension are "caused mainly because of an imperfect understanding of the term," according to Chris Steward.[15] The BNET Business Dictionary defines a *strategic partnership* as

> structured collaboration between organizations to take joint advantage of market opportunities, or to respond to customers more effectively than could be achieved in isolation. Strategic partnering occurs both in and between the public and private sectors. Besides allowing information, skills, and resources to be shared, a strategic partnership also permits the partners to share risk.[16]

This description appears quite satisfactory. Unfortunately, as with the case in IR regarding contested concepts, the definition is complicated by quasi-synonyms. Frequently the term *strategic alliance* is substituted for *strategic partnership* in the organization studies literature. William Bergquist and colleagues define a strategic alliance as a "pact between two or more organizations to achieve a mutual goal or set of goals."[17] To nonspecialists, the boundaries between "strategic partnership" and "strategic alliance" appear fuzzy and need not preoccupy us here.[18] The distinction may be semantic or in terms of scale—"alliance" conjuring up a joint venture of larger enterprises. Indeed, any business preference for labeling relations as "alliances" rather than "partnerships" is most likely due to the potential legal connotations held by the latter term, according to Joan Roberts, though the reverse is likely to obtain in international politics.[19] Hence the organization studies literature on "strategic alliances" is quite apposite to strategic partnerships.[20] A final word of caution here: the term *strategic alliance* is also used as a form of longhand for "alliances" in IR. This is often used by policymakers or analysts, as the redundant adjective of *strategic* presumably gives it a more highfalutin ring.[21] It can safely be banished from our vocabulary without forfeit.

Therefore, adapting the definition above to an IR context, a strategic partnership represents structured collaboration between states (or other actors) to take joint advantage of economic opportunities, or to respond to security challenges more effectively than could be achieved in isolation. More specifically, a strategic partnership may be considered a form of enhanced bilateral cooperation between two states (or other actors) that brings them into closer alignment on security and economic issues in order to reduce uncertainties and aggregate capabilities toward mutual challenges. It is foremost a form of security cooperation, but one that contains an important economic element, and as it progresses, it will typically be undergirded by efforts to expand cooperation into other spheres, including cultural cooperation. Such partnering can span both state and non-state collaboration, allowing the pooling of resources and sharing of risk in dealing with joint challenges. In the words of the Chinese Ministry of Foreign Affairs, "By 'partnership,' it means that the cooperation should be equal-footed, mutually beneficial and win-win. The two sides should base themselves on mutual respect and mutual trust, endeavor to expand converging interests and seek common ground on the major issues while shelving differences on the minor ones."[22] Moreover, Satish Kumar and others attest that "these partnerships are considered strategic in nature because of the importance of the issues involved and the long-term nature of cooperation that is visualized."[23] This echoes the Chinese Ministry's understanding that "by 'strategic,' it means that the cooperation should be long-term and stable."[24]

We must determine for ourselves, with the assistance of the definition and accompanying framework below, if a so-called strategic partnership genuinely merits the appellation or whether it simply represents the vapid application of a high-sounding label to an inconsequential—and therefore "false"—partnership. In the latter case, a major Indian study questions whether "a less serious but equally palatable nomenclature can be devised for relationships that are not as comprehensive and far reaching" as that intimated by the label "strategic partnership."[25]

Characteristics of a Strategic Partnership

Following from this basic interpretation, a number of typical characteristics will aid us in identifying and delineating the strategic partnership as a security alignment. First, genuine strategic partners coalesce under a broad "system principle," a common purpose that serves to justify collaboration. This has its basis in shared assumptions or axioms about how international politics works, or should work. Examples might include the "Beijing consensus," a "rules-based order," or "multipolarity." This takes the place of a specifically designated threat to be deterred, as typical in an alliance.

Second, unlike alliances then, strategic partnerships are primarily "goal-driven" rather than "threat-driven" arrangements. As Prashanth Parameswaran recounts, "the main purpose of strategic partnerships is to both address common challenges and seize joint opportunities, rather than countering a particular country or group."[26] Thus, no "enemy" state is identified by the partnership as a "threat," though the partnership may be concerned with joint security "issue-areas"—such as terrorism, proliferation, or transnational crime. This is not to say it won't find itself in some form of ideological or political antagonism with other alignments with differing or opposing goals.

Third, they entail low commitment costs due to their typically informal nature. Though they may be enunciated through treaties or declarations and associated confidence-building measures (CBMs), these will seldom bind the partners into such rigid or dangerous commitments as are typically found in alliance defense pacts. "These partnerships, unlike the Cold War type of alliances, do not bind nations to support each other on all strategic issues in all situations," according to Satish Kumar and others.[27] By allowing partners to retain a greater degree of autonomy and flexibility, members are not subject to the intense abandonment-entrapment dynamic of more conventional military alliances.[28]

Fourth, such partnerships are typically catalyzed by economic as well as security concerns. For example, some form of free trade agreement (FTA) or economic partnership agreement (EPA) often forms part of the larger strategic partnership "package." Though the security and diplomatic "superstructure" of strategic partnership takes precedence, the evidence suggests that economic and cultural "substructure" will almost invariably accompany them. This comports with an Indian study's classification of the paradigm as "a strong relationship bound primarily by security and defence ties."[29] Though they evince some congruities with other forms of alignment, considered in this book and elsewhere, they are distinctive enough to form a coherent paradigm quite independent of these.

Theoretical Base

Despite its undoubted salience as a new form of security cooperation in the post–Cold War international system, academics appear to have been exceedingly reluctant to address the phenomenon from a conceptual or theoretical point of view. However, building on some of the pioneering work by Sean Kay, Vidya Nadkarni, as well as this author, a new generation of scholars less wedded to the Cold War conventional military alliance paradigm of alignment have started to place the phenomenon under the conceptual microscope.[30] Strategic partnerships as a new form of security alignment are here to stay and must therefore be integrated into the larger body of alignment theory and the IR research traditions in general. As IR scholars have incrementally advanced our understanding of this new phenomenon, it has become possible to incorporate their work in order to reinforce the analytical framework presented below.

The phrase originated in the business world, where it is ingrained in the disciplines of business and organization studies. Indeed, these fields have long been grappling with analogous problems and limitations with the term. In contrast, in international politics, the term has been so widely misused and misconstrued as to seriously undermine its utility. Sometimes, policymakers or analysts have simply importuned the phrase to place a rhetorical seal on high-profile interstate agreements. After all, Feng Huiyun notes "the interplay of 'strategic' and 'partnership' could mean nothing or a lot in world politics."[31] This has led David Envall and Ian Hall to question whether strategic partnerships really constitute security *alignment* or rather a type of security *practice*.[32] They base this critique on pointing to the undeveloped or even conflictual nature of some so-called strategic partnerships. But this variance in the depth or quality of partnerships is to be expected. As Feng and Huang testify, "The Chinese do not expect every strategic partnership to carry the same weight. They accept that some partnerships are going to be less substantial than others."[33] They noted that it was problematic that Beijing had labeled very weak agreements of little substance (e.g., China-Zimbabwe) the same as more concrete and expansive security dyads, such as China-Russia. According to Kay, "The evidence shows that some strategic partnerships have considerable meaning, whereas others are vague in purpose and structure."[34] The same might be said about various examples of other forms of alignment, be they alliances, coalitions, ententes, or nonaggression pacts.

With such qualifications duly noted, it is feasible to selectively draw upon the wide literature relating to the phenomenon in the business and organization studies literature to fashion an analytical framework fit for the purpose of understanding its behavioral dynamics.[35] Organization studies is especially well fitted to the task since it is designed, according to one of the flagship journals in the discipline, to "promote the understanding of organizations, organizing and the organized, and the social relevance of that understanding."[36] Not only did the term *strategic partnership* originate from this discipline, but organizational theories have already been constructively applied to other major issues in IR such as crisis management, military innovation, and nuclear weapons safety, to good effect.[37] Thus the case for a novel and cross-disciplinary approach to fill the analytical gaps left by traditional alignment theories is compelling.

Additionally, a survey of relevant policy documents appertaining to specific strategic partnerships and associated academic studies suggests a variety of options for structuring our analysis. Some studies present strategic partnerships according to "sectors" of cooperation: for example, diplomatic, economic, and military, or through a "narrative" of their development.[38] Others have advanced specific models such as the "threat-interest" model of partnership or the "rationale-development-evaluation" mode.[39] This chapter seeks to incorporate these contributions. While the analytical framework that follows is largely anchored in the conceptual bases of organization studies, undoubtedly there are various aspects of all the main IR traditions—realism, liberalism, and constructivism—that can be productively spliced into the following discussion.

Analytical Framework: Strategic Partnership

Following these cues and drawing on the mainstays of organizational theories that are transferrable to IR, I formulate a dedicated analytical framework here to examine strategic partnerships through their "life cycle."[40] With reference to Roberts and Karthik Iyer, the framework considers three sequential stages of development across a "collaboration continuum": formation, implementation, and evaluation.[41] More recent works have adopted derivatives of this three-stage model of strategic partnerships, as noted above, and this model echoes the symmetry of the three-phase approach to security communities.[42] The model looks at the different dimensions of the strategic partnership's activities: the *vertical* hierarchy within each state and the *horizontal* areas of cooperation. It also identifies that while strategic partnerships often begin as bilateral state-to-state enterprises, they can expand their membership to incorporate new partners or become embedded in the form of interlocking "networks" within a multilateral organization, as we shall discover in the Shanghai Cooperation Organisation (SCO) case study.

Formation Stage

During the formation stage of a strategic partnership, state leaders will be concerned with three key factors: responding to environmental "uncertainty"; identifying "strategic fit"; forging a "system principle." "Leadership" itself is a key driver in the formation stage. It should be noted that factors driving the formation process will continue to operate at subsequent stages as foundations and reference points for implementation and evaluation.

First, according to Mytelka, strategic partnerships are formed in reaction to "uncertainty" in the international environment. By responding jointly to conditions of uncertainty, partners are able to expand the range of capabilities at their disposal and distribute risk.[43] Prospective partners essentially seek to mitigate some of the competitive elements of the international security environment through joining forces to reduce bilateral tensions and to create new organizational capabilities based on their shared enterprise. Feng concurs that they are designed in the initial phase "to reduce uncertainties and build trust between . . . two nations, not to cope with challenges from a third party."[44] Therefore, unlike alliances, strategic partnerships are not explicitly "threat-based," or "balancing," arrangements, though this does not preclude cooperation on security and defense matters or shared geopolitical aims (or even forms of "*soft* balancing"/"hedging").

Second, prospective partners are cultivated on the basis of their "strategic fit."[45] Potential strategic partners will be considered on the basis of mutual interests, shared values, and desired capabilities. Feng suggests that "in the preliminary phase" or the "thin" stage of partnership it is "mainly based upon common interests instead of shared values or identities between states."[46] It is only subsequently that "a value-based partnership, therefore, can be seen as the second phase or the 'thick' stage of partnership, which is based on shared practices, rules, and identities."[47] From an instrumental point of view, a partner must bring some "value-added" to the relationship, be it complementary economic resources, organizational expertise, or diplomatic leverage. The ability to access a partner's capabilities and expertise in order to *learn* is also an important determining factor for the participants, according to Bergquist and others.[48] The expectation is that exposure to a partner's capabilities and methods may enhance one's own, as well as develop new synergies of joint cooperation. Furthermore, strategic partnerships are relatively easy to enter into due to their informality and low commitment costs in comparison to subscribing to a formal military alliance pact. Thus, "they do not have the stigma of a multilateral alliance, which may be presumed to be a power bloc meant to countervail some big power or another power bloc."[49] They are thus less risky in the contemporary strategic environment, due to their non-provocative and nonthreatening nature.

Third, once such a partner has been identified on the basis of the above criteria, they will typically seek to codify their mutual cooperation in some form. Their agreed common purpose will be embodied in the notion of a "system principle." Roberts notes that all "organizations must have a system principle, a reason for being."[50] The absence of such a principle is a reliable way to identify a *false* partnership. The system principle is usually fabricated around the common interests and values that together may constitute a joint worldview. Subsequent to such an accord, in the "closing stage" of formation, the system principle is distilled into a set of specific common *goals* for the partnership. Alan McLennan and Rod Troutbeck identify that the essence of a strategic partnership is "the coupling of autonomous units to work collaboratively for a common goal and shared objectives."[51] Richard Hall reminds us that "the important point is that the goal of any organization is an abstraction distilled from the desires of members and pressures from the environment and internal system."[52] But goals can be malleable, evolve over time, and be subject to differing interpretations by the respective partners. Charles Perrow contends that the real or "operative; goals" of the partnership may be dissimulated behind a veil of "official" goals for international consumption.[53] Furthermore, as with any form of alignment, each member state is likely to pursue its own national goals (or "hidden agendas") even *within* the partnership. Jingdong Yuan neatly encapsulates the range of typical or potential goals that they may be founded upon:

The goals of strategic partnerships can vary from the minimum and defensive (confidence building and no undercutting of partners' core interests) to the aspirational and maximalist short of alliance formation (coordination of policies at global and regional level; significant military cooperation; support of each other's key positions at international forums), states pursuing them are driven by normative (supporting democracy), politico-economic, and hedging-balancing needs.[54]

Finally, leadership is a key driver in the formation stage. James Austin posits that strategic partnership building is an elite-driven process through formation, goal-setting, and beyond, with "significant support and direct involvement from top leaders a key ingredient in the partnership's prospects."[55] This is supported in the case of China, where "almost all strategic partnerships are established or upgraded during top leaders' state visits."[56] Parameswaran calls such occurrences "action-forcing events" that come to define and embody the purposes, functions, and nature of such partnerships.[57]

Implementation Stage

Strategic partnerships, once formed, "must contend with a challenge quite different from the challenge of creation—the challenge of implementation and, in particular the challenge of building and maintaining relationships."[58] The implementation stage is concerned with the fabrication of an organizational structure as a means to facilitate and mediate interaction between partners. Again, the absence of this will reliably denote a false partnership. This is the "basic mechanism that make all organizations work: procedures for deliberation, decision-making, and implementation."[59] This may vary in its degree of formalization, but as O. N. Mehrotra notes, even if "such relations are generally not institutionalized" in strategic partnerships, they will be structured.[60] According to Parameswaran, "The structure of the strategic partnership and its component parts are usually ultimately detailed either in one initial joint statement issued at the outset or several of them over time."[61]

Organizational structure is an extremely complicated affair. A partnership of two states (or multistate international organizations), each with its own government and bureaucracy, represents a "meta organization" of infinite complexity.[62] This level of organizational complexity will vary in accordance with the number of partners and their respective "sizes." In the latter case, a China-Russia partnership will be a far more complex configuration than one between Israel-Turkey, for instance, due to the fact that they are great powers with all the demographic, economic, military, historical, and institutional intricacy that entails. Due to these factors, every strategic partnership will be uniquely designed. Additionally, and importantly, such partnerships will sometimes be closely connected or even embedded in existing multilateral institutional frameworks. According to Feng and Huang, "When strategic partnerships are built with member states of important regional organizations such as the EU, ASEAN or the Shanghai Cooperation Organisation (SCO), cooperation is usually framed with reference to cooperation with these organizations."[63] McLennan and Troutbeck affirm that "the principles, concepts and processes of strategic partnering are universal, but the form is flexible and should be developed and modified to suit the circumstances and the situation."[64] However, the empirical record attests to a basic schema for strategic partnerships that states are now beginning to replicate.

In general terms, according to Bergquist, Betwee, and Meuel, "The complex system that is formed includes a nonhierarchical structure, a collaboration-based culture, and a relatively equitable distribution of power and authority among the partnership's chief participants."[65] The structure of the strategic partnership outlines the respective roles and responsibilities of its members. It lays out the policies, procedures, and rules to be observed and the bureaucratic components on a *vertical* hierarchy—executive, ministerial, military, financial, public—of each state that will interact within the partnership. Closely related is the demarcation of the horizontal scope of the partnership through *horizontal* areas of cooperation, designated by sectors (e.g., diplomatic/security, defense/military, societal, and cultural collaboration). The Indian case provides the following example of horizontal areas:

> They pertain to core areas of national interest like supply of defence equipment and technology, military exercises, cooperation in the field of nuclear energy, trade and investments, diplomatic support on critical issues, cooperation in science and technology, education, agriculture, information and communication technology, banking, insurance, and various other sectors.[66]

Given that the strategic partnership concept originated in the business world, it is entirely appropriate that economic cooperation is usually at the forefront of collaborative activities. The operation of organizational governance, channels for communication and knowledge sharing (including intelligence information) are all fixed at this stage. By examining the multifarious linkages between the states on both vectors, we can ascertain the degree to which the partners are "coupled": loosely, moderately, or tightly, with a direct bearing on likely cohesion, somewhat mirroring the differential between "loose" and "tight" security communities detailed in Chapter 4.[67] Richard Hall contends:

> There appears to be strong evidence that particular degrees of vertical, horizontal, or spatial complexity are related to organizational cohesion and continuity in particular situations. If an organization chooses an inap-

propriate form or is unable, for whatever reason—economic, personnel, tradition, leadership—to adapt its structure to changed situations, it will likely soon be in trouble.[68]

The implementation stage consolidates the "system principle" by codifying the general purpose and goals of the partnership in some form of institutional structure to advance collaborative activities. It also concomitantly fabricates a joint organizational "identity" and "culture" by generating organizationally based values, practices, systems, symbols, and beliefs, though it must be noted that strategic partnering does not aim at a merger or "amalgamation" of identity such as is evidenced in security communities.[69] This endorses Feng's prediction that "interests" will be the primary driver in the formation stage and that values will follow in this latter stage as the partnership needs to be consolidated, as noted above. Organizational structure thus governs the interaction of the partner states within the relationship. It also influences the behavior of other actors in relation to the partnership itself. A flawed organizational structure, weakly held or poorly defined goals, inherent power imbalances, or conflicts between partners will impede the partnership's successful implementation and its survival as a cohesive security actor.

Evaluation Stage

Once a strategic partnership is implemented, it can be said to have entered an ongoing "evaluation" stage. The partnership can be judged against a set of metrics by which its success and future prospects may be evaluated. Of course, organizational leaders and other officials will offer their own, usually positive, appraisal of the institution's progress and achievements, and these are worth taking note of. But IR specialists have suggested a number of ways by which a strategic partnership could be evaluated. An Indian think tank has devised a shorthand way of quantifying its range of strategic partnerships through the application of a crude points system based on "substance," "sustainability," and "potentiality,"[70] whereas Parameswaran suggests looking at "periodic-based evaluation, event-based evaluation, and strategic evaluation."[71] Lastly, Feng provides four categories of strategic partnership depending upon their level of integration and cohesion, with examples shifting between the "simple partnership," "security partnership," "economic partnership," and "full partnership."[72] These methods are perfectly serviceable, but in going deeper conceptually, from an organizational perspective, it is necessary to revisit the formation stage for validation of the strategic partnership's efficacy. The strategic partnership may be deemed as successful to the degree that it is achieving its goals, the common interests and values converge, and it accommodates the mutual perspectives of the members.[73]

First, and most appositely, the partnership must be gauged against its success in achieving its respective goals. Chris Steward argues that "true strategic partnerships only exist where both parties have demonstrated actual commitment, through action as well as words."[74] Otherwise they may be considered inconsequential or "false" partnerships unworthy of the title, the short-lived US-Russian "strategic partnership" of the early 1990s providing a ready example. States within the partnership must be diligently working toward the attainment of organizational goals and be able to demonstrate real progress based upon the implementation strategy. Hall states that "the determination of a goal for collective action becomes a standard by which collective action is judged."[75] This may be evaluated by "functional area," with political/diplomatic, defense, and economic goals the most important.[76] Nick Bisley, however, reminds us that "these are not just the aims articulated in public—which can be at some remove from the internal goals—but also those recognized by analysts and policy makers."[77]

Second, the system principle acts as a "halo" over interstate collaboration, against which underlying common interests and values are identified. This must be consistently validated by the words and actions of member states individually and collectively. Leadership summits and statements and the declared and actual outputs of partner interaction are the benchmarks. If the partnership remains credible and their interests and values remain in accord, the partnership will be maintained and may deepen or expand over time. Progress may also be reflected in rhetorical "upgrades" in its status—using the Australia-Japan case, for example. As it passed from formation to implementation, its status was successively upgraded from an initial "Creative Partnership" in 2002[78] to a "Comprehensive Strategic Relationship" in 2006,[79] to a "Strategic Partnership" in 2007,[80] to its current incarnation as "Special Strategic Partnership" (2014).[81]

Third, it is important to evaluate the issue of mutual perceptions within the partnership, echoing the intra-alliance politics framework examined in Chapter 2. Through this perspective, we can identify issues that may strengthen or challenge the partnership's integrity such as historical legacies, ideologies, or cultural affinities or clashes. Indeed, in the process of formation and implementation, one of the tasks to vouchsafe the partnership's success may be to gloss over historical, cultural, or ideological differences, obfuscating them or subordinating them to the newly established "system principle." The Saudi-US "strategic partnership" is illustrative of this axiom—theoretically being "allied" but in reality almost completely at odds over their national preferences.[82] Mutual perceptions extend beyond the country's leadership and elite to popular opinion, even in more authoritarian societies, where the empirical record shows such regimes carefully cultivating "grassroots" support for their new relationships. The empirical record suggests that partners will organize national events to profile the cultures of their new associates and raise public awareness, echoing the security communities perspective.

Together, these evaluation criteria give us some indication of the durability and potential longevity of the strategic partnership. As Yuan concludes, "There do exist different variations of partnerships, the extent to which they can be truly 'strategic' depends really on the degree and depth of shared interests, the level of cooperation and coordination of policies, and the substance and potentials of future expansion of ties in geopolitical, geo-economic, and just simply economic terms."[83] Assuming the partnership is performing well against these criteria, it has the potential to *expand* and *evolve*, adapting to its internal and external environments and building its capacities. In the first instance, new strategic partners may be sought out for "strategic fit" and invited to join the existing ones. For example, the Sino-Russian strategic partnership expanded into Central Asia through individual bilateral partnerships and the SCO (as indicated earlier in this chapter). In the second instance, the nature and purpose of the strategic partnership may be transformed by the process of integration and "coupling," also known as the "collaboration multiplier." In this process, cooperation in one area will spill over into others, and the more this happens, the more the partner states will identify with one another's joint interests.[84] Ultimately, organizational goals may be reconfigured or the strategic partnership may tighten and deepen its institutional structure toward building a closer relationship, perhaps maturing into a fully fledged alliance or other form of security organization, like the SCO, which is built upon a network of interlocking strategic partnerships, as examined in Chapter 7. As Feng identifies, even "'full partnership' does not equal a formal alliance, but is rather a soft balancing strategy with the potential to become a military alliance in the future."[85] Alternatively, or in addition, it could even evolve over time into a security community, thus indicating the overlap between paradigms, as discussed in the concluding chapter (Chapter 8).

Conversely, Roberts argues that "no organization lasts forever. But most traditional organizations develop with the assumption that they will be permanent if they are successful at their mission."[86] There are a plethora of factors that can erode the partnership's future prospects, signaling the end of the collaboration continuum: external pressures, shifting goals, changes in partner status, hidden agendas, cultural friction, or simply the lack of available resources or motivation for further "capacity-building." Any or all of these factors can contribute to the termination of a partnership—the "exit stage"—though it may be maintained for an indefinite period of time as a hollow or false partnership. Individual partnerships and indeed perhaps the model of alignment itself may not be designed for perpetuity. From this point of view, Mytelka maintains, strategic partnerships are "seen as temporary arrangements, endangered by opportunism, lack of trust and power games."[87]

Conclusion

The strategic partnership paradigm is the most novel form of security alignment considered in this book. Detailed background discussion about its significance and inadequate definitions has therefore been required to establish its utility and justify its inclusion in our repertoire of alignment paradigms. Succinctly stated, such partnerships involve structured collaboration between states (or other actors) to take joint advantage of economic opportunities, or to respond to security challenges more effectively than could be achieved in isolation. This fully comports with our conception of "alignment" explored in Chapter 1. The term is meaningful when a "true" partnership exhibits the necessary characteristics enumerated above and concrete evidence of its bureaucratic existence and achievements can be provided. Absent these factors, it may be consigned as a "false" partnership (and thus wrongly labeled). As Kumar and others remind us, "It is in the nature of things that some partnerships are more comprehensive than others, depending on the number of areas in which the two sides can fruitfully and actively engage to mutual benefit and the scope and depth of their relations."[88]

Correspondingly, there is no well-developed IR theoretical literature upon which to directly ground an analytical framework. This is a significant shortcoming given the ever-multiplying presence of such strategic partnerships in the international system among great and small powers alike. Little effort has been made to account for strategic partnerships as a new form of security alignment using existing realist/alliance theory (Chapter 2) or constructivist applications of security community theory (Chapter 4), though these perspectives may have some limited and/or contextual application. Instead, this chapter has reached outside the IR discipline to the field of organization studies literature in order to assemble a suitable first-cut analytical framework. Informed by relevant aspects of IR theory, induction of empirical evidence, and a gradually accumulating scholarship on the phenomenon, I have fashioned a practically oriented analytical framework to consider such a partnership's life cycle from its formation, implementation, and evaluation, mirroring Adler and Barnett's security communities approach and more obliquely that of alliance theory. At each stage in the partnership's development, the framework reveals the motivations for cooperation, how such collaboration will be structured, and how its objectives are set and assessed.

Notes

1. Ministry of Foreign Affairs of the People's Republic of China, "China Maintains with Brazil Long-Term and Stable Strategic Partnership Based on Mutual Benefit."
2. See, for example: Rozman, "Sino-Russian Relations"; North Atlantic Treaty Organization, "Fact Sheet: NATO–EU Relations"; White House Office of the Press Secretary, "Fact Sheet: United States and India."
3. See Envall and Hall, "Asian Strategic Partnerships."
4. Feng and Huang, "China's Strategic Partnership Diplomacy," p. 7.
5. Terada, "Thirty Years of the Australia-Japan Partnership in Asian Regionalism"; Togo, "Regional Security Cooperation in East Asia."
6. Tellis, "Seeking Alliances and Partnerships," p. 28.
7. Cited in Feng and Huang, "China's Strategic Partnership Diplomacy," p. 4.
8. European Strategic Partnerships Observatory (ESPO), "Our Project."
9. Feng and Huang, "China's Strategic Partnership Diplomacy," p. 7.
10. Several writers in the field of IR use the term *alliance* liberally when they are in fact referring to a strategic partnership (e.g., Misra, "Shanghai 5 and the Emerging Alliance in Central Asia"). Conversely, Robert Person uses the term *strategic partnership* in its correct context yet creates confusion by then using the term *strategic alliance* (which is almost the same thing in business) to refer to what should be correctly termed simply an *alliance* in IR (Person, "Crouching Tiger, Hidden Jargon").
11. The sole exception I encountered was Kay, "What Is a Strategic Partnership?" Though Goldstein, "An Emerging China's Emerging Grand Strategy," offers a brief but compelling definition in the course of discussing China's grand strategy. Nadkarni, *Strategic Partnerships in Asia*, provides a thoughtful appreciation of a number of Asian case studies.
12. Feng and Huang, "China's Strategic Partnership Diplomacy," p. 4.
13. For example, see Silver, *Strategic Partnering*; Bergquist, Betwee, and Meuel, *Building Strategic Relationships*; Mytelka, *Strategic Partnerships*; Alter and Hage, *Organizations Working Together;* and Steward, *Developing Strategic Partnerships*.
14. Mytelka, *Strategic Partnerships*, p. 1.
15. Steward, *Developing Strategic Partnerships*, p. xi.
16. BNET Business Dictionary, "Strategic Partnership" [Accessed June 2007], http://www.businessdictionary.com/
17. Bergquist, Betwee, and Meuel, *Building Strategic Relationships*, p. 27.
18. Roberts, *Alliances, Coalitions and Partnerships*.
19. Ibid., p. 27.
20. For example, see Yoshino and Rangan, *Strategic Alliances*; Kuglin, *Building, Leading, and Managing Strategic Alliances*.
21. Denmark and Hosford, *Securing South Korea*
22. Wen, "Speech by H. E. Wen Jiabao: Vigorously Promoting Comprehensive Strategic Partnership Between China and the European Union."
23. Kumar et al. *India's Strategic Partners*, p. 1. Italics added.
24. Wen, "Speech by H. E. Wen Jiabao."
25. Kumar et al., *India's Strategic Partners,* p. 14.
26. Parameswaran, "Explaining US Strategic Partnerships in the Asia-Pacific Region," p. 265.
27. Kumar et al., *India's Strategic Partners,* p. 1.
28. See Chapter 2.
29. *Russia & India Report*, "Russia Tops the List of India's Strategic Partners."

30. Kay, "What Is a Strategic Partnership?"; Nadkarni, *Strategic Partnerships in Asia*.

31. Feng, "The New Geostrategic Game," p. 11.

32. See Envall and Hall, "Asian Strategic Partnerships."

33. Feng and Huang, "China's Strategic Partnership Diplomacy," p. 15.

34. Kay, "What Is a Strategic Partnership?" p. 16.

35. Organizational studies is itself quite interdisciplinary in its approach but has a long academic pedigree. For key works see March and Simon, *Organizations*; Hall, *Organizations*; Dawson, *Analysing Organisations*; Weber, *The Theory of Social and Economic Organization*; Taylor, *The Principles of Scientific Management*.

36. See *Organization Studies*, "Description."

37. Allison and Zelikov, *Essence of Decision*; Posen. *The Sources of Military Doctrine*; Sagan, *The Limits of Safety*.

38. See for example: White House Office of the Press Secretary, "Fact Sheet: United States and India," which breaks up cooperation into "civil-nuclear," "economy," "democracy," "energy and the environment," "security," "technologies," and "public health" sectors. Anderson, "The Limits of Sino-Russian Strategic Partnership," divides the analysis into (bilateral relations): "politics and society," "trade and economic," and "demilitarization and border demarcation." Rozman, "Sino-Russian Relations," provides an interrogative narrative of this partnership's evolution.

39. Feng, "The New Geostrategic Game."

40. Earlier iterations thereof appearing in Wilkins, "The Russo-Chinese Strategic Partnership."

41. See Roberts, *Alliances, Coalitions and Partnerships*; Iyer, "Learning in Strategic Alliances"; Austin, *The Collaboration Challenge*, p. 23. The term *stage* rather than *phase* is used here to distinguish from, and avoid confusion with, the security communities perspective.

42. See Parameswaran, "Explaining US Strategic Partnerships in the Asia-Pacific Region."

43. Mytelka, *Strategic Partnerships*.

44. Feng, "The New Geostrategic Game," p. 9.

45. See Bergquist, Betwee, and Meuel, *Building Strategic Relationships*, pp. 69–70; Austin, *The Collaboration Challenge*, p. xii.

46. Feng, "The New Geostrategic Game," p. 12.

47. Ibid.

48. Bergquist, Betwee, and Meuel, *Building Strategic Relationships*, p. 72.

49. Kumar et al., *India's Strategic Partners*, p. 1.

50. Roberts, *Alliances, Coalitions and Partnerships*, p. 24.

51. McLennan and Troutbeck, "Building Strategic Partnerships," p. 3.

52. Hall, *Organizations*, p. 251.

53. Perrow, "The Analysis of Goals in Complex Organizations."

54. Yuan, "Useful Alignments or Just Convenient Labels?" p. 2.

55. Austin, *The Collaboration Challenge*, p. 53.

56. Feng and Huang, "China's Strategic Partnership Diplomacy," p. 14.

57. Parameswaran, "Explaining US Strategic Partnerships in the Asia-Pacific Region," p. 274.

58. Bergquist, Betwee, and Meuel, *Building Strategic Relationships*, p. 87.

59. Wallander, "Institutional Assets and Adaptability," p. 711.

60. Mehrotra, "Indo-Russian Strategic Partnership," p. 80.

61. Parameswaran, "Explaining US Strategic Partnerships in the Asia-Pacific Region," p. 271.

62. Ahrne and Brunsson, "Organizations and Meta-Organizations."

63. Feng and Huang, "China's Strategic Partnership Diplomacy," p. 10.

64. McLennan and Troutbeck, "Building Strategic Partnerships," p. 12.

65. Bergquist, Betwee, and Meuel, *Building Strategic Relationships*, p. 19.

66. Kumar et al., *India's Strategic Partners,* p. 1.

67. Wallace, *Strategic Partnerships*, p. 10.

68. Hall, *Organizations*, p. 62.

69. Parker, *Organizational Culture and Identity*.

70. Kumar et al., *India's Strategic Partners*.

71. Parameswaran, "Explaining US Strategic Partnerships in the Asia-Pacific Region," p. 273.

72. Feng, "The New Geostrategic Game," p. 15.

73. Bergquist, Betwee, and Meuel, *Building Strategic Relationships*, p. 70.

74. Steward, *Developing Strategic Partnerships*, p. 35.

75. Hall, *Organizations*, p. 251.

76. Kumar et al., *India's Strategic Partners,* p. 1.

77. Bisley, *Building Asia's Security*, p. 79.

78. Ministry of Foreign Affairs, Japan, "Joint Press Statement by Prime Minister John Howard and Prime Minister Junichiro Koizumi."

79. The developing relationship went through a number of semantic evolutions, beginning as a "partnership" (1995), then a "creative partnership" (2002), followed by a "strategic partnership" (2007) to "comprehensive strategic partnership" (2008) to "comprehensive strategic, security and economic partnership" (2009).

80. Ministry of Foreign Affairs, Japan. "Prime Minister Abbott and Prime Minister Abe Joint Statement"; Ministry of Foreign Affairs, Japan. "Prime Minister Shinzo Abe's Interview with *The Australian*."

81. Ministry of Foreign Affairs, Japan, "Japan-Australia Joint Declaration on Security Cooperation."

82. Cordesman, *Saudi National Security and the Saudi-US Strategic Partnership*.

83. Yuan, "Useful Alignments or Just Convenient Labels?" p. 3.

84. Austin, *The Collaboration Challenge*, p. 72.

85. Feng, "The New Geostrategic Game," p. 16.

86. Roberts, *Alliances, Coalitions and Partnerships*, p. 30.

87. Mytelka, *Strategic Partnerships*, p. 73.

88. Kumar et al., *India's Strategic Partners,* p. 1.

7

The Shanghai
Cooperation Organisation

The Shanghai Cooperation Organisation (SCO) has assumed mount-
ing significance in the context of Asia Pacific security alignment.[1] After
two decades of steady institutional progress, Stephen Aris contends that the
"SCO is rapidly developing into an important player in the Asian regional
landscape."[2] Indeed, Zhao Huasheng, the director of the Center for SCO
Studies at Fudan University, contends that the "SCO has the potential to
develop into the most influential regional organization in this part of the
world."[3] Hence, there are several compelling reasons to include this in our
study of regional alignment dynamics, all of which resonate with the book's
initial orientating themes of "order," "architecture," and "region."

First, the SCO, spearheaded by the Sino-Russian strategic partnership,
in "Moscow and Beijing's view, is for other governments to organise a multipolar order in which other centres of power counterbalance the lone superpower or hegemon."[4] Geir Flikke attests that "both are status-seekers in
international affairs, with the SCO serving as a vehicle for and manifestation of their transformed relationship, but also as a platform for claiming
wider ambitions in international affairs."[5] And these ambitions are backed
by formidable power resources. As Pál Dunay observes, "The makeup of
the SCO is . . . impressive. The group of members and observers entail ten
states, 2.8 billion people, 34 million square kilometers, the control of 47
percent of the world's gas reserves and half of the world's nuclear weapon
states."[6] Now that India and Pakistan have become full members, the SCO's
critical mass will henceforth multiply further, as discussed below.[7] This
enormous potential would allow it to form a significant counterweight to
the Trilateral Security Dialogue (TSD) and extended US alliance system
discussed in Chapter 3. Thus, Paul Dibb posits that "this is starting to look

141

like the beginnings of a new continental alignment opposed to US hegemony and maritime dominance."[8] At the 2016 Summit meeting, Presidents Xi Jinping and Vladimir Putin enunciated their intentions to create "a new Eurasian-centered concept of security clearly aimed to counter the maritime alliances of the United States," in the assessment of Michael Green.[9]

Second, the SCO is now firmly established as a key component of security architecture in Asia Pacific, although its core focus began in Central Asia. As such it is indicative of Sino-Russian efforts to build "a new architecture of global security."[10] This places it into competition with the ASEAN family of regional institutions discussed in Chapter 5. William Cole and Erik Jensen advise us that "it may itself pose as a viable alternative for multilateral organizations in Asia."[11] Indeed, it is emblematic of new efforts on the part of Beijing to shape regional/global architecture to its tastes, with Niklas Swanström affirming that the "SCO is primarily a Chinese organization, in the sense that China is the main funder and its driving engine."[12] Thus, it can be considered as a proving ground for Chinese approaches to order and alignment, advanced variously under the labels of "new security concept," "peaceful rise/development," "new state-to-state relations," "harmonious world," "win-win relations," and the "China dream" (to date).[13] Aris views it as "a crucial test case of China's regional strategy, especially given that there is already evidence of the Chinese leadership seeking to replicate its approach to the SCO in other regions of the world."[14] It likewise represents a major platform of Russia's attempted "pivot" toward the Asia Pacific, according to Alexander Lukin.[15]

Lastly, it is also to a large degree a "regionalist" project, since it is designed "to create a new security model for Central Asia," according to Yevgeny Kozhokin.[16] Interestingly, Michael Clarke discerns that this model "exhibits both 'soft' (promoting a sense of regional awareness/community) and 'hard' (regionalism formalized by interstate arrangements) elements of regionalism."[17] One of its major functions is to harness the geopolitically and geo-economically significant Central Asian "hinterland"—an area rich in key strategic resources—for privileged Chinese and Russian use. The Central Asian states are important because "each is supported by some combination of rich resources, critical geostrategic positioning, and other assets such as military bases that gives it persuasive clout in foreign policy matters."[18] It is also designed to exclude Western interference in this region. From this perspective, it is worth remembering that the combined region sits astride what early twentieth-century geopolitical writer Halford Mackinder dubbed the "Heartland" of the "World Island." In his writings, Mackinder argued that control of this region would lead to dominance of the entire Eurasian continent and serve as a platform for global domination—the greatest danger to offshore "maritime balancers" such as the TSD.[19]

On these bases, the SCO is finally attracting the attention it deserves from strategic commentators and academics—as it should, since, in the estimation of Alyson Bailes and Pál Dunay, "The SCO both channels and illuminates many of the most interesting issues and themes of Asian security today."[20] In the decade I first began work on this topic, the relevant literature has mushroomed. Analyses of the SCO are diverse in their perspectives and interpretations and, until very recently, have largely failed to convincingly grapple with how this novel organization represents a new form of security alignment. In this chapter, I seek to assist in overcoming this shortcoming by applying the dedicated analytical framework outlined in Chapter 6 to structure and enhance our understanding of this ambiguous case study.

The SCO as an Alignment

Neither Alliance nor Security Community

As in the case of ASEAN (Chapter 5) and variations of US alliances (Chapter 3), the initial question to pose is: exactly what type of alignment is the SCO? This question is followed by: how can we make analytical/conceptual sense of it? These are difficult questions given that, at present, as Matthew Crosston laments, "there is little analysis of the SCO in terms of its theoretical makeup."[21] The SCO, with the Sino-Russian axis as its heart, certainly conforms to our prior definitions of *alignment* in Chapter 1, which shall not be repeated here. According to Matthew Oresman, it is clearly identifiable as a "political community with an operational capability."[22] Moreover, it deliberately *excludes* non-Eurasian powers from its membership, evidenced by the fact that the United States has pointedly been denied "observer" status. In recognition of this, two of the field's most prominent practical and theoretical analysts of the phenomenon, Michael Green and Rajan Menon, respectively, have specifically labeled it a "new alignment"[23] and an "alignment," in recent works. The term has now taken hold in some of the more specialist literature as well.[24]

Nevertheless, as anticipated, many analysts have reached for the conventional alliance paradigm (Chapter 2) to characterize the SCO, consequently resulting in some skewed understandings. Oresman states that "a reasoned analysis indicates that the SCO . . . does not fit in the Cold War paradigms often applied to it by observers."[25] Not surprisingly, since Zhang Deguang, the first SCO Secretary General, declared that "it is not an ordinary organization of cooperation. On the one hand, the SCO cooperation on security is not carried out in the way of a traditional military bloc such as

NATO; on the other hand, its economic cooperation is not aimed at closer integration as in the EU."[26] It is therefore quite inaccurate at present to describe the SCO as akin to a "NATO East" or "China's NATO."[27] On the other hand, it is evidently much more than a simple security dialogue forum, like many of the "ASEAN-plus" institutions (discussed previously in Chapter 5). As Thomas Ambrosio notes, "a cursory examination of its founding documents and later statements illustrates that the SCO is not meant to be just another intergovernmental 'talking shop.'"[28]

As a consequence, according to Aris, the SCO is theoretically seen as problematic "because it does not fit western 'alliance' or 'EU-security [community]' paradigms."[29] The SCO does not qualify as an alliance, since it eschews a formal military defense pact and has no integrated military command structure. It does, however, embody various other treaties and plainly focuses on military/security cooperation. For instance, the SCO does incorporate a mutual assistance clause ("immediate consultations") among members faced with separatist or terrorist uprisings. Tumurkhuleg Tugsbilguun, in his detailed investigation into whether the SCO constitutes an "alliance," concludes that though it displays some alliance-type properties, it does not conform to generally accepted definitions of such.[30] As a corollary, he concludes that "traditional alliance theory has a limited application to explaining the phenomenon of SCO."[31]

Likewise, it cannot be accommodated comfortably through the "security community" paradigm. Unlike ASEAN, it has produced no definitive blueprint for creating a security community, and its grounding in the Sino-Russian strategic partnership makes it structurally distinct from this paradigm. Nevertheless, some congruities with this paradigm are to be detected, with the work of Marc Lanteigne highlighting the presence of "identity" and "norms" within the SCO, factors commonly associated with the security communities/constructivist approach.[32]

A Strategic Partnership "Network"

The SCO, as its instigators are at pains to point out, is a new (or nontraditional) form of alignment, one that subsumes a few of the common traits of alliance and security community but exhibits unfamiliar or novel characteristics of cooperation. Jingdong Yuan argues that Beijing is "promoting *a new type of state-to-state relationship based on partnership rather than alliance.*"[33] Therefore, its relations with Central Asian states and with its major partner, Russia, can be specifically framed through strategic partnership paradigm outlined in Chapter 6. As Farkhad Tolipov reminds us, "This is a special type of cooperation based on long-term relations, permanent common strategic interests, and cooperation in practically all spheres based on shared or close security interest . . . and close positions on key international issues."[34]

But the SCO as an alignment is more complex than this might suggest and deviates slightly from the basic (bilateral) model heretofore proposed. More accurately, this alignment case study operates at the intersection of the Sino-Russian strategic partnership and both powers' network of bilateral partnerships with individual Central Asian states, upon which is superimposed the institutional apparatus of the SCO itself. As Ambrosio points out, "This alignment is underpinned by a complex, comprehensive, and growing network of agreements which have institutionalized the bilateral relationship and elevated it beyond typical, ad hoc arrangements."[35] Let us briefly illustrate these important intersections to sketch out the "network approach" adopted here.

First, it is necessary to indicate the central role played by the bilateral Sino-Russian strategic partnership, as this served as the precondition for the creation of the SCO and remains its central locus of action.[36] Fu Ying attests that "the Chinese-Russian relationship is a stable strategic partnership and by no means a marriage of convenience: it is complex, sturdy, and deeply rooted."[37] Therefore, according to Zhao Huasheng, "the SCO was a natural outcome of the development of the Sino-Russian strategic partnership."[38] With this great power alignment as its nucleus, Andrew Korybko believes that "the SCO, although being a multilateral framework, essentially functions as a bilateral entity for larger Russian-Chinese cooperation, using Central Asia as a practice ground for future applications elsewhere."[39]

Second, while the bilateral Sino-Russian strategic partnership undoubtedly forms the raison d'être and core of the larger SCO, intraorganizational relations among China, Russia, and the various Central Asian states are more complex than a simple "2+4" formula might suggest. The SCO is rather the embodiment of multiple strategic partnership dyads into a combined institutional form: a "strategic partnership network." Many transactions within the membership are not actually conducted through institutional channels but rather done bilaterally. It is therefore nested in a web of associated treaties and agreements. Ambrosio states that such "treaty nestedness holds that states accede to international agreements which are embedded or nested in other international agreements to create a complex, interconnected, and self-reinforcing structure of bilateral and multilateral ties."[40] Headed by the Sino-Russian strategic partnership, it subsumes existing or desired strategic partnerships between these two powers and the individual Central Asian states (e.g., China-Kazakhstan, China-Tajikistan, Russia-Uzbekistan). Shirin Akiner notes that "not only do these different sets of relationships intersect all the other sets, forming interlocking and overlapping sub-clusters, they are also extremely fluid, constantly fluctuating."[41]

Drawing on organizational networking theory, she identifies that "although it has the attributes of a formal Organization, in essence it is a loosely meshed network which embraces and encourages diverse linkages and clusters. This openness and flexibility sparks synergies by facilitating and multiplying ties between partners with common interests and complementarities."[42] This essential characteristic should be borne in mind throughout the following analysis.

The extension of the SCO beyond Central Asia and across wider Eurasia (the "SCO-plus" model) is specifically discussed in the last section of this chapter. Moreover, it should be noted that the accession of India and Pakistan as full members in 2017 is likely to have significant ramifications in the future. This issue is also dealt with briefly in the section preceding the chapter's conclusions. However, at the time the book was completed, neither substantive empirical evidence nor significant relevant literature was available to fully analyze the impact of this development on the case study, and this must therefore be treated as a prospective avenue for further research. Finally, as with the previous case studies, the narrative of the SCO's development is woven into the analytical framework and not presented separately in advance (see Appendix).

Analytical Framework: Stages of Strategic Partnership

There has been an increasing tendency to apply theories of organization or institution to enhance our understanding of the SCO, as seen in the work of Timur Dadabaev, who draws upon functionalism,[43] and Weiqing Song, who adopts a similar framework to the one adopted here, examining "organizational formalization, functional cooperation and membership enlargement."[44] On this basis, the main text now tracks the development of the SCO using the "strategic partnership" analytical framework set out in Chapter 6. It examines and further elaborates upon the drivers and dynamics behind its formation, mode of implementation, and organizational structure before proceeding to an evaluation of its successes and failures, and concluding with its prospects for future advancement.[45]

Formation Stage

This section accounts for the formation of the SCO, examining the key factors of environmental "uncertainty," "strategic fit," "system principle," and "leadership." It should be noted that it is widely acknowledged that the formation of the SCO and its continued evolution remain in many ways quite inseparable from that of the Sino-Russian strategic partnership at its core, as reflected in the following analysis. Indeed, Aris notes that "it is possible to see SCO as a barometer of the state of Russo-Chinese relations, as up to the present time the development of SCO has mirrored the evolution of their bilateral relationship."[46]

Environmental uncertainty. To understand the formation of the SCO in 2001, we must first go back to the extraordinary Sino-Russian rapprochement of the early to mid-1990s, out of which their strategic partnership and the Shanghai Five (S5) grouping emerged.[47] Aris records that "the momentum created by the upturn in bilateral relations between Moscow and Beijing provided the driving force for the development of the SCO."[48] Since the collapse of the Sino-Soviet alliance in the late 1950s, Beijing-Moscow relations had been highly antagonistic, characterized by ideological warfare and extensive militarization of their common land borders.[49] Throughout the Cold War, a potential Sino-Soviet conflict remained a serious possibility. In 1969, there was a brief border clash between Soviet and Chinese troops on the Ussuri River, and Moscow apparently contemplated a preemptive nuclear strike against the People's Republic of China (PRC) to disable its nascent atomic weapons capability.[50] In the early 1970s, the Henry Kissinger–Richard Nixon missions to Beijing resulted in a cautious diplomatic alignment between the PRC and the United States against their common foe—the Soviet Union.[51] This remained the case through the later Cold War period, until Moscow's own rapprochement with Washington from 1985 onward. Yet the transformation of the international system resulting from the end of the Cold War and collapse of the Soviet bloc also had profound effects upon the Eurasian and Central Asian security environment, creating space for a reordering of security relationships in this region.

On these bases, the formation of the strategic partnership was animated by extreme "uncertainty" in a seemingly unipolar post–Cold War order dominated by the United States. Thus, Lanteigne notes, "The fracturing of the Soviet Union provided just such a catalyst not only for the Central Asian states but also for Russia and China."[52] From Beijing's perspective, the collapse of the Warsaw Pact and Soviet Union voided their own tacit alignment with the United States, since Washington no longer needed the PRC to counterbalance Moscow. Indeed, the United States had led the charge in criticizing and isolating the PRC after the 1989 Tiananmen Square crackdown and resultant Western arms embargo. As a newly assertive and "unilateralist" Washington, no longer contained by the Eastern bloc, flexed its muscles internationally, Beijing increasingly began to view US policy with resentment and alarm. US military demonstrations in the Taiwan Strait in 1996 outraged the Chinese Communist Party (CCP), which considered relations with the "renegade province" of Taiwan a strictly "internal matter." American humiliation of China continued with the bombing of the Chinese embassy in Belgrade (1999) and the interception of a US spy plane over Chinese territory in 2001, as well as heightened rhetoric of an emerging "Chinese threat." As it became clear that Washington was not only maintaining but enhancing its bilateral alliance system in Asia Pacific, despite the absence of its original raison d'être—the Soviet threat—Beijing recognized it was now the potential target (dubbed by Washington as a "strategic competitor"). Chien Peng-Cheng notes that "China consider[ed] American attempts to establish, maintain or strengthen strategic alliances with countries in Asia as potentially threatening to China's military and economic security."[53] When Moscow took steps to mend fences with the PRC, "Beijing was happy to respond favorably to Russia's attempts over recent decades to build a partnership."[54]

For Moscow's part, initial high hopes that the Russian Federation would become a true member of the West and equal partner with Washington were quickly dashed only years after the Kremlin had ended the Cold War largely through Mikhail Gorbachev's "new thinking" approach to foreign policy. Moscow's immediate post–Cold War pro-Western or "Atlanticist" stance was rebuffed by the United States and European Union (EU), who appeared more concerned with humbling than accommodating their former communist foe.[55] This Western snub caused Russian policy to swing toward a "Eurasianist" approach. Key elements of this foreign policy turn included reassertion of Russian influence in the "near abroad," including Central Asia, and a decision to bury the hatchet with China. Russian policymakers, "disappointed with what they saw as unfulfilled pledges of American and European assistance and irritated by talk of NATO's eastward expansion, began to pay more attention to Asia."[56] Thus began a concerted effort to repair and enhance bilateral relations with the PRC and establish joint condominium in eastern Eurasia. Quite simply, "the West was ignoring Russia and sanctioning China (for Tiananmen), so the two turned to each other."[57]

Strategic fit. As the strategic partnerships framework predicts, the response to environmental "uncertainty" is to search for partners with a good "strategic fit."[58] In this sense, in Swanström's words, Russia was deemed "the perfect partner for a rising China."[59] In 1994, Beijing and Moscow agreed to label their enhanced bilateral relations as a "constructive partnership." Huiyun Feng notes that "the major purpose of the 'constructive partnership' [was] to reduce mutual fears originating from uncertainty and threats from each other."[60] Various confidence-building measures (CBMs) acted to dispel border tensions and allow for progressive demilitarization of their neighboring regions as perceptions were rapidly transformed from "threat" to "friend." The corollary was that "unlike during the

Cold War, China and Russia no longer fear engaging in a shooting war."[61] This development led to the "strategic partnership" declaration in 1996 (the third Sino-Russian Joint Statement on "partnership of strategic coordination"),[62] alongside the formation of the Shanghai Five mechanism (with Kazakhstan, Kyrgyzstan, and Tajikistan), the precursor to the SCO. This was followed by steadily expanding CBMs, such as the Treaty on Deepening Military Trust in Border Regions (1996), Treaty on Reduction of Military Forces in Border Regions (1997), and the axial Treaty of Good-Neighborliness and Friendly Cooperation (2001).

The S5/SCO aimed at bringing Astana, Bishkek, Dushanbe, and Tashkent (later in 2001) into the new Sino-Russian security fold. The leaders of the so-called Stans were likewise faced with acute uncertainty. As Aris notes: "As a result of the internal uncertainty and competition for authority within less developed states, their political and security landscapes are dominated by the prevailing authorities' desire to ensure the strength and stability of their position as the pinnacle of this authority."[63] The primary reason that the Central Asian states embraced the protection of the great powers under the S5/SCO umbrella was "regime security." The governments of Central Asia found their form of authoritarian dictatorship under siege by global trends that apparently favored liberal democracy, a movement championed by the American "End of History" philosophy and manifested in a series of apparently democratic uprisings in other former Soviet countries. Yuan argues that "concern over the impact of contagious 'colored revolutions' in the region has led Central Asian governments to seek greater ties with Russia and, to some extent, with China for regime stability and security."[64] In this respect, it was natural for the smaller states of Central Asia to pursue protection and patronage from their powerful neighbors against external forces. This entirely dovetailed with Moscow's thinking. As David Hale notes, "the Russians have supported incumbent regimes in Central Asia because they have been long-standing allies."[65]

The formation stage was also predicated upon the "strategic fit" between China and Russia, and between these powers and their Central Asian neighbors. Bailes and Dunay note that "China and Russia, for their part, are linked by their status as nuclear weapon states, permanent membership of the UN Security Council and long experience (in Russia's case, now ended) of Communist rule."[66] A high degree of economic complementarity, compatibility of domestic regimes, and a shared worldview served to unite the partners. While China sought access to advanced Russian military technology, now that it was embargoed by the West, the ailing Russian economy desperately needed trade and investment from its rising neighbor. They also became mutually aware of the increasing importance of Central Asia and sought to collaborate rather than compete in some form of a new "great game" toward this pivotal local region.[67] For Moscow, the motivators were primarily geopolitical: reasserting waning influence in its former Soviet backyard. Without cooperation with Beijing in Central Asia, Russia might well find itself increasingly marginalized. Meanwhile, for Beijing, Marcel de Haas writes, "the SCO is a vehicle for China to advance its economic aims in Central Asia."[68] This objective is highly reciprocal, as Henry Plater-Zyberk identifies that "the four Central Asian members of the SCO saw the two regional super-powers and economic locomotives as natural allies."[69] These states were happy to encourage investment and infrastructure assistance from Beijing and Moscow to facilitate the export of their rich natural resources and underwrite their national economic development.

The SCO was formed as a vehicle for various cooperative endeavors, not only to secure Central Asia from nontraditional security (NTS) threats emanating from restive terrorist, criminal, or separatist groups, but to protect the vulnerable eastern and southern flanks for China and Russia, respectively. With respect to ensuring "peace and stability in the region," according to Bailes and Dunay, "The SCO's primary focus remains defined in the 2001 Convention on Combating Terrorism, Separatism and Extremism."[70] These so-called three evils form a nexus of NTS threats across the Central Asian region, often emanating from neighboring Afghanistan. SCO cooperation was therefore designed to target groups such as the Islamic Movement of Uzbekistan, Hizb-ut-Tahrir, and the East Turkestan Islamic Movement across the region. In addition to instability in Chechnya and Kyrgyzstan (e.g., the Tulip Revolution), China's Xinjiang Uighur Autonomous Region was a serious cause for concern. As Yuan identifies, "Beijing is particularly concerned with the spill-over effect of the resurgent terrorist activities in Central Asia on Xinjiang and its Uighur ethnic group."[71] A common inward-facing threat based upon these lines therefore acted as a catalyst for the formation of the SCO, mirroring this aspect of the ASEAN Security Community (ASC) case study.

But there is an interesting twist to this "natural" alignment of interests. This grouping contains a strong element of *pactum de contrahendo*, in other words, a means of mutually "restraining" partners as well as aligning toward common purposes. De Haas determines that "Chinese cooperation with Russia is aimed not only at restraining American power but also at precluding close cooperation towards China between Moscow and Washington."[72] In this sense, James Bosbotinis argues that China aims at "'containing' Russia and minimizing external influences on the Western flank, enabling it to focus on the Asia-Pacific."[73] Interestingly, their partnership also embodies an "exclusionary" clause within the current Sino-Russian Treaty (2001) prohibiting either country from joining other alliances or blocs considered prejudicial to the other's sovereignty and security.[74] For

Moscow, alignment with China is a way of mediating relations with a potential rival or foe and avoiding a contest for hegemony in Central Asia. As Zakir Chotaev has pointed out, the SCO is a "structure that allows Moscow to control and limit Beijing's activities in Central Asia."[75] This dynamic is also true for the Central Asian states themselves. Though they welcome Chinese economic largesse, they prefer political/cultural ties with Russia and remain dependent on many logistical and infrastructural assets under Moscow's control. Indeed, "the region remains Russia's sphere of influence due to historical reasons and therefore Central Asian states remain cautious with regard to China's growing presence."[76] By balancing the two major powers within the organization, they escape domination by one power or both jointly. Thus, "to Kazakhstan, the SCO is not only a channel for its cooperation with China and Russia, but also a means to balance relations among the two dominant powers."[77]

System principle. The organization's founding in 2001 was swiftly followed by the SCO Charter (2002), which outlines the "system principle," the raison d'être for its existence. First, the SCO is aimed at "strengthening mutual confidence and good-neighbourly relations among the member countries."[78] Beyond this statement of good-neighborliness, it is designed for "maintenance and strengthening of peace, security and stability in the [Central Asian] region and promotion of a new democratic, fair and rational political and economic international order."[79] The first objective testifies to the inward-looking focus of the SCO, ensuring regional and regime security against transnational and NTS threats, especially the nexus between the "three evils" of terrorism, separatism, and extremism. Second, this regional alignment has externally oriented objectives—publicly seeking "establishment of a new, democratic, just and rational order," though underlining that it is not "targeted at any third party country." The operational content of these objectives and the efforts to implement them through "functional areas of cooperation" are considered at length in the following section of this chapter.

Leadership. As the framework predicts, leadership has been key in the formation of the strategic partnership. Aris affirms that "the SCO, like ASEAN, has adopted a model of cooperation driven more by political elites, at least in the initial development stage."[80] Bilateral strengthening occurred under the tenure of President Boris Yeltsin and continued to be pushed vigorously by his successor Vladimir Putin, under whom the actual SCO was founded (2001). The CCP under President Hu Jintao was also a strong advocate of increased Sino-Russian cooperation and the SCO. Hale notes that "China has played a major leadership role in encouraging them to come together in an organization to promote both security and economic cooperation."[81] What is remarkable is the investment that the Chinese leadership has put into the creation of the SCO. Thus, Pan Guang attests that "China has actively pushed forward the institutionalization of the SCO since its foundation."[82]

Implementation Stage

This section considers the results of "a conscious choice by the organization to focus on the implementation of the agenda and programmes discussed and developed in the mid-2000s."[83] Rather than fully list the vast range of summits, treaties, and other agreements in full here (see Appendix), this section now seeks to present a simplified picture of an extraordinary, complex networked "meta-organization." As noted above, "a treaty network consists of a number of agreements which create an interconnected and interlocking web of obligations and responsibilities."[84] This "network" element, identified earlier by Akiner, results in "a mind-bendingly complex structure—metaphorically speaking, a multi-dimensional game of noughts and crosses."[85]

Notwithstanding, in accord with the strategic partnership framework provided, Song points out "a well-defined hierarchy and functional specialization," which can be assembled into vertical and horizontal institutional axes.[86] The section ends with an appreciation of the development of an organizational culture arising from this official structure and derived from its official charter. Lastly, it should be noted that much of the formal and informal institutional makeup of the SCO strongly reflects the activities of the Sino-Russian strategic partnership at its core. Therefore, references to the former may ostensibly stand as representing those of the latter throughout the following analysis.

Organizational hierarchy. Though in its official declarations the SCO conforms to the basic principles of a "strategic partnership," namely, a "spirit of mutual trust, mutual advantage, equality, mutual consultations, respect for cultural diversity and aspiration for joint development,"[87] as the framework predicts, the reality is more complicated. There are several notable and interlocking structural characteristics of the SCO. First to note is its present domination by Beijing and Moscow (and perhaps soon also by India, as a result of its membership in 2017). Though relations between members are officially equal, these great powers clearly outclass the other members in terms of economic and military power, allowing them to monopolize the organization in every way.

Second, stemming from this is a blurring of the boundaries between bilateralism and multilateralism—its "networked" facet. The "core" Sino-

Russian bilateral strategic partnership is embedded in a multilateral context. However, as alluded to above, it is difficult to adjudge where bilateralism ends and multilateralism begins. Unusually, Tolipov notes that "Russian-Chinese security cooperation paradoxically manifests itself as bilateralism within SCO multilateralism."[88] However, countering potential domination of the SCO by China and Russia are various intraorganizational bilateral strategic partnerships.

Within this broader context, the SCO has elaborated an intricate framework of organizational interaction, "coupling" the member states along a vertical hierarchy. Further information is provided by the SCO's organizational chart (Figure 7.1). At the apex of the organizational hierarchy are the Heads of State Council and Heads of Government Council, the highest decisionmaking bodies. These councils meet annually for summit meetings, which rotate between the member states. This arrangement is noteworthy because it ensures that power remains in the hands of the leadership of sovereign states, rather than being devolved to a transnational body. Thus, "the direction of the SCO is predominately conceived by the national elites."[89] As Aris notes, "the summit of the national leaderships is the most important event in the SCO's calendar and defines the direction of the organization for the forthcoming year."[90] Multinational policy initiatives are implemented by a Council of National Coordinators, an "SCO body coordinating and directing day-to-day activities of the Organization."[91] The member states are also bureaucratically represented

Figure 7.1 The Structure of the Shanghai Cooperation Organisation

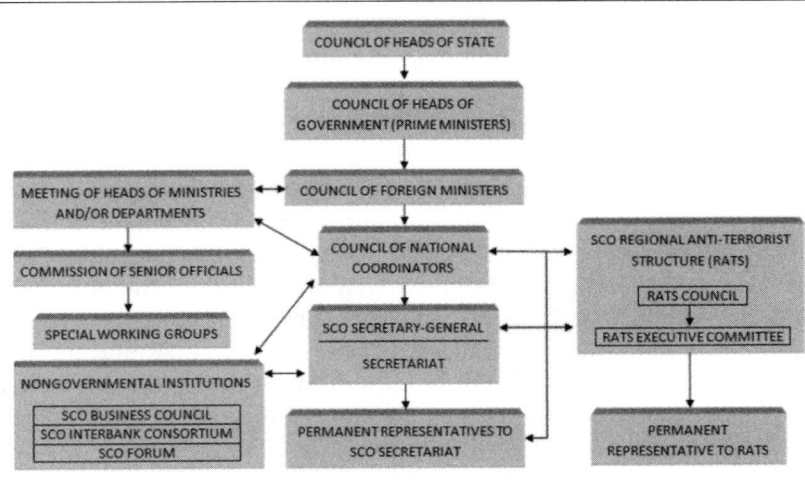

by speakers of Parliament; secretaries of security councils; foreign ministers; ministers of defense, emergency relief, economy, transportation, culture, education, healthcare; heads of law enforcement agencies; supreme
courts and courts of arbitration; and prosecutors general, who meet as
required to coordinate joint policy.[92]

The SCO has two major permanent organs. The Secretariat is the
"bureaucratic backbone of the organization"[93] based in Beijing, with a
Secretary-General appointed on a three year rotating basis. According to
the charter, the Secretariat functions as the

> main permanent executive body of the SCO and carries out coordination,
> information-analytical, legal and organizational and technical support of
> activities of the Organization, develops proposals on enhancing of cooper-
> ation within the SCO and international relations of the Organization,
> supervises the implementation of decisions of SCO bodies.[94]

The second permanent structure is the Regional Anti-Terrorist Structure (RATS), with an executive committee director, similarly appointed.
The RATS, located in Tashkent, governs joint responses to the "three
evils"—one of the organization's core activities. Beyond this are a plethora
of associated commissions, special working groups, and nongovernmental
organizations.[95] Lastly, the SCO maintains external *interorganizational
relationships*, holding observer status in the UN General Assembly and
having Memoranda of Understanding with ASEAN, the Collective Security
Treaty Organization (CSTO), and Commonwealth of Independent States.
Together, based upon the 2001 SCO Charter (as the organization's foundational document), the various councils/meetings and permanent organs
serve to lock "the parties into predictable and reliable patterns of behaviour,
as well as conflict resolution mechanisms which can ensure that issues that
do arise do not undermine the relationship."[96]

Functional areas of collaboration. As with any organization, the SCO
"seeks to be relevant to the member states and help them achieve both
their practical and political goals."[97] The remit of the organization is extensive, with the SCO Charter specifying a wide range of issue-areas for
cooperation. Indeed, from its modest beginnings, it now engages in such
"areas as politics, trade and economy, defense, law enforcement, environment protection, culture, science and technology, education, energy, transport, credit and finance, and also other areas of common interest."[98] In
accord with the framework presented in Chapter 6, this section collates
these activities in four key "functional areas of cooperation": diplomatic
and strategic collaboration, security and military coordination, economic
interaction, and sociocultural exchange.

Diplomatic and strategic collaboration. Coordinated policy on the grand strategic and diplomatic front serves as a penumbra under which other functional areas operate. Now "it has clear principles that it promotes within the international system," embodied in the "system principle."[99] Indeed, policy declarations have included a Sino-Russian declaration on "A New 21st-Century World Order."[100] The joint diplomatic outlook for the SCO proposes a multipolar world, a stronger emphasis on the UN, and a new security model for Central Asia. It opposes military alliance blocs, US hegemony, and attempts by the West to intervene in Central Asia or elsewhere to impose their preferred liberal democratic principles. Aris demonstrates that "integral to this has been a number of high-profile joint statements on contemporary international events and the international system in general. This common narrative on international relations is now evident within the SCO, in particular in the common declarations issued at the annual SCO summit."[101] When using the SCO as a diplomatic platform, Richard Weitz posits that "Chinese and Russian leaders appreciate that their combined statements resonate louder than the pronouncements of each government speaking unilaterally."[102] Specific examples of successes and failures on this score are evaluated in the next section of this chapter.

Security and military coordination. In addition to general organization-framing policies and pronouncements, cooperation on security and military issues lend gravitas to this diplomatic grandstanding. Indeed, Aris declares that "security cooperation forms the main focus of the SCO."[103] In this respect, the SCO engages in an array of NTS cooperation, primarily concerning its objective of fighting terrorism, separatism, and extremism in Central Asia and beyond, as well as more conventional forms of military-defense cooperation. Pan asserts that "regional security cooperation must be based on 'comprehensive security' with the handling of conventional security threats combined closely with the handling of non-conventional threats."[104]

The organization's official mission to tackle the three evils of terrorism, separatism, and extremism is charged to the RATS, in addition to each member state's national efforts. RATS collects and analyzes data on terrorist groups, conducts studies on WMD, and prepares and coordinates antiterrorist legislation, building upon bilateral intelligence-sharing agreements.[105] This extends to agreements on cybersecurity or "information war," including a 2009 accord that took a strong stance against those seeking to use the Internet to undermine another's "political, economic, and social systems." Using the phrase "mass psychologic[al] brainwashing," the agreement declared that the dissemination of information "harmful to the spiritual, moral and cultural spheres of other states" represented a major "security threat."[106] A team of experts on international information security has also been set up. Other transnational threats such as criminal organizations, drug trafficking, and illegal migration fall under the ambit of RATS, in cooperation with the CSTO. Related to this, "Afghanistan is both a factor of regional instability helping to drive the current SCO members together, and a state that shares several prima facie objectives with them."[107] The establishment of an SCO-Afghanistan Contact Group and granting of Observer status is recognition of this.[108]

Interestingly, rather than "whole of government" responses, as are seen in the West and elsewhere, "all the members have a distinctly militarized approach to combating 'new threats,'" according to Bailes and Dunay.[109] To this purpose, the SCO members engage in military staff exchange and education programs and share intelligence and other assets. The organization commenced regular military exercises from 2005, euphemistically dubbed "Peace Missions."[110] In 2014, Russia and China also engaged in a joint naval drill in the East China Sea.[111] In fact, de Haas argues, such regularized defense cooperation actually has "little to do with warfare against terrorism," but more to do with "the practice of conventional warfare, employing all services except for nuclear forces."[112] War planning scenarios are often predicated on potential "breakaway" provinces or separatist or terrorist insurrections (e.g., Taiwan, Caucasus). As Liselotte Odgaard notes, in conformity with the analytical framework, "these include the benefits of training for both China and Russia, enabling them to *learn* from the practices of their partner."[113] Increasing doctrinal and technological interoperability through such exercises neatly dovetails with the third leg of military/security cooperation: arms transfers. Russia and, to a lesser extent, China supply the region with the bulk of its military hardware. This is underwritten by service, support, training, and in some cases, production rights for Russian hardware.[114] Arms transfers form a significant tranche of intraregional trade, the topic to which we now turn.

Economic interactions. As the framework indicates, economic relations also act as a prime mover in regional collaboration. Indeed, "economic development has been a constant priority for SCO."[115] Chinese industrial power, combined with Russian and Central Asian energy resources, create an economic bloc of great potential behind the diplomatic front of the SCO. Various efforts are under way aimed at realizing some form of Eurasian economic integration: SCO Business Council; action plan for reduction of trade barriers; working groups on e-commerce, customs, quality inspection, investment promotion, transport; creation of SCO Development Fund and Business Forum; Interbank Association (2006–2007). Eventually, a free trade area is envisaged, slated for 2020. Such initiatives complement, but also vie with, Russia's Eurasian Economic Union (EEU), which includes all of the SCO members except China, with which the SCO has signed a memorandum of understanding (MOU). But Beijing also has a range of its own economic policies that impact the SCO, which are aimed at unifying the historical "Silk Road" region. These policies fall under the umbrella term "Belt and Road Initiative" (BRI) (previously "One Belt, One Road" [OBOR]) and include the Asian Infrastructure Investment Bank (AIIB), in which Russia participates.[116]

Joint energy extraction and infrastructure projects are also among the organization's key priorities. The SCO has emerged as a "convenient platform for concluding energy deals, also on a bilateral level."[117] Cooperation occurs in the oil and gas sectors, joint exploration of new hydrocarbon sources, and water management projects.[118] China has major petroleum holdings in Kazakhstan and major oil pipeline projects are in motion to supply the PRC, with the Atasu-Xinjiang pipeline, Eastern Siberia–Pacific Ocean oil pipeline, and Central Asia natural gas pipeline as exemplary initiatives.[119] While economic exchanges are viewed as a part of the SCO's remit, in line with Pan's assertion, de Haas highlights that "economic cooperation is also regarded from a security dimension: fighting poverty will also remove the grounds of the 'three evils,' i.e. terrorism, separatism and extremism."[120]

"Soft power" and sociocultural exchange. The final functional area of cooperation within the SCO is collaboration on "soft power" issues, exemplified across a range of intraregional cultural connections. First, in 2002, a Declaration on Cultural Cooperation was issued, with the Chinese culture minister stating that "cultural exchanges and cooperation among SCO member states will play an irreplaceable role in promoting mutual understanding and traditional friendship among the six peoples, and further all-round cooperation among the six countries."[121] Subsequent efforts to build people-to-people linkages have included sporting events, joint festivals and exhibitions, student and academic exchange programs, professional training, youth exchanges, and tourism, according to Pan.[122] These are in addition to a wide range of bilateral youth, media, and language exchanges held between China and Russia. Second, like ASEAN, the SCO has Track II support from various epistemic communities, specifically the SCO Forum, and within its member states. Prestigious think tanks in China, such as the Shanghai Academy for Social Sciences, have a Centre for SCO Studies.[123]

Finally, any established institution will give rise to a distinct organizational culture, including what constructivists term *norms.*[124] This culture formally or informally shapes patterns of behavior and interaction in the organization and can form a distinct part of its identity. Emilian Kavalski posits that "SCO's pattern of dynamic interactions intimates the emergence of a particular institutional culture and identity."[125] First, the SCO is strictly an intergovernmental multilateral organization, with a strong emphasis on national sovereignty and personal control by national elites (per ASEAN). Aris records that "the SCO's permanently functioning organs are reliant on state resources, and are largely restricted in their mandate to the implementation of decisions and policy developed by the annual summit of the Council of Heads of State."[126] The SCO therefore remains emphatically intergovernmental, and as Akiner reminds us, "although the great majority of the initiatives that have been undertaken within the framework of SCO have not involved the Organisation as a whole, they nevertheless reflect its aims and principles."[127]

Second, the SCO's organizational identity and ideology rests upon a clearly articulated set of norms known as the "Shanghai Spirit," which closely adhere to the strategic partnership framework's prediction that a unifying "system principle" will emerge to mediate the organization (and echoing the "ASEAN way" in the previous case study). These entail the following "Principles" as specified in the SCO Charter: "mutual respect of sovereignty, independence, territorial integrity of States and inviolability of State borders, non-aggression, non-interference in internal affairs, non-use of force or threat of its use in international relations, seeking no unilateral military superiority in adjacent areas."[128] It is this mutual understanding and expectations of "correct" or "appropriate" behavior that provide cohesion to the SCO's meetings and activities. In effect, the respect for state sovereignty and noninterference in domestic politics of the member states sits well with the priority of internal security and regime security in the region (again, echoing the ASC's norms). "From this perspective," Aris notes, "the 'Shanghai spirit' is conceived not as a formal structure of regulations, but a shared set of beliefs and principles that should guide the progression of the organization."[129] Third, it will be apparent that these conform closely to China's own normative conceptions of a "new security concept" (adopted by SCO in 2012),[130] "harmonious world," and its subsequent permutations. Kavalski alerts us that "the region has gradually been socialized into Beijing's worldview through the promotion of various initiatives for regional cooperation ultimately consolidated in the Shanghai Cooperation Organization."[131]

Evaluation Stage

In official pronouncements at summit meetings, Beijing and Moscow have naturally lauded the achievements of the SCO and described their bilateral relationship as reaching a "new level in principle."[132] From such pronouncements, Swanström concludes, "it seems evident that the bilateral relations are at an all-time high and that the shared vision of partnership between Russia and China has never been clearer."[133] But organizational rhetoric has limited utility in reaching a thorough evaluation of the SCO. On the other hand, analysts are divided in their overall evaluations of the SCO and Sino-Russian partnership at its core. First, Western analysts, principally in the United States, have taken a negative view, strangely divided between those that focus on its *strength*—a new "alliance" to threaten the West[134]—and those who focus on its *weakness*—a "marriage of convenience," without substance.[135] But this misses the point, as Odgaard argues, since "Russia and China are looking for a different type of strategic partnership, which calls for different assessment criteria compared to those used to assess relationships with Western participation."[136]

Perhaps more appositely, Chinese and Russian analysts have evinced a more nuanced and positive evaluation of the SCO. Stephen Blank identifies that "Chinese analysts highly praise the SCO and believe it to be the crowning achievement of their Central Asian policy."[137] Mikhail Troitskiy notes, "Russian mainstream analysts do not treat the SCO as an attempt at a traditional collective security arrangement. Nor do they write it off—as outside observers tend to do—as a loose grouping of states that have nothing more in common than reservations about Western policies and positions."[138]

To properly evaluate the progress of the SCO as an organization and its cohesion and effectiveness as a security alignment presents certain difficulties. As Akiner notes, "It is not easy to sum up the achievements of SCO, since much of what is happening is not immediately visible."[139] In accord with the analytical framework for evaluating strategic partnerships and drawing upon the contesting perspectives offered by analysts noted above, this section now proceeds first to evaluate its progress, or lack thereof, with regard to its stated goals (strategic/diplomatic, security/military, economic). It then looks at the conflicts and synergies among its members' interests and values before finishing with consideration of mutual perspectives among the membership. The chapter concludes with an assessment of its possible expansion or evolution.

Strategic and diplomatic collaboration. In terms of the SCO's overarching goals, it seems that moderate success has been attained in the grand-strategic and diplomatic areas. First, the Chinese and Russian leadership have successfully utilized the SCO as a larger platform from which to channel their objectives of seeking a "multipolar world" and "new political and economic world order." In practical terms, "as permanent members of the UNSC, China and Russia have been making full use of that platform to take a common stand on contentious security issues regarding Kosovo, Iraq, Iran, Sudan, Zimbabwe, Libya and Syria."[140] Moreover, by aligning together, they are also able to endorse and defend some of their own more controversial domestic policies in the international arena. Thus, "Russia and China have offered each other support on Taiwan, Tibet, and Xinjiang; and Chechnya, respectively."[141] They have also opposed Western policies such as NATO expansion (without much success),[142] as well as missile defense deployments and creeping militarization of space by the United States.[143] Moreover, the centripetal attraction of this Sino-Russian worldview is clear from the association of observer states and dialogue partners and as a model for other states otherwise un-enamored with the Western *weltanschauung*. De Haas states that by "its mere existence [it] shows the world that alternatives to American domination of security issues exist."[144]

And yet, there have been strains in this understanding as each of the major powers seeks to constrain the other (and any undermining of the "system principle"), while continuing to pursue its own national interests. For example, the SCO did not endorse Russia's 2008 foray into Georgia, which was in violation of its own "system principle." Nor did it recognize Moscow-sponsored breakaway republics of South Ossetia and Abkhazia, though it was more low-key in criticizing the Crimean and Ukrainian adventures in 2014. On the other hand, Beijing has not been pleased with Russian collaboration with Vietnam in the contested waters of the South China Sea.[145]

Second, as a vehicle for securing Central Asia within the Sino-Russian orbit, mitigating bilateral rivalry, and excluding Western interference, the SCO appears successful in imposing a form of Eurasian "Monroe Doctrine." Its initial agreements on border demarcation and additional CBMs have done much to reduce intra-regional tensions. Not only has a mixture of Sino-Russian political, military, and economic support buttressed the regime security of the Central Asian states, but development assistance and capacity-building against internal threats such as separatism, fundamentalism, and terrorism have undoubtedly prevented the region from slipping into anarchy and violence in the post-Soviet era. Yet, the SCO failed to help with the 2010–2011 Kyrgyzstan uprising, in which ethnic tensions spilled into riots between Kyrgyzstanis and Uzbeks and the removal of Kurmanbek Bakiyev from the presidency.[146] Thus Charles Ziegler points out that "the SCO's inability, or unwillingness, to assume an active role in addressing the violent events of June 2010 in Kyrgyzstan, or those of July 2012 in the Gorno-Badakhshan region of Tajikistan, highlighted the organization's limitations."[147] The conflicting principles of combating ethnic disturbance and nonintervention stymied effective organizational support.

The cordoning off of Central Asia to Western influence was also undermined when Uzbekistan (2001–2005) and Kyrgyzstan (2001–2014) hosted US bases for a period during the "War on Terror." But once Washington succumbed to the temptation to berate local regimes for their democratic and human rights deficits, these forces ended up being expelled. The decision was announced in the first case at the 2005 SCO Summit in

Astana and in the second case at a 2009 press conference of the Kyrgyz and Russian presidents.[148] In any event, it seems that Western interest and presence in this pivotal region has now been ceded to China and Russia by default, with Akhilesh Pillalamarri noting that the United States "does not have a clear, long-term plan to engage with the region, which ranks low on its list of geopolitical priorities."[149]

Security and military coordination. Stepping down a level to the security and military sphere, the SCO has been active to good effect. First, cooperation on NTS threats under the combined rubric of the "three evils" has produced tangible results. According to Aris, "there has been a marked decrease in the perceived threat of major terrorist bombings or attacks in the SCO space in the time since the RATS began its work."[150] Accurate figures are not available, but RATS claims to have trained over 1,000 personnel and averted hundreds of attacks, notably coordinating with national agencies during the 2008 Beijing Olympics and 2011 Astana Winter Asian games.

Second, the European Policy Centre notes that "since the SCO's formation, militant separatist activity in Central Asia has calmed down noticeably."[151] For Beijing, having the cooperation of its Central Asian border states in tracking and intercepting Uighur separatist-activists has been invaluable. Now "the threat from Islamic inspired terrorism and separatism in China has declined substantially and the SCO is seen by the Chinese authorities as a key element in this."[152] As for transnational criminal challenges, "tangible achievements have been claimed for this activity" as exemplified by Operation KANAL-2006 involving more than 74,000 personnel and resulting in the seizure of more than 19 tons of narcotics.[153]

Due to a "securitization" element running through most collaborative activities in Central Asia, there have been multiplier effects from these achievements on overall "regime security," one of the main goals of the SCO. This is cardinal since "the SCO is a cooperative vehicle judged by the region's elites primarily on its ability to contribute to the main security concerns as they perceive them: internal challenges to their regime security."[154] In addition to peace of mind on Uighur separatism for China, Beijing and Moscow also provided cover against Western denunciations of the Andijan crackdown on dissidents in Uzbekistan in 2005, something all the Central Asian states are concerned about.[155] There are also important ramifications for economic cooperation, since "this has allowed economic programs to begin against the background of a more stable security environment."[156]

In the background to this NTS cooperation is defense collaboration of a more traditional stamp. The SCO has been used as a stage for significant military maneuvers, principally involving Chinese and Russian forces. According to Nick Bisley, these have "showed the SCO's growing ability to manage military cooperation and coordination, which is a notable achievement for an international security organization."[157] The innocuous-sounding Peace Missions have become a biannual feature of the SCO's calendar since 2005.[158] In concordance with the overall system principle above, these joint exercises send signals on political and strategic intent to external parties, with several of these drills indirectly aimed at conflict scenarios relevant to potential conflict scenarios in the Taiwan Strait and Caucasus, among others. They concurrently provide an opportunity to showcase Russian military technology to eager Chinese buyers, which forms a major pillar of Sino-Russian interaction. Since the US/EU arms embargo following the Tiananmen Square massacre of 1989, Moscow has delivered advanced technology such as Su-27 fighters, Su-30 multirole aircraft, Mi-8 and Mi-17 helicopters, Il-76 transport planes, Il-78M in-flight refueling tankers, T-72 MBTS, *Kilo* class diesel-electric submarines, and *Sovremenny*-class destroyers to China, with the Su-35 combat aircraft recently added to the list. The widespread use of Russian and Chinese equipment increases military interoperability between the SCO partners, as does the presence of Russian bases. Moreover, Moscow has assisted China with its satellite program, manned space flight, and nuclear weapons program.[159] This tight defense relationship provides substantial benefits to both the leaders of the SCO. As Alexander Korolev concludes, "China-Russia military relations have begun moving into the initial stages of deep institutionalization."[160]

Lastly, following the inter-organizational track of the SCO, Moscow has also connected the SCO to the Moscow-dominated Collective Security Treaty Organization (CSTO) defense mechanism through a "military assistance concept."[161] This further expands the capability and remit of military/defense cooperation, but it should be remembered that from Moscow's perspective, the CSTO, as a weak form of military alliance, rivals the SCO as a preferred mechanism of Central Asian security management.[162] We must also remember, however, that both Russia and China have undertaken unilateral military exercises close to joint borders, such as People's Liberation Army's (PLA's) NORTHERN SWORD-2005 and STRIDE-2009, 2014, 2015, 2016, and Russia's *TSENTR*-2008, 2011, 2015 and *VOSTOK*-2010, 2014.[163]

Economic interaction. The SCO was not officially aimed at economic integration, but it has increasingly coalesced as an unofficial economic "bloc." As "an emerging platform for regional economic cooperation," according to Chinese vice foreign minister Cheng Guoping, it has already registered some significant economic achievements and shows even greater potential, though there are some caveats to this assessment below.[164] According to data from the World Bank, the aggregate gross domestic product (GDP) of the SCO in 2015 was US$12.6 trillion, up from US$1.28 trillion at the time of the organization's establishment in 1996.[165] It is estimated that China's trade with other SCO members—Kazakhstan, Kyrgyzstan, Russia, Tajikistan, Uzbekistan—has increased more than tenfold since 1996 from US$6.69 billion to US$83.76 billion in 2015.[166] During the same time period, China's exports to them have been increased by US$44 billion, while imports from them increased by US$32 billion.[167]

At the SCO Heads of State Meeting in 2012, China and Russia pledged to increase bilateral trade to US$100 billion by 2015 (it reached US$95 billion despite sanctions against Russia)[168] and to US$200 billion by 2020.[169] In addition, in 2014 China's investment in Russia grew by 80 percent.[170] Much of the cooperation in the economic sphere aimed at trade and in particular energy supplies rests upon ambitious schemes for regional infrastructure development intersecting with the EEU and BRI, as noted earlier in this chapter. Vice Minister Cheng announced that "the member states, guided by the Program of Multilateral Trade and Economic Cooperation, have actively promoted trade and investment facilitation and carried out sound cooperation in transportation, energy, telecommunications, agriculture and other fields."[171] China and Russia have offered US$900 million and US$500 million respectively toward infrastructure development in Central Asia.[172] Former president Hu Jintao promised that China will offer a loan of US$10 billion to support economic cooperation within SCO.[173] Plans are afoot for continued gas and oil pipeline construction that will facilitate energy supplies from Russia to China, through the region and from the region to China, as well as bilateral deals between the two leading states.[174] Another milestone occurred in 2014 when Russia confirmed a US$400 billion deal for the supply of natural gas to the PRC.[175]

As the strategic partnership paradigm entails a significant economic pillar, these activities reinforce its larger security purposes detailed above. Zhao Huasheng considers that "in the long run, economic cooperation will be the most important and active factor for pushing ahead the SCO."[176] Yet there are some complications on the economic front. As noted above, China has its own national economic vision for the region as embodied in the BRI and AIIB initiatives, whereas Russia has its concept of EEU to compete with these. Though concerns were raised about the competitive nature of these initiatives, Samuel Charap, John Drennan, and Pierre Noël maintain that "the emerging cooperation between the BRI and the Eurasian Economic Union (EEU) is also indicative of the new Russia–China modus operandi."[177] The outcome remains to be seen.

Moreover, the Central Asian states and Russia are wary of too much economic integration, such as Beijing's desired Free Trade Area proposal, since they believe China would dominate this. Accordingly, "it is arguable that the speed of institutionalization is driven by China and is against Russia and the Central Asian Republics' desire for it to evolve slowly."[178] On the other hand, Russian proposals for an SCO "energy club" have likewise received a tepid response from the other members, with Beijing unhappy about Moscow's reliability in providing promised supplies. Notably, Russia is also afraid that it is becoming a raw materials appendage of China. Quite simply, Dimitri Trenin asserts that "Russia is a less important trading partner to China than China is to Russia."[179] While Russia is the world's second-largest arms supplier and has provided China with a wide range of military hardware, this core plank in their economic relationship entails some friction. As a customer, China has created tension by driving hard bargains on cost and technology transfer and violated past agreements by reverse-engineering aircraft samples.[180] Though Moscow desires orders, it is seemingly unwilling to supply its most cutting-edge technologies to the PRC at this time, which led to a decline in arms transfers in recent years. In 2015, however, Russia finally agreed to supply Su-35 combat aircraft to China on the basis of an intellectual property agreement they made in 2008.

Lastly, the achievements of the SCO may be circumscribed by its relative paucity of institutional resources. In particular, the Secretariat budget is quite limited given the scope of its aspirations to oversee all the economic projects proposed (like ASEAN). Yuan reminds us of the limits of SCO cooperation, noting that "despite the many declarations, signed agreements, and proposed projects, actual implementation is constrained due to resource limitation and the diversity of interests and priorities among member states."[181] Also, Mikhail Karpov points out that trade synergy, and thus volumes, may have reached a "structural ceiling," at least between the two main partners.[182] Further economic progress may require deeper integration, or additional membership, which may form the raison d'être for the recent accession of India.

Interests and values. As with any alignment, the SCO is united by a set of underlying common interests and values. But it will be a "complex" of intersecting but sometimes divergent interests in multiple spheres. As Yuan points out: "There are different relationships within: between China and Russia; China's and Russia's relationships with the Central Asian states; and those between the latter themselves. Given the differences in history, preferences, and interests, each has its unique priorities and focuses."[183] We will examine these below. Certainly, analysts have pointed to the narrowness in the overlap of common interests, with Troitskiy contending that "whereas NATO was founded on its members' long term commonality of values and similar threat perceptions, the SCO unites countries with diverging security and external economic agendas."[184] Again, let us examine this claim.

Prima facie, under the broad doctrine of the SCO's "system princi-ple," each member is able to interpret cooperation in ways acceptable and satisfying to their own national interests. At present, the SCO is seen as a relatively low-cost, low-risk mechanism under which joint interests can be served or accommodated. Plater-Zyberk notes that "most of the SCO's initiatives have been driven by China" as a "senior partner."[185] He contin-ues that as long as this also serves Russian interests, "Moscow does not seem to mind playing second fiddle in the SCO."[186] Indeed, Aris notes that "it has been suggested that the SCO is only as strong as the Russian-Chinese relationship, and that this relationship is inherently limited and only maintained by a common interest in creating a counterbalance to US interests."[187] Nevertheless, let us not forget that Beijing has strong incen-tives for strategic cooperation with Russia. Bosbotinis reminds us that "the securing of China's western flank enables it to maintain its current eastward focused military posture, prioritize the development of power-projection capabilities and enhance China's position in the western Pacific and South China Sea."[188] Moreover, Russia remains a major regional player and cannot be allowed to slip into the European, US, or Indian orbit, as this would seriously undermine Chinese security. Hence the notion of SCO as *pactum de contrehendo*, as noted earlier. Likewise, Moscow benefits to a degree from having China on its side, as it increas-ingly faces down NATO to its West over Crimea and Ukraine, without having to worry about its "strategic rear."

Nevertheless, Weitz records that "Chinese and Russian policies regard-ing a range of important subjects are still largely uncoordinated and some-times in conflict."[189] In particular, Oksana Antonenko argues, "China favors an SCO with an emphasis on economics, while Russia prioritizes secu-rity."[190] Though Russia and China are closely cooperating at present, Moscow has misgivings about Beijing's long-term ambitions. As a conse-quence, the Kremlin fears that it will be potentially overawed as the PRC's military and economic power continues to eclipse that of its partner, though this situation may be partially mitigated by the accession of India in 2017. For this reason, Tugsbilguun notes, from a "hard" security perspective, Moscow continues to place a firm emphasis on its relations with Central Asia in the context of the CSTO, which it naturally dominates.[191]

One of the key problems in managing divergent national interest in an organization with a diverse membership is the tendency for stronger pow-ers to dominate the weak. This must be especially so due to the divergence in power between the membership identified above. On the one hand, Weitz sees the SCO simply as "the institutional manifestation" of "shared Chinese and Russian interests."[192] S. Enders Wimbush notes that "Central Asian countries have yet to work together to advance common interests in the face of large-power competition, and there is little prospect of this happening in the near future."[193] On the other hand, the "Shanghai spirit" serves as a certain safeguard for the weaker members, with Ruslan Maksutov noting that "the smaller powers of the SCO are still able to outline their national interest . . . and . . . articulate them within the frameworks provided by the organization."[194]

Moreover, there are also frictions between the four Central Asian republics themselves, which "have different strategic interests and have taken different paths to development. They hold conflicting views on the handling of security threats, which are often informed by the degree of openness tolerated by their regimes."[195] For example, there are latent tensions between Kazakhstan and Uzbekistan for primacy in Central Asia, while the "Kazakh leadership has publicly vowed to prevent the SCO from becoming an anti-Western bloc."[196] Astana even maintains an active role in the NATO Partnership for Peace as a means of hedging against domination by the Sino-Russian leadership.[197]

Since the SCO does not conform to the accepted values of Western analysts, this aspect of the SCO has received scant attention and its significance has even been dismissed due to the absence of "liberal" values. However, the SCO, with China and Russia at its head, does in fact represent a distinct set of particular values, expressed through its overarching system principle, noted above. The similarity of the regime types in the SCO, which range in degrees of authoritarianism and the leadership style, speaks to a continued compatibility, further reinforced by the values espoused on the international stage by these states. Ideologically speaking, "China and Russia share a communist authoritarian legacy, which makes them associate stability with authoritarian control rather than democratic participation."[198] The internally focused aspect of the SCO system principle, embodied in "Shanghai Spirit," upholds the right to espouse and practice authoritarian control and provides moral and potentially logistical support for "antirevolutionary" activities. In practice, Beijing and Moscow "promote norms, particularly on cyber issues and human rights, which reinforce internal control and limit external oversight or capacity to influence events across borders."[199] All of this is quite acceptable to Central Asian states as well. Awareness of and conformity to these principles means "the SCO brand of multilateralism provides a political framework that defines right and wrong state conduct and a forum for policy dialogue that limits regional conflict."[200]

Following from this are issues of mutual perspectives, often based on ethnic, cultural, or linguistic affinities or discrepancies. Skeptics are right to question the level of mutual trust among the SCO members. Because of its diverse national makeup, grounded in several distinct civilizational groupings—Sinic, Slavic, Turkic, and others—it therefore "lacks a "transnational social basis."[201] At the core of the SCO are mutual Sino-Russian perceptions. According to Swanström, "both Chinese and Russian officials express their perceptions of mistreatment and culturally defined misperceptions between both countries."[202] For Beijing, Trenin notes that "despite their confidence in Putin, the Chinese feel a distinct cultural divide between themselves and the Russians. The Russians feel the same."[203] He continues that "Post-Soviet Russia is frankly unattractive to many Chinese, who see it as disorganized, backward and uncivilized."[204] Consequently, "while this feeling is almost never made explicit, the Chinese have quietly written off Russia as a country that is in an absolute and relative decline."[205] For Moscow, annoyance at transborder pollution from Chinese industry and fears of illegal migration into its sparsely populated Far Eastern provinces have sparked xenophobic fears of creeping "Sinicization." Indeed, Weitz notes that "one reason Chinese and Russian officials consider these immigration and pollution problems security issues is that they generate animosity and distrust towards China by many Russians."[206] Overemphasizing such contradictions has led several commentators to argue China and Russia are natural opponents and that their current alignment is only a tactical "axis of convenience."[207]

Feelings toward China and Russia in Central Asia are also suitably mixed. For its part, "China encompasses a good portion of Central Asia and shares ethnic and historical populations, languages, and cultures with the former Soviet states it borders."[208] Much play is made of historic linkages through the fabled "Silk Road," but today China aims squarely at promoting its culture through Confucius Institutes to overcome the language barriers in particular. But the Central Asian states are wary of Chinese cultural, demographic, and economic penetration. As Wimbush notes, "Having only recently scrubbed much of Russia's heavy veneer from their politics and cultures, Central Asians are unlikely to stand quietly as their fragile, emerging national societies are challenged by a new, albeit richer, imperial power."[209] Sébastien Peyrouse concludes that "in relation to cultural questions and long-term outlook, Central Asian experts hold pessimistic views of China."[210] On the other hand, Tugsbilguun notes that during Moscow's long imperial presence in the region, "close bonds were formed between Russia and Central Asian nations in the areas of politics, economy, defense, culture, language, social life and ideology."[211] It bestowed them with large Russian ethnic diasporas, as well as linguistic and cultural affinities. But it also left deep suspicions of Russia's intentions based upon its historical record. In addition, there exists friction between the Central Asian states themselves, based upon national historical or ethnic tensions. Akiner considers that "relations between them are brittle, complicated by disagreements over such issues as border security and water management."[212]

Although there are tensions in mutual perspectives, as Akiner argues, "there are also sustained efforts to address these issues and to contain, if not eradicate, such concerns."[213] Effusive rhetoric about the "Shanghai Spirit" is now being reinforced by a package of people-to-people CBMs such as joint education, tourism, and cultural exchanges. For example, 2006 and 2007 saw the "Year of Russia" in China and the "Year of China" in Russia, respectively. There are also plans for an SCO university.[214] The need for sociocultural support for the SCO is deemed a priority, with Aris arguing that "wider people-to-people links are vital for the longevity and development of the SCO."[215] The results of such initiatives so far have been mixed, with Dadabaev noting that "there is an increasing gap between the image of political elites with respect to the SCO and the general public"[216] A Pew Research Center poll found the following: in Russia, positive views on China increased from 64 percent in 2014 to 79 percent in 2015, while in China, positive views on Russia decreased from 66 percent in 2014 to 51 percent in 2015.[217] As with the ASC project then, the SCO has much work to do toward building a sense of community or investment in a common destiny among its respective publics.

External Dimension: An "SCO-Plus"?

There are two thrusts to any future expansion of the SCO. The first is widening. It may either expand its range of operations or its actual membership. The SCO, as it stands, is a regionally confined and inward-looking security alignment. As de Haas identifies, "An essential difference between the organizational development of the SCO and NATO remains the fact that NATO is aimed primarily at external security risks whereas the SCO concentrates strongly on security within the territory covered by its member states."[218] Therefore Anatoly Torkunov argues that the SCO "would perhaps be more effective if it emerged from its Central Asian 'cocoon' . . . [in order to] . . . give higher priority to the Asia Pacific region."[219] This is effectively a call for the SCO to "go out of area"; that is, to take an active role beyond its national boundaries into the wider Asia Pacific region. So far, the organization has concentrated on internal consolidation rather than external projection, but this could change in the future as the SCO grows more durable and confident. To date, "consensus had still not been reached among member states regarding the geographical range of the SCO."[220]

In 2010, criteria for new membership were promulgated: members must be in Eurasia, have diplomatic relations with all SCO members, be an observer/dialogue partner, and not be subject to any UN sanctions. After ending a moratorium on new membership, the SCO has begun to expand, with India and Pakistan having joined in 2017. This will have a massive impact upon its future trajectory. The addition of these powers will increase the SCO's aggregate power and influence, while changing its internal and external dynamics in unforeseen ways, including importing the Indo-Pakistani conflict into its midst. Waiting in the wings are Iran, Afghanistan, and Mongolia as observer states, while Belarus, Sri Lanka, and Turkey are "dialogue partners."[221] Of the other most obvious candidates, Turkmenistan remains aloof in its "strict neutrality."[222] Additionally, de Haas notes that "in practice the observer states participate in many of the activities of the SCO, such as annual summits and as observers in military exercises. Their position is specifically mentioned in the regulations of the 'SCO Energy Club.' Therefore their status is more than simply 'observer.'"[223] There is no space here to discuss the posture of each of these states in relation to the SCO, but it is very notable that several bilateral "strategic partnership" dyads, such as Russia-India, Russia-Iran, and China-Pakistan, already exist, thus further reinforcing their affiliation and alignment with the SCO in practice. As David Shambaugh concludes, "the SCO has begun to evolve into a broader and more comprehensive organization, reflecting Beijing's goal of building strategic partnerships."[224]

In the same vein, when the observer states, dialogue partners, and interorganizational relationships of the SCO are factored in, we can envisage an incipient "SCO-plus" model, somewhat analogous to the ASEAN-plus model of expansion. Akihiro Iwashita dubs this the "SCO plus alpha" format.[225] Moreover, the SCO already has institutional linkages with the Commonwealth of Independent States and CSTO, as mentioned above, and could consider expanding its scope by emulating either ASEAN or NATO, developing mechanisms analogous to NATO's "Partnership for Peace," for example.[226] Indeed, Masayuki Masuda considers that "building external relations will be an important part of improving the organization's problem-solving ability."[227]

The second thrust for expansion is deepening. In addition to expanding its range of functional areas of cooperation to include new initiatives, perhaps into the area of space or cybersecurity, [228] this could mean the simple strengthening of institutional "coupling" on the vertical axis (more treaties, agreements, memoranda, etc.), or it could entail evolution into a more robust or deeply rooted form of security alignment. It has been stressed throughout that neither SCO nor the Sino-Russian strategic partnership qualifies as or intends to become a conventional military alliance. Sergei Lavrov, former Russian minister of foreign affairs, claims "the SCO had no intention of setting up a military alliance."[229] Indeed, most analysts concur that "it is unlikely that their bilateral cooperation or the SCO will, in the near-to-mid-term, develop into a military alliance."[230] Moscow and China can leverage the specter of an alliance to place pressure on opponents, for example, by conducting military exercises to intimidate their "near abroad," although as Swanström notes, "the step from military exercises to a *bona fide* alliance is exceedingly long."[231] Yet Korolev reminds us that "not announcing an 'alliance' by China and Russia does not mean that an 'alliance' is not possible or not ready. Rather, delaying the official announcement, or not making such an announcement, may be beneficial for both China and Russia at the current time."[232] Indeed, he has characterized the China-Russia partnership as "on the verge of an alliance," which might perhaps indicate the potential applicability of the "virtual alliance" model outlined in Chapter 2. Igor Ivanov also asserts that "if needed, the ties can be converted into an alliance relationship without long preparation."[233] Indeed, some Russian and Chinese commentators have again begun to bandy about the terms *alliance* or *de facto alliance*[234] more openly in recent years.

On the other hand, it is unlikely to emerge as a security community comparable to the EU or ASEAN in the near future. Even so, Aris notes that "although the SCO is still a long way away from being considered a security community, it has been able to contribute to the region's states slowly accepting a regional approach to addressing certain security challenges."[235] Wu Xinbo concurs that "the SCO will also likely have both normative and practical impacts on East Asia community building."[236] Indeed, such conjectures ought to be moot points, as the architects of the SCO have continuously argued that it represents a form of "new state-to-state relations." Thus Akiner concludes that "SCO is a product of this 'environment': it is pragmatic, mobile, fashioned to respond to current needs. Its durability will be determined by whether or not it can remain relevant. This in turn will depend on its capacity for adaptation and transformation."[237]

Conclusion

Rather than apply ill-fitting analytical frameworks designed to explain the alliance and security community paradigms of alignment, this chapter has employed a new framework grounded in organization studies to improve our understanding of the SCO. By casting the SCO as "a loose, network-type organisation with a broad-brush approach to achieving its aims" involving subsets of strategic partnership dyads orbiting around a Sino-Russian core, we can more accurately capture its nature, purpose, and dynamics.[238] As Song records, "the SCO is an organization with multifaceted purposes, including regional stability, anti-radicalism, energy security and anti-foreign influence."[239] Indeed, it will be remembered that both in the SCO's system principle and in Beijing's foreign policy is an embedded antipathy to alliances. As Odgaard reiterates, "China is not looking for allies, it is looking for strategic partners with common strategic interests with China that makes policy coordination worthwhile without entailing collective defense commitments."[240] This does not mean that realist, liberalist, or constructivist elements drawn from the opposing paradigms are not useful for understanding threats, interests, values, and norms, but underlines the fact that new forms of alignment such as this do not perfectly conform to the existing paradigms and frameworks. By tracking the development of the SCO through its collaboration continuum, from formation to implementation, and then using the framework to evaluate its progress and deficiencies, we can gain a superior appreciation of its behavioral dynamics.

When evaluating the SCO/Sino-Russian strategic partnership, we must also be alert to ethnocentric and ideological biases from some Western sources. Because it subscribes to a "system principle" at odds with that espoused by the Western allies and its member states are not fully fledged democracies, there is a tendency to perceive the SCO as lacking in legitimacy or effectiveness.[241] For example, in a highly superficial appraisal, Joseph Nye dismisses the prospects of the Sino-Russian strategic partnership based upon the predictably false assumption that it should be measured against the prospects of becoming a fully fledged alliance.[242] Akiner suggests that for such analysts, "The mere existence of a body that is neither Western-led nor inspired by Western models is regarded as an affront."[243] Hence, Bailes and Dunay conclude "the SCO may be a rare case of an organization that is relatively effective but not generally regarded— by other institutions, outside powers and some elements in its own member states—as legitimate."[244]

Nevertheless, the SCO has achieved notable success in embedding itself in the alphabet soup of multilateral institutions in Asia Pacific. Lanteigne concludes, "In its brief history, the SCO has the distinction of evolving into one of the most potentially powerful regional organizations to appear in post–Cold War Asia. It remains an indispensable forum for strategic cooperation for the former Soviet Central Asian states as well as an essential conduit between East and Central Asia."[245] Respondents to the *Asia Pacific Security Survey Report 2008* voted the SCO the third most effective regional institution, behind ASEAN and ASEAN+3 (Chapter 5). This placed it far ahead of the US alliance network (Chapter 3), which was in tenth place.[246] In this sense, Masuda indicates that it serves as "a rebuttal or counterpoint to the military alliance strategy of the United States."[247] By offering a plausible alternative to the ideology championed by Washington and a new mechanism for global, pan-regional, and Central Asian regional security governance, the members "engage in social competition with the West, framing the SCO as a rivalling security alternative to a U.S.-led security System."[248] Indeed, the SCO serves as a relatively successful prototype of the Sinic worldview and Beijing's preferred vision of regional and global security order. With the deepening and widening of the SCO "family" now occurring, its transformative potential for the international system is enormous.

Appendix: List of Summits of Shanghai Cooperation Organisation and Shanghai Five

Year	Date	Summit	State	Place	Agreements
1996	April 26	1st Shanghai Five	China	Shanghai	• Agreement on Confidence-Building in the Military Field in Border Areas Between China, Russia, Kazakhstan, Kyrgyzstan and Tajikistan ("Shanghai Declaration")
1997	April 24	2nd Shanghai Five	Russia	Moscow	• Agreement on Mutual Reduction of Military Forces in Border Areas Between China, Russia, Kazakhstan, Kyrgyzstan and Tajikistan
1998	June 3	3rd Shanghai Five	Kazakhstan	Almaty	• Joint Statement of Participants of the Almaty Meeting
1999	August 25	4th Shanghai Five	Kyrgyzstan	Bishkek	• Bishkek Declaration
2000	July 5	5th Shanghai Five	Tajikistan	Dushanbe	• Dushanbe Declaration
2001	June 14	6th Shanghai Five	China	Shanghai	• Declaration on Establishment of the SCO • The Shanghai Convention on Fight Against Terrorism, Separatism and Extremism
2001	September 14	1st Shanghai Cooperation Organisation (SCO)	Kazakhstan	Almaty	• Declaration of Establishment of Regular Meetings of Heads of Governments Mechanism

continues

Appendix: Continued

Year	Date	Summit	State	Place	Agreements
					• Memorandum Among Governments of Member States on the Basic Goals and Directions of Regional Economic Cooperation and Launch of Process on Creating Favorable Conditions in the Field of Trade and Investments
2002	June 7	2nd SCO	Russia	Saint Petersburg	• The Charter of SCO • Agreement on Regional Anti-Terrorist Structure • Declaration of Heads of SCO Member States
2003	May 29	3rd SCO	Russia	Moscow	• Moscow Declaration
2004	January 15	3rd SCO	China	Beijing	• Major Ceremony of the Establishment of the SCO Secretariat
2004	June 17	4th SCO	Uzbekistan	Tashkent	• Tashkent Initiative • Convention on the Privileges and Immunities of the SCO • Agreement on the Host Country of the Secretariat Between the People's Republic of China and the SCO • Joint Declaration to Cooperate in Fighting Terrorism; Launched Executive Committee of the SCO Regional Counter-terrorism Structure
2005	July 5	5th SCO	Kazakhstan	Astana	• Astana Declaration • Resolution on Approving the Vision of the SCO Member States to Combat Terrorism, Separatism and Extremism
2006	June 15	6th SCO	China	Shanghai	• Joint Declaration on the Fifth Anniversary of the SCO
2007	August 16	7th SCO	Kyrgyzstan	Bishkek	• Treaty on Long-Term Good-Neighborliness, Friendship and Cooperation
2008	August 28	8th SCO	Tajikistan	Dushanbe	• Dushanbe Declaration

continues

Appendix: Continued

Year	Date	Summit	State	Place	Agreements
2009	June 16	9th SCO	Russia	Yekaterinburg	• Yekaterinburg Declaration • SCO Counter-Terrorism Convention • SCO Regulations on Political Diplomatic Measures and Mechanisms of Response to Events Jeopardising Regional Peace, Security and Stability • Agreement on Cooperation in the Field of Ensuring International Information Security • Agreement on Training of Officers for Counter-Terrorism Agencies
2010	June 11	10th SCO	Uzbekistan	Tashkent	• Tashkent Declaration • Action Plan for 2010–2011
2011	June 15	11th SCO	Kazakhstan	Astana	• Astana Declaration on the Tenth Anniversary of the SCO • Anti-Drug Strategy for 2011–2016
2012	June 7	12th SCO	China	Beijing	• Declaration on Building a Region with Lasting Peace and Common Prosperity • The Strategic Plan for the Medium-Term Development of the SCO
2013	September 13	13th SCO	Kyrgyzstan	Bishkek	• Bishkek Declaration • Framework to Implement the Treaty on Long-Term Good-Neighborliness, Friendship and Cooperation • Action Plan for 2013–2017
2014	September 12	14th SCO	Tajikistan	Dushanbe	• Dushanbe Declaration • Amendments of "For SCO Membership Program" and "Memo Template of Duties for Application to Join SCO"
2015	July 10	15th SCO	Russia	Ufa	• Ufa Declaration • Agreement on Border Defense Cooperation Among the SCO Member States

continues

Appendix: Continued

Year	Date	Summit	State	Place	Agreements
2016	June 24	16th SCO	Uzbekistan	Tashkent	• Development Strategy Until 2025 of the SCO • A 2016–2018 Cooperation Program on Combating Terrorism, Separatism and Extremism Among the SCO Member States • Tashkent Declaration on the Fifteenth Anniversary of the SCO • Approval of the Action Plan for 2016–2020 on Implementation of the SCO Development Strategy Towards 2025 • Memorandum of the Obligations on the Entry of the Republic of India to the SCO • Memorandum of the Obligations on the Entry of the Islamic Republic of Pakistan to the SCO
2017	June 9	17th SCO	Kazakhstan	Astana	• Astana Declaration • The Decisions of the SCO Heads of State Council on Granting India and Pakistan the Status of SCO Member State • The SCO Convention on Countering Extremism signed
2018	June 10	18th SCO	China	Qingdao	• Qingdao Declaration • Approval of the Action Plan for 2018–2022 to Implement the Provisions of the Treaty of Long-Term Neighbourliness, Friendship and Cooperation Between the Member States • Approval of the Programme of Cooperation Between the Member States in Countering Terrorism, Separatism and Extremism for 2019–2021

continues

Appendix: Continued

Year	Date	Summit	State	Place	Agreements
2018	June 10	18th SCO	China	Qingdao	• Memorandum of Understanding to Encourage Cooperation in the area of Micro-, Small and Medium Businesses Between Ministries of Member States

Notes

1. My sincere gratitude goes to Jingdong Yuan and Stephen Aris for their assistance with this chapter.
2. Aris, "A New Model of Asian Regionalism," p. 453.
3. Zhao, "Security Building in Central Asia and the Shanghai Cooperation Organization," p. 286.
4. Menon, "The Limits of Chinese–Russian Partnership," p.110.
5. Flikke, "Sino-Russian Relations Status Exchange or Imbalanced Relationship?" p. 168.
6. Dunay, "Not Beyond Limits."
7. Michel, "SCO Set to Expand, Adding India and Pakistan."
8. Dibb, "Australia–United States," p. 44.
9. Green, "Should America Fear a New Sino-Russian Alliance?" p. 1.
10. Cited in Akiner, "The Shanghai Cooperation Organisation," p. 6.
11. Cole and Jensen, "Norms and Regional Architecture," p. 266.
12. Swanström, "Transformation of the Sino-Russian Partnership," p. 6.
13. Clarke, "China and the Shanghai Cooperation Organization," p. 1.
14. Aris, *Eurasian Regionalism*, p. 2.
15. Lukin, "Russia's Pivot to Asia."
16. Kozhokin, "Russo-Chinese Collaboration on the World Scene," p. 163.
17. Clarke, "China and the Shanghai Cooperation Organization," p. 123.
18. Wimbush, "Great Games in Central Asia," pp. 280–281.
19. Mackinder, "The Geographical Pivot of History," pp. 421–437.
20. Bailes and Dunay, "The Shanghai Cooperation Organization as a Regional Security Institution," p. 2.
21. Crosston, "The Pluto of International Organizations," p. 284.
22. Oresman, "Letter from the Editor," p. 3.
23. Green, "Should America Fear a New Sino-Russian Alliance?" p. 1.
24. Menon, "The Limits of Chinese-Russian Partnership," p. 113.
25. Oresman and Chargynov, "The Shanghai Cooperation Summit," p. 6.
26. Cited in Kavalski, "Shanghaied into Cooperation," p. 138.
27. Castillo, "SCO: Rise of NATO East?"; Roney, "The Shanghai Cooperation Organization"; Korotun, "Russia-China."
28. Ambrosio, "Catching the 'Shanghai Spirit,'" p. 1322.
29. Aris, *Eurasian Regionalism*, p. 52.

30. Tugsbilguun, "Does the Shanghai Cooperation Represent an Example of a Military Alliance?"

31. Ibid., p. 100.

32. Lanteigne, "'In Medias Res': The Development of the Shanghai Co-operation Organization as a Security Community."

33. Yuan, "China's Role in Establishing and Building the Shanghai Cooperation Organization," p. 869. Italics added.

34. Tolipov, "On the Role of the Central Asian Cooperation Organization Within the SCO," p. 9.

35. Ambrosio, "The Architecture of Alignment," p. 135.

36. See Kaczmarski, *Russia-China Relations in the Post-crisis International Order*; Rozman, *The Sino-Russian Challenge to the World Order*; Lukin. *The Bear Watches the Dragon*.

37. Ying, "How China Sees Russia," p. 96.

38. Zhao, "Security Building in Central Asia and the Shanghai Cooperation Organization."

39. Korybko, "Washington's Nightmare Comes True."

40. Ambrosio, "The Architecture of Alignment," p. 112.

41. Akiner, "The Shanghai Cooperation Organisation," p. 9.

42. Cited in Ibid.

43. Dadabaev, "Shanghai Cooperation Organization (SCO) Regional Identity Formation from the Perspective of the Central Asia States."

44. Song, "Interests, Power and China's Difficult Game in the Shanghai Cooperation Organization," p. 90.

45. Interestingly, Aris also applies a three "phase" model (institutional building, agenda expanding, and implementation). Aris, *Eurasian Regionalism*.

46. Aris, "A New Model of Asian Regionalism," p. 460.

47. Wilson, *Strategic Partners*; Wishnick, *Mending Fences*.

48. Aris, "Spreading the 'Shanghai Spirit,'" p.159.

49. Jersild, *The Sino-Soviet Alliance*; Quested, *Sino-Russian Relations*; Westad, *Brothers in Arms*.

50. For background, see Westad, *Brothers in Arms*.

51. Ross, *China, the United States, and the Soviet Union*.

52. Lanteigne, "'In Medias Res,'" p. 606.

53. Chung, "The Shanghai Cooperation Organization: China's Roles and Influence in Central Asia," p. 993.

54. Trenin, *True Partners?* p. 15.

55. See Tsygankov, *Russia's Foreign Policy*.

56. Ying, "How China Sees Russia," p. 97.

57. Dittmer, "Political and Cultural Roots of the Sino-Russian Partnership," p. 22.

58. Trenin, *True Partners?* p. 15.

59. Swanström, "Transformation of Sino-Russian Partnership," p. 3.

60. Feng, "The New Geostrategic Game," p. 20.

61. Weitz, *China-Russia Security Relations*, p. vii.

62. Ministry of Foreign Affairs of the People's Republic of China, "China and Russia: Partnership of Strategic Coordination." For the full text of the statement, see United Nations, "Letter dated 2 May 1996 from the Permanent Representatives of China and the Russian Federation to the United Nations Addressed to the Secretary-General."

63. Aris, "The Shanghai Cooperation Organisation," p. 478.

64. Yuan, "China's Role in Establishing and Building the Shanghai Cooperation Organization," p. 865.

65. Hale, "The Outlook for Economic Integration in East Asia," p. 68.

66. Bailes and Dunay, "The Shanghai Cooperation Organization as a Regional Security Institution," p. 8.

67. Fingar, *The New Great Game.*

68. De Haas, *The Shanghai Cooperation Organisation,* p. 34.

69. Plater-Zyberk, *Who's Afraid of the SCO?* p. 1.

70. Bailes and Dunay, "The Shanghai Cooperation Organization as a Regional Security Institution," p. 24.

71. Yuan, "China's Role in Establishing and Building the Shanghai Cooperation Organization," p. 858.

72. De Haas, *The Shanghai Cooperation Organisation,* p. 36.

73. Bosbotinis, "Sustaining the Dragon, Dodging the Eagle and Barring the Bear?" p. 67.

74. Weitz, *China-Russia Security Relations*, p. 35.

75. Cited in Troitskiy, "A Russian Perspective on the Shanghai Cooperation Organization," p. 34.

76. Yuan, "China's Role in Establishing and Building the Shanghai Cooperation Organization," p. 860.

77. Zhao, "Security Building in Central Asia and the Shanghai Cooperation Organization," p. 289.

78. Shanghai Cooperation Organisation, "Brief Introduction to Shanghai Cooperation Organisation."

79. Shanghai Cooperation Organisation, "Charter of the Shanghai Cooperation Organisation," p. 2.

80. Aris, "The Shanghai Cooperation Organisation," p. 477.

81. Hale, "The Outlook for Economic Integration in East Asia," p. 67.

82. Pan, "A Chinese Perspective on the Shanghai Cooperation Organization," p. 49.

83. Aris, *Eurasian Regionalism*, p. 6.

84. Ambrosio, "The Architecture of Alignment," p. 123.

85. Akiner, "The Shanghai Cooperation Organisation," p. 9.

86. Song, "Interests, Power and China's Difficult Game in the Shanghai Cooperation Organization," p. 92.

87. Shanghai Cooperation Organisation, "Charter of the Shanghai Cooperation Organisation," p. 1.

88. Tolipov, "On the Role of the Central Asian Cooperation Organization within the SCO," p. 164.

89. Aris, "The Shanghai Cooperation Organisation: 'Tackling the Three Evils,'" p. 476.

90. Aris, *Eurasian Regionalism*, p. 22.

91. Shanghai Cooperation Organisation, "Charter of the Shanghai Cooperation Organisation," p. 6.

92. Ibid., "Brief Introduction to Shanghai Cooperation Organisation."

93. Aris, *Eurasian Regionalism*, p. 24.

94. Shanghai Cooperation Organisation, "Charter of the Shanghai Cooperation Organisation," p. 7.

95. Details can be found at the Secretariat's website, http://eng.sectsco.org [accessed October 2018].

96. Ambrosio, "The Architecture of Alignment," p. 122.

97. Oresman and Chargynov, "The Shanghai Cooperation Summit," p. 6.

98. Shanghai Cooperation Organisation, "Charter of the Shanghai Cooperation Organisation," p. 2.

99. Aris, *Eurasian Regionalism*, p. 137.

100. Cited in Azarkan, "The Interests of the Central Asian States and the Shanghai Cooperation Organization," p. 396.

101. Aris, "Spreading the 'Shanghai Spirit,'" pp. 159-60.

102. Weitz, *China-Russia Security Relations*, p. 37.

103. Aris, *Eurasian Regionalism*, p. 28.

104. Pan, "SCO's Success in Security Architecture."

105. The official website for RATS is http://www.ecrats.org/en.

106. Gjelten, "Seeing the Internet as an 'Information Weapon.'"

107. Bailes and Dunay, "The Shanghai Cooperation Organization as a Regional Security Institution," p. 19.

108. Flikke, "Sino-Russian Relations Status Exchange or Imbalanced Relationship?" p. 159.

109. Bailes and Dunay, "The Shanghai Cooperation Organization as a Regional Security Institution," p. 22.

110. Muraviev, "Comrades in Arms."

111. Keck, "China, Russia Military Ties Deepen with Naval Drill in East China Sea."

112. De Haas, *The Shanghai Cooperation Organisation*, p. 17.

113. Odgaard, "Beijing's Quest for Stability in Its Neighborhood," p. 47. Italics added.

114. Weitz, "Kazakhstan-China Military Exchanges Continue."

115. Akiner, "The Shanghai Cooperation Organisation," p. 14.

116. Putz, "China's Silk Road Belt Outpaces Russia's Economic Union."

117. De Haas, *The Shanghai Cooperation Organisation*, p. 23.

118. Freeman, "New Strategies for an Old Rivalry?"

119. Yuan, "China's Role in Establishing and Building the Shanghai Cooperation Organization," p. 860; Bosbotinis, "Sustaining the Dragon, Dodging the Eagle and Barring the Bear?" pp. 71, 77.

120. De Haas, *The Shanghai Cooperation Organisation*, p. 29.

121. *Xinhua,* "Culture Ministers of SCO Member States Meet in Beijing."

122. Pan, "The SCO's Success in Security Architecture."

123. Shanghai Academy for Social Sciences website can be found at http://www.coscos.org.cn/sub5.htm.

124. Lanteigne, "'In Medias Res.'"

125. Kavalski, "Shanghaied into Cooperation," p. 141.

126. Aris, "Spreading the 'Shanghai Spirit,'" p. 157.

127. Akiner, "The Shanghai Cooperation Organisation," p. 13.

128. Shanghai Cooperation Organisation, "Charter of the Shanghai Cooperation Organisation," p. 3.

129. Aris, "Spreading the 'Shanghai Spirit,'" pp. 158–159.

130. Ministry of Foreign Affairs of the People's Republic of China, "Declaration of the Heads of State of the Member States of the Shanghai Cooperation Organization on Building a Region of Lasting Peace and Common Prosperity."

131. Kavalski, "Shanghaied into Cooperation," p. 132.

132. Rodkiewicz, "Putin in Shanghai."

133. Swanström, "Transformation of the Sino-Russian Partnership," p. 3.

134. Adomanis, "A Russian-China Alliance Is Emerging, and It Will Be a Disaster for the West."

135. Lo, *Axis of Convenience*; Lamothe-Cadet, "A Relationship of Convenience."

136. Odgaard, "Beijing's Quest for Stability in Its Neighborhood," pp. 44–45.

137. Blank, "The Shanghai Cooperative Organization: Post-Mortem or Prophecy," p. 16.

138. Troitskiy, "A Russian Perspective on the Shanghai Cooperation Organization," p. 30.

139. Akiner, "The Shanghai Cooperation Organisation," p. 24.

140. Trenin, "True Partners?" p. 28.

141. Ibid., p. 26.

142. Menon, "The Limits of Chinese-Russian Partnership," p. 109.

143. Shanghai Cooperation Organisation, "The Tashkent Declaration of the Fifteenth Anniversary of the Shanghai Cooperation Organization."

144. De Haas, *The Shanghai Cooperation Organisation,* p. 37.

145. Blank, "Russia and Vietnam Team Up to Balance China."

146. International Crisis Group, "China's Central Asia Problem," p. 17.

147. Ziegler, "Central Asia, the Shanghai Cooperation Organization, and American Foreign Policy," p. 502.

148. Centre for Research on Globalization, "U.S. Military Base in Uzbekistan to Counter Russia in Central Asia"; Pillalamarri, "The United States Just Closed Its Last Base in Central Asia"; Miller and Wich, *Becoming Asia,* p. 271.

149. Pillalamarri, "The United States Just Closed Its Last Base in Central Asia."

150. Aris, "The Shanghai Cooperation Organisation," p. 474.

151. Hu, "The Shanghai Cooperation Organisation: A New Regional Kid on the Block?"

152. Aris, "The Shanghai Cooperation Organisation," p. 473.

153. Maksutov, "The Shanghai Cooperation Organization," p. 17.

154. Aris, "The Shanghai Cooperation Organisation," p. 462.

155. Ibid., p. 468.

156. Ibid., p. 472.

157. Bisley, *Building Asia's Security,* p. 41.

158. Peace Mission exercises were conducted in 2005, 2007, 2009, 2010, 2012, 2013, 2014, 2016. Meick, "China-Russia Military-to-Military Relations," pp. 24–27.

159. Dittmer, "Political and Cultural Roots of the Sino-Russian Partnership," p. 27.

160. Korolev, "On the Verge of an Alliance," p. 15.

161. De Haas and Beerthuizen, "The Shanghai Cooperation Organization," p. 5.

162. Official website for CSTO is at http://www.odkb.gov.ru/start/index_aengl.htm. The CTSO is not fully investigated in this book because its regional coverage compromises the specific focus on the broader "Asia Pacific."

163. Ministry of National Defense, People's Republic of China, "Nine Changes in Stride-2015 Zhurihe Series Exercise"; Ministry of National Defense, People's Republic of China, "Stride 2016-Zhurihe B Exercise Wraps Up"; Cozad, "PLA Joint Training and Implications for Future Expeditionary Capabilities"; McDermott, "*Tsentr* 2015: Testing Mobility and Strategic Messaging"; McDermott, "Russian Combat Training: Quantity Versus Quality"; Norberg, *Training to Fight,* pp. 11–12.

164. Cheng, Gouping, "The Shanghai Cooperation Organization: A Cause Worth Ceaseless Efforts."

165. World Bank, "World Development Indicators."

166. Observatory of Economic Complexity, "China."

167. Ibid.

168. Feng, "The New Geostrategic Game," p. 32.

169. *Xinhua,* "China, Russia Pledge Closer Economic Cooperation Amid Global Adversity."

170. Ying, "How China Sees Russia," p. 98.

171. Cheng, "The Shanghai Cooperation Organization: A Cause Worth Ceaseless Efforts.

172. Maksutov, "The Shanghai Cooperation Organization," p. 20.

173. Dzyubenko, "China to Expand C. Asian Presence with $10 bln in Loans."

174. Blagov, "Arms, Energy and Commerce in Sino-Russian Relations," pp. 8–11.

175. Koch-Weser and Murray, "The China-Russia Gas Deal."

176. Zhao, "Security Building in Central Asia and the Shanghai Cooperation Organization," p. 311.

177. Charap, Drennan, and Pierre Noël, "Russia and China," p. 33.

178. Aris, "A New Model of Asian Regionalism," p. 462.

179. Trenin, "True Partners?" p. 33.

180. Rousseau, "The Tortuous Sino-Russian Arms Trade Analysis."

181. Yuan, "China's Role in Establishing and Building the Shanghai Cooperation Organization," p. 867.

182. Karpov, "Will the Russian-Chinese 'Strategic Partnership' Last Until 2020?" p. 9.

183. Yuan, "China's Role in Establishing and Building the Shanghai Cooperation Organization," p. 867.

184. Troitskiy, "A Russian Perspective on the Shanghai Cooperation Organization," p. 35.

185. Plater-Zyberk, *Who's Afraid of the SCO?* p. 5.

186. Ibid., p. 6.

187. Aris, "The Shanghai Cooperation Organisation," p. 459.

188. Bosbotinis, "Sustaining the Dragon, Dodging the Eagle and Barring the Bear?" p. 67.

189. Weitz, *China-Russia Security Relations*, p. 2.

190. Antonenko, "The EU and the Shanghai Cooperation Organisation," p. 5.

191. Tugsbilguun, "Does the Shanghai Cooperation Represent an Example of a Military Alliance?" p. 81.

192. Weitz, *China-Russia Security Relations*, p. 41.

193. Wimbush, "Great Games in Central Asia," p. 258.

194. Maksutov, "The Shanghai Cooperation Organization," p. 5.

195. Azarkan, "The Interests of the Central Asian States and the Shanghai Cooperation Organization," p. 397.

196. Aris, *Eurasian Regionalism*, p. 85.

197. North Atlantic Treaty Organization, "Relations with Kazakhstan."

198. Odgaard, "Beijing's Quest for Stability in its Neighborhood," p. 51.

199. Charap, Drennan, and Pierre Noël, "Russia and China," p. 37.

200. Odgaard, "Beijing's Quest for Stability in Its Neighborhood," p. 52.

201. Hu, "The Shanghai Cooperation Organisation."

202. Swanström, "Transformation of the Sino-Russian Partnership," p. 8.

203. Trenin, "True Partners?" p. 13.

204. Ibid., p. 23.

205. Ibid., p. 16.

206. Weitz, *China-Russia Security Relations*, p. 16.

207. Lo, *Axis of Convenience,* p. 2; Lamothe-Cadet, "A Relationship of Convenience."

208. Wimbush, "Great Games in Central Asia," p. 260.

209. Ibid., p. 266.

210. Peyrouse, "Power Differential and Security Issues in Central Asia," p. 104.

211. Tugsbilguun, "Does the Shanghai Cooperation Represent an Example of a Military Alliance?" p. 80.

212. Akiner, "The Shanghai Cooperation Organisation," p. 10.

213. Ibid., p. 9.

214. Aris, *Eurasian Regionalism*, p. 6.

215. Ibid., p. 33.

216. Dadabaev, "Shanghai Cooperation Organization (SCO) Regional Identity Formation from the Perspective of the Central Asia States," p. 109.

217. Cited in Baev, "Russia's Pivot to China Goes Astray."

218. De Haas, *The Shanghai Cooperation Organisation*, p. 57.

219. Torkunov, "Groundwork for the Future," p. 25.

220. Masuda, "China's SCO Policy in the Regional Security Architecture," p. 13.

221. Schleifer, "Turkey: With EU Talks Stalled, Erdogan Suggests Ankara May Join SCO."

222. Seryaev, "The Permanent Neutrality of Turkmenistan."

223. De Haas, *The Shanghai Cooperation Organisation*, p. 5.

224. Shambaugh, "China Engages Asia: Reshaping the Regional Order," p. 74.

225. Iwashita, "The Shanghai Cooperation Organization and Japan—Moving Together to Reshape the Eurasian Community," p. 25.

226. Weitz, "Building a NATO-SCO Dialogue."

227. Masuda, "China's SCO Policy in the Regional Security Architecture," p. 8.

228. Shanghai Cooperation Organisation, "SCO Member State Experts from Competent Authorities Discuss IT Cooperation"; Ministry of Foreign Affairs of the People's Republic of China, "SCO Hosts First Joint Online Counter-Terrorism Exercise in China"; Wood, "China Conducts Anti-Terror Cyber Operations with SCO Partners."

229. Cited in Plater-Zyberk, *Who's Afraid of the SCO?* p. 5.

230. Yeung and Bjelakovic, "The Sino-Russian Strategic Partnership," p. 257.

231. Swanström, "Transformation of the Sino-Russian Partnership," p. 12.

232. Korolev, "On the Verge of an Alliance," p. 15.

233. Ivanov, *Rossiysko-Kitayskiy Dialog: Model 2015*, p. 6.

234. Karaganov, "Izbezhat Afganistana-2."

235. Aris, "The Shanghai Cooperation Organisation: 'Tackling the Three Evils,'" p. 478.

236. Wu, "Chinese Perspectives on Building an East Asian Community in the Twenty-First Century," p. 63.

237. Akiner, "The Shanghai Cooperation Organisation," p. 24.

238. Ibid., p. 22.

239. Song, "Interests, Power and China's Difficult Game in the Shanghai Cooperation Organization (SCO)," p. 86.

240. Odgaard, "Beijing's Quest for Stability in Its Neighborhood," p. 41.

241. Weitz, *China-Russia Security Relations*.

242. Nye, "A New Sino-Russian Alliance?"

243. Akiner, "The Shanghai Cooperation Organisation," p. 19.

244. Bailes and Dunay, "The Shanghai Cooperation Organization as a Regional Security Institution," p. 3.

245. Lanteigne, "'In Medias Res,'" p. 605.

246. Baker and Fox, *Asia Pacific Security Survey Report 2008*, p. 28.

247. Masuda, "China's SCO Policy in the Regional Security Architecture," p. 2.

248. Flikke, "Sino-Russian Relations Status Exchange or Imbalanced Relationship?" p. 163.

8

Rethinking Alignment

This book has formulated a set of theoretically grounded analytical frameworks on alignment and applied them as a means to systematize our understanding of the most prominent case studies in the Asia Pacific.

This exercise confirms three general propositions. First, the alliance (redux), security community, and strategic partnership paradigms are all distinctive variations of the phenomenon of *alignment*. Their differing nature, purpose, and behaviors necessitate custom-designed and specifically calibrated analytical tools, rather than a "one-theory fits all" approach. Second, the examination of alignment theory as it is presented here shows the progressive accretion of intellectual frameworks from initial system-level conceptions (traditional alignment theory) to the interstate level (intra-alliance politics), through the community level (security community), to a totally novel approach that considers alignments from an organizational perspective (strategic partnership). Therefore, Chapters 2, 4, and 6 together serve to chart the progress of alignment theorizing through an accumulation of multiple "layers" of scholastic understanding. And third, concomitant with this theoretical progression is an empirical evolution observed through the comparative case studies. Beginning with the Trilateral Security Dialogue (TSD), an alignment with its roots in the immediate postwar alliance paradigm that has now mutated in form and purpose, to the later Cold War ASEAN Security Community (ASC), and finishing with the Shanghai Cooperation Organisation (SCO), a product of the post–Cold War period, we can also deduce a changing pattern of alignment paradigms through the course of Chapters 3, 5, and 7.

In relation to these general observations, this section now supplies some closing reflections on the book's empirical and theoretical findings, in

183

particular seeking to provisionally draw out synergies between cases and paradigms that have emerged in the course of this study.

Asia Pacific: Three Case Studies

In order to increase our understanding of the macro processes occurring in the Asia Pacific security environment, this book has cast a conceptual spotlight on three key alignment groupings: the TSD "virtual" alliance, the ASEAN security community, and the SCO strategic partnership "network." This section now reflects upon what the three analytical frameworks contribute to our understanding of the empirical case studies. Rather than repeat the conclusions found at the end of each case study chapter that gauge current issues and future trajectories for each of them, this section comments more broadly on the findings regarding their implications for understanding alignment behavior. The section ends with preliminary observations regarding the important question of *inter*-alignment relationships, which represents a potentially rich avenue for further research.

First, the TSD trilateral "virtual" alliance case study (Chapter 3) was critically examined as a variant of the heretofore dominant alliance paradigm of alignment, using the intra-alliance politics framework. With its realist/liberal-constructivist conceptual bifurcation, this framework highlights the two main driving forces behind this new alignment grouping: "interests" and "values," as explicitly stated in the three countries' policy documents. As the latest TSD joint statement affirms, the alignment "rests on the unshakable foundation of shared interests and values, including a commitment to a rules-based international order, respect for international law, open economies, and the peaceful resolution of disputes."[1] Importantly, this framework serves as an extension of the widely employed conventional balance of power/balance of threat (BOP/BOT) model of alliance/alignment theorizing, while concomitantly overcoming some of its explanatory limitations. As Steven David reminds us: "Balance of power theory emphasizes that the determinants of alignment come overwhelmingly from the structure of the international system, particularly the actual and potential threats that states face. Accordingly, the internal characteristics of the states are usually not considered relevant in influencing alignments."[2]

As the foregoing statement of the TSD's purpose indicates, it is not officially or explicitly identified as a threat-based alignment, though it maintains a strong hedge against such an eventuality. In many respects, TSD's behavioral dynamics are better captured by the intra-alliance politics framework than by the BOP/BOT model. By relocating to the state (unit) level of analysis and using a combination of material-ideational drivers as explanatory tools, this new framework is able to fill important gaps in our understanding of the formation, management, and prospects of the TSD virtual alliance that a purely system-level analysis misses. By reconceptualizing notions of "insecurity," as manifested in the so-called intra-alliance security dilemma, for example, it achieves enhanced understanding of internal dynamics affecting alliance behavior. In essence, it captures the crucial details of interstate and intrastate behavioral dynamics that are not factored into the orthodox BOP/BOT theoretical canon. In sum, the findings of Chapter 3 have demonstrated that this modified intra-alliance politics framework can be effectively applied to contemporary alliances in all their variants to provide significant new insights into alignment dynamics.

Next, the application of a suitably modified analytical framework, based upon the foundational work of Karl Deutsch, and Emmanuel Adler and Michael Barnett, to the ASEAN security community case study (Chapter 5) also exposed significant findings. Importantly, it confirmed that "the idea of security community is also distinct from that of an alliance."[3] It is a different paradigm altogether, with states aligning for the purposes of both internal and external "war avoidance" in preference to traditional "collective defense" (a characteristic the SCO also shares to a certain degree). As such, a distinct set of analytical tools is needed to understand its alignment dynamics, and different benchmarks are required to assess its effectiveness. As Amitav Acharya points out: "ASEAN's approach to regional cooperation has differed not only from the conventional process of alliance building, in the sense of being inspired exclusively by a common external threat; it has also differed from integrationalist models exemplified by the EU, which remains the most important example of a regional security community."[4]

As well as accounting for intramural behavior, the application of the modified analytical framework provided here has indicated the importance of external factors bearing upon internal relations. First, the case study findings have validated the need to reincorporate some realist elements back into the dominant constructivist-based security community framework. The ASC throughout its life span has remained conscious of security threats both from within and from outside the ASEAN. Nevertheless, important new literature that has looked at a security community's external orientation allows us to perceive how the ASC as an alignment has largely eschewed traditional military balancing, instead building an overarching institution across the region in the form of "ASEAN-plus." By emphasizing this characteristic of security communities, it becomes clearer that states are in alignment, while using different tools, such as "soft power" or "soft balancing," to protect and advance their collective interests, principally by seeking to "socialize" or "enmesh" the region's major powers. Lastly, it is worth noting that the ASC's ability to operate as a cohesive alignment is predicated upon the effective functioning of intramural relations. As Acharya observes, "resisting marginalization in a multipolar environment would be impossible for ASEAN unless it holds together as a group."[5]

Finally, the SCO "strategic partnership" network represents the most novel and understudied case (Chapter 7). Due to its nonconformity to existing international relations (IR) paradigms of alignment, it has been necessary to formulate its precepts from scratch with the assistance of literature appertaining to business/organization studies, from which the term originated. Distilling an analytical framework from this literature, as well as relevant aspects of IR that can be brought to bear, I have provided a first-cut model to account for its nature, purpose, and behavioral dynamics. The application of this new framework has allowed us to track the development of the SCO case study from its genesis in the Sino-Russian strategic partnership of the 1990s to the present, as it stands on the cusp of further expansion across Eurasia. Developed outside the Cold War traditional alliance paradigm in the early part of the twenty-first century, it champions close security cooperation among China and Russia within a wider multilateral (Central Asian) regional context and beyond. While elements of common interest and shared values are certainly familiar motivators for cooperation that can be captured under the intra-alliance politics framework, the structure and purpose of the SCO is distinct from Western military alliances or the former Sino-Soviet pact. Now the Sino-Russian strategic partnership alongside the SCO is emerging as an alternative "pole" of geopolitical attraction, for those excluded by the US-alliance or ASEAN "clubs." It represents a new Eurasian model in counterpoint to the long-standing American "San Francisco system" and the more recent ASEAN-plus efforts at regional community. It fits neither the orthodox alliance nor security community paradigms and therefore requires new tools for analysis. This may explain why the SCO "has remained one of the world's least-known and least-analyzed multilateral groups."[6]

The main focus of this book has been to probe the internal dynamics and external orientations of each of the three alignment groupings that span the Asia Pacific. But a brief word may be said specifically on how these three alignments interact with one another. There are three relevant points to make here. The first, as alluded to throughout the preceding analysis, is the incipient formation of three regional blocs—largely a competitive bipolarity between the TSD and SCO, with the ASC caught in the middle. Michael Green and Bates Gill contend that "if these kinds of minilateral security arrangements begin to view one another as 'containment' mechanisms, 'exclusionary blocs,' or potential rivals, the result will not be positive for regional security."[7] In some ways, geopolitical rivalry between the emerging continental (SCO) and maritime (TSD) alignments places the third alignment, the ASC, not powerful enough to stand alone, in the unenviable position of having to "choose sides." As previously noted, so far the ASC members have sought to avoid this predicament by seeking to mediate great power tensions and rivalries through their ASEAN-plus institutional efforts. Shaun Narine argues,

> ASEAN is, even now, serving a useful and even essential role as a mediator between the great powers of the region. East Asia constitutes a unique security environment wherein several great and rising powers will compete with each other for followers and influence into the foreseeable future. As a bloc of "follower" states, this reality provides ASEAN with the opportunity to influence regional events.[8]

However, this role is now increasingly undermined by the sharpening geopolitical competition in the region, which has resulted in the leaders of the opposing TSD and SCO blocs courting allegiance from the ASC members. Acharya notes that "the principle of ASEAN's neutrality is unravelling. While both the United States and China continue to pay lip service to ASEAN centrality, their policies have chipped away at its principal corollary—ASEAN neutrality."[9] While the TSD has sought association with certain Southeast Asian states (Singapore, Indonesia, Vietnam), Beijing has adopted a more "hands off approach," though this may be changing, notably with shifts in alignment toward China visible in Thailand, the Philippines, Laos, and Cambodia. Barry Desker argues that "Beijing's approach is significant as most Southeast Asian states prefer not to have to choose between alignment with the US and alignment with China and have adopted 'hedging' strategies in their relationships with the two powers."[10] Yet, as tensions between emerging Washington-led and Beijing-led power blocs heighten, the pressure to take sides will only increase.

These tensions are already being played out to some extent within the ASC's pan-regional security architecture, the ASEAN-plus institutions. These institutions are beginning to develop into an arena in which the other powerful alignments conduct their rivalries despite the ASC's past effort to mediate/socialize these powers into a stable and secure regional environment. As Andrew Carr and Joanne Wallis note, "there is concern that the great powers are not so much cooperating through the same institutions as they are competing via the institutions through which they have the most influence."[11] For example, the TSD powers "stressed the value of the East Asia Summit (EAS) as a Leaders-led forum for strategic dialogue and reiterated the importance of strengthening the EAS as the premier forum in the region."[12] Beijing courts the ASEAN+3 as the preferred mechanism for security dialogue since it pointedly excludes the United States and Australia. Additionally, the centrality of the ASEAN-plus institutions is also under threat from "China's expanding vision of, and approaches to, regionalism," which revolve around the SCO and a suite of related instruments such as the Belt and Road Initiative (BRI) and Asian Infrastructure Investment Bank (AIIB).[13]

Yet, on the other hand, Stephen Aris speculates, due to their multilateral institutional nature, "There is significant potential for inter-regional cooperation between ASEAN and SCO on a number of common interests and within a framework of common perceptions and values."[14] Given that both these organizations and their associated institutional apparatus are more focused upon regionalism in Asia and Eurasia, there may be potential for some form of concordance in terms of region and community-building that is absent from the US-led alliance project.

Following from this, and further complicating the picture, it should also be remembered that core membership of the three alignments examined here also enjoys wider support from "peripheral" members or associates. The TSD remains part of a broader US alliance system that notably includes South Korea and nominally the Philippines and Thailand. The United States also has a "virtual" alliance relationship with Taiwan and "strategic partnerships" with India and Singapore, making it possible to speak of a TSD-plus model. For the SCO, the accession of India and Pakistan at the time of writing, as well as the observer states (Iran, Mongolia, Belarus, and Afghanistan) and the dialogue partners (Sri Lanka, Turkey, Armenia, Azerbaijan, Cambodia, and Nepal) also add to the critical mass of this alignment (an SCO-plus model). The ASEAN-plus model, already discussed, indicates the format through which the ASC seeks wider affiliation. Each of these alignment cores seeks to encourage adherence to its own vision of order, while acting as a "pole" of attraction. Bruce Russett and Curtis Lamb stipulate that "a pole is not a single state, but a group of nations joined by linkages of varying types and strengths; and the ability of a pole to generate allegiances can be weakened as easily by inadequate attention to its bonds as by military failures or an eroding power base."[15]

Lastly, it should be recognized that while the alignments studied here are nominally "exclusive," there are some crosscutting alignments between members of each grouping. As Michael Ward points out: "overlapping and cross-cutting alliance memberships are quite prevalent in inter-state relations. Given the broadness of the notion of alignment, it should be no surprise that the degree of alignment on subsets of issues and within subsets of nations will vary; that is they will be overlapping and cross-cutting."[16] To give one prominent example, Singapore is at the center of the ASC and yet it remains closely affiliated with the TSD-plus through its "strategic partnership" with the United States and via the FPDA, which includes Australia. This also demonstrates that regional and international alignments are a complex web of interactions, with the presence of "bilaterals" nested in "plurilaterals" (sometimes called "minilaterals") and "plurilaterals" nested in "multilaterals," according to William Tow and Brendan Taylor.[17]

Toward a "Grand Theory" of Alignment?

As indicated in Chapter 1, the phenomenon of alignment is fundamental to workings of the international system and a core concern of IR. In this vein, the book has endeavored toward advancing a more complex, nuanced, and holistic understanding of the phenomenon moving beyond system-level explanations by focusing primarily upon the interstate level of analysis. The phenomenon, as this book has argued, is long overdue for a reconstitution of its underlying theoretical bases to better address how existing paradigms of alignment have evolved and to account for newly emergent paradigms. With all of the case studies in this book claiming to be aligning as much against NTS as traditional military-territorial ones, the very nature of security alignment appears to be undergoing significant changes by departing to some degree from its original conception of military-territorial collective defense. The TSD has continued to list terrorism, transnational crime, infectious diseases, human security, and cybersecurity as priorities for security cooperation, even as these have taken a back seat to North Korean nuclear dangers and Chinese provocations in the South China Sea.[18] Likewise, Stéphanie Martel notes that "ASEAN has also made 'non-traditional security' (NTS) a central element of its approach to community-building."[19] And the SCO's latest summit declaration highlighted, among others, terrorism, violent extremism, transnational crime, sustainable development, and environmental issues as joint security priorities.[20] This book has sought to update and reformulate existing paradigms and present modified analytical frameworks that acknowledge these sea changes.

Though the traditional alliance paradigm and the theories developed to explain it remain necessary conceptual foundations of any alignment theory (Chapter 2), they are not entirely sufficient to extrapolate on all aspects of alliances and certainly not adequate to explain newer forms of alignment such as the security community and strategic partnership archetypes. Tow advises us that "the 'hybridization' of state-centric and asymmetrical security challenges will likely yield future mechanisms that may not fit the theoretical explanations and rationales for those alliance, alignment or coalition models which are most familiar to us."[21] By incorporating new conceptual tools into our theoretical repertoire, we can enhance our overall understanding of alignment as a "holistic" phenomenon as well as enhancing paradigm-specific results. Indeed, Tow affirms that "theories explaining the future of security partnerships will need to clarify such complexities more effectively than now is the case if the evolution of alliance, alignment and coalition politics is to be adequately understood and applied."[22]

Though the formulation of a "grand theory" remains beyond the scope of this book, the preceding study has edged us toward a potentially more unified understanding of alignment. Though the basic explanatory power to traditional structural theories of alignment remains an important point of departure and some elements of BOP/BOT necessarily permeate the analytical frameworks presented here, it does not fully capture the complex behavioral dynamics of highly differentiated paradigms. Notably, analysis of the case studies has shown that the framework's equal coverage of both internal dynamics and external factors increases their utility and somewhat corrects the exclusive system-level bias of the traditional structuralist approaches that have heretofore dominated alignment theorizing.

It has been emphasized throughout this study that different paradigms of alignment require separately constructed analytical frameworks to understand them. The empirical analysis has also revealed some interesting intersections between the paradigms and their associated analytical frameworks. These intersections may point the way for further research into a more overarching or unified grand theory of alignment. Moreover, despite their origins in competing research traditions—realism, liberalism and constructivism, and constructivism and organizational studies—this study has uncovered some uniformities and overlaps in their theoretical bases and the corresponding analytical frameworks.

First, the intra-alliance politics framework rectifies some shortcomings of the system-level BOP/BOT theory of alliance/alignment (Chapter 2). Alex Bellamy argues that "traditional alliance theories, with their emphasis on objective goods such as pre-political 'national interests' and degrees of obligation and mutuality, downplay the social and relational aspects of transnational security relationships."[23] By incorporating ideational factors such as ideology, domestic politics, and norms from liberal and constructivist approaches, we gain a more composite picture of allied relations. This recognition draws attention toward synergy with constructivist approaches to security communities. Emmanuel Adler and Patricia Greve note, "In the context of the security community mechanism, alliances or alignments are rooted in mutual trust and collective identity (even if they might have been a matter of expediency in their origins); this quells the internal and external security dilemma for states within a security community."[24] In other words, in some ways, alliances can be security communities or at least demonstrate some of the properties thereof, and hence be subject to the application of some aspects of security community theory.

This dynamic cuts both ways. Using the security community framework, we can discern that security communities in practice have been subject to external/internal "insecurity" dynamics normally corresponding to the alliance paradigm. Even Adler and Barnett, the authors of the seminal work on security communities, acknowledge that such alignments may be shaped by "external threat" perceptions, at least in initial stages. Noting its focus on an external threat from Vietnam in its early years, Acharya attests that "ASEAN functioned more as a sub-regional alliance than a regional security community."[25] Likewise, other scholars have also pointed to the presence of both balancing and associative efforts in ASEAN. Ralf Emmers notes that, "in short, collective defense alignments and cooperative security institutions may operate side by side, but separately."[26] Empirically, the presence of some form of military alliance guarantee has overlaid the development of a security community. While the EU/NATO case would be exemplary, this also applies to the ASEAN case, which gained traditional security assurance first through the Southeast Asia Treaty Organization (SEATO) and subsequently through bilateral/multilateral arrangements with external powers, either bilaterally with the United States or multilaterally through the Five Power Defense Arrangements (FPDA). Hence, "Southeast Asia is therefore often said to accommodate a dual security system, one ranging from bilateral military arrangements to multilateral expressions of cooperative security."[27] This suggests that security communities may not therefore be able to independently evolve in the absence of military power-balancing conditions.

Moreover, if a security community becomes cohesive enough to become a "regional fortress," as M. J. Reese argues, then threat perceptions toward an external "other" may subsequently (re)emerge. The ASC case study also indicated that for all the emphasis on NTS threats, more traditional territorial disputes are remerging, at least for some members, due to conflict with the People's Republic of China (PRC) in the South China Sea. In addition, according to the case study findings, the focus on domestic politics in the intra-alliance politics perspective is also something that requires greater attention in the security community perspective. Andrej Tusicisny argues that the disposition of "public opinion" needs to be taken into account in building trust among communities, and the ASC case study has pointed toward the tensions arising from the diversity of regimes that comprise its membership and the difficulties associated with achieving trust or we-feeling among non-liberal states: a problem also arguably undermining the SCO.[28] Thus, this issue also typically appears to a greater or lesser degree in both alliances and strategic partnerships.

Finally, the strategic partnership framework points to several significant convergences with the prior perspectives and therefore represents an invaluable addition to our taxonomy of alignment. First, it displays a remarkable resemblance with the security community perspective in the way it develops in three phases, or rather "stages." In the formation stage, it indicated that "insecurity" or "uncertainty" in the system primes such partnerships, à la traditional alliance theory, and that they are often based upon shared interests and values (conceived as "strategic fit"), as captured in the intra-alliance politics framework. That "leadership" is a prime mover in alliances and security communities as well as strategic partnerships has also been amply demonstrated: each requires political entrepreneurship on the part of state leaders. Likewise, the notion of "system principle" dovetails with notions of alliance "ideology" and security community "we-feeling." It is also the repository for "norms" of behavior common to both the alliance and security community perspectives. This is starkly evident in the case of the SCO's "Shanghai Spirit" and other norms of behavior, which partly replicate the "ASEAN way." According to Christopher Len, the "'ASEAN way' is in many ways, similar to the SCO's 'Shanghai Spirit' of mutual trust and benefit, equality, consultation, respect for different civilizations, and common prosperity."[29] Indeed, Marc Lanteigne goes as far as claiming that "the SCO must now be studied not only as a security community but also as an evolving regional community, one which is growing in confidence and expanding its interests well beyond its original mandates."[30]

Second, the notion of an implementation stage is equally applicable to the institutional development of alliances and security communities, once formed, as is the notion of "organizational culture" developed around increasing interaction patterns. Notable here is the use of leader's summit meetings and "2+2" foreign and defense minister meetings across all the forms of alignment considered. Also, both strategic partnerships and security communities use the term *coupling* to determine how closely institutional bonds intertwine. Third, the evaluation stage overlaps with the need to match criteria for nascent/ascendant/mature security community phases of that model. In addition, the importance of mutual perceptions is stressed in all three frameworks. Lastly, it should be noted that all three perspectives, explicitly or implicitly, acknowledge that building alignments is about capabilities aggregation, in line with traditional structural accounts, and consequentially generating institutional capabilities.

These putative points of convergence notwithstanding, how we classify a certain alignment as "alliance," "security community," or "strategic partnership" will determine how we perceive and evaluate it. Ascertaining what form of alignment a case represents dictates which analytical framework is most appropriate to capture its behavioral dynamics. For example, if the ASEAN alignment is misconstrued as an "alliance" and consequentially inappropriate analytical tools are applied, this will lead to fundamental misunderstandings as to its nature and purpose. Likewise, the same erroneous application of "alliance" labels to the SCO, or indeed the absence of any categorization, can have equally detrimental consequences.

Moreover, in practice "alliances" have evolved well beyond the limits of the traditional theories designed to explain the paradigm in the 1970s through 1980s, as the TSD case illustrates. As reiterated throughout this book, the Western political and scholarly attachment to the alliance paradigm has impeded our understanding of the broader phenomenon of alignment. Quite simply, Hugh White contends, "America's NATO experience has left it with a deep attachment to alliances and a tendency to exaggerate their value."[31] We now live in a changed world, in which a more finessed understanding of alignment is imperative. As Parag Khanna identifies, we now live "in a world of alignments, *not* alliances."[32] This book has provided an intensive analysis of the three major alignment groupings in the Asia Pacific region using specifically designed theoretical models. On the basis of the revised taxonomy of alignment, the analytical frameworks that accompany them, and the application of these to the key alignments in the Asia Pacific, it adds up to a comprehensive compendium of alignment behavior in both theory and practice.

Notes

1. US Department of State, "Australia–Japan–United States Trilateral Strategic Dialogue Ministerial Joint Statement."
2. David, "Explaining Third World Alignment," p. 234.
3. Acharya, *Constructing a Security Community in Southeast Asia*, p. 18.
4. Ibid., p. 285.
5. Acharya, "ASEAN 2030," p. 6.
6. Bailes and Dunay, "The Shanghai Cooperation Organization as a Regional Security Institution," p. 1.
7. Green and Gill, "Unbundling Asia's New Multilateralism," p. 25.
8. Narine, "ASEAN in the Twenty-First Century," p. 380.
9. Acharya, "The Myth of ASEAN Centrality?" p. 277.
10. Desker, "Why War Is Unlikely in Asia," p. 3.
11. Carr and Wallis, "An Introduction to Asia-Pacific Security," p. 11.
12. Ministry of Foreign Affairs, Japan, "Japan–United States–Australia Trilateral Strategic Dialogue Joint Statement."
13. Acharya, "The Myth of ASEAN Centrality?" p. 277.
14. Aris, "A New Model of Asian Regionalism," p. 464.
15. Russett and Lamb, "Global Patterns of Diplomatic Exchange," p. 37.
16. Ward, *Research Gaps in Alliance Dynamics*, p. 11.
17. See Tow and Taylor, *Bilateralism, Multilateralism and Asia-Pacific Security.*
18. White House, "Australia–Japan–United States Trilateral Leaders Meeting Joint Media Release"; US Department of State, "Australia–Japan–United States Trilateral Strategic Dialogue Ministerial Joint Statement."

19. Martel, "From Ambiguity to Contestation," p. 550.

20. Shanghai Cooperation Organisation, "Information Report Following the Meeting of the Council of Heads of State of the Shanghai Cooperation Organisation Member States."

21. Tow, "Alliances and Alignments in the Twenty-First Century," p. 16.

22. Ibid.

23. Bellamy, *Security Communities and Their Neighbours*, p. 6.

24. Adler and Greve, "When Security Community Meets Balance of Power," p. 71.

25. Acharya, *Constructing a Security Community in Southeast Asia*.

26. Emmers, *Cooperative Security and the Balance of Power in ASEAN and the ARF*, p. 1.

27. Emmers, "The Role of the Five Power Defence Arrangements in Southeast Asian Security Architecture," p. 87.

28. Tusicisny, "Security Communities and Their Values."

29. Len, "Energy Security Cooperation in Asia," p. 169.

30. Lanteigne, "'In Medias Res': The Development of the Shanghai Co-Operation Organization as a Security Community," p. 621.

31. White, "Alliances and Order in the 'Asian Century,'" p. 167.

32. Khanna, *The Second World*, p. 324. Italics added.

Acronyms

ACSA	Acquisition and Cross-Servicing Agreement
ADF	Australian Defence Force
ADIZ	Air Defense Identification Zone
ADMM	ASEAN Defense Ministers Meeting
AFTA	ASEAN Free Trade Area
AIIB	Asian Infrastructure Investment Bank
ANZUS	Australia, New Zealand, United States Security Treaty
APEC	Asia Pacific Economic Cooperation
APSC	ASEAN Political-Security Community
ARF	ASEAN Regional Forum
ASA	Association of Southeast Asia
ASC	ASEAN Security Community
ASEAN	Association of Southeast Asian Nations
ASEM	Asia-Europe Meeting
BMD	ballistic missile defense
BOP	balance of power
BOT	balance of threat
BRI	Belt and Road Initiative
CBM	confidence-building measure
CCP	Chinese Communist Party
CICA	Conference on Interaction and Confidence Building Measures in Asia
CLMV	Cambodia, Laos, Myanmar, and Vietnam
CMI	Chiang-Mai Initiative
COC	Code of Conduct

CSCAP	Council for Security Cooperation in Asia Pacific
CSTO	Collective Security Treaty Organization
DOC	Declaration on Conduct
DPRK	Democratic People's Republic of Korea
EAS	East Asia Summit
ECSC	European Coal and Steel Community
EEU	Eurasian Economic Union
EEZ	Exclusive Economic Zone
EPA	economic partnership agreement
EU	European Union
FDI	foreign direct investment
FPDA	Five Power Defense Arrangement
FTA	free trade agreement
GCC	Gulf Cooperation Council
HADR	humanitarian assistance and disaster relief
IAP	intra-alliance politics
IISS	International Institute for Strategic Studies
IR	international relations
ISA	intelligence sharing agreement
ISIL	Islamic State in Iraq and the Levant
ISR	intelligence, surveillance, and reconnaissance
JGSDF	Japan Ground Self-Defense Force
JSDF	Japan Self-Defense Forces
MOU	Memorandum of Understanding
NAFTA	North American Free Trade Agreement
NATO	North Atlantic Treaty Organization
NIC	newly industrialized country
NTS	nontraditional security
OBOR	One Belt, One Road
OSCE	Organization for Security and Co-operation in Europe
PLA	People's Liberation Army
PRC	People's Republic of China
PSI	Proliferation Security Initiative
RATS	Regional Anti-Terrorist Structure (SCO)
RCEP	Regional Comprehensive Economic Partnership
RSC	regional security complex
SCO	Shanghai Cooperation Organisation
SDCF	Security and Defense Cooperation Forum
SEANWFZ	Southeast Asian Nuclear Weapons Free Zone
SEATO	Southeast Asia Treaty Organization
TAC	Treaty of Amity and Cooperation
TPP	Trans Pacific Partnership

TSD	Trilateral Security Dialogue
UKUSA	United Kingdom–United States of America
UN	United Nations
UNCLOS	United Nations Convention for the Law of the Sea
US	United States
USFJ	US Forces in Japan
WMD	weapons of mass destruction
ZOPFAN	Zone of Peace, Freedom, and Neutrality

Bibliography

Acharya, Amitav. "Arguing About ASEAN: What Do We Disagree About?" *Cambridge Review of International Affairs*, vol. 22, no. 3 (2009): 493–499.

———. "ASEAN 2030: Challenges of Building a Mature Political and Security Community." ADBI Working Paper 441. Tokyo: Asian Development Bank Institute, 2013.

———. "Collective Identity and Conflict Management in Southeast Asia." In Adler and Barnett, *Security Communities,* 198–227.

———. *Constructing a Security Community in Southeast Asia: ASEAN and the Problem of Regional Order.* London: Routledge, 2001.

———. "The Emerging Regional Architecture of World Politics." *World Politics,* vol. 59, no. 4 (July 2007): 629–653.

———. "Ideas, Identity, and Institution Building from the 'ASEAN Way' to the 'Asia-Pacific Way'?" *Pacific Review,* vol. 10, no. 3 (1997): 319–346.

———. "The Myth of ASEAN Centrality?" *Contemporary Southeast Asia: A Journal of International and Strategic Affairs,* vol. 39, no. 2 (2017): 273–279.

———. "Remaking Southeast Asian Studies: Doubt, Desire and the Promise of Comparisons." *Pacific Affairs,* vol. 87, no. 3 (2014): 463–483.

———. "The Strong in the World of the Weak: Southeast Asia in Asia's Regional Architecture." In Green and Gill, *Asia's New Multilateralism,* 172–191.

———. *Why Is There No NATO in Asia? The Normative Origins of Asian Multilateralism.* Cambridge, MA: Weatherhead Center for International Affairs, Harvard University, 2005.

Acharya, Amitav, and See Seng Tan. "Betwixt Balance and Community: America, ASEAN, and the Security of Southeast Asia." *International Relations of the Asia-Pacific,* vol. 6, no. 1 (2005): 37–59.

Adib-Moghaddam, Arshin. "Regional Security Complex Theory: A Critical Examination." *International Studies Journal,* vol. 3, no. 1 (2006): 25–40.

Adler, Emmanuel. *Communitarian International Relations.* London: Routledge, 2005.

————. "Europe's New Security: A Pluralistic Security Community." In Beverly Crawford (ed.), *The Future of European Security,* 287–326. Berkeley: University of California Press, 1992.

————. "Imagined (Security) Communities: Cognitive Regions in International Relations." *Millennium,* vol. 26, no. 2 (1997): 249–277.

————. "Seeds of Peaceful Change: The OSCE's Security Community-Building Model." In Adler and Barnett, *Security Communities,* 119–160.

————. "Seizing the Middle Ground: Constructivism in World Politics." *European Journal of International Relations,* vol. 3, no. 3 (1997): 319–363.

————. "The Spread of Security Communities: Communities of Practice, Self-Restraint, and NATO's Post–Cold War Transformation." *European Journal of International Relations*, vol. 14, no. 2 (2008): 195–230.

Adler, Emmanuel, and Michael Barnett. "A Framework for the Study of Security Communities." In Adler and Barnett, *Security Communities,* 29–65.

———— (eds.). *Security Communities.* Cambridge: Cambridge University Press, 1998.

Adler, Emmanuel, and Beverly Crawford (eds.). *The Convergence of Civilizations.* Toronto, ON: University of Toronto Press, 2006.

Adler, Emmanuel, and Patricia Greve. "When Security Community Meets Balance of Power: Overlapping Regional Mechanisms of Security Governance." *Review of International Studies,* vol. 35, no. 1 (2009): 59–84.

Adomanis, Mark. "A Russian-China Alliance Is Emerging, and It Will Be a Disaster for the West." *Forbes,* May 20, 2014.

Agius, Christine. "Social Constructivism." In Collins, *Contemporary Security Studies,* 50–68.

Ahrne, Göran, and Nils Brunsson. "Organizations and Meta-Organizations." *Scandinavian Journal of Management,* vol. 21, no. 4 (2005): 429–449.

Akaha, Tsuneo, and David Arase (eds.). *The US-Japan Alliance: Balancing Soft and Hard Power in East Asia.* London: Routledge, 2009.

Akimoto, Daisuke. *The Abe Doctrine: Japan's Proactive Pacifism and Security Strategy.* Basingstoke, UK: Palgrave Macmillan, 2018.

————. "Exercising the Right to Collective Self-Defense? An Analysis of 'Japan's Peace and Security Legislation.'" *Zeitschrift für Japanisches Recht,* vol. 21, no. 41 (2016): 137–164.

Akiner, Shirin. "The Shanghai Cooperation Organisation: A Networking Organisation for a Networking World." Global Strategy Forum, June 2010, pp. 1–20.

Akrasanee, Narongchai. "Issues in ASEAN Economic Regionalism." In Karl D. Jackson and M. Hadi Soesastro (eds.), *ASEAN Security and Economic Development*, 71–83. Berkeley: University of California Press, 1984.

Alagappa, Mutihiah (ed.). *Asian Security Order: Instrumental and Normative Features.* Stanford: Stanford University Press, 2003.

————. *Asian Security Practice: Material and Ideational Influences.* Palo Alto, CA: Stanford University Press, 1998.

Allison, Graham. *Destined for War: Can America and China Escape Thucydides's Trap?* London: Scribe Publications, 2017.

Allison, Graham, and Philip Zelikov. *Essence of Decision: Explaining the Cuban Missile Crisis.* Reading, MA: Addison-Wesley, 1999.

Alter, Catherine, and Jerald Hage. *Organizations Working Together.* London: Sage, 1993.

Ambrosio, Thomas. "The Architecture of Alignment: The Russia-China Relationship and International Agreements." *Europe-Asia Studies*, vol. 69, no. 1 (2017): 110–156.

―――. "Catching the 'Shanghai Spirit': How the Shanghai Cooperation Organization Promotes Authoritarian Norms in Central Asia." *Europe-Asia Studies*, vol. 60, no. 8 (2008): 1321–1344.

Anderson, Jennifer. "The Limits of Sino-Russian Strategic Partnership." *Adelphi Paper* 315. New York: Oxford University Press, 1997.

Antonenko, Oksana. "The EU and the Shanghai Cooperation Organisation." Online Paper, No Date. http://src-h.slav.hokudai.ac.jp/kaken/iwashita2007/01antonenko-eng.pdf.

Arase, David. "Non-traditional Security in China-ASEAN Cooperation." *Asian Survey,* vol. 50, no. 4 (2010): 808–833.

Aris, Stephen. *Eurasian Regionalism—The Shanghai Cooperation Organisation.* London: Palgrave Macmillan, 2011.

―――. "A New Model of Asian Regionalism: Does the Shanghai Cooperation Organisation Have More Potential than ASEAN?" *Cambridge Review of International Affairs*, vol. 22, no. 3 (2009): 451–467.

―――. "The Shanghai Cooperation Organisation: 'Tackling the Three Evils'. A Regional Response to Non-traditional Security Challenges or an Anti-Western Bloc?" *Europe-Asia Studies*, vol. 61, no. 3 (2009): 457–482.

―――. "Spreading the Shanghai Spirit: A Chinese Model of Regionalization in Post-Soviet Central Asia." In Kavalski (ed.) *China and the Global Politics of Regionalization*. 153–164. Aldershot: Ashgate, 2009.

Armitage, Richard, and Joseph Nye. "The U.S.-Japan Alliance: Anchoring Stability in Asia." CSIS Report, Washington DC, 2012.

Ashizawa, Kuniko. "Australia-Japan-US Trilateral Strategic Dialogue and the ARF: Extended Bilateralism or a New Minilateral Option?" In Jürgen Haacke and Noel M. Morada (eds.). *Cooperative Security in the Asia-Pacific: The ASEAN Regional Forum*. London: Routledge, 2011.

Asia-Pacific Partnership on Clean Development and Climate. "Overview." Accessed October 1, 2011. http://www.asiapacificpartnership.org/english/about.aspx.

Associated Press. "Philippines to 'Set Aside' South China Sea Tribunal Ruling to Avoid Imposing on Beijing." *The Guardian*, December 17, 2016.

Association of Southeast Asian Nations. "AFTA & FTAs." Accessed October 2, 2011. http://www.aseansec.org/4920.htm.

Association of Southeast Asian Nations. *Agreement on the Common Effective Preferential Tariff Scheme for the ASEAN Free Trade Area*, Singapore, January 1992.

―――. *ASEAN Agreement on Transboundary Haze Pollution*. Kuala Lumpur, June 2002. http://haze.asean.org/2016/09/asean-agreement-on-transboundary-haze-pollution-2.

―――. "ASEAN Leaders' Declaration on the 50th Anniversary of ASEAN." August 8, 2017.

―――. "ASEAN Member States." Accessed November 3, 2011. http://www.aseansec.org/18619.htm.

―――. "ASEAN Political-Security Community Blueprint." 2009.

―――. "ASEAN Security Community Plan of Action." Accessed November 3, 2011. http://www.aseansec.org/16826.htm.

―――. "ASEAN Vision 2020." Kuala Lumpur, December 1997. http://asean.org/?static_post=asean-vision-2020.

————. "Cebu Declaration on East Asian Energy Security." Cebu, January 2007. http://dfat.gov.au/international-relations/regional-architecture/eas/pages/cebu -declaration-on-east-asian-energy-security.aspx.

————. "The Founding of ASEAN." Accessed November 2, 2011. http://www .asean.org/asean/about-asean/history.

————. "Regional Comprehensive Economic Partnership (RCEP)." October 3, 2016. http://asean.org/?static_post=rcep-regional-comprehensive-economic-partnership/.

Association of Southeast Asian Nations Wildlife Enforcement Network. "About Us." Accessed November 3, 2011. http://www.aseanwen.org/index.php?option=com _content&view=article&id=47&Itemid=55.

Auslin, Michael. *The End of the Asian Century: War, Stagnation, and the Risks to the World's Most Dynamic Region.* New Haven, CT: Yale University Press, 2017.

————. "Shaping a Pacific Future: Washington's Goal for the Trilateral Strategic Dialogue." In Tow et al., *Assessing the Trilateral Security Dialogue,* 11–22.

Austin, James. *The Collaboration Challenge.* San Francisco: Jossey-Bass, 2000.

Australian Agency for International Development. "East Asia Regional." Accessed November 3, 2011. http://www.ausaid.gov.au/countries/eastasia/regional/Pages /home.aspx.

Australian Department of Defence. "Australia-Japan Bilateral Exercise Concludes." April 23, 2016. https://news.defence.gov.au/media/media-releases/australia-japan -bilateral-exercise-concludes.

————. *Australia's National Security: A Defence Update 2003.* Canberra, 2003.

————. *Australia's National Security: A Defence Update 2005.* Canberra, 2005.

————. *Defence 2000: Our Future Defence,* Canberra, 2000.

————. *2013 Defence White Paper.* Canberra, May 2013. http://www.defence.gov .au/whitepaper/2013.

————. *2016 Defence White Paper.* Canberra, February 2016. http://www.defence .gov.au/WhitePaper.

Australian Government. *Australia in the Asian Century.* Canberra, October 2012. http://www.defence.gov.au/whitepaper/2013/docs/australia_in_the_asian_century _white_paper.pdf.

Australian Minister for Foreign Affairs. "China's Announcement of an Air-Defence Identification Zone over the East China Sea." November 26, 2013. http:// foreignminister.gov.au/releases/Pages/2013/jb_mr_131126a.aspx?ministerid=4.

Australian Strategic Policy Institute. "Global Jigsaw: ASPI's Strategic Assessment 2008." Barton, ACT: Australian Strategic Policy Institute, 2008.

Ayoob, Mohammed. "Defining Security: A Subaltern Realist Perspective." In Keith Krause and Michael C. William (eds.), *Critical Security Studies,* 121–146. Minneapolis: University of Minnesota Press, 1997.

————. "From Regional System to Regional Society: Exploring Key Variables in the Construction of Regional Order." *Australian Journal of International Affairs,* vol. 53, no. 3 (1999): 247–260.

Ayson, Robert. *Asia's Security.* New York: Palgrave Macmillan, 2015.

Ayson, Robert, and Desmond Ball (eds.). *Strategy and Security in the Asia-Pacific.* Crows Nest, NSW: Allen & Unwin, 2006.

Azarkan, Ezeli. "The Interests of the Central Asian States and the Shanghai Cooperation Organization." *Ege Academic Review,* vol. 10, no. 1 (2010): 395–420.

Ba, Alice. "ASEAN Centrality Imperiled? ASEAN Institutionalism and the Challenges of Major Power Institutionalization." In Emmers (ed.). *ASEAN and the Institutionalization of East Asia,* 114–129.

————. "On Norms, Rule Breaking, and Security Communities: A Constructivist Response." *International Relations of the Asia-Pacific,* vol. 5, no. 2 (2005): 255–266.

————. "Who Is Socializing Whom? Complex Engagement in Sino-ASEAN Relations." *Pacific Review,* vol. 19, no. 2 (2006): 157–179.

Baev, Pavel K. "Russia's Pivot to China Goes Astray: The Impact on the Asia-Pacific Security Architecture." *Contemporary Security Policy,* vol. 37, no. 1 (2016): 89–110.

Bailes, Alyson J. K., and Pál Dunay. "The Shanghai Cooperation Organization as a Regional Security Institution." In Bailes et al., *The Shanghai Cooperation Organization,* 1–29.

Bailes, Alyson J. K., Pál Dunay, Pan Guang, and Mikhail Troitskiy. *The Shanghai Cooperation Organization.* SIPRI Policy Paper No. 17. Stockholm: SIPRI, 2007.

Baker, Richard W., and Galen W. Fox. *Asia Pacific Security Survey Report 2008.* Honolulu: East West Center, 2008. Accessed December 30, 2008. http://www .eastwestcenter.org/system/tdf/private/apss2008_1.pdf?file=1&type=node&id=32273.

Baldino, Daniel, and Andrew Carr. "The End of 2%: Australia Gets Serious About Its Defence Budget." *The Conversation,* February 26, 2016. http://theconversation .com/the-end-of-2-australia-gets-serious-about-its-defence-budget-53554.

Baldino, Daniel, Juliet Pietsch, David Lundberg, and John Rees. *Contemporary Challenges to Australian Security.* London: Palgrave Macmillan, 2011.

Baldwin, David A. (ed.). *Neorealism and Neoliberalism: The Contemporary Debate.* New York: Columbia Press, 1993.

Ball, Desmond. "Reflections on Defence Security in East Asia." RSIS Working Paper 237. Singapore: S. Rajaratnam School of International Studies, 2012.

————. "Security Cooperation Between Japan and Australia: Current Elements and Future Prospects." In Brad Williams and Andrew Newman (eds.). *Japan, Australia and Asia Pacific Security,* 164-185. New York: Routledge, 2006.

————. "The US-Australian Alliance: History and Prospects." Working Paper, no. 330. Strategic and Defence Studies Centre, Australian National University, Canberra, 1999.

————. "Whither the Japan-Australia Security Relationship?" APSNet Policy Forum, September 21, 2006. https://nautilus.org/apsnet/0632a-ball-html.

Baltrusaitis, Daniel F. *Coalition Politics and the Iraq War.* Boulder, CO: Lynne Rienner, 2010.

Baral, L. S. "Nepal and Non-Alignment." *International Studies,* vol. 20, no. 1 (1981): 257–272.

Barnett, Michael. *Dialogues in Arab Politics: Negotiations in Regional Politics.* New York: Columbia University Press, 1998.

Barnett, Michael, and F. Gregory Gause III. "Caravans in Opposite Directions: Society, State and the Development of a Community in the Gulf Cooperation Council." In Adler and Barnett (eds.). *Security Communities,* 161–197.

Barnett, Michael N., and Jack S. Levy. "Domestic Sources of Alliances and Alignments: The Case of Egypt, 1962–73." *International Organization,* vol. 45, no. 3 (1991): 369–395.

Barry, Mark P. "Korean Reunification Would Cast Off China's Shadow." *World Policy,* June 11, 2012. https://worldpolicy.org/2012/06/11/korean-reunification-would -cast-off-chinas-shadow.

Basu Das, Sanchita (ed.). *Achieving the ASEAN Economic Community 2015: Challenges for Member Countries & Business.* Singapore: Institute of Southeast Asian Studies, 2012.

Baylis, John, Steve Smith, and Patricia Owens. *The Globalization of World Politics: An Introduction to International Relations*, Fifth edition. Oxford: Oxford University Press, 2011.

Bayly, Christopher, and Tim Harper. *Forgotten Armies: The Fall of British Asia 1941–1945*. London: Penguin Books, 2004.

Becker, Patricia. *Illiberal Security Communities: A Revised Concept and the Empirical Example of ASEAN*. Munich: GRIN Publishing, 2004.

Beeson, Mark. "American Hegemony and Regionalism: The Rise of East Asia and the End of the Asia-Pacific." *Geopolitics*, vol. 11, no. 4 (2006): 541–560.

——— (ed.). *Contemporary Southeast Asia: Regional Dynamics, National Differences*. New York: Palgrave Macmillan, 2004.

———. *Institutions of the Asia-Pacific: ASEAN, APEC and Beyond*. London: Routledge, 2009.

———. *Regionalism and Globalization in East Asia: Politics, Security and Economic Development*. Basingstoke, UK: Palgrave, 2007.

Beeson, Mark J., and Alex J. Bellamy. *Securing Southeast Asia: The Politics of Security Sector Reform*. London: Routledge, 2008.

Bell, Christopher M. "Thinking the Unthinkable: British and American Naval Strategies for an Anglo-American War, 1918–1931." *International History Review*, vol. 19, no. 4 (1997): 789–808.

Bell, Coral. *Dependent Ally: A Study of Australia's Relations with the United States and the United Kingdom Since the Fall of Singapore*. Canberra: Australian National University Press, 1984.

———. "Foreword." In Taylor, *Australia as an Asia Pacific Power*.

Bellamy, Alex J. *Security Communities and Their Neighbours: Regional Fortresses or Global Integrators?* Basingstoke, UK: Palgrave, 2004.

Berger, Samuel. "The US Stake in Greater Asian Integration." *Global Asia*, vol. 1, no. 1 (2006): 25–27.

Berger, Thomas. "From Sword to Chrysanthemum: Japan's Culture of Anti-militarism." *International Security*, vol. 17, no. 4 (1993): 119–50.

Bergquist, William H., Juli Betwee, and David Meuel. *Building Strategic Relationships*. San Francisco: Jossey-Bass, 1995.

Beukel, Erik. "ASEAN and ARF in East Asia's Security Architecture: The Role of Norms and Powers." Danish Institute for International Studies (DIIS) Report 4 (2008).

Bisley, Nick. "Asian Security Architectures." In Tellis and Wills, *Strategic Asia 2007*, 341–368.

———. *Building Asia's Security*, (Adelphi 408). London and New York: Routledge, 2009.

Bitzinger, Richard. "Military Modernization in the Asia-Pacific: Assessing New Capabilities." In Tellis, Marble, and Tanner (eds.). *Strategic Asia 2010–2011*, 79–112.

Blagov, Sergei. "Arms, Energy and Commerce in Sino-Russian Relations." *China Brief*, vol. 7, no. 16 (2007). https://jamestown.org/program/arms-energy-and-commerce-in-sino-russian-relations.

Blank, Stephen. "Russia and Vietnam Team Up to Balance China." *The National Interest*, April 7, 2014. http://nationalinterest.org/commentary/russia-vietnam-team-balance-china-10195.

———. "The Shanghai Cooperative Organization: Post-mortem or Prophecy." *China and Eurasia Forum Quarterly*, vol. 3. no. 2. (2005): 13–18.

Blumenthal, David, Randall Schriver, Mark Stokes, L. C. Russell Hsiao, and Michael Mazza. "Asian Alliances in the 21st Century." *Project 2049 Institute*, August 30, 2011. http://www.aei.org/wp-content/uploads/2011/10/Asian-Alliances -21st-Century.pdf.

Booth, Ken. "Alliances." In John Baylis et al. (eds.). *Contemporary Strategy I,* 258– 309. New York: Holmes & Meier, 1987.

Booth, Ken, and Nicholas Wheeler. *The Security Dilemma: Fear, Cooperation and Trust in World Politics.* Basingstoke, UK: Palgrave Macmillan, 2007.

Borthwick, Mark. *Pacific Century: The Emergence of Modern Pacific Asia.* Boulder, CO: Westview Press, 2007.

Bosbotinis, James. "Sustaining the Dragon, Dodging the Eagle and Barring the Bear? Assessing the Role and Importance of Central Asia in Chinese National Strategy." *China & Eurasia Forum Quarterly*, vol. 8, no. 1 (2010): 65–81.

Bracken, Paul. *Fire in the East: The Rise of Asian Military Power and the Second Nuclear Age.* New York: HarperCollins, 2000.

———. "How to Think About Korean Unification." *Orbis,* vol. 42, no. 3 (1998): 409–422.

Brady, David. "The Poverty of Liberal Economics." *Socio-Economic Review,* vol. 1, no. 3 (2003): 369–409.

Brands, Hal. *American Grand Strategy in the Age of Trump.* Washington, DC: Brookings Institution, 2018.

Brawley, Mark R., and Pierre Martin. "Kosovo, Alliance Politics and NATO." In Martin, Pierre, and Mark R. Brawley (eds.). *Alliance Politics, Kosovo, and NATO's War: Allied Force or Forced Allies?* 1–10. New York: Palgrave, 2000.

Bremberg, Niklas. *Diplomacy and Security Community-Building: EU Crisis Management in the Western Mediterranean.* Abingdon, UK: Routledge, 2016.

———. "The European Union as Security Community-Building Institution: Venues, Networks and Co-operative Security Practices." *Journal of Common Market Studies,* vol. 53, no. 3 (2015): 674–692.

Brewster, David. *India as an Asia Pacific Power.* Abingdon, UK: Routledge, 2011.

Bristow, Damon. "The Five Power Defence Arrangements: Southeast Asia's Unknown Regional Security Organization." *Contemporary Southeast Asia,* vol. 27, no. 1 (2005): 1–20.

Bronfenbrenner, M. "The Dilemma of Liberal Economics." *The Journal of Political Economy,* vol. 54, no. 4 (1946): 334–346.

Bryant-Tokalau, Jenny, and Ian Frazer (eds.). *Redefining the Pacific? Regionalism Past, Present and Future.* Aldershot, UK: Ashgate, 2006.

Buchan, Alistair. "Problems of an Alliance Policy: An Essay in Hindsight." In Michael Howard (ed.). *The Theory and Practice of War,* 293–310. Bloomington: Indiana University Press, 1965.

Bull, Hedley. *The Anarchical Society.* London: Macmillan, 1999.

Bundy, Barbara, Stephen D. Burns, and Kimberly V. Weichel (eds.). *The Future of the Pacific Rim.* London: Praeger, 1994.

Burchill, Scott, Andrew Linklater, Richard Devatak, Jack Donnely, Terry Nardin, Matthew Paterson, Christian Reus-Smit, and Jacqui True. *Theories of International Relations,* Fourth edition. New York: Palgrave, 2009.

Burton, J. W. *International Relations: A General Theory.* Cambridge: Cambridge University Press, 1965.

Buszynski, Leszek. *SEATO: The Failure of Alliance Strategy.* Singapore: Singapore University Press, 1983.

Buzan, Barry. "The Level of Analysis Problem in International Relations Reconsidered." In Ken Booth and Steve Smith (eds.). *International Relations Theory Today,* 198–216. Cambridge, MA: Polity Press, 1997.

———. *People, States and Fear.* New York: Harvester Wheatsheaf, 1991.

———. "Security Architecture in Asia: The Interplay Between the Regional and Global Levels." *Pacific Review*, vol. 16, no. 2 (2003): 143–173.

Buzan, Barry, Charles Jones, and Richard Little. *The Logic of Anarchy: Neorealism to Structural Realism.* New York: Columbia University Press, 1993.

Buzan, Barry, Morten Kelstrup, Pierre Lemaitre, and Elzbieta Tromer. *The European Security Order Recast: Scenarios for the Post-Cold War Era.* London: Pinter, 1990.

Buzan, Barry, and Ole Wæver. *Regions and Powers: The Structure of International Security.* Cambridge: Cambridge University Press, 2003.

Buzan, Barry, Ole Wæver, and Jaap de Wilde. *Security: A New Framework for Analysis.* Boulder, CO: Lynne Rienner, 1998.

Caballero-Anthony, Mely. "Non-traditional Security Challenges, Regional Governance, and the ASEAN Political-Security Community (APSC)." In Ralf Emmers (ed.). *ASEAN and the Institutionalization of East Asia,* 1–14. London: Routledge, 2012.

———. "Non-traditional Security and Multilateralism in Asia." In Michael Green and Bates Gill (eds.). *Asia's New Security Multilateralism*, 306–328. New York: Columbia University Press, 2009.

Caballero-Anthony, Mely, and Ralf Emmers. "Understanding the Dynamics of Securitizing Non-Traditional Security." In Mely Caballero-Anthony, Ralf Emmers, and Amitav Acharya (eds.). *Non-Traditional Security in Asia: Dilemmas in Securitisation,* 1–12. Aldershot, UK: Ashgate Publishing, 2006.

Calder, Kent E. *Asia's Deadly Triangle: How Arms, Energy, and Growth Threaten to Destabilize Asia-Pacific.* Sonoma, CA: Nicholas Brealey Publishers, 1997.

———. "Securing Security Through Prosperity: The San Francisco System in Comparative Perspective." *Pacific Review*, vol. 17, no. 1 (2004): 135–157.

Calder, Kent E., and Francis Fukuyama (eds.). *East Asian Multilateralism: Prospects for Regional Stability.* Baltimore: Johns Hopkins University Press, 2008.

Calder, Kent E., and Min Ye. *The Making of Northeast Asia.* Stanford: Stanford University Press, 2010.

Calvocoressi, Peter, and Ben Wint. *Total War: The Story of World War II.* London: Penguin Press, 1972.

Camilleri, Jospeh A., Larry Marshall, Michális S. Michael, and Michael T. Siegel (eds.). *Asia-Pacific Geopolitics: Hegemony vs Human Security.* Cheltenham, UK: Edward Elgar, 2007.

Campbell, Kurt M. "The End of Alliances? Not So Fast." *The Washington Quarterly,* vol. 27, no. 2 (2004): 151–163.

Capie, David. "The Bilateral-Multilateral Nexus in Asia's Defense Diplomacy." In Tow and Taylor, *Bilateralism, Multilateralism and Asia-Pacific Security,* 115–131.

———. "Evolving Attitudes to Peacekeeping in ASEAN." In Katsuya Tsukamoto (ed.). *New Trends in Peacekeeping: In Search of a New Direction,* 111–125. Tokyo: National Institute for Defence Studies, 2015.

———. "Explaining ASEAN's Resilience: Institutions, Path Dependency, and Asia's Emerging Architecture." In Emmers, *ASEAN and the Institutionalization of East Asia,* 168-179.

Capie, David, and Paul Evans. *The Asia-Pacific Security Lexicon.* Singapore: Institute of Southeast Asian Studies, 2007.

Carr, Andrew, and Joanne Wallis. "An Introduction to Asia-Pacific Security." In Wallis and Carr, *Asia-Pacific Security: An Introduction,* 1–22.

Carter, Ashton B., William J. Perry, and John D. Steinbruner. *A New Concept of Cooperative Security.* Washington, DC: Brookings Institution, 1992.

Castells, Manuel. "Four Asian Tigers with a Dragon Head: A Comparative Analysis of the State, Economy, and Society in the Asian Pacific Rim." In Richard Appelbaum and Jeffrey Henderson (eds.). *States and Development in the Asian Pacific Rim,* 33–70. Newbury Park, London, New Delhi: Sage, 1992.

Castillo, Adam. "SCO: Rise of NATO East?" *Diplomatic Courier,* August 18, 2008. http://www.css.ethz.ch/content/specialinterest/gess/cis/center-for-securities -studies/en/services/digital-library/articles/article.html/90108.

Centre for Research on Globalization, "U.S. Military Base in Uzbekistan to Counter Russia in Central Asia." August 25, 2012. https://www.globalresearch.ca/u-s -military-base-in-uzbekistan-to-counter-russia-in-central-asia/32484.

Cha, Victor D. *Alignment Despite Antagonism: The United States–Korea–Japan Security Triangle.* Palo Alto, CA: Stanford University Press, 1999.

———. "Complex Patchworks: U.S. Alliances as Part of Asia's Regional Architecture. *Asia Policy,* vol. 11, no. 1 (2011): 27–50.

———. "The Geometry of Asia's Architecture: Traditional and Transnational Security." In Charles W. Freeman III and Michael J. Green (eds.). *Asia's Response to Climate Change and Natural Disasters: Implications for an Evolving Regional Architecture,* 99–116. Washington, DC: Center for Strategic and International Studies, 2010.

———. *North Korea: The Impossible State.* New York: Harper-Collins, 2012.

———. *Powerplay: The Origins of the American Alliance System in Asia.* Princeton, NJ: Princeton University Press, 2016.

Chang, Jun Yan. "Essence of Security Communities: Explaining ASEAN." *International Relations of the Asia-Pacific,* vol. 16, no. 3 (2016): 335–369.

Chanlett-Avery, Emma, and Bruce Vaughn. "Emerging Trends in the Security Architecture in Asia: Bilateral and Multilateral Ties Among the United States, Japan, Australia, and India." *CRS Report for Congress,* January 7, 2008.

Charap, Samuel, John Drennan, and Pierre Noël. "Russia and China: A New Model of Great-Power Relations." *Survival,* vol. 59, no. 1 (2017): 25-42.

Chase, Michael. *Taiwan's Security Policy: External Threats and Domestic Politics.* Boulder, CO: Lynne Rienner, 2008.

Chellaney, Brahma. *Asian Juggernaut: The Rise of China, India, and Japan.* London: HarperCollins, 2010.

Cheng, Gouping, "The Shanghai Cooperation Organization: A Cause Worth Ceaseless Efforts." Keynote Speech by Vice Foreign Minister Cheng Guoping at the Lanting Forum, May 29, 2012. https://www.fmprc.gov.cn/mfa_eng/zxxx_662805 /t936026.shtml.

Chidley, Colleen. "Towards a Framework of Alignment in International Relations." *Politikon,* vol. 41, no. 1 (2014): 141–157.

Chinwanno, Chulacheeb. "Thailand's Security Policy: Bilateralism or Multilateralism?" In Tow and Taylor, *Bilateralism, Multilateralism and Asia-Pacific Security,* 68–84.

Chizov, Vladimir. "The 30th Anniversary of the Helsinki Final Act and the Problems of the OSCE." *Helsinki Monitor,* vol. 16, no. 3 (2005): 176–179.

Choi, Anjin, and William T. Tow. "Bridging Alliances and Asia Pacific Multilateralism." In Tow and Taylor, *Bilateralism, Multilateralism and Asia-Pacific Security*, 21–38.

Choi, Young Jong. "South Korea's Regional Strategy and Middle Power Activism." *Journal of East Asia Affairs*, vol. 23, no. 1 (2009): 47–67.

Chung, Chien. "Confidence-Building Measures in the South China Sea." In Hung-Mao Tien and Ten-jen Cheng (eds.) *The Security Environment in the Asia-Pacific*, 259–305. Armonk, N.Y.: M.E. Sharpe, 2000.

Chung, Chien-peng. "The Shanghai Cooperation Organization: China's Changing Influence in Central Asia." *The China Quarterly*, vol. 180 (December 2004): 989–1009.

Ciorciari, John D. *The Limits of Alignment: Southeast Asia and the Great Powers Since 1975*. Washington, DC: Georgetown University Press, 2010.

Clark, Cal, and K. C. Roy. *Comparing Development Patterns in Asia*. Boulder, CO: Lynne Rienner, 1997.

Clarke, Michael. "China and the Shanghai Cooperation Organization: The Dynamics of 'New Regionalism,' 'Vassalization,' and Geopolitics in Central Asia." In Emilian Kavalski (ed.). *The New Central Asia: The Regional Impact of International Actors*, 116–147. London: World Scientific and Imperial College Press, 2009.

Clinton, Hillary. "America's Pacific Century." *Foreign Policy*, October 11, 2011. https://foreignpolicy.com/2011/10/11/americas-pacific-century.

Cole, Bernard D. *Taiwan's Security: History and Prospects*. London: Routledge, 2006.

Cole, William, and Erik G. Jensen. "Norms and Regional Architecture: Multilateral Institution Building in Asia and Its Impact on Governance and Democracy." In Green and Gill, *Asia's New Multilateralism*, 243–278.

Collier, David, Fernando D. Hidalgo, and Andra O. Maciuceanu. "Essentially Contested Concepts: Debates and Applications." *Journal of Political Ideologies*, vol. 11, no.3 (2006): 211–246.

Collins, Alan. "Bringing Communities Back: Security Communities and the Association of Southeast Asian Nations' Plural Turn." *Cooperation and Conflict*, vol. 49, no. 2 (2014): 276–291.

——— (ed.). *Contemporary Security Studies*. Oxford: Oxford University Press, 2009.

———. "Forming a Security Community: Lessons from ASEAN." *International Relations of the Asia-Pacific*, vol. 12, no. 2 (2007): 203–225.

———. *The Security Dilemmas of South East Asia*. London: Macmillan, 2000.

Cooper, Andrew, Richard A. Higgott, and Kim Richard Nossal. *Relocating Middle Powers: Australia and Canada in a Changing World Order*. Melbourne: Melbourne University Press, 1993.

Cooper, Zack, and Andrew Shearer. "Thinking Clearly About China's Layered Indo-Pacific Strategy." *Bulletin of the Atomic Scientists*, vol. 73, no. 5 (2017): 305–311.

Cordesman, Anthony H. *Saudi National Security and the Saudi-US Strategic Partnership*. Washington, DC: Center for Strategic and International Studies, 2010.

———. "Evolving US Views on Asia's Future Institutional Architecture." In Green and Gill, *Asia's New Multilateralism*, 33–54.

———. "U.S.-Japan-Korea: Creating a Virtual Alliance." *PacNet* 47, Pacific Forum CSIS, December 3, 1999. https://csis-prod.s3.amazonaws.com/s3fs-public/legacy_files/files/media/csis/pubs/pac9947.pdf.

——— (ed.). *U.S.-Korea-Japan Relations: Building Toward a "Virtual Alliance."* Honolulu: Center for Strategic and International Studies, 1999.

Cossa, Ralph A., and Brad Glosserman. "The Pivot Is Dead, Long Live the Pivot." *Comparative Connections*, May 2017, 1–10. http://cc.csis.org/wp-content/uploads /2017/05/1701_overview.pdf.

———. "US-Japan Defense Cooperation: Has Japan Become the Great Britain of Asia?" *Issues and Insights*, vol. 5, no. 3 (2005): 1-21.

Cossa, Ralph A., Brad Glosserman, Michael A. McDevitt, Nirav Patel, James Przystup, and Brad Roberts. *The United States and the Asia-Pacific Region: Security Strategy for the Obama Administration.* Center for a New American Security, February 2009. https://csis-prod.s3.amazonaws.com/s3fs-public/legacy_files/files /media/csis/pubs/issuesinsights_v09n01.pdf.

Cotterell, Arthur. *Western Power in Asia: Its Slow Rise and Swift Fall 1415–1999.* Hoboken, NJ: John Wiley & Sons, 2010.

Council for Security Cooperation in Asia Pacific. "About Us." http://www.cscap .org/index.php?page=about-us.

Cox, Michael. "Beyond the West: Terrors in Transatlantic." *European Journal of International Relations*, vol. 11, no. 2 (2005): 203–233.

Cox, Robert T. "Middlepowermanship, Japan and the Future of World Order." *International Journal*, vol. 44, no. 4 (1999): 823–862.

Cozad, Mark R. "PLA Joint Training and Implications for Future Expeditionary Capabilities." Testimony presented before the US-China Economic and Security Review Commission, January 21, 2016. https://www.rand.org/content/dam/rand /pubs/testimonies/CT400/CT451/RAND_CT451.pdf.

Crosston, Matthew. "The Pluto of International Organizations: Micro-Agendas, IO Theory, and Dismissing the Shanghai Cooperation Organization." *Comparative Strategy*, vol. 32, no. 3 (2013): 283–294.

Crump, Thomas. *Asia-Pacific: A History of Empire and Conflict.* London: Hambeldon, 2007.

Dadabaev, Timur. "Shanghai Cooperation Organization (SCO) Regional Identity Formation from the Perspective of the Central Asia States." *Journal of Contemporary China*, vol. 23, no. 85 (2014): 102–118.

Dakhlallah, Farah. "The League of Arab States and Regional Security: Towards an Arab Security Community?" *British Journal of Middle Eastern Studies*, vol. 39, no. 3 (2012): 393–412.

David, Steven R. "Explaining Third World Alignment." *World Politics,* vol. 43, no. 2 (1991): 233–256.

Davies, Matthew. "Multilateralism and Security Communities." In Wallis and Carr, *Asia-Pacific Security: An Introduction,* 223–239.

Davison, Rémy. "Introduction: The Asia Pacific Century?" In Michael Kelly Connors, Rémy Davison, and Jörn Dosch (eds.). *The New Global Politics of the Asia Pacific*, Second edition, 1–21. New York: Routledge, 2012.

———. "Introduction: Asia's 'Great Game'?" In Michael Kelly Connors and Rémy Davison (eds.). *The New Global Politics of the Asia Pacific*, Third edition, 1– 28. New York: Routledge, 2017.

Dawson, Sandra. *Analysing Organisations,* Third edition. London: Macmillan, 1996.

De Haas, Marcel (ed.). *The Shanghai Cooperation Organisation: Towards a Full-Grown Security Alliance?* The Hague: Netherlands Institute of International Relations Clingendael, 2007.

Denmark, Abraham M., and Zachary M. Hosford. *Securing South Korea: A Strategic Alliance for the 21st Century.* Washington, DC: Center for New American

Security, 2010. Accessed October 3, 2018. https://www.cnas.org/publications /reports/securing-south-korea-a-strategic-alliance-for-the-21st-century.

Dent, Christopher M. *East Asian Regionalism*. London: Routledge, 2008.

Desker, Barry. "Why War Is Unlikely in Asia." *RSIS Commentaries,* June 27, 2008. Accessed October 3, 2018. https://www.rsis.edu.sg/rsis-publication/rsis/1091 -why-war-is-unlikely-in-asia.

Deutsch, Karl. *The Analysis of International Relations.* Englewood Cliffs, NJ: Prentice-Hall, 1968.

Deutsch, Karl, Sidney Burrell, and Robert Kann. *Political Community and the North Atlantic Area.* Princeton, NJ: Princeton University Press, 1957.

DeWit, Andrew. "Japan's Renewable Power Prospects." In Jeff Kingston (ed.). *Critical Issues in Contemporary Japan*, 120–134. Abingdon, UK: Routledge, 2014.

Dewitt, David. "Common, Comprehensive, and Cooperative Security." *Pacific Review,* vol. 7, no. 1 (1994): 1–15.

Dibb, Paul. "America and the Asia-Pacific Region." In Ayson and Ball, *Strategy and Security in the Asia-Pacific*, 173–190.

———. "Australia–United States." In Taylor, *Australia as an Asia-Pacific Regional Power*, 33-49.

DiMaggio, Paul J., and Walter W. Powell. "The Iron Cage Revisited: Institutional Isomorphism and Collective Rationality in Organizational Fields." *American Sociological Review*, vol. 48, no. 2 (1983): 147–160.

Dinerstein, Herbert S. "The Transformation of Alliance Systems." *The American Political Science Review*, vol. 59, no. 3 (1965): 589–601.

Dirlik, Arif. "The Asia-Pacific Idea: Reality and Representation in the Invention of Regional Structure." *Journal of World History*, vol. 3, no. 1 (1992): 55–79.

——— (ed.). *What's in a Rim? Critical Perspectives on the Pacific Region Idea.* Taipei: SMC Publishing, 1993.

Ditrych, Ondrej. "Security Community: A Future Idea for a Troubled Concept?" *International Relations*, vol. 28, no. 3 (2014): 350–366.

Dittmer, Lowell. "Political and Cultural Roots of the Sino-Russian Partnership." In Robert E. Bedeski and Niklas Swanström (eds.). *Eurasia's Ascent in Energy and Geopolitics: Rivalry or Partnership for China, Russia, and Central Asia?*, 16–33. Abingdon, UK: Routledge, 2012.

Doyle, Michael. "Liberalism and World Politics." *American Political Science Review,* vol. 80, no. 4 (1986): 1151–1169.

Dudden, Alexis. "Okinawa Today: Spotlight on Henoko." In Jeff Kingston (ed.). *Critical Issues in Contemporary Japan*. Boston: Credo, 2013.

Duffield, John. "Asia-Pacific Institutions in Comparative Perspective." In Alagappa, *Asian Security Practice,* 243–270.

———. "Asia-Pacific Security Institutions in Comparative Perspective." In Ikenberry and Mastanduno, *International Relations Theory and the Asia Pacific*, 243–270.

———. *Power Rules: The Evolution of NATO's Conventional Force Posture.* Stanford: Stanford University Press, 1995.

Duffield, John S., Cynthia Michota, and Sara Ann Miller. "Alliances." In Paul Williams (ed.). *Security Studies: An Introduction,* 291–306. London: Routledge, 2008.

Dunay, Pál. "Not Beyond Limits: The Prospects of the Shanghai Cooperation Organization (SCO)." *GCSP Policy Paper* 5, Geneva Centre for Security Policy,

August 2010. http://www.gcsp.ch/News-Knowledge/Publications/Not-Beyond
-Limits-The-Prospects-of-the-Shanghai-Cooperation-Organization-SCO.

Dunne, Tim, Milja Kurki, and Steve Smith. *International Relations Theories: Discipline and Diversity*, Second edition. Oxford: Oxford University Press: 2010.

Dupont, Alan. *East Asia Imperiled: Transnational Challenges to Security*. Cambridge: Cambridge University Press, 2001.

Dzyubenko, Olga. "China to Expand Central Asian Presence with $10 Billion in Loans." *Reuters*, December 6, 2012.

Economist. "Not Whaling but Drowning." March 11, 2010. http://www.economist.com/node/15663372.

Economy, Elizabeth C. *The Third Revolution: Xi Jinping and the New Chinese State*. Oxford: Oxford University Press, 2018.

Edwards, Peter. "Permanent Friends?: Historical Reflections on the Australian-American Alliance." Lowy Institute paper. Lowy Institute of International Policy, Sydney, 2005.

Emmers, Ralf (ed.). *ASEAN and the Institutionalization of East Asia*. New York: Routledge, 2011.

———. *Cooperative Security and the Balance of Power in ASEAN and the ARF*. London: RoutledgeCurzon, 2003.

———. "The Influence of the Balance of Power Factor Within the ASEAN Regional Forum." *Contemporary Southeast Asia*, vol. 23, no. 2 (2001): 275–291.

———. "The Role of the Five Power Defence Arrangements in Southeast Asian Security Architecture." In Tow and Taylor, *Bilateralism, Multilateralism and Asia-Pacific Security,* 87–99.

———. "Southeast Asia's New Security Institutions." In Vinod K. Aggarwal and Min Gyo Koo (eds.). *Asia's New Institutional Architecture: Evolving Structures for Managing Trade, Financial, and Security Relations,* 181–213. Leipzig: Springer, 2008.

Emmers, Ralf, Mely Caballero-Anthony, and Amitav Acharya. *Studying Non-Traditional Security in Asia: Trends and Issues*. Singapore: Marshall Cavendish Academic, 2006.

Emmers, Ralf, and See Seng Tan. "The ASEAN Regional Forum and Preventive Diplomacy." In Emmers, *ASEAN and the Institutionalization of East Asia,* 89–102.

Emmerson, Donald K. "'Southeast Asia': What's in a Name?" *Journal of Southeast Asian Studies,* vol. 15, no. 1 (1984): 1–21.

Emmott, Bill. *Rivals: How the Power Struggle Between China, India and Japan Will Shape Our Next Decade*. San Diego, CA: Harcourt, 2008.

Envall, H. D. P. "Community Building in Asia? Trilateral Cooperation in Humanitarian Assistance and Disaster Relief." In Tatsumi, *US-Japan-Australia Security Cooperation,* 51–60.

Envall, H. D. P., and Ian Hall. "Are India and Japan Potential Members of the Great Power Club?" In Wallis and Andrew, *Asia-Pacific Security: An Introduction*, 63–82.

———. "Asian Strategic Partnerships: New Practices and Regional Security Governance." *Asian Politics & Policy*, vol. 8, no. 1 (2016): 87–105.

Erlanger, Steven. "Gulf War Alliance: 6 Years Later, Seams Fray." *New York Times,* November 5, 1997, p. 6.

European Strategic Partnerships Observatory. "Our Project." Accessed June 1, 2016. http://strategicpartnerships.eu/about-us-project.

Evans, Gareth. "Cooperative Security and Intrastate Conflict." *Foreign Policy,* no. 96 (1994): 3–22.

Evans, Paul. "The Concept of Eastern Asia." In Colin Mackerras. *Eastern Asia: An Introductory History,* Third edition, 7–14. Sydney: Longman, 2000.

Faiola, Anthony. "Japan to Join U.S. Policy on Taiwan." *Washington Post*, February 18, 2005.

Farrell, Mary, Bjorn Hettne, and Luk Langenhove. *Global Politics of Regionalism.* New York: Pluto, 2005.

Fawcett, Louise, and Andrew Hurrell (eds.). *Regionalism in World Politics*. Oxford: Oxford University Press, 1996.

Feng Huiyun. "The New Geostrategic Game: Will China and Russia Form an Alliance Against the United States?" *Danish Institute for International Studies Report* 7 (2015).

Feng Zhongping and Jing Huang. "China's Strategic Partnership Diplomacy: Engaging with a Changing World." *European Strategic Partnerships Observatory Working Paper* 8 (June 2014).

Feng, Zhu. "TSD—Euphemism for Multiple Alliance?" In Tow et al. *Assessing the Trilateral Security Dialogue*, 41–50.

Fingar, Thomas (ed.). *The New Great Game: China and South and Central Asia in the Era of Reform.* Stanford: Stanford University Press, 2016.

Flemes, Daniel. "Creating a Regional Security Community in Southern Latin America: The Institutionalisation of the Regional Defence and Security Policies." *SSRN Working Paper Series,* 2006.

———. "Emerging Middle Powers' Soft Balancing Strategy: State and Perspectives of the IBSA Dialogue Forum." GIGA Working Paper 57 (2007). http://www .giga-hamburg.de/index.php?file=workingpapers.html&folder=publikationen.

Flikke, Geir. "Sino-Russian Relations Status Exchange or Imbalanced Relationship?" *Problems of Post-Communism*, vol. 63, no. 3 (2016): 159–170.

Fort, Bertrand, and Douglas Webber (eds.). *Regional Integration in East Asia and Europe: Convergence or Divergence?* New York: Routledge, 2006.

Fouse, David. "Japan's 'Values-oriented Diplomacy." *The New York Times*, March 21, 2007. http://www.nytimes.com/2007/03/21/opinion/21iht-edfouse.4978402 .html.

Franke, Benedikt. "Africa's Evolving Security Architecture and the Concept of Multilayered Security Communities." *Cooperation and Conflict,* vol. 43, no. 3 (2008): 313–340.

Franklin, John K. *The Hollow Pact: Pacific Security and the Southeast Asia Treaty Organization.* Fort Worth: Texas Christian University, 2007.

Freeman, Carla P. "New Strategies for an Old Rivalry? China-Russia Relations in Central Asia After the Energy Boom." *Pacific Review* (2017): 1–20.

Freistein, Katja. "A Living Document': Promises of the ASEAN Charter." *Pacific Review*, vol. 26, no. 4 (2013): 407–429.

French, Howard W. *Everything Under the Heavens: How the Past Helps Shape China's Push for Global Power.* New York: Alfred A. Knopf, 2017.

Friedberg, Aaron L. *A Contest for Supremacy: China, America, and the Struggle for Mastery in Asia.* New York: W. W. Norton, 2012.

———. "Ripe for Rivalry: Prospects for a Multipolar Asia." *International Security,* vol. 18, no. 3 (1994): 5–33.

———. "Will Europe's Past Be Asia's Future?" *Survival*, vol. 42, no. 3 (2000): 147–160.

Friedman, George. *The Next 100 Years: A Forecast for the 21st Century.* New York: Anchor Books, 2010.

Friedman, George, and Meredith Lebard. *The Coming War with Japan.* New York: St. Martin's Press, 1991.

Friedman, Thomas L., and Michael Mandelbaum. *That Used To Be Us: How America Fell Behind in the World It Invented and How We Can Come Back.* New York: Farrar, Straus and Giroux, 2011.

Friedrichs, Jörg. "East Asian Regional Security: What the ASEAN Family Can (Not) Do." *Asian Survey,* vol. 52, no. 4 (2012): 754–776.

Frost, Ellen L. *Asia's New Regionalism.* Boulder, CO: Lynne Rienner, 2008.

Gady, Franz-Stefan. "Why Japan Lost the Bid to Build Australia's New Subs." *The Diplomat,* April 27, 2016. http://thediplomat.com/2016/04/why-japan-lost-the-bid-to-build-australias-new-subs.

Galbreath, David. *The Organization for Security and Co-operation in Europe.* London: Routledge, 2007.

Garafano, John F. "A Security Community for Asia? Power, Institutions and the ASEAN Regional Forum." *Asian Survey,* vol. 42, no. 3 (2002): 502–521.

Garran, Robert. *Tigers Tamed: The End of the Asian Miracle.* Manoa, HI: University of Hawaii Press, 1998.

Gentner, Heide Haruyo. "ASEAN: Cooperative Disaster Relief After the Tsunami." In *Südostasien Aktuell: Journal of Current Southeast Asian Affairs,* vol. 24, no. 4 (2006): 3–9. http://www.ssoar.info/ssoar/bitstream/handle/document/33920/ssoar-suedostaktuell-2006-4-gentner-ASEAN_Cooperative_disaster_relief_after.pdf?sequence=1.

George, Alexander L., and Andrew Bennett. *Case Studies and Theory Development in the Social Sciences.* Cambridge, MA: MIT Press, 2004.

Gibler, Douglas. *International Military Alliances: 1648–2008.* Washington DC: CQ Press, 2009.

Gibney, Frank. *The Pacific Century: America and Asia in a Changing World.* New York: Scribner's Sons, 1992.

Gilley, Bruce. "Not So Dire Straits: How the Finlandization of Taiwan Benefits U.S. Security." *Foreign Affairs,* vol. 89, no. 1 (2010): 44–60.

Giuliani, Rudolph W. "Toward a Realistic Peace: Defending Civilization and Defeating Terrorists by Making the International System Work." *Foreign Affairs,* vol. 86, no. 5 (2007): 2–18.

Gjelten, Tom. "Seeing the Internet as an "Information Weapon." NPR. September 23, 2010. https://www.npr.org/templates/story/story.php?storyId=130052701.

Glaser, Bonnie S. *Armed Clash in the South China Sea.* New York: Council on Foreign Relations, 2012.

Glaser, Bonnie S., and Brad Glosserman. *Promoting Confidence Building Across the Taiwan Strait.* Washington, DC: Center for Strategic and International Studies, 2008.

Global Security. "Keen Sword." Accessed October 1, 2018. https://www.globalsecurity.org/military/ops/keen-sword.htm.

Goh, Evelyn. "Conceptualizing the Relationship Between Bilateral and Multilateral Security Approaches in East Asia." In Tow and Taylor, *Bilateralism, Multilateralism and Asia-Pacific Security,* 169–182.

———. "Great Powers and Hierarchical Order in Southeast Asia: Analyzing Regional Security Strategies." *International Security,* vol. 32, no. 3 (2008): 113–157.

———. "Hierarchy and the Role of the United States in the East Asian Security Order." *International Relations of the Asia-Pacific,* vol. 8, no. 3 (2008): 353–377.

————. "Institutions and the Great Power Bargain in East Asia: ASEAN's Limited 'Brokerage' Role." In Emmers (ed.). *ASEAN and the Institutionalization of East Asia,* 105–121.

Goldman, Emily O., and Thomas Mahnken (eds.). *The Information Revolution in Military Affairs in Asia.* London: Palgrave McMillan, 2004.

Goldstein, Avery. "An Emerging China's Emerging Grand Strategy: A Neo-Bismarckian Turn?" In G. John Ikenberry and Michael Mastanduno (eds.). *International Relations Theory and the Asia-Pacific,* 57–106. New York: Columbia University Press, 2003.

————. *Rising to the Challenge: China's Grand Strategy and International Security.* Stanford: Stanford University Press, 2005.

Goldstein, Joshua S., and Jon C. Pevehouse. *International Relations,* Seventh edition. London: Longman, 2005.

Goldstein, Morris. *The Asian Financial Crisis: Causes, Cures, and Systemic Implications.* Washington, DC: Institute for International Economics, 1998.

Gonzalez, Guadalupe, and Stephan Haggard. "The United States and Mexico: A Pluralistic Security Community?" In Adler and Barnett, *Security Communities,* 295–332.

Göran, Ahrne, and Nils Brunsson. "Organizations and Meta-Organizations." *Scandinavian Journal of Management,* vol. 21, no. 4 (2005): 429–449.

Gordon, Sandy. "Widening Horizons: Australia's New Relationship with India." Australian Strategic Policy Institute, May 2007.

Green, Michael J. "Is Japan a Fading Strategic Asset for the US?" In Chandler, Clay, Heang Chhor, and Brian Salsberg (eds.). *Reimagining Japan.* San Francisco: Viz Media, 2011: 214–219.

————. "Should America Fear a New Sino-Russian Alliance?" *Foreign Policy,* August 13, 2014. http://foreignpolicy.com/2014/08/13/should-america-fear-a-new-sino-russian-alliance.

————. "Strategic Asian Triangles." In Saadia Pekkanen, John Ravenhill, and Rosemary Foot (eds.). *The Oxford Handbook of the International Relations of Asia,* 758-774. Oxford: Oxford University Press, 2014.

Green, Michael J., and Patrick M. Cronin (eds.). *The U.S.-Japan Alliance: Past, Present, and Future.* New York: Council on Foreign Relations Press, 1999.

Green, Michael J., and Bates Gill. "Unbundling Asia's New Multilateralism." In Green and Gill, *Asia's New Multilateralism,* 1–32.

———— (eds.). *Asia's New Multilateralism: Cooperation, Competition, and the Search for Community.* New York: Columbia University Press, 2009.

Gries, Peter Hays. "The Koguryo Controversy, National Identity, and Sino-Korean Relations Today." *East Asia,* vol. 22, no. 4 (2005): 3–17.

The Guardian. "Malcolm Turnbull Tells Shinzo Abe He's Disappointed About Whaling Resumption." December 19, 2015. https://www.theguardian.com/australia-news/2015/dec/19/malcolm-turnbull-tells-shinzo-abe-hes-disappointed-about-whaling-resumption.

Haacke, Jürgen. "ASEAN's Diplomatic and Security Culture: A Constructivist Assessment." *International Relations of the Asia-Pacific,* vol. 3, no. 1 (2003): 57–87.

Haas, Ernst B. *Beyond the Nation-State: Functionalism and International Organization.* Stanford: Stanford University Press, 1964.

Haas, Michael (ed.). *Asian and Pacific Regional Cooperation: Turning Zones of Conflict into Arenas of Peace.* New York: Palgrave Macmillan, 2013.

————. "Successful Security Communities." In Haas (ed.). *Asian and Pacific Regional Cooperation,* 135–161.

Haggard, Stephan. *The Politics of the Asian Financial Crisis.* Washington, DC: Institute for International Economics, 2000.

Hale, David. "The Outlook for Economic Integration in East Asia." In K. E. Calder and F. Fukuyama (eds.). *East Asian Multilateralism: Prospects for Regional Stability,* 58–77. Baltimore, MD: Johns Hopkins University Press, 2008.

Hall, Richard H. *Organizations: Structures, Processes and Outcomes.* Englewood Cliffs, NJ: Prentice Hall, 1990.

Harris, Stuart, and Richard Cooper. "The US-Japan Alliance." In Robert Blackwill and Paul Dibb (eds.). *America's Asian Alliances,* 31–60. Cambridge, MA: MIT Press.

Hartley, Keith, and Todd Sandler. "NATO Burden-Sharing: Past and Future." *Journal of Peace Research,* vol. 36, no. 6 (1999): 665–680.

Hemmer, Christopher, and Peter J. Katzenstein. "Why Is There No NATO in Asia? Collective Identity, Regionalism, and the Origins of Multilateralism." *International Organization,* vol. 42, no. 2 (1988): 575–607.

Heo, Uk, Terence Roehrig, and Jungmin Seo. *Korean Security in a Changing East Asia.* Westport, CT: Prager, 2007.

Herndon, David. "Sun Sets on Keen Sword Exercise." US Air Force. December 10, 2010. https://www.af.mil/News/Article-Display/Article/114701/sun-sets-on-keen -sword-exercise.

Hessbruegge, Jan Arno. "The Shanghai Cooperation Organization: A Holy Alliance for Central Asia?" *Al-Nakhlah* (Spring 2004): 13–21.

Hettne, Bjorn. "Beyond the 'New' Regionalism." *New Political Economy,* vol. 10, no. 4 (2005): 543–571.

Hettne, Bjorn, Andras Inotai, and Osvaldo Sunkel. *Globalism and the New Regionalism.* London: Macmillan, 1999.

Higgins, Andrew. "ASEAN Struggles to Cope with Rival Claims in the South China Sea." *Washington Post,* August 27, 2012. https://www.washingtonpost.com/world /asean-struggles-to-cope-with-rival-claims-in-the-south-china-sea/2012/08/27 /6b184fde-f04d-11e1-b74c-84ed55e0300b_story.html.

Higgot, Stephen A., and Kim Richard Nossal. "Australia and the Search for a Security Community in the 1990's." In Adler and Barnett (ed.). *Security Communities,* 265–294.

Hirabayashi, Hiroshi. "Responses to PacNet #56—Korea-Japan: Enough Is Enough!" *PacNet,* Number 56R, Pacific Forum, September 18, 2012. http://csis.org/files /publication/Pac1256R.pdf.

Holbraad, Carsten. *Middle Powers in International Politics.* London: Macmillan, 1984.

————. "The Role of Middle Powers." *Cooperation and Conflict,* vol. 7, no. 2 (1971): 77–90.

Homer. *The Iliad.* Translated by M. M. Wilcock. London: Bristol Classical Press, 1996.

Hopf, Ted. "The Promise of Constructivism in International Relations Theory." *International Security,* vol. 23, no. 1 (1998): 171–200.

Horelick, Arnold. "The Soviet Union's Asian Collective Security Proposal: A Club in Search of Members." *Pacific Affairs,* vol. 47, no. 3 (1974): 269–285.

Hsueh, Chienwu. "ASEAN and Southeast Asian Peace: Nation Building, Economic Performance, and ASEAN's Security Management." *International Relations of the Asia-Pacific,* vol. 16, no. 1 (2016): 27–66.

Hu, Richard Weixing. "The Shanghai Cooperation Organisation: A New Regional Kid on the Block?" *European Policy Centre.* February 18, 2008. http://www.epc .eu/prog_details.php?cat_id=6&pub_id=880&prog_id=3.

Hughes, Christopher. *Japan's Foreign and Security Policy Under the "Abe Doctrine": New Dynamism or New Dead End?* Palgrave Macmillan, 2015.

Hughes, Christopher, and Elis Krauss. "Japan's New Security Agenda." *Survival,* vol. 49, no. 2 (2007): 157–176.

Human Rights Watch. "Philippines: Duterte's 'Drug War' Claims 12,000+ Lives." January 18, 2018. https://www.hrw.org/news/2018/01/18/philippines-dutertes -drug-war-claims-12000-lives.

Hurrell, Andrew. "An Emerging Security Community in South America?" In Adler and Barnett, *Security Communities,* 228–264.

Huxley, Tim. *Defending the Lion City: The Armed Forces of Singapore.* St. Leonards, Australia: Allen & Unwin, 2000.

Hveem, Helge. "Explaining the Regional Phenomenon in an Era of Globalization." In Richard Stubbs and Geoffrey R. D. Underhill (eds.). *Political Economy and the Changing Global Order,* 70–81. Oxford: Oxford University Press, 2000.

Ikenberry, G. John. "A New Order in East Asia." In Calder and Fukuyama (ed.). *East Asian Multilateralism,* 217–233.

Ikenberry, G. John, and Takashi Inoguchi. *Reinventing the Alliance: US-Japan Security Partnership in an Era of Change.* Basingstoke, UK: Palgrave, 2003.

Ikenberry, G. John, and Michael Mastanduno (eds.). *International Relations Theory and the Asia Pacific.* New York: Columbia University Press, 2003.

Ikenberry, G. John, and Jitsuo Tsuchiyama. "Between Balance of Power and Community: The Future of Multilateral Security Co-operation in the Asia-Pacific." *International Relations of the Asia-Pacific,* vol. 13, no. 3 (2013): 69–94.

Inbar, Efriam. "Regional Implications of the Israeli-Turkish Strategic Partnership." *Middle Eastern Review of International Affairs,* vol. 5, no. 2 (2001): 48–65.

Information Office of the State Council of the People's Republic of China. "China's National Defense in 2010." Beijing, March 2011. http://eng.mod.gov.cn/Data base/WhitePapers/2010.htm.

———. "The Diversified Employment of China's Armed Forces." Beijing, April 2013. http://aseanregionalforum.asean.org/files/library/ARF%20Defense%20White %20Papers/China-2013.pdf.

———. *White Paper: China's National Defence in 2004.* Beijing, December 2004.

International Crisis Group. "China's Central Asia Problem." Asia Report Number 244, February 27, 2013. https://www.crisisgroup.org/europe-central-asia/central -asia/china-s-central-asia-problem.

International Institute for Strategic Studies. "IISS-Asia Singapore." Accessed October 1, 2018. https://www.iiss.org/contact-us/singapore.

Ivanov, Igor (ed.). *Rossiysko-Kitayskiy Dialog: Model 2015* [Russia-China Dialogue: The Model 2015]. Moscow: Russian International Affairs Council, 2015.

Iwashita, Akihiro. "The Shanghai Cooperation Organization and Japan—Moving Together to Reshape the Eurasian Community." In Akihito Iwashita (ed.). *Toward a New Dialogue on Eurasia: The Shanghai Cooperation Organization and Its Partners,* 21–26. Japan: The Slavic Research Center, 2007.

Iyer, Karthik N. S. "Learning in Strategic Alliances: An Evolutionary Perspective." *Academy of Marketing Science Review,* vol. 2002, no. 10 (2002). http://www .amsreview.org/articles/iyer10-2002.pdf.

Jain, Purnendra. "Japan-Australia Security Ties and the United States: The Evolution of the Trilateral Dialogue Process and Its Challenges." *Australian Journal of International Affairs*, vol. 60, no. 4 (2006): 521–535.

Jain, Purnendra, and John Bruni. "American Acolytes: Tokyo, Canberra and Washington's Emerging Pacific Axis?" In Brad Williams (ed.). *Australia-Japan Defence and Security Relations*, 89–106. Abingdon, UK: Routledge, 2006.

———. "Japan, Australia and the United States: Little NATO or Shadow Alliance?" *International Relations of the Asia-Pacific*, vol. 4, no. 2 (August 1, 2004): 265–285.

Jansen, Marius B. *The Making of Modern Japan*. Cambridge, MA: Harvard University Press, 2000.

Japan Times. "Abe Cites Need for Japan to Fully Exercise Right to Collective Self-Defense." March 1, 2016. http://www.japantimes.co.jp/news/2016/03/01/national/politics-diplomacy/abe-cites-need-japan-fully-exercise-right-collective-self-defense.

Jersild, Austin. *The Sino-Soviet Alliance: An International History*. Chapel Hill: The University of North Carolina Press, 2014.

Jimbo, Ken. "Japan-US-Australia Cooperation on Capacity Building in Southeast Asia." In Tatsumi, *US-Japan-Australia Security Cooperation*, 61–76.

Job, Brian. "The Track 2 Diplomacy: Ideational Contribution to the Evolving Asian Security Order." In Alagappa, *Asian Security Order Instrumental and Normative Features*, 241–279.

Johnson, Chalmers. *Japan: Who Governs? The Rise of the Developmental State*. New York: W. W. Norton, 1995.

———. *MITI and the Japanese Miracle: The Growth of Industrial Policy, 1925–1975*. Stanford: Stanford University Press, 1982.

———. *Nemesis: The Last Days of the American Republic*. New York: Metropolitan Books, 2007.

Johnston, Alastair Iain. "Is China a Status Quo Power?" *International Security*, vol. 27, no. 4 (2003): 5–56.

Jones, David Martin, and Nicole Jenne. "Weak States' Regionalism: ASEAN and the Limits of Security Cooperation in Pacific Asia." *International Relations of the Asia-Pacific*, vol. 16, no. 2 (2016): 209–240.

Jones, David Martin, and Michael L. R. Smith. "Making Process, Not Progress: ASEAN and the Evolving East Asian Regional Order." *International Security*, vol. 32, no. 1 (2007): 148–184.

Jones, Lee. "Explaining the Failure of the ASEAN Economic Community: The Primacy of Domestic Political Economy." *Pacific Review*, vol. 29, no. 5 (2016): 647–670.

Jordaan, Eduard. "The Concept of a Middle Power in International Relations: Distinguishing Between Emerging and Traditional Middle Powers." *Politikon*, vol. 30, no. 1 (2003): 165–181.

Kacowicz, Arie M. "Explaining Zones of Peace: Democracies as Satisfied Powers?" *Journal of Peace Research*, vol. 32, no. 3 (1995): 265–276.

———. *Pluralistic Security Communities and "Negative" Peace in the Third World*. Madison: University of Wisconsin, 1993.

Kaczmarski, Marcin. *Russia-China Relations in the Post-crisis International Order*. New York: Routledge, 2015.

Kamp, Karl-Heinz, and Wolf Langheld. "The Military Adaptation of the Alliance." NATO Adaptation Initiative Supporting Paper, GLOBSEC Policy Institute,

2017. https://www.globsec.org/wp-content/uploads/2017/03/GNAI-The-Military
-Adaptation-of-the-Alliance.pdf.

Kan, Paul Rexton, Bruce E. Bechtol Jr., and Robert M. Collins. *Criminal Sovereignty: Understanding North Korea's Illicit International Activities.* Carlisle, PA: Strategic Studies Institute, 2010.

Kang, David C. "Getting Asia Wrong: The Need for New Analytical Frameworks." *International Security,* vol. 27, no. 4 (2003): 57–85.

———. *Rising China.* New York: Columbia University Press, 2008.

Kaplan, Lawrence S. *NATO Divided, NATO United: Evolution of an Alliance.* Westport, CT: Greenwood Publishing Group, 2004.

Kaplan, Robert D. *Asia's Cauldron: The South China Sea and the End of a Stable Pacific.* New York: Random House, 2014.

———. *Monsoon: The Indian Ocean and the Future of American Power.* New York: Random House, 2010.

———. *The Return of Marco Polo's World: War, Strategy, and American Interests in the Twenty-First Century.* New York: Random House, 2018.

Karaganov, Sergei. "Izbezhat' Afganistana-2" [To Avoid Afghanistan-2]. *Vedomosti,* July 28, 2014. www.vedomosti.ru/opinion/news/29501801/izbezhat-afganistana-2.

Karpov, Mikhail. "Will the Russian-Chinese 'Strategic Partnership' Last Until 2020? Plausible Thoughts on an 'Implausible' Scenario." *Policy Paper Series— China Studies Centre,* University of Sydney, May 2015.

Katsumata, Hiro. *ASEAN's Cooperative Security Enterprise: Norms and Interests in the ASEAN Regional Forum.* London: Palgrave, 2009.

———. "Establishment of the ASEAN Regional Forum: Constructing a 'Talking Shop' or a 'Norm Brewery'?" *Pacific Review,* vol. 19, no. 2 (2006): 181–198.

———. "Mimetic Adoption and Norm Diffusion: 'Western' Security Cooperation in Southeast Asia?" *Review of International Studies,* vol. 37, no. 2 (2011): 557–576.

Katzenstein. Peter J. (ed.). *The Culture of National Security.* New York: Columbia University Press, 1996.

———. "Introduction: Alternative Perspectives on National Security." In Katzenstein, *The Culture of National Security,* 1–32.

———. *Rethinking Japanese Security: Internal and External Dimensions.* London: Routledge, 2008.

———. *A World of Regions: Asia and Europe in the American Imperium.* Ithaca, NY: Cornell University Press, 2005.

Katzenstein, Peter J., and Takashi Shiraishi (eds.). *Beyond Japan: The Dynamics of East Asian Regionalism.* Ithaca, NY: Cornell University Press, 2006.

Katzenstein, Peter J., and Rudra Sil. "Rethinking Asian Security: A Case for Analytical Eclecticism." In J. J. Suh, Peter Katzenstein, and Allen Carlson (eds.). *Rethinking Security in East Asia: Identity, Power, and Efficiency,* 1–33. Palo Alto, CA: Stanford University Press, 2004.

Kautalya. *The Arthashastra.* Translated by L. N. Rangarajan. London: Penguin, 1992.

Kavalski, Emilian. "Do as I Do." In Emilian Kavalski (ed.). *China and the Global Politics of Regionalization,* 1–18. Surrey, UK: Ashgate, 2009.

———. "Shanghaied into Cooperation: Framing China's Socialization of Central Asia." *Journal of Asian and African Studies,* vol. 45, no. 2 (2010): 131–145.

Kay, Sean. "What Is a Strategic Partnership?" *Problems of Post-Communism,* vol. 47, no. 3 (2000): 15–24.

Keck, Zachary. "China, Russia Military Ties Deepen with Naval Drill in East China Sea." *The Diplomat*, May 2, 2014. https://thediplomat.com/2014/05/china-russia -military-ties-deepen-with-naval-drill-in-east-china-sea.

Kegley, Charles W., and Gregory A. Raymond. *When Trust Breaks Down: Alliance Norms and World Politics.* Columbia: University of South Carolina Press, 1990.

Kegley, Charles W., and Eugene R. Wittkopf. *World Politics: Trend and Transformation*, Fifth edition. New York: St. Martin's Press, 1995.

Keohane, Robert O. *International Institutions and State Power: Essays in International Relations Theory.* Boulder, CO: Westview, 1989.

Keohane, Robert O., and Joseph S. Nye. *Power and Interdependence: World Politics in Transition.* Boston: Little, Brown, 1977.

Khanna, Parag. *The Second World: Empires and Influence in the New Global Order.* New York: Random House, 2008.

Khoo, Nicholas. "The ASEAN Security Community: A Misplaced Consensus." *Journal of Asian Security and International Affairs*, vol. 2, no. 2 (2015): 180–199.

———. "Deconstructing the ASEAN Security Community: A Review Essay." *International Relations of the Asia Pacific*, vol. 4, no. 1 (2004): 35–46.

Khurana, G. S. "Proliferation Security Initiative: An Assessment." *Strategic Analysis,* vol. 28, no. 2 (2004): 237–248.

Kim, Choong-nam. "Redefining ROK's Strategic Posture in the Twenty-First Century." *International Journal of Korean Studies*, vol. 11, no. 2 (2007): 26–66.

Kim, Eun Mee. *The Four Asian Tigers: Economic Development and the Global Political Economy.* San Diego, CA: Academic Press, 1998.

Kim, Kyuryoon, and Byung-Duck Hwang. *New Approach to the Costs/Benefits of Korean Unification: Adopting Comprehensive Research Factors and Seeking Alternatives.* Seoul: Korean Institute for National Unification, 2011.

Kim, Samuel S. *The Two Koreas and the Great Powers.* Cambridge: Cambridge University Press, 2006.

Kim, Sung Chul, and Michael D. Cohen (eds.). *North Korea and Nuclear Weapons: Entering the New Era of Deterrence.* Washington, DC: Georgetown University Press, 2017.

Kim, Sung-Han. "From Blood Alliance to Strategic Alliance: Korea's Evolving Strategic Thought Toward the United States." *Korean Journal of Defense Analysis,* vol. 22 (2010): 265–281.

Kim, Tongfi. "Asia's Minilateral Moment." *The Diplomat*, June 13, 2017. https://thediplomat.com/2017/06/asias-minilateral-moment.

Koch-Weser, Iacob, and Craig Murray. "The China-Russia Gas Deal: Background and Implications for the Broader Relationship." U.S.-China Economic and Security Review Commission, June 9, 2014. https://www.uscc.gov/sites/default /files/Research/China%20Russia%20gas%20deal_Staffbackgrounder.pdf.

Korolev, Alexander. "On the Verge of an Alliance: Contemporary China-Russia Military Cooperation." *Asian Security,* April 30, 2018. https://www.tandfonline.com /doi/full/10.1080/14799855.2018.1463991.

Korotun, Lada. "Russia-China: SCO Military Alliance Challenges US-NATO Unipolar World." *Global Research*, September 7, 2008. http://www.globalresearch.ca /russia-china-sco-military-alliance-challenges-us-nato-unipolar-world/10104.

Korybko, Andrew. "Washington's Nightmare Comes True: The Russian-Chinese Strategic Partnership Goes Global (I)." *Oriental Review*, August 21, 2014, http://orientalreview.org/2014/08/21/washingtons-nightmare-comes-true-the -russian-chinese-strategic-partnership-goes-global-i.

Koschut, Simon. *Normative Change and Security Community Disintegration: Undoing Peace.* New York: Palgrave Macmillan, 2016.

———. "Regional Order and Peaceful Change: Security Communities as a Via Media in International Relations Theory." *Cooperation and Conflict*, vol. 49, no. 4 (2014): 519–535.

Kozhokin, Yevgeny. "Russo-Chinese Collaboration on the World Scene." RIA Novosti/Renmin Ribao, 2002.

Kraft, Herman Joseph S. "Driving East Asian Regionalism: The Reconstruction of ASEAN's Identity." In Emmers, *ASEAN and the Institutionalization of East Asia*, 61–74.

Krasner, Stephen D. *International Regimes.* New York: Cornell University Press, 1983.

Kubicek, Paul. "The Commonwealth of Independent States: An Example of Failed Regionalism?" *Review of International Studies,* vol. 35, no. 1 (2009): 237–256.

Kuchins, Andrew C. "Russia's Relations with China and India: Strategic Partnerships, Yes; Strategic Alliances, No." *Demokratizatsiya*, vol. 9, no. 2 (2001): 259–275.

Kuglin, Fred A. *Building, Leading, and Managing Strategic Alliances.* In collaboration with Jeff Hook. New York: Amacom, 2002.

Kumar, Satish, S. D. Pradhan, Kanwal Sibal, Rahul Bedi, and Bidisha Ganguly. *India's Strategic Partners: A Comparative Assessment.* New Delhi: Foundation for National Security Research, 2011.

Kwon, Goohoon. "A United Korea: Reassessing North Korean Risks." *Goldman Sachs Global Economics Paper* 188, September 21, 2009.

Kyle, Keith. *Suez: Britain's End of Empire in the Middle East.* London: I. B. Tauris, 2003.

LaFeber, Walter. *The Clash The Clash: U.S.-Japanese Relations Throughout History.* New York: Norton, 1998.

Lake, David A., and Patrick M. Morgan (eds.). *Regional Orders: Building Security in a New World.* University Park: Pennsylvania State University Press, 1997.

Lam, Peng Er, and Tai-Wei Lim. *The Rise of China and India: A New Asian Drama.* London: World Scientific, 2009.

Lamothe-Cadet, Amanda M. "A Relationship of Convenience: The Russo-Chinese Strategic Partnership." Daniel K. Inouye Asia-Pacific Center for Security Studies, September 26, 2014.

Lankowski, Michael. "America's Asian Alliances in a Changing World." *Australian Journal of International Affairs,* vol. 57, no. 1 (2003): 113–124.

Lansford, Tom. *A Bitter Harvest: U.S. Foreign Policy and Afghanistan.* Aldershot, UK: Ashgate, 2003.

Lanteigne, Marc. "'In Media Res': The Development of the Shanghai Co-operation Organization as a Security Community." *Pacific Affairs*, vol. 79, no. 4 (2006–2007): 605–622.

Lawrence, Susan V. "Miles to Go." *Far Eastern Economic Review*, November 26, 1998.

Lee, Chung-Min. "Coping with Giants: South Korea's Responses to China's and India's Rise." In Tellis, Tanner, and Keough, *Strategic Asia 2011–12,* 161–194.

Lee, Jae-Seung. "Rethinking APEC's Security Agenda: The Challenges of Functional Expansion." *Issues & Studies*, vol. 46, no. 4 (2010): 73–100.

Lee, Sook-Jong. "Korean Perspectives on East Asian Regionalism." In Calder and Fukuyama, *East Asian Multilateralism,* 198–213.

Lego, Jera. "Why ASEAN Can't Ignore the Rohingya Crisis." *The Diplomat*, May 17, 2017. https://thediplomat.com/2017/05/why-asean-cant-ignore-the-rohingya-crisis.

Legro, Jeffery W. "Which Norms Matter? Revisiting the 'Failure' of Internationalism." *International Organization,* vol. 51, no. 1 (1997): 31–63.

Leifer, Michael. "The ASEAN Peace Process: A Category Mistake." *Pacific Review*, vol. 12, no.1 (1999): 25–38.

———. "The ASEAN Regional Forum: Extending ASEAN's Model for Regional Security." *Adelphi Paper* 302. Oxford: Oxford University Press, 1996.

Le Mière, Christian. "The Return of Gunboat Diplomacy." *Survival*, vol. 53, no. 5 (2011): 53–68.

Len, Christopher. "Energy Security Cooperation in Asia: An ASEAN-SCO Energy Partnership?" In Mark Hong and Teo Kah Beng (eds.). *Energy Perspectives in Singapore and the Region,* 156–176. Singapore: Institute of Southeast Asian Studies, 2007.

Lewis, Mark Edward. "Warring States Political History." In Michael Loewe and Edward L. Shaughnessy (eds.). *The Cambridge History of Ancient China: From the Origins of Civilization to 221 B.C.,* 587–649. Cambridge: Cambridge University Press, 1999.

Liff, Adam P. "Japan's Defense Policy: Abe the Evolutionary." *Washington Quarterly*, vol. 38, no. 2: 79–99.

Lim, Robyn. "Australia's Stake in Asia Pacific Regional Security." In Peter King and Yoichi Kibata (eds.). *Peace Building in the Asia Pacific Region: Perspectives from Japan and Australia,* 76-87. St. Leonards, Australia: Allen & Unwin, 1996.

Limaye, Satu. "Why ASEAN Is Here to Stay and What That Means for the US." *The Diplomat*, August 30, 2016. http://thediplomat.com/2016/08/why-asean-is-here-to-stay.

Lindley-French, Julian. "Adapting NATO to an Unpredictable and Fast-Changing World." *NATO Review,* February 19, 2018. https://www.nato.int/docu/review/2018/Also-in-2018/adapting-nato-to-an-unpredictable-and-fast-changing-world-defence-alliance-security/EN/index.htm.

Liska, George. *Nations in Alliance: The Limits of Independence.* Baltimore: Johns Hopkins Press, 1962.

Liu, Mingfu. *The China Dream: Great Power Thinking and Strategic Power Posture in the Post-American Era.* New York: CN Times Books, 2015.

Lo, Bobo. *Axis of Convenience: Moscow, Beijing, and the New Geopolitics.* Washington, DC: Brookings Institution Press, 2008.

———. "A Wary Embrace: What the China-Russia Relationship Means for the World." *Lowy Institute Papers*, April 3, 2017. https://www.lowyinstitute.org/publications/wary-embrace.

Loo, Bernard F. W. "Is There an Arms Race in Asia?" *RSIS Commentary* 149 (2010).

Lorell, Mark. *Troubled Partnership: History of US-Japan Collaboration on the FS-X Fighter.* London: Routledge, 1996.

Lowy Institute. "Asia Power Index." Accessed October 1, 2018. https://power.lowyinstitute.org.

Lukin, Alexander. *The Bear Watches the Dragon: Russia's Perceptions of China and the Evolution of Russian-Chinese Relations Since the Eighteenth Century.* New York: Routledge, 2016.

———. *China and Russia: The New Rapprochement.* Cambridge, UK: Polity, 2018.

————. "Russia's Pivot to Asia: Myth or Reality?" *Strategic Analysis*, vol. 40, no. 6 (2016): 573–589.

Luthi, Lorenz M. *The Sino-Soviet Split: Cold War in the Communist World*. Princeton, NJ: Princeton University Press, 2008.

Luttwak, Edward N. *The Rise of China vs. the Logic of Strategy*. Cambridge, MA: Harvard University Press, 2012.

Lyon, Rod and William Tow. "The Future of the US–Australian Security Relationship." *Asian Security*, vol. 1, no. 1 (2005): 25–52.

Ma, Ying. *Regionalism and Developing Countries*. Beijing: China Social Science Press, 2002.

Machiavelli, Niccolò. *The Prince*. Translated by George Bull. London: Penguin, 1961.

Mack, Andrew, and John Ravenhill (eds.). *Pacific Cooperation: Building Economic and Security Regimes in the Asia-Pacific Region*. Sydney: Allen & Unwin, 1994.

Mackinder, Halford J. "The Geographical Pivot of History." *The Geographical Journal*, vol. 23, no. 4 (1904), reprinted in *The Geographical Journal*, vol. 170, no. 4 (2004).

Mahbubani, Kishore. *Can Asians Think?* New York: Times Publishers, 2004.

————. *The New Asian Hemisphere: The Irresistible Shift of Global Power to the East*. New York: Public Affairs, 2008.

Maksutov, Ruslan. "The Shanghai Cooperation Organization: A Central Asian Perspective." SIPRI Project Paper, Stockholm International Peace Research Institute, 2006.

Malcolm, Neil. "The 'Common European Home' and Soviet European Policy." *International Affairs*, vol. 65, no. 4 (1989): 659–676.

Malley, Paul. "Spies Like Us: ASIS Training Japanese." *The Australian*, March 21, 2015. http://www.theaustralian.com.au/national-affairs/foreign-affairs/spies-like-us-asis-training-japanese/news-story/e875461b152ec4ce7058f5a0a900302b.

Mandelbaum, Michael. *Reconstructing the European Security Order*. New York: Council on Foreign Relations, 1990.

Manyin, Mark E., Emma Chanlett-Avery, Mary Beth Nikitin, and Mi Ae Taylor. "U.S.–South Korea Relations." *Congressional Research Service* (December 8, 2010). http://www.dtic.mil/dtic/tr/fulltext/u2/a536036.pdf.

Maoz, Zeev. "The Street-Gangs of World Politics: The Origins, Management, and Termination of International Alliances." In John A. Vasquez (ed.). *What Do We Know About War?* 114–141. New York: Rowman and Littlefield, 2000.

March, James G., and Herbert A. Simon. *Organizations*, Second edition. Cambridge, MA: Blackwell, 1994.

Martel, Stéphanie. "From Ambiguity to Contestation: Discourse(s) of Non-traditional Security in the ASEAN Community." *Pacific Review*, vol. 30, no. 4 (2017): 549–565.

Massie, Justin. "Canada's (In)dependence in the North American Security Community: The Asymmetrical Norm of Common Fate." *American Review of Canadian Studies*, vol. 37, no. 4 (2007): 493–516.

Masuda, Masayuki. "China's SCO Policy in the Regional Security Architecture." Policy Research Brief, Tokyo Foundation, December 21, 2010. http://www.tokyofoundation.org/en/articles/2010/china2019s-sco-policy.

Mathur, Arpita. "Japan's Approach to Regionalism: Outlook Towards the EAS and EAC." *Strategic Analysis,* vol. 33, no. 5 (2009): 675–685.

Maull, Hanns W. "The European Security Architecture: Conceptual Lessons for Asia-Pacific Security Cooperation." In Amitav Acharya and Evelyn Goh (eds.). *Reassessing Security Competition in the Asia-Pacific,* 253–274. Cambridge, MA: BCISA, 2007.

———. "Security Cooperation in Europe and Pacific Asia: A Comparative Analysis." *Journal of East Asian Affairs*, vol. 19, no. 2 (2005): 67–108.

McDermott, Roger. "Russian Combat Training: Quantity Versus Quality." *Eurasia Daily Monitor*, vol. 8, no. 108 (2011). https://jamestown.org/program/russian -combat-training-quantity-versus-quality.

———. "Tsentr 2015: Testing Mobility and Strategic Messaging." *Eurasia Daily Monitor*, vol. 12, no. 170 (2015). https://jamestown.org/program/tsentr-2015 -testing-mobility-and-strategic-messaging.

McDougall, Derek. *Asia Pacific in World Politics*. London: Lynne Rienner, 2007.

McGregor, Richard. *Asia's Reckoning: China, Japan, and the Fate of U.S. Power in the Pacific Century*. New York: Viking, 2017.

McLennan, Alan, and Rod Troutbeck. "Building Strategic Partnerships." June 2002. http://esvc000907.wic056u.server-web.com/pdfs/Building_strategic _partnerships.pdf.

Mearsheimer, John J. "Back to the Future: Instability in Europe After the Cold War." *International Security,* vol. 19, no. 1 (1990): 5–56.

———. *The Tragedy* of *Great Power Politics*. New York: Norton, 2001.

Medcalf, Rory. "An Alliance for the Indo-Pacific." *The Interpreter* (Lowy Institute), March 7, 2011. https://www.lowyinstitute.org/the-interpreter/alliance-indo -pacific.

———. "Squaring the Triangle: An Australian Perspective on Asian Security Minilateralism." In Tow et al., *Assessing the Trilateral Security Dialogue*, 23–32.

Mehrotra, O. N. "NATO Eastward Expansion and Russian Security." *Strategic Analysis,* vol. 22, no. 8 (1998): 1225–1235.

———. "Indo-Russian Strategic Partnership in the Current World Order." In Shams Ud Bin (ed.). *India and Russia: Towards a Strategic Partnership*, 97–112. New Delhi: Lancer Books, 2001.

Mehta, Aaron. "'Pivot to the Pacific' Is Over, Senior U.S. Diplomat Says." *Defense News*, March 14, 2017.

Meick, Ethan. "China-Russia Military-to-Military Relations: Moving Toward a Higher Level of Cooperation." US-China Economic and Security Review Commission, March 20, 2017.

Menon, Rajan. *The End of Alliances*. Oxford: Oxford University Press, 2007.

———. "The Limits of Chinese-Russian Partnership." *Survival*, vol. 51, no. 3 (2009): 99–130.

Mérieau, Eugenie. "Thailand's Deepening Authoritarian Rule." *East Asia Forum*, January 30, 2018. http://www.eastasiaforum.org/2018/01/30/thailands-deepening -authoritarian-rule.

Michel, Casey. "SCO Set to Expand, Adding India and Pakistan." *The Diplomat*, June 6, 2017. http://thediplomat.com/2017/06/sco-set-to-expand-adding-india-and-pakistan.

Michishita, Narushige. "Alliance After Peace in Korea." *Survival,* vol. 41, no. 3 (1999): 68–83.

Miller, Alice Lyman, and Richard Wich. *Becoming Asia: Change and Continuity in Asian International Relations Since World War II*. Stanford: Stanford University Press, 2011.

Miller, David. *The Cold War: A Military History.* New York: St. Martin's Press, 1998.

Miller, Eric A., and Arkady Toritsyn. "Bringing the Leader Back In: Internal Threats and Alignment Theory in the Commonwealth of Independent States." *Security Studies,* vol. 14, no. 2 (2005): 325–363.

Ministry of Defense, Japan. *Defense of Japan 2005.* Tokyo, 2005. http://www.mod .go.jp/e/publ/w_paper/2005.html.

———. *Defense of Japan 2013.* Tokyo, 2013. http://www.mod.go.jp/e/publ/w _paper/2013.html.

———. *Defense of Japan 2016.* Tokyo, 2016. http://www.mod.go.jp/e/publ/w _paper/2016.html.

Ministry of Foreign Affairs, Indonesia. *Deplu Paper on ASEAN Security Community.* Tabled at the ASEAN Ministerial Meeting in Cambodia, June 16–18, 2003.

Ministry of Foreign Affairs, Japan. "Australia–Japan–United States Trilateral Strategic Dialogue Joint Statement." Manila, August 7, 2017. https://www.mofa.go.jp /files/000279008.pdf.

———. "Japan-Australia Joint Declaration on Security Cooperation." Tokyo, March 13, 2007. http://www.mofa.go.jp/region/asia-paci/australia/joint0703.html.

———. "Japan–United States–Australia Trilateral Strategic Dialogue Joint Statement." Tokyo, June 27, 2008. https://www.mofa.go.jp/region/asia-paci/australia /joint0806-2.html.

———. "Japan–United States–Australia Trilateral Strategic Dialogue Joint Statement." Tokyo, July 25, 2016. http://www.mofa.go.jp/a_o/ocn/page3e_000514 .html.

———. "Japan-U.S. Joint Declaration on Security: Alliance for the 21st Century." April 17, 1996. http://www.mofa.go.jp/region/n-america/us/security/security .html.

———. "Joint Press Statement by Prime Minister John Howard and Prime Minister Junichiro Koizumi: Australia-Japan Creative Partnership." May 1, 2002. http:// www.mofa.go.jp/region/asia-paci/pmv0204/joint.html.

———. "Prime Minister Abbott and Prime Minister Abe Joint Statement: Special Strategic Partnership for the 21st Century." Canberra, July 8, 2014. http:// www.mofa.go.jp/files/000044543.pdf.

———. "Prime Minister Shinzo Abe's Interview with *The Australian*: 'Special Relationship' Between Australia and Japan Begins." July 8, 2014. http://www .mofa.go.jp/p_pd/ip/page4e_000114.html.

———. "Trilateral Strategic Dialogue Joint Statement Australia–Japan–United States." Sydney, March 18, 2006. http://www.mofa.go.jp/region/asia-paci/australia /joint0603-2.html.

Ministry of Foreign Affairs, People's Republic of China. "China and Russia: Partnership of Strategic Coordination." http://www.fmprc.gov.cn/mfa_eng/ziliao _665539/3602_665543/3604_665547/t18028.shtml.

———. "China Maintains with Brazil Long-Term and Stable Strategic Partnership Based on Mutual Benefit." http://www.fmprc.gov.cn/mfa_eng/ziliao_665539 /3602_665543/3604_665547/t18025.shtml.

———. "Declaration of the Heads of State of the Member States of the Shanghai Cooperation Organization on Building a Region of Lasting Peace and Common Prosperity." Beijing, June 7, 2012. http://www.fmprc.gov.cn/mfa_eng/wjdt _665385/2649_665393/t939149.shtml.

———. "Nine Changes in Stride 2015 Zhurihe Series Exercise." *China Military Online,* June 3, 2015. http://eng.mod.gov.cn/Opinion/2015-06/03/content_4588253 .htm.

Ministry of National Defense, People's Republic of China. "SCO Hosts First Joint Online Counter-Terrorism Exercise in China." *China Military Online*, October 15, 2015. http://eng.mod.gov.cn/Database/MOOTW/2015-10/15/content_4624404 .htm.

————. "Stride 2016-Zhurihe B Exercise Wraps Up." *China Military Online*, August 18, 2016. http://eng.chinamil.com.cn/view/2016-08/18/content_7214473.htm.

Minnich, James M. *The North Korean People's Army: Origins and Current Tactics.* Annapolis, MD: Naval Institute Press, 2005.

Misra, Amalendu. "Shanghai 5 and the Emerging Alliance in Central Asia: The Closed Society and Its Enemies." *Central Asian Survey*, vol. 20, no. 3 (2001): 305–321.

Mitzen, Jennifer. "Security Communities and the Unthinkabilities of War." *Annual Review of Political Science*, vol. 19, no. 1 (2016): 229–248.

Modelski, George. "The Study of Alliances: A Review." *Journal of Conflict Resolution*, vol. 7, no. 4 (1963): 769–776.

Möller, Frank. "Capitalizing on Difference: A Security Community or/as a Western Project." *Security Dialogue,* vol. 34, no. 3 (2003): 315–328.

————. *Thinking Peaceful Change: Baltic Security Policies and Security Community Building.* Syracuse, NY: Syracuse University Press, 2007.

Moravcsik, Andrew. "Taking Preferences Seriously: A Liberal Theory of International Politics." *International Organization*, vol. 51, no. 4 (Autumn 1997): 513–553.

Morgan, David A. "Regional Security Complexes and Regional Order." In Lake and Morgan, *Regional Orders: Building Security in a New World,* 20-42.

Morgan, Patrick. "Liberalism." In Collins, *Contemporary Security Studies,* 35–43.

Morgenthau, Hans J. "Alliances in Theory and Practice." In Arnold Wolfers (ed.). *Alliance Policy in the Cold War*, 184–212 Westport, CT: Greenwood Press, 1976.

————. *Politics Among Nations*, Sixth edition. New York: McGraw-Hill, 1985.

Morrison, Charles. "Track 1/Track 2 Symbiosis in Asia-Pacific Regionalism." *Pacific Review,* vol. 17, no. 4 (2004): 547–565.

Morris-Suzuki, Tessa. "Japan's 'Comfort Women': It's Time for the Truth (in the Ordinary, Everyday Sense of the Word)." *Japan Focus*, vol. 5, no. 3 (March 1, 2007). http://apjjf.org/-Tessa-Morris-Suzuki/2373/article.html.

Morrow, James D. "Alliances and Asymmetry: An Alternative to the Capability Aggregation Model of Alliances." *American Journal of Political Science*, vol. 35, no. 4 (1991): 904–933.

Mossop, Joanna. "Australia v Japan: Whaling in the International Court of Justice." *New Zealand Yearbook of International Law*, vol. 7 (2009): 169.

Mouritzen, Hans. "Peace for the Wrong Reason? Towards a European Security Community: A Rejoinder to Moller." *Security Dialogue*, vol. 34, no. 3 (2003): 329–332.

Mousseau, Michael. "The Nexus of Market Society, Liberal Preferences, and Democratic Peace: Interdisciplinary Theory and Evidence." *International Studies Quarterly,* vol. 47, no. 4 (2003): 483–510.

Mulgan, Aurelia G. "The US-Japan Security Relationship in a New Era." In Denny Roy (ed.). *The New Security Agenda in the Asia-Pacific Region,* 237–296. New York: St. Martin's Press, 1997.

Muraviev, Alexey D. "Comrades in Arms." *Journal of Asian Security and International Affairs*, vol. 1, no. 2 (2014): 163–185.

Mytelka, Lynn K. (ed.). *Strategic Partnerships: States, Firms and International Competition*. London: Pinter, 1991.

Nadkarni, Vidya. *Strategic Partnerships in Asia: Balancing Without Alliances*. New York: Routledge, 2010.

Nanda, Prakash (ed.). *Rising India: Friends and Foes*. Olympia Fields, IL: Lancer, 2007.

Narine, Shaun. "ASEAN in the Twenty-First Century: A Sceptical Review." *Cambridge Review of International Affairs*, vol. 22, no. 3 (2009): 369–386.

————. "Forty Years of ASEAN: A Historical Review." *Pacific Review*, vol. 21, no. 4 (2008): 411–429.

National Institute for Defense Studies. "Southeast Asia: Challenges in Creating an 'ASEAN Political-Security Community.'" In *East Asian Strategic Review*, 127–158. Tokyo: National Institute for Defense Studies, 2012.

Navarro, Peter. *Crouching Tiger: What China's Militarism Means for the World*. New York: Prometheus Books, 2015.

Nayar, Baldev Raj, and T. V. Paul. *India in the World Order: Searching for Major Power Status*. Cambridge: Cambridge University Press, 2003.

Nesadurai, Helen E. S. "ASEAN During the Life of the *Pacific Review*: A Balance Sheet on Regional Governance and Community Building." *Pacific Review*, vol. 30, no. 6 (2017): 938–951.

Neumann, Iver B. "A Region-Building Approach to Northern Europe." *Review of International Studies*, vol. 20, no. 1 (1994): 53–74.

New Zealand Ministry of Foreign Affairs & Trade. *Statement of Intent 2011–2014*. Wellington, April 2011.

Ngoma, Naison. "SADC: Towards a Security Community?" *African Security Review*, vol. 12, no. 3 (2003): 17–28.

Nolan, Janne E. *Global Engagement: Cooperation and Security in the 21st Century*. Washington, DC: Brookings Institution, 1994.

Noland, Sherman Robinson, and Li-gang Liu. "The Costs and Benefits of Korean Unification—Alternative Scenarios." *Asian Survey*, vol. 38, no. 8 (1998): 801–814.

Norberg, Johan. *Training to Fight: Russia's Major Military Exercise 2011–2014*. Stockholm: Swedish Defense Research Agency, December 2015.

North Atlantic Treaty Organization. "Fact Sheet: NATO–EU Relations." July 2016. http://www.nato.int/nato_static_fl2014/assets/pdf/pdf_2016_07/20160630_1607 -factsheet-nato-eu-en.pdf.

————. "Relations with Kazakhstan." December 12, 2017. http://www.nato.int /cps/en/natohq/topics_49598.htm.

Nye, Joseph S. "A New Sino-Russian Alliance?" *Project Syndicate,* January 12, 2015. https://www.project-syndicate.org/commentary/russia-china-alliance-by -joseph-s-nye-2015-01?barrier=accesspaylog.

Oberdorfer, Don. *The Two Koreas: A Comparative History*. New York: Basic Books, 2001.

Observatory of Economic Complexity. "China." Data extracted in 2017 from http:// atlas.media.mit.edu/en.

Odgaard, Liselotte. "Beijing's Quest for Stability in Its Neighborhood: China's Relations with Russia in Central Asia." *Asian Security*, vol. 13, no. 1 (2017): 41–58.

Ong, Russell. "'Peaceful Evolution,' 'Regime Change' and China's Political Security." *Journal of Contemporary China*, vol. 16, no. 53 (2007): 717–727.

Oppermann, Daniel. *Hedley Bull: From Pluralism to Solidarism.* Munich: GRIN Verlag GmbH, 2007.

Oresman, Matthew, and Zamir Chargynov. "The Shanghai Cooperation Summit: Where Do We Go from Here?" *China and Eurasia Forum Quarterly*, vol. 3, no. 2 (2005): 5–6.

Organization Studies. "Description." March 7, 2017. https://us.sagepub.com/en-us/nam/journal/organization-studies#description.

Osborne, Milton. *South East Asia: An Illustrated Introductory History.* Sydney: Allen & Unwin, 1988.

Osgood, Robert E. *Alliances and American Foreign Policy.* Baltimore: Johns Hopkins Press, 1968.

Ota, Fumio. *The US-Japan Alliance in the 21st Century: A View of the History and a Rationale for Its Survival.* Honolulu: University of Hawaii Press, 2006.

Pan, Guang. "A Chinese Perspective on the Shanghai Cooperation Organization. In Bailes et al., *The Shanghai Cooperation Organization,* 45–58.

———. "The SCO's Success in Security Architecture." In Ron Huisken (ed.). *The Architecture of Security in the Asia-Pacific,* 33–44. Canberra: ANU Press, 2009.

Papp, Daniel S. "The Gulf War Coalition: The Politics and Economics of a Most Unusual Alliance." In Willam Head and Earl Tilford (eds.). *The Eagle in the Desert,* 21–46. London: Praeger, 1996.

Parameswaran, Prashanth. "Explaining US Strategic Partnerships in the Asia-Pacific Region: Origins, Developments and Prospects." *Contemporary Southeast Asia: A Journal of International and Strategic Affairs*, vol. 36, no. 1 (2014): 262–289.

Parker, J. S. F. "The United Arab Republic." *International Affairs,* vol. 38, no. 1 (1968): 15–28.

Parker, Martin. *Organizational Culture and Identity.* London: Sage, 2000.

Pasicolan, Paolo, and Balbina Y. Hwang. "The Vital Role of Alliances in the Global War on Terrorism." *Backgrounder,* no. 1607 (2002). https://www.heritage.org/homeland-security/report/the-vital-role-alliances-the-global-war-terrorism.

Paul, T. V. (ed.). *The India-Pakistan Conflict: An Enduring Rivalry.* Cambridge: Cambridge University Press, 2005.

———. "India's Role in Asia: A Rising Regional Power." In Shambaugh and Yahuda, *International Relations of Asia,* 173–196.

Paul, T. V., and John A. Hall (eds.). *International Order and the Future of World Politics.* Cambridge: Cambridge University Press, 1999.

Paul, T. V., James J. Wirtz, and Michel Fortmann (eds.). *Balance of Power: Theory and Practice in the 21st Century.* Palo Alto, CA: Stanford University Press, 2004.

Pempel, T. J. (ed.). *Remapping East Asia: The Construction of a Region.* New York: Cornell University Press, 2005.

Perlez, Jane. "Singaporean Tells China U.S. Is Not in Decline." *New York Times,* September 6, 2012.

Perrow, Charles. "The Analysis of Goals in Complex Organizations." *American Sociological Review,* vol. 26, no. 6 (1961): 854–866.

Person, Robert. "Crouching Tiger, Hidden Jargon: The Sino-Russian Partnership." *Stanford Journal of International Relations*, vol. 3, no. 1 (2001). http://www.stanford.edu/group/sjir/3.1.10_person.html.

Petersen, Kira. *The Concept of Power in International Relations.* Cambridge, MA: Harvard University, 2011.

Peyrouse, Sébastien. "Power Differential and Security Issues in Central Asia: Threat Perceptions of China." In Robert Bedeski and Niklas Swanström (eds.). *Eura-*

sia's Ascent in Energy and Geopolitics: Rivalry or Partnership for China, Russia, and Central Asia? 92-107. Abingdon, UK: Routledge, 2012.

Phadnis, Urmila, and Sivananda Patnaik. "Non-Alignment as a Foreign Policy Strategy: A Case Study of Sri Lanka." *International Studies,* vol. 20, no. 1 (1981): 223–238.

Pierre, Andrew J. *Coalitions Building and Maintenance: The Gulf War, Kosovo, Afghanistan, and the War on Terrorism.* Washington, DC: Georgetown University, Institute for the Study of Diplomacy, 2002.

Pike, Francis. *Empires at War: A Short History of Modern Asia Since WWII.* London: I. B. Tauris, 2011.

Pillalamarri, Akhilesh. "The United States Just Closed Its Last Base in Central Asia." *The Diplomat,* June 10, 2014. http://thediplomat.com/2014/06/the-united -states-just-closed-its-last-base-in-central-asia.

Plater-Zyberk, Henry. *Who's Afraid of the SCO?* Surrey: Conflict Studies Research Centre, Defence Academy of the United Kingdom, 2007.

Pollack, Jonathan D. "The Major Powers and the Two Koreas: An Uneasy Transition." *Korean Journal for Defense Analysis,* vol. 21, no. 1 (2009): 1–9.

———. *No Exit: North Korea, Nuclear Weapons and International Security.* Adelphi 418-19. Abingdon, UK: Routledge for International Institute for Strategic Studies, 2011.

Pollack, Jonathan D., and Chung Min-Lee. *Preparing for Korean Unification: Scenarios and Implications.* Santa Monica: RAND, 1999. http://www.rand.org /pubs/monograph_reports/2007/MR1040.pdf.

Poole, Avery. "Cooperation in Contention: The Evolution of ASEAN Norms." York Centre for International and Security Studies (YCISS) Working Paper 44. Toronto: York University, 2007.

Posen, Barry N. *The Sources of Military Doctrine: France, Britain, and Germany Between the World Wars.* Ithaca, NY: Cornell University Press, 1984.

Pouliot, Vincent. "The Alive and Well Transatlantic Security Community: A Theoretical Reply to Michael Cox." *European Journal of International Relations,* vol. 12, no. 119 (2002): 120–127.

Prantl, Jochen. "Five Principles for a New Security Order in the Asia Pacific." *PacNet* 38, Pacific Forum CSIS, June 18, 2012. http://csis.org/publication/pacnet -38-five-principles-new-security-order-asia-pacific.

Price, Richard, and Christian Reus-Smit. "Dangerous Liaisons? Critical International Theory and Constructivism." *European Journal of International Relations,* vol. 4, no. 3 (1998): 169–195.

Putz, Catherine. "China's Silk Road Belt Outpaces Russia's Economic Union." *The Diplomat,* March 10, 2016. http://thediplomat.com/2016/03/chinas-silk-road -belt-outpaces-russias-economic-union.

Quested, R. K. I. *Sino-Russian Relations: A Short History.* London: Routledge, 2005.

Qiu, Jin. "The Politics of History and Historical Memory in China-Japan Relations." *Journal of Chinese Political Science,* no. 11 (2006): 25–53.

Rachman, Gideon. *Easternization: Asia's Rise and America's Decline from Obama to Trump and Beyond.* New York: Other Press, 2017.

Ravenhill, John. *APEC and Construction of Pacific Rim Regionalism.* Cambridge: Cambridge University Press, 2001.

———. "Cycles of Middle Power Activism: Constraint and Choice in Australian and Canadian Foreign Policies." *Australian Journal of International Affairs,* vol. 52, no. 3 (1998): 309–327.

Reese, M. J. "Destructive Double Standards: Great Powers and the Security Community Paradox." Paper presented at the International Studies Association Convention, San Diego, March 22–25, 2006.

Repeta, Lawrence. "Japan's 2013 State Secrecy Act—The Abe Administration's Threat to News Reporting." *Japan Focus*, vol. 12, no. 10 (March 3, 2014). http:// apjjf.org/2014/12/10/Lawrence-Repeta/4086/article.html.

Reudiger Frank. "A New Foreign Policy Paradigm: Perspectives on the Role of South Korea as a Balancer." Policy Forum 05-35A, NAPSNet Policy Forum, April 25, 2005. http://nautilus.org/napsnet/napsnet-policy-forum/a-new-foreign -policy-paradigm-perspectives-on-the-role-of-south-korea-as-a-balancer.

Rice, Condoleezza. "Rethinking the National Interest: American Realism for a New World." *Foreign Affairs*, vol. 87, no. 4 (2008): 2–14.

Rich, Motoko. "Japanese Government Urges Another Increase in Military Spending." *New York Times*, August 30, 2016. http://www.nytimes.com/2016/08/31 /world/asia/japan-defense-military-budget-shinzo-abe.html?_r=0.

Rich, Paul B. *The Dynamics of Change in Southern Africa.* Basingstoke, UK: Macmillan, 1994.

Richardson, Louise. *When Allies Differ: Anglo-American Relations During the Suez and Falklands Crises.* New York: St. Martin's Press, 1996.

Richelson, Jeffrey T., and Desmond Ball. *The Ties That Bind: Intelligence Cooperation Between the UKUSA Countries.* Sydney: Allen and Unwin, 1985.

Rieker, Pernille (ed.). *External Governance as Security Community Building: The Limits and Potential of the European Neighbourhood Policy.* London: Palgrave Macmillan UK, 2016.

Riker, William H. *Theory of Political Coalitions.* New Haven, CT: Yale University Press, 1962.

Risse-Kappen, Thomas. *Cooperation Among Democracies.* Princeton, NJ: Princeton University Press, 1995.

Roberts, Christopher B. *ASEAN Regionalism: Cooperation, Values and Institutionalization.* New York: Routledge, 2012.

———. "ASEAN, the 'South China Sea' Arbitral Award, and the Code of Conduct: New Challenges, New Approaches." *Asian Politics & Policy*, vol. 10, no. 2 (2018): 190–218.

———. "State Weakness and Political Values: Ramifications for the ASEAN Community." In Emmers, *ASEAN and the Institutionalization of East Asia,* 11–26.

Roberts, Joan M. *Alliances, Coalitions and Partnerships: Building Collaborative Organizations.* Gabriola Island, Canada: New Society Publishers, 2004.

Robertson, Jeffery. "South Korea as a Middle Power: Capacity, Behaviour and Now Opportunity." *International Journal of Korean Unification Studies,* vol. 16, no. 1 (2007): 151–174.

Rodkiewicz, Witold. "Putin in Shanghai: A Strategic Partnership on Chinese Terms." *The Centre for Eastern Studies*, May 21, 2014. https://www.osw.waw.pl /en/publikacje/analyses/2014-05-21/putin-shanghai-a-strategic-partnership -chinese-terms.

Roney, Tyler. "The Shanghai Cooperation Organization: China's NATO?" *The Diplomat*, September 11, 2013. http://thediplomat.com/2013/09/the-shanghai -cooperation-organization-chinas-nato-2.

Rosen, Daniel H. "China and the Impracticality of Closed Regionalism." In Calder and Fukuyama, *East Asian Multilateralism,* 143–167.

Ross, Robert S. (ed.). *China, the United States, and the Soviet Union: Tripolarity and Policy Making in the Cold War.* New York: M. E. Sharpe, 1993.

——— (ed.). *East Asia in Transition: Toward a New Regional Order.* New York: M. E. Sharpe, 1995.

Ross, Robert S., and Zhu Feng (eds.). *China's Ascent: Power, Security, and the Future of International Politics.* Ithaca, NY: Cornell University Press, 2008.

Rousseau, Richard. "The Tortuous Sino-Russian Arms Trade Analysis." *Eurasia Review* (June 9, 2012). https://www.eurasiareview.com/09062012-the-tortuous-sino-russian-arms-trade-analysis.

Rowan, Joshua P. "The U.S.-Japan Security Alliance, ASEAN, and the South China Sea Dispute." *Asian Survey,* vol. 45, no. 3 (2005): 414–436.

Rozman, Gilbert. *Northeast Asia's Stunted Regionalism: Bilateral Distrust in the Shadow of Globalization.* Cambridge: Cambridge University Press, 2004.

———. *The Sino-Russian Challenge to the World Order: National Identities, Bilateral Relations, and East Versus West in the 2010s.* Washington, DC: Woodrow Wilson Center Press, 2014.

———. "Sino-Russian Relations: Will the Strategic Partnership Endure?" *Demokratizatsiya,* vol. 6, no. 2 (1998): 396–415.

RSIS-Macarthur Conference on Regional Security Cooperation. "Building Institutional Coherence in Asia's Security Architecture: The Role of ASEAN." Singapore, November 24–25, 2009.

Rudd, Kevin. "The First National Security Statement to the Australian Parliament." Canberra, December 4, 2008.

Ruggie, John Gerard. *Constructing the World Polity: Essays on International Institutionalization.* London: Routledge, 1998.

———. "Territoriality and Beyond: Problematizing Modernity in International Relations." *International Organization,* vol. 47, no. 1 (1993): 139–174.

Rüland, Jürgen. "Southeast Asian Regionalism and Global Governance: 'Multilateral Utility' or 'Hedging Utility'?" *Contemporary Southeast Asia,* vol. 33, no. 1 (2011): 83–112.

Russett, Bruce M. "Components of an Operational Theory of International Alliance Formation." *Journal of Conflict Resolution,* vol. 12, no. 3 (September 1968): 285–381.

———. "An Empirical Typology of International Military Alliances." *Midwest Journal of Political Science,* vol. 15, no. 2 (1971): 262–289.

———. *Grasping the Democratic Peace: Principles for a Post Cold War World.* Princeton, NJ: Princeton University Press, 1994.

———. "A Neo-Kantian Perspective: Interdependence and International Organizations in Building Security Communities." In Adler and Barnett, *Security Communities,* 368–394.

Russett, Bruce M., and W. Curtis Lamb. "Global Patterns of Diplomatic Exchange, 1963–64." *Journal of Peace Research,* vol. 6, no. 1 (1969): 37–54.

Russia & India Report. "Russia Tops the List of India's Strategic Partners: Study." January 20, 2012. http://indrus.in/articles/2012/01/20/russia_tops_the_list_of_indias_strategic_partners_study_14573.html.

Sagan, Scott D. *The Limits of Safety: Organizations, Accidents and Nuclear Weapons.* Princeton, NJ: Princeton University Press, 1995.

Sahashi, Ryo. "Australia, Japan, and US Trilateral Cooperation in the Regional Security Architecture." In Tatsumi, *US-Japan-Australia Security Cooperation,* 37–50.

————. "The Rise of China and the Transformation of Asia-Pacific Security Architecture." In Tow and Taylor, *Bilateralism, Multilateralism and Asia-Pacific Security,* 135–156.

Sajjanhar, Ashok. "India and the Shanghai Cooperation Organization." *Diplomat*, June 19, 2016. http://thediplomat.com/2016/06/india-and-the-shanghai-cooperation -organization.

Sakwa, Richard. "Senseless Dreams and Small Steps: The CIS and CSTO Between Integration and Cooperation." In Maria R. Freire and Roger E. Kanet (eds.). *Key Players and Regional Dynamics in Eurasia: The Return of the Great Game,* 195–214. New York: Palgrave Macmillian, 2010.

Salmon, Trevor. "The European Union: Just an Alliance or a Military Alliance?" *Journal of Strategic Studies*, vol. 29, no. 5 (2007): 813–842.

Samuels, Richard. *3.11: Disaster and Change in Japan*. Ithaca, NY: Cornell University Press, 2013.

Satake, Tomohiko. "The Origin of Trilateralism?: The U.S.-Japan-Australia Security Relations in the 1990s." *International Relations of the Asia-Pacific,* vol. 11, no. 1 (2011): 87–114.

Schleifer, Yigal. "Turkey: With EU Talks Stalled, Erdogan Suggests Ankara May Join SCO." *Eurasianet*, January 28, 2013. http://www.eurasianet.org/node/66460.

Schlossstein, Steven. *Asia's New Little Dragons: The Dynamic Emergence of Indonesia, Thailand, and Malaysia.* Chicago: Contemporary Books, 1991.

Schoff, James L. "The Evolution of US-Japan-Australia Security Cooperation." In Tatsumi, *US-Japan-Australia Security Cooperation,* 37–50.

Schroeder, Paul. "Alliances, 1815–1945: Weapons of Power and Tools of Management." In Klaus Knorr (ed.). *Historical Dimensions of National Security Problems,* 227–263. Lawrence, KS: Allen Press, 1976.

Seryaev, Yazmurad. "The Permanent Neutrality of Turkmenistan." *Diplomat*, November 1, 2015. http://www.diplomatmagazine.com/the-permanent-neutrality -of-turkmenistan.

Shambaugh, David. "China Engages Asia: Reshaping the Regional Order." *International Security*, vol. 29, no. 3 (2004): 64–99.

———— (ed.). *Power Shift: China and Asia's New Dynamic.* Berkeley: University of California Press, 2005.

Shambaugh, David, and Michael B. Yahuda (eds.). *International Relations of Asia.* Lanham, MD: Rowman and Littlefield, 2014.

Shanghai Cooperation Organisation. "Brief Introduction to the Shanghai Cooperation Organisation." Accessed June 3, 2010. http://www.sectsco.org/EN/brief.asp.

————. "Charter of the Shanghai Cooperation Organisation." June 7, 2002. Accessed June 3, 2010. http://eng.sectsco.org/load/203013.

————. "Information Report Following the Meeting of the Council of Heads of State of the Shanghai Cooperation Organisation Member States." June 10, 2018. http://eng.sectsco.org/news/20180610/443710.html.

————. "Main Page." Accessed June 3, 2010. http://www.sectsco.org/EN/index .asp#.

————. "SCO Member State Experts from Competent Authorities Discuss IT Cooperation." News, January 13, 2017. http://eng.sectsco.org/news/20170113/195008 .html.

————. "The Tashkent Declaration of the Fifteenth Anniversary of the Shanghai Cooperation Organization." Tashkent, June 24, 2016. http://eng.sectsco.org/load /207886.

Sheehan, Michael. *The Balance of Power: History and Theory*. London: Routledge, 1995.

Sheen, Seongho. "A Smart Alliance in the Age of Complexity: ROK-US Alliance in the 21st Century." *EAI Issue Briefing*, MASI 2009-02. June 1, 2009. http://www.eai.or.kr/data/bbs/eng_report/200908061732413.pdf.

Shore, Sean M. "No Fences Make Good Neighbors: The Development of the US-Canadian Security Community." In Adler and Barnett, *Security Communities*, 333–367.

Signorino, Curtis S., and Jeffery M. Ritter. "Tau-b or Not Tau-b: Measuring the Similarity of Foreign Policy Positions." *International Studies Quarterly*, vol. 43, no. 1 (1999): 115–144.

Silkett, Wayne A. "Alliance and Coalition Warfare." *Parameters*, vol. 23, no. 2 (Summer 1993): 74–85.

Silver, David A. *Strategic Partnering*. New York: McGraw-Hill, 1993.

Simon, Sheldon W. "ASEAN and Southeast Asia: Remaining Relevant." In Shambaugh and Yahuda, *International Relations of Asia*, 189–205.

———. "The United States, Japan, and Australia: Security Linkages to Southeast Asia." In Tow et al., *Assessing the Trilateral Security Dialogue*, 51–58.

Singh, Bhubhindar. "The Development of Japanese Security Policy: A Long-Term Defensive Strategy." In *Asia Policy*, no. 19 (January 2015): 49–64.

Siracusa, Joseph M. "John Howard, Australia, and the Coalition of the Willing." *Yale Journal of International Affairs* (Winter/Spring 2006): 39–49.

Smith, Gary, and David Lowe. "Howard, Downer and the Liberals' Realist Tradition." *Australian Journal of Politics and History*, vol. 51, issue. 3 (2005): 459–472.

Smith, Hazel (ed.). *Reconstituting Korean Security: A Policy Primer*. Tokyo: United Nations University, 2007.

Smith, Martin A., and Graham Timmins (eds.). *Uncertain Europe: Building a New European Security Order?* London: Routledge, 2007.

Smith, Sheila A. "A Strategy for the U.S.-Japan Alliance." *Policy Innovation Memorandum 19*, Council on Foreign Relations, April 25, 2012. https://www.cfr.org/report/strategy-us-japan-alliance.

Smith, Stephen. "Trilateral Strategic Dialogue: Joint Statement." Media Release, Australian Minister for Foreign Affairs and Trade, June 27, 2008. http://www.foreignminister.gov.au/releases/2008/fa-s080627.html.

Snyder, Glenn. *Alliance Politics*. Ithaca, NY: Cornell University Press, 1997.

———. "Alliances, Balance, Stability." *International Organization*, vol. 45, no. 1 (1991): 121–142.

———. "The Security Dilemma in Alliance Politics." *World Politics*, vol. 36, no. 4. (July 1984): 461–495.

Snyder, Scott. *China's Rise and the Two Koreas: Politics, Economics, Security*. Boulder, CO: Lynne Rienner, 2009.

———. "Is It Time for the U.S.–Japan–South Korea Virtual Alliance To Get Real?" *Asia Unbound*, Council on Foreign Relations, January 17, 2012. http://blogs.cfr.org/asia/2012/01/17/is-it-time-for-the-u-s-japan-south-korea-virtual-alliance-to-get-real.

———. *South Korea at the Crossroads: Autonomy and Alliance in an Era of Rival Powers*. New York: Columbia University Press, 2018.

———. *The US–South Korea Alliance: Meeting New Security Challenges* (Boulder, CO: Lynne Rienner, 2012).

Soderbaum, Fredrik, and Timothy M. Shaw (eds.). *Theories of New Regionalism: A Palgrave Reader.* London: Palgrave, 2003.

Soeya, Yoshihide. "Japan: Normative Constraints Versus Structural Imperatives." In Muthiah Alagappa (ed). *Asian Security Practice*, 198-233. Stanford: Stanford University Press, 1998.

Solana, Javier. "The EU-Russia Strategic Partnership." Speech by the High Representative Designate of the European Union for Common Foreign and Security Policy, Stockholm, October 13, 1999. http://www.consilium.europa.eu/uedocs /cms_data/docs/pressdata/EN/discours/59417.pdf.

Solingen, Etel. "East Asian Regional Institutions: Characteristics, Sources, Distinctiveness." In Pempel, T. J. (ed.). *Remapping East Asia: The Construction of a Region.* Ithaca, NY: Cornell University Press, 2005.

———. *Regional Orders at Century's Dawn.* Princeton, NJ: Princeton University Press, 1998.

Song, Weiqing. "Interests, Power and China's Difficult Game in the Shanghai Cooperation Organization (SCO)." *Journal of Contemporary China*, vol. 23, no. 85 (2014): 85–101.

Sperling, James, and Emil Kirchner. *Recasting the European Order: Security Architectures and Economic Cooperation.* Manchester, UK: Manchester University Press, 1997.

Spykman, Nicholas John. *The Geography of the Peace.* New York: Harcourt, Brace and Company, 1944.

Starr, Harvey. "Democracy and War: Choice, Learning and Security Communities." *Journal of Peace Research,* vol. 29, no. 2 (1992): 207–213.

———. *War Coalitions.* Lexington, MA: Lexington Books, 1972.

State Council Information Office of the People's Republic of China. *China's Policies on Asia-Pacific Security Cooperation.* White Paper, Beijing, January 2017. http:// english.gov.cn/archive/white_paper/2017/01/11/content_281475539078636.htm.

Steans, Jill, and Lloyd Pettiford. *Introduction to International Relations: Perspectives and Themes,* Second edition. Upper Saddle River, NJ: Prentice Hall, 2005.

Steward, Chris. *Developing Strategic Partnerships.* Brookfield, VT: Gower, 1999.

Storey, Ian, Ralf Emmers, and Daljit Singh (eds.). *The Five Power Defence Arrangements at Forty.* Singapore: Institute of Southeast Asian Studies, 2011.

Stubbs, Richard. "The ASEAN Alternative? Ideas, Institutions and the Challenge to Global Governance." *Pacific Review,* vol. 21, no. 4 (2008): 451–467.

Sukma, Rizal. "The ASEAN Political and Security Community (APSC): Opportunities and Constraints for the R2P in Southeast Asia." *Pacific Review*, vol. 25, no. 1 (2012): 135–152.

Sun Tzi. *The Art of War.* Translated by Ralph D. Sawyer. New York: Barnes & Noble, 1994.

Sutter, Robert. "The United States in Asia: Durable Leadership." In Shambaugh and Yahuda, *International Relations of Asia,* 93–114.

Swanström, Niklas. "Transformation of the Sino-Russian Partnership: From Cold War to the Putin Era." In Robert Bedeski and Niklas Swanström (eds.). *Eurasia's Ascent in Energy and Geopolitics: Rivalry or Partnership for China, Russia, and Central Asia?* Abingdon, UK: Routledge, 2012.

Talesco, Christian. "How East Timor's Democracy Is Making It an Outcast." *Foreign Policy*, May 10, 2016. http://foreignpolicy.com/2016/05/10/how-east-timors -democracy-is-making-it-an-outcast-asean-southeast-asia.

Tan, See Seng. "Southeast Asia in Search of Security Community: Can ASEAN Go Beyond Crisis, Consequentiality and Conceptual Convenience?" Unpublished paper, permission for citation granted.

Tanaka, Akihiko. "Trilateral Strategic Dialogue: A Japanese Perspective." In Tow et al., *Assessing the Trilateral Security Dialogue*, 33–40.

Tatsumi, Yuki. "Introduction." In Tatsumi, *US-Japan-Australia Security Cooperation*, 15–22.

——— (ed.). *US-Japan-Australia Security Cooperation: Prospects and Challenger.* Washington, DC: Stimson Center, April 2015. http://www.stimson.org/sites/default/files/file-attachments/US-Japan_Australia-WEB.pdf.

Taylor, Alastair M. "Malaysia, Indonesia—and Maphilindo." *International Journal*, vol. 19, no. 2 (1964): 155–171.

Taylor, Brendan (ed.). *Australia as an Asia-Pacific Regional Power: Friendships in Flux?* London: Routledge, 2007.

———. "Conceptualizing the Bilateral-Multilateral Security Nexus." In Tow and Taylor, *Bilateralism, Multilateralism and Asia-Pacific Security*, 8–18.

Taylor, Brendan, and Desmond Ball. "Australia-Japan." In Taylor, *Australia as an Asia-Pacific Regional Power*, 50–59.

Taylor, Brendan, and William Tow. "Challenges to Building an Effective Asia-Pacific Security Architecture." In Green and Gill, *Asia's New Multilateralism*, 329–349.

Taylor, Frederick W. *The Principles of Scientific Management.* New York: Harper & Row, 1911.

Tellis, Ashley J., Andrew Marble, and Travis Tanner (eds.). *Strategic Asia 2010–2011: Asia's Rising Power and America's Continued Purpose.* Seattle: National Bureau of Asian Research, 2010.

Tellis, Ashley J., and Michael Wills (eds.). *Strategic Asia 2005–2006: Military Modernization in an Era of Uncertainty.* Seattle: National Bureau of Asian Research, 2005.

Tellis, Ashley J. "Seeking Alliances and Partnerships: The Long Road to Confederationism in U.S. Grand Strategy." In Tellis, Denmark, and Chaffin, *Strategic Asia 2014–15*, 3–32.

Tellis, Ashley J., Abraham M. Denmark, and Greg Chaffin (eds.). *Strategic Asia 2014–15: U.S. Alliances and Partnerships at the Center of Global Power.* Seattle: National Bureau of Asian Research, 2014.

Tellis, Ashley J., Travis Tanner, and Jessica Keough (eds.). *Strategic Asia 2011–12: Asia Responds to Its Rising Powers—China and India.* Seattle: National Bureau of Asian Research, 2011.

Tellis, Ashley J., and Michael Wills (eds.). *Strategic Asia 2007: Domestic Political Change and Grand Strategy.* Seattle: National Bureau of Asian Research, 2007.

Terada, Takashi. "Thirty Years of the Australia-Japan Partnership in Asian Regionalism: Evolution and Future Directions." *Australian Journal of International Affairs*, vol. 60, no. 4 (2006): 536–551.

Tertrais, Bruno. "The Changing Nature of Military Alliances." *The Washington Quarterly*, vol. 27, no. 2 (2004): 133–150.

Thayer, Carlyle. "The Five Power Defence Achievements: The Quiet Achiever." *Security Challenges*, vol. 3, no. 1 (2007): 71–96.

———. "The Rise of China and India: Challenging or Reinforcing Southeast Asia's Autonomy." In Tellis, Tanner, and Keough, *Strategic Asia 2011–12*, 313–346.

Thucydides. *History of the Peloponnesian War.* Translated by Charles Forster Smith. Cambridge, MA: Harvard University Press, 1991.

Tilly, Charles. "International Communities: Secure and Otherwise." In Adler and Barnett, *Security Communities*, 397–412.

Togo, Kazuhiko. "Regional Security Cooperation in East Asia: What Can Japan and Australia Usefully Do Together?" *Australian Journal of International Affairs,* vol. 65, no. 1 (2011): 40–60.

Tolipov, Farkad. "On the Role of the Central Asian Cooperation Organization within the SCO." *Central Asia and the Caucasus,* vol 3, no. 27 (2004): 146–154.

Toloraya, Georgy. "Russian Policy in Korea in a Time of Change." *Korean Journal of Defense Analysis,* vol. 21, no. 1 (2009): 67–84.

Torkunov, Anatoly. "Groundwork for the Future." *International Affairs* (Moscow), vol. 52, no. 2 (2006): 25.

Tow, William T. "Alliances and Alignments in the Twenty-First Century." In Brendan Taylor (ed.). *Australia as an Asia Pacific Power: Friendships in Flux.* London: Routledge, 2007: 12–29.

———. "Asia's Competitive 'Strategic Geometries': The Australian Perspective." *Contemporary Southeast Asia,* vol. 30, no. 1 (2008): 29–51.

———. "'Contingent Trilateralism': Applications for the Trilateral Security Dialogue." In William Tow, Mark Thomson, Yoshinobu Yamamoto and Satu Limaye (eds.). *Asia-Pacific Security: US, Australia and Japan and the New Security Triangle,* 23–38. London: Routledge, 2007.

——— (ed.). *Security Politics in the Asia-Pacific: A Regional-Global Nexus?* Cambridge: Cambridge University Press, 2009.

———. "Tangled Webs: Security Architectures in Asia." *ASPI Paper.* Barton, ACT: Australian Strategic Policy Institute, 2008.

———. "The Trilateral Strategic Dialogue: Facilitating Community-Building or Revisiting Containment." In William Tow and Michael Austin, Rory Medcalf, Akihiko Tanaka, Zhu Feng, and Sheldon Simon. *Assessing the Trilateral Security Dialogue,* 1–19. National Bureau of Asian Research Special Report 16, Seattle, 2008.

Tow, William T., and Russel Trood. "The 'Anchors': Collaborative Security, Substance or Smokescreen?" In Brad Williams and Andrew Newman (eds.) *Japan, Australia and Asia-Pacific Security,* 70–88. London: Routledge, 2006.

Tow, William T., and Amitav Acharya. "Obstinate or Obsolete?: The US Alliance Structure in the Asia-Pacific." Working Paper 2007/4, Department of International Relations, Australian National University, December 2007.

Tow, William T., Michael Austin, Rory Medcalf, Akihiko Tanaka, Zhu Feng, and Sheldon Simon. *Assessing the Trilateral Security Dialogue.* National Bureau of Asian Research Special Report 16, Seattle, 2008.

Tow, William T., and H. D. P. Envall. "The United States, Asia, and 'Convergent Security.'" *Policy Background Paper* 7, MacArthur Security Initiative, Australian National University, December 13, 2011.

Tow, William T., and Satu Limaye. "What's China Got to Do with It? U.S. Alliances, Partnerships in the Asia-Pacific." *Asian Politics & Policy,* vol. 8, no. 1 (2016): 7–26.

Tow, William T., and Brendan Taylor (eds.). *Bilateralism, Multilateralism and Asia-Pacific Security: Contending Cooperation.* London: Routledge, 2013.

———. "What Is Asian Security Architecture?" *Review of International Studies,* vol. 36, no. 1 (2010): 95–116.

Trenin, Dmitri. "True Partners? How Russia and China see Each Other." *Centre for European Reform* (February 2012).

Trofimenko, Henry. "The Third World and the US-Soviet Competition: A Soviet View." *Foreign Affairs,* vol. 59, no. 5 (1981): 1021–1040.

Troitskiy, Mikhail. "A Russian Perspective on the Shanghai Cooperation Organization." In Alyson J. K. Bailes, Pál Dunay, Pan Guang, and Mikhail Troitskiy. *The Shanghai Cooperation Organization,* 30–44. SIPRI Policy Paper No. 17. Stockholm: SIPRI, 2007.

Tsunekawa, Keiichi. "Building Asian Security Institutions Under the Triple Shocks: Competitive, Complementary, or Juxtaposed?" In Vinod K. Aggarwal and Min Gyo Koo (eds.). *Asia's New Institutional Architecture: Evolving Structures for Managing Trade, Financial and Security Relations,* 59–89. Leipzig: Springer, 2008.

———. "Why So Many Maps There? Japan and Regional Cooperation." In Pempel, T. J. (ed.). *Remapping East Asia: The Construction of a Region,* 101–148. Ithaca, NY: Cornell University Press, 2005.

Tsygankov, Andrei P. *Russia's Foreign Policy: Change and Continuity in National Identity,* Third edition. New York: Rowman and Littlefield Publishers, 2013.

Tugsbilguun, T. "Does the Shanghai Cooperation Represent an Example of a Military Alliance?" *Mongolian Journal of International Affairs,* no. 15–16 (2008–2009): 59–107.

Tusicisny, Andrej. "Security Communities and Their Values: Taking the Masses Seriously." *International Political Science Review,* vol. 28, no. 4 (2007): 425–449.

United Nations. "Letter Dated 2 May 1996 from the Permanent Representatives of China and the Russian Federation to the United Nations Addressed to the Secretary-General." Documents, General Assembly, 51st session, 1996. http://www.un.org/documents/ga/docs/51/plenary/a51-127.htm.

US Department of Defense. *East Asia Strategy Report.* Washington, DC, 1998. http://ryukyu-okinawa.net/downloads/usdod-easr98.pdf.

———. *The National Defense Strategy of the United States of America.* Washington, DC, March 2005. http://www.colonelby.com/teachers/krichardson/Grade%2012/Carleton%20-%20Int%20Law%20Course/Week%2010/USDefenseStrategy.pdf.

———. *Quadrennial Defense Review Report.* Washington, DC, February 6, 2006. http://archive.defense.gov/pubs/pdfs/QDR20060203.pdf.

———. *Summary of the 2018 National Defense Strategy of the United States of America.* Washington, DC, January 2018. http://nssarchive.us/wp-content/uploads/2018/01/2018-National-Defense-Strategy-Summary.pdf.

US Department of State. "Australia–Japan–United States Trilateral Strategic Dialogue Ministerial Joint Statement." Washington, DC, August 6, 2017. https://www.state.gov/r/pa/prs/ps/2017/08/273216.htm.

———. "Trilateral Strategic Dialogue Joint Statement." Washington, DC, March 20, 2006. https://2001-2009.state.gov/r/pa/prs/ps/2006/63411.htm.

———. "Trilateral Strategic Dialogue Joint Statement." Washington, DC, September 21, 2009. https://2009-2017.state.gov/r/pa/prs/ps/2009/sept/129443.htm.

US Office of the Secretary of Defense. *Military and Security Developments Involving the People's Republic of China 2016.* Annual Report to Congress. Washington, DC, May 13, 2016. http://www.defense.gov/Portals/1/Documents/pubs/2016%20China%20Military%20Power%20Report.pdf.

Van Wagenen, Richard W. *Research in the International Organization Field: Some Notes on a Possible Focus.* Princeton, NJ: Center for Research on World Political Institutions, 1952.

Väyrynen, Raimo. "Stable Peace Through Security Communities? Steps Towards Theory Building." In Arie M. Kacowicz et al. (eds.). *Stable Peace Among Nations,* 157–193. Lanham, MD: Rowman & Littlefield, 2000.

Vogel, Ezra. *Japan as Number One.* Cambridge, MA: Harvard University Press, 1979.

Wæver, Ole. "Insecurity, Security, and Asecurity in the West European Non-War Community." In Adler and Barnett, *Security Communities,* 69–118.

———. "Securitization and Desecuritization." In R. Lipschutz (ed.). *On Security,* 46–86. New York: Columbia University Press, 1995.

Wallace, Robert. *Strategic Partnerships: An Entrepreneur's Guide to Joint Ventures and Alliances.* Chicago: Dearborn Trade, 2004.

Wallander, Celeste A., "Institutional Assets and Adaptability: NATO After the Cold War." *International Organization,* vol. 54, no. 4 (2000): 705–735.

Wallander, Celeste A., and Robert O. Keohane. "Risk, Threat and Security Institutions." In Helga Haftendorn et al. (eds.). *Imperfect Unions: Security Institutions over Time and Space,* 21–47. Oxford: Oxford University Press, 1999.

Wallensteen, Peter. *Towards a Security Community in the Baltic Region: Patterns of Peace and Conflict.* Uppsala: Baltic University Secretariat, 1993.

Wallis, Joanne, and Andrew Carr (eds.). *Asia-Pacific Security: An Introduction.* Washington, DC: Georgetown University Press, 2016.

Walt, Stephen. *The Origins of Alliances.* Ithaca, NY: Cornell University Press, 1987.

———. "Why Alliances Endure or Collapse." *Survival,* vol. 39, no. 1 (1997): 156–179.

Walton, David, and Emilian Kavalski (eds.). *Power Transition in Asia.* London: Routledge, 2017.

Waltz, Kenneth N. "The Emerging Structure of International Politics." *International Security,* vol. 18, no. 2 (1993): 44–79.

———. *Man, the State and War.* New York: Columbia University Press, 1959.

———. *Theory of International Politics.* Reading, MA: Addison-Wesley, 1979.

Ward, Michael D. *Research Gaps in Alliance Dynamics.* Denver, CO: University of Denver, 1982.

Watanabe, Akio. "Japan and Australia: A Comparison of Their Strategies for Coexistence with Asia and America." In Peter King and Yoichi Kabata (eds.). *Peace Building in the Asia Pacific Region,* 6–15. NSW: Allen & Unwin, 1996.

Weber, Max. *The Theory of Social and Economic Organization.* Translated by Talcott Parsons and Alexander M. Henderson. New York: Free Press, 1974.

Weidenfeld, Werner, Caio Koch-Weser, and Walther Stutzle (eds.). *From Alliance to Coalitions: The Future of Transatlantic Relations.* Guetersloh, Germany: BertelsmannStiftung, 2006.

Weitsman, Patricia. "Alliance Cohesion and Coalition Warfare: The Central Powers and the Triple Entente." *Security Studies,* vol. 12, no. 3 (2003): 79–113.

———. *Dangerous Alliances.* Stanford: Stanford University Press, 2004.

Weitz, Richard. "Building a NATO-SCO Dialogue." *European Dialogue,* March 14, 2011. http://eurodialogue.org/Building-a-NATO-SCO-dialogue.

———. *China-Russia Security Relations: Strategic Parallelism Without Partnership or Passion?* Carlisle, PA: Strategic Studies Institute, US Army War College, 2008.

————. "Kazakhstan-China Military Exchanges Continue." *Eurasia Daily Monitor*, vol. 9, no. 206 (2012).

Wen, Jiabao. "Speech by H. E. Wen Jiabao: Vigorously Promoting Comprehensive Strategic Partnership Between China and the European Union." The China-EU Investment and Trade Forum, Brussels, May 6, 2004.

Wendt, Alexander. "Anarchy Is What States Make of It." *International Organization*, vol. 46, no. 2 (1992): 391–425.

————. "Constructing International Politics." *International Security*, vol. 20, no. 1 (1995): 71–81.

————. *Social Theory of International Politics.* Cambridge: Cambridge University Press, 1999.

Wesley, Michael. "Irresistible Rise of the Indo-Pacific." *The Australian*, May 4, 2011.

————. *There Goes the Neighbourhood.* Sydney, Australia: UNSW Press, 2011.

Westad, Odd A. (ed.). *Brothers in Arms: The Rise and Fall of the Sino-Soviet Alliance.* Washington, DC: Woodrow Wilson Center Press, 1998.

Wheeler, Nicholas. *Saving Strangers: Humanitarian Intervention in International Society.* Oxford: Oxford University Press, 2000.

White, Hugh. "Alliances and Order in the 'Asian Century.'" In Tow and Taylor, *Bilateralism, Multilateralism and Asia-Pacific Security,* 157–168.

————. *The China Choice: Why America Should Share Power.* Melbourne: Black, 2013.

————. "Should Australia Form an Alliance with Japan?" Video on ANU TV, Australian National University, December 19, 2012. http://www.youtube.com/watch?v=7zKvzkvk0Mk.

————. "Why War in Asia Remains Thinkable." *Survival*, vol. 50, no. 6 (2008): 85–104.

White House. "Australia–Japan–United States Trilateral Leaders Meeting Joint Media Release." November 15, 2014. Accessed November 20, 2014. https://obamawhitehouse.archives.gov/the-press-office/2014/11/15.

————. *National Security Strategy of the United States of America.* Washington, DC, February 2015.

————. *National Security Strategy of the United States of America.* Washington, DC, December 2017.

White House Office of the Press Secretary. "Fact Sheet: United States and India: Strategic Partnership." New Delhi, March 2, 2006. https://2001-2009.state.gov/p/sca/rls/fs/2006/62422.htm.

Wiberg, Håkan, "The Nordic Security Community: Past, Present, Future." In Bertil Heurlin and Hans Mouritzen (eds.). *Danish Foreign Policy Yearbook,* 121–137. Copenhagen: Danish Institute of International Affairs, 2000.

Wight, Martin. *Power Politics.* London: Leicester University Press, 1978.

Wilkins, Thomas S. "Alignment, Not Alliance: The Shifting Paradigm of International Security Cooperation." *Review of International Studies,* vol. 38, no. 1 (2012): 53–76.

————. "Analytical Eclecticism in Theorizing Japanese Security Policy." *Asian Security,* vol. 4, no. 3 (2008): 1–6.

————. "Analyzing Coalition Warfare from an Intra-Alliance Politics Perspective: The Normandy Campaign 1944." *Journal of Strategic Studies*, vol. 29, no. 6 (2006): 1121–1150.

————. "Australia and Middle Power Approaches to Asia Pacific Regionalism." *Australian Journal of Political Science*, vol. 52, no. 1 (2017): 110–125.

————. "Coalition Formation and Management in the Asia-Pacific Region: The Case of an American-Japanese-Australian Combination." *Ritsumeikan Journal of Asia Pacific Studies,* vol. 14 (2004): 153–170.

————. "From Strategic Partnership to Strategic Alliance? Australia-Japan Security Ties and the Asia-Pacific." *Asia Policy,* vol. 20 (2015): 81–111.

————. "'The New Pacific Century' and the Rise of China: An International Relations Perspective." *Australian Journal of International Affairs,* vol. 64, no. 4 (2010): 381–405.

————. "The Russo-Chinese Strategic Partnership: A New Form of Security Cooperation?" *Contemporary Security Policy,* vol. 29, no. 2 (2008): 358–383.

————. "Towards a 'Trilateral Alliance?' Understanding the Role of Expediency and Values in American-Japanese-Australian Relations." *Asian Security,* vol. 3, no. 3 (2007): 251–278.

Willetts, Peter. *The Non-Aligned Movement: The Origins of Third World Alliance.* London: Pinter Publishers, 1983.

Williams, Michael C. "From Alliance to Security Community: NATO, Russia, and the Power of Identity." *Millennium Journal of International Studies,* vol. 29, no. 2 (2000): 357–387.

Wilson, Jeanne Lorraine. *Strategic Partners: Russian-Chinese Relations in the Post-Soviet Era.* London: M. E. Sharpe, 2004.

Wimbush, S. Enders. "Great Games in Central Asia." In Tellis, Tanner, and Keough, *Strategic Asia 2011–12,* 259–284.

Wishnick, Elizabeth. *Mending Fences: The Evolution of Moscow's China Policy from Brezhnev to Yeltsin.* Seattle: University of Washington Press, 2001.

Wolf, Charles. "Korean Reunification and Reconstruction: Circumstances, Costs, and Implications." *Regional Economic Implications of DPRK Security Behavior: The "Bold Switchover" Conference,* Beijing, January 18-19, 2006. http://www.nbr.org/downloads/pdfs/PSA/BS_Conf06_Wolf.pdf.

Wolf, Charles, and Kamil Akramov. *North Korean Paradoxes: Circumstances, Consequences, and Costs of Korean Unification.* Santa Monica, CA: RAND, 2005. http://www.rand.org/pubs/monographs/2005/RAND_MG333.pdf.

Woo, Wing Thye, Jeffrey Sachs, and Klaus Schwab (eds.). *The Asian Financial Crisis: Lessons for a Resilient Asia.* Cambridge, MA: MIT Press, 2000.

Wood, Bernard. "Canada and Southern Africa: A Return to Middle Power Activism." *The Round Table,* vol. 315 (1990): 280–290.

Wood, Christopher. *The Bubble Economy: Japan's Extraordinary Speculative Boom of the '80s and the Dramatic Bust of the '90s.* Jakarta: Equinox Publishing, 2005.

Wood, Peter. "China Conducts Anti-Terror Cyber Operations with SCO Partners." *China Brief,* vol. 15, no. 20 (October 19, 2015): 1–3.

Woodman, Stewart. "Beyond Armageddon? The Shape of Conflict in the Twenty-First Century." In Denny Roy (ed.). *The New Security Agenda in the Asia-Pacific Region.* London: Macmillan, 1997.

World Bank. "World Development Indicators." Last Updated March 23, 2017. http://databank.worldbank.org.

Wu, Xinbo. "Chinese Perspectives on Building an East Asian Community in the Twenty-First Century." In Green and Gill, *Asia's New Multilateralism,* 55–77.

Xinhua. "China, Russia Pledge Closer Economic Cooperation Amid Global Adversity." June 5, 2012.

————. "Culture Ministers of SCO Member States Meet in Beijing." April 13, 2002.

Yahuda, Michael. *The International Politics of the Asia-Pacific,* Third edition. London: Routledge, 2009.

Yeung, Christina, and Nebojsa Bjelakovic. "The Sino-Russian Strategic Partnership." *Journal of Slavic Military Studies,* vol. 23, no. 2 (2010): 243–281.

Ying, Fu. "How China Sees Russia: Beijing and Moscow Are Close, but Not Allies." *Foreign Affairs,* vol. 95, no. 1 (January/February 2016): 96–105.

Yoshino, Michael Y., and U. Srinivasa Rangan. *Strategic Alliances: An Entrepreneurial Approach to Globalization.* Boston: Harvard Business School Press, 1995.

Yuan, Jingdong. "China's Role in Establishing and Building the Shanghai Cooperation Organization (SCO)." *Journal of Contemporary China,* vol. 19, no. 67 (2010): 855–869.

———. "Useful Alignments or Just Convenient Labels? Dissecting China's Strategic Partnerships Since the End of the Cold War." Paper presented at the International Association Asia-Pacific Conference, Hong Kong, June 25–27, 2016.

Yuzawa, Takeshi. "The Fallacy of Socialization? Rethinking the ASEAN Way of Institution-Building." In Emmers, *ASEAN and the Institutionalization of East Asia,* 75–88.

———. *Japan's Security Policy and the ASEAN Regional Forum: The Search for Multilateral Security in the Asia-Pacific.* London and New York: Routledge, 2007.

Zehfuss, Maja. *Constructivism in International Relations: The Politics of Reality.* Cambridge: Cambridge University Press, 2002.

Zhao, Huasheng. "Security Building in Central Asia and the Shanghai Cooperation Organization." *Slavic Eurasian Studies* (Slavic Research Center, Hokkaido University), no. 2 (2004): 283–314. http://src-h.slav.hokudai.ac.jp/coe21/publish/no2_ses/4-2_Zhao.pdf.

Ziegler, Charles E. "Central Asia, the Shanghai Cooperation Organization, and American Foreign Policy: From Indifference to Engagement." *Asian Survey,* vol. 53, no. 3 (2013): 484–505.

Index

Abandonment-entrapment dyad, 32, 53, 62, 127

Acquisition and Cross-Servicing Agreements (ACSAs), 59

ADF. *See* Australian Defence Force

ADIZ. *See* Air Defense Identification Zone

Adler, Emanuel, 11, 69, 71, 75f, 185, 190

AFTA. *See* ASEAN Free Trade Area

Agendas, 10

AIIB. *See* Asian Infrastructure Investment Bank

Air Defense Identification Zone (ADIZ), 60

Alignment: alliances and, 12, 14, 23, 193; ASC and, 89, 90, 91–93, 114–115, 183, 186; behavior, 19; cases, 19; Cold War and, 4, 19; credibility of, 51; definition of, 13, 117*n*26, 143; dialogue and, 28; dynamics, 185; exclusivity criterion of, 69; grand theory of, 189–193; in India, 8; in IR, 13, 186; NTS and, 17; perspectives, 5; as phenomenon, 183, 189; policy, 8, 13; realism and, 136; relationships and, 69; SCO and, 143–146, 159, 183; security and, 3; security community and, 67, 69, 83, 84, 85*n*26, 92; strategic partnerships and, 128, 135–136; theories, 3–4, 18, 24, 76, 128, 183, 189–193; TSD

and, 183; types of, 192–193; values and, 48; virtual alliances as, 43–45

Alliances, 4, 15–16, 183; alignment and, 12, 14, 23, 193; behavior, 32, 35; bias, 24; bilateral, 41–42, 51; BOT theory and, 30–31; building, 185; burden-sharing, 30, 35–36, 51; cohesion of, 28, 29, 32–33, 35, 36, 48, 58; Cold War and, 14, 24–25, 36, 61, 123–124, 127; conceptual understanding of, 23; cooperation, 33; culture and, 33; defense pacts, 127; definition of, 23–27, 37*n*9; dissolution of, 31; diversity and, 33; dynamics of, 23; foreign policy and, 170–171; formation of, 77; institutionalized, 29, 35; institutions, 33; intra-alliance politics and, 28–36; management of, 30; memberships, 188; motivations of, 46; NATO and, 27–28, 36; negotiations and, 34; in New Delhi, 8; norms of, 35–36, 58–61; NTS and, 25; old-style, 13; organizational structure of, 34; pacts, 24; policy and, 15, 24; preservation, 29; quasi, 25, 61; reciprocity and, 35; regional, 9; relationships and, 28, 58, 59; resilience of, 48; SCO and, 144; security community and, 82, 190; Sino-Russian strategic partnership

241

244 *Index*

CSCAP. *See* Council for Security Cooperation in Asia Pacific
CSOs. *See* Civil society organization
CSTO. *See* Collective Security Treaty Organization
Culture, 133; alliances and, 33; cooperation and, 126, 132; SCO and, 167; sociocultural exchange and SCO, 157–158; strategic partnership and, 134–135; transnational civic, 77–78

Declaration on Conduct (DOC), 110
Declaration on Cultural Cooperation, 157
Defense pacts, alliances, 127
Democracy, 105–106
Democratic People's Republic of Korea (DPRK), 10, 62
Desecuritization, 6
Deutsch, Karl, 68–69, 91, 185
Dialogue, alignment and, 28
Dilemmas, 10, 31–32, 36, 91
Diplomacy, 107, 113–114
Disintegration, 71, 81–82, 106
Disputes, 101, 108
Dissolution, 31, 71, 84
Diversity, alliances and, 33
DOC. *See* Declaration on Conduct
Domestic politics, 33–35, 56–58
DPRK. *See* Democratic People's Republic of Korea

East Asia Summit (EAS), 2, 6, 12, 17, 69, 187
East Asian Regional Security Complex, 7
Economic cooperation, 132, 144
Economic interactions, of SCO, 156–157, 162–164
Economic partnership agreement (EPA), 127
Economy, 1, 9, 76, 98
ECSC (European Coal and Steel Community), 97
EEU. *See* Eurasian Economic Union
EEZ. *See* Exclusive economic zone
Elites, 99, 101, 105
Energy security, 109
Entrapment, 32, 53, 62
Environmental uncertainty, SCO and, 147–148
EPA. *See* Economic partnership agreement

EU. *See* European Union
EU/NATO case, 83, 191
Eurasian Economic Union (EEU), 156–157, 163
European Coal and Steel Community. *See* ECSC
European Policy Centre, 161
European Strategic Partnerships Observatory, 124
European Union (EU), 89
Exclusive economic zone (EEZ), 58
Exclusivity criterion, of alignment, 69
Extramural security, 114
Extremism, 151, 155

FDI. *See* Foreign Direct Investment
Five Power Defense Arrangement (FPDA), 12, 96, 188, 191
Foreign Direct Investment (FDI), 98
Foreign policy, 33–34, 170–171
Formation stage, 129–131, 146–147
FPDA. *See* Five Power Defense Arrangement
Frames, 79
Framing concepts, 10–13
Free trade agreement (FTA), 48, 127
Free Trade Area, 163
Freedom, 54
Freedom of press, 34–35
FTA. *See* Free trade agreement
Functionalism, 146
Fundamentalism, 160

Gas, 103
GCC. *See* Gulf Cooperation Council
GDP. *See* Gross domestic product
Geo-economics, 1
Geography, power and, 30
Geopolitics, 1, 9, 53, 186–187
Governance, of ASC, 108
Greve, Patricia, 11
Gross domestic product (GDP), 162–163
Groupings, 4
Gulf Cooperation Council (GCC), 78
Gulf War, 51

HADR. *See* Humanitarian assistance and disaster relief
Hall, Richard, 132–133
Heterogeneity of states, 33
Hub-and-spoke system, 42–43, 51, 89

About the Book

The complex security dynamics of the pivotal Asia Pacific region, involving disparate and contentious power blocs, clearly have implications far beyond the region itself. Thomas Wilkins sheds new light on those dynamics, providing a rich framework for better understanding the nature of security alignments in Asia Pacific, as well as a reexamination of the dominant forces at play: the US alliance system, ASEAN, and the Shanghai Cooperation Organisation.

Thomas S. Wilkins is senior lecturer in international security at the University of Sydney.